LETTERS
FROM
PRISON
AND OTHER ESSAYS

" LETTERS FROM PRISON

AND OTHER ESSAYS

// Adam Michnik

Translated by
MAYA LATYNSKI

Foreword by
CZESŁAW MIŁOSZ

Introduction by
JONATHAN SCHELL

University of California Press
Berkeley • Los Angeles • London

The Publisher wishes to thank the Alfred Jurzykowski Foundation, Inc., New York, N.Y. and the Polish American Congress, Chicago, Ill., for their generous contributions toward the publication of this important work.

Most of the essays published in this volume were first published underground in Poland and in London by Aneks publishers.

University of California Press
Berkeley and Los Angeles, California
University of California Press, Ltd.
London, England

Library of Congress Cataloging in Publication Data

Michnik, Adam.
  Letters from prison and other essays.

  Translation from Polish.
  1. Poland—Politics and government—1980–   —Addresses, essays, lectures. 2. Michnik, Adam—Addresses, essays, lectures. 3. Political prisoners—Poland—Correspondence. I. Title.
DK4442.M53 1985   943.8′056   85-1196
ISBN 0-520-05371-0 (alk. paper)

Printed in the United States of America

1 2 3 4 5 6 7 8 9

Special thanks to David Ost, Terry Repak, Barbara Torunczyk, Jonathan Schell, and Lawrence Weschler.

// Contents

// Foreword

by Czesław Miłosz

// Let me begin by quoting the words of Mahatma Gandhi: "If a government does a grave injustice, the subject must withdraw cooperation wholly or partially, sufficient to wean the ruler from wickedness. In each case conceived by me there is an element of suffering whether mental or physical. Without such suffering it is not possible to attain freedom."

Today, toward the end of the century that has seen the triumph of Gandhi's action in his country, it is legitimate to ask whether these words of the prophet of nonviolence are not a little too idealistic. We hear often the argument that because the British Empire respected the law, passive resistance had a chance of success, while the modern totalitarian or police state does not recognize any bounds to the exercise of its power. Confronted with such a state, is nonviolence, as a philosophy, and a tactic of the individual, possible? True, Gandhi himself recognized its difficulties. He said that "the practice of nonviolence requires fearlessness and courage of the highest order. I am painfully aware of my failings." And yet Gandhi did not have for his adversary a state that sends in its tanks against workers' unions.

Our very natural tendency to place the possible in the past leads us often to overlook the acts of our contemporaries who defy the presumably unmovable order of things, and accomplish what at first sight has seemed impossible or improbable. And yet if a man appears today who represents the philosophy of nonviolence, he merits being known and honored. I could pronounce here the names of Lech Wałęsa and of other Polish leaders of Solidarity. This time, however, I want to concentrate upon a man who propagates nonviolence in his writings, and in doing so provides a foundation of theory for his own activity. I have in mind Adam Michnik, whom I am privileged to count among my friends, and who was sentenced by the Polish courts in June 1985 to three years of prison. I shall try to present him first as the author of books that he has written in his brief moments of liberty, but mostly in his jails.

Adam Michnik, born in 1946 in Warsaw, son of a prewar communist militant, and himself a zealous Marxist in his early youth, has undergone an evolution, the description of which in his essays makes fascinating reading. He speaks of the influence of books, some found at home, some borrowed not quite legally from public libraries where they were placed in the departments of the "prohibita." He discovered a discrepancy between the real history of the twentieth century and that presented in the official textbooks and histories. Since that discrepancy was at the center of his thought, he started to reflect upon the role of the intellectuals as servants of the party, as makers of a smoke screen to disguise the truth.

Having decided to become an intellectual, though a different sort of intellectual, he studied history at the university and simultaneously engaged in opposition activities. Since 1965 he has often been arrested. Expelled from the university and sentenced in 1968 to three years of prison, he became a factory worker while continuing to study history. He came to delineate his field of action: (1) to see clearly, to call the intellectuals to overcome fear, and never to lie; (2) to redefine the relations between the intellectuals and the two main forces capable of changing Poland—the workers and the Church.

Michnik's book *The Church, The Left, A Dialogue,* sent clandestinely to Paris and published in 1977, marks a decisive turn in the political climate of his country. The relations between the majority of the Polish intellectuals and the Catholic Church were not cordial during the first half of the century; these two worlds seemed even to be hostile to each other. The Church has undergone profound changes, however, since the end of the war. It ceased to be the Church of the peasants, and attracted more and more young people of high intellectual caliber into its ranks as clergy and parishioners. Thanks to its defense of the individual against the power of the state, and to its courage during the Stalinist period, the Church became a natural ally of all those who wanted to introduce freedom into public life. The evolution of the intellectuals was leading them in the same direction. The dialogue proposed by Michnik had nothing to do with the famous dialogues between Marxists and Christians, which always ended by drafting the latter into the service of the revolution. Rather the goal was to unite the two forces called to work in a nonviolent manner toward the transformation of society. This transformation was to begin, according to Michnik, the moment when society learned to consider itself as a *subject*, rather than as an object manipulated by those who govern.

After the workers' spontaneous demonstrations in Radom in 1976, cruelly crushed by the police, Michnik became one of the founders of KOR—Committee for the Defense of Workers—and diligently set about implementing his aim: an alliance between the intellectuals and the workers. Incessantly harassed by the police, who arrested and tried to intimidate its members, the Committee remained faithful to the principle of legal, open, and nonviolent action. The strike of Gdansk in 1980, which led to the creation of Solidarity, accomplished in practice what Michnik had envisioned in theory: an alliance of intellectuals, workers, and the Church, and the principles of legality and nonviolence. And if Solidarity has preserved—a rare thing in similar cases—its nonviolent character, the merit for this is due to the foundations laid by Michnik and his companions. He himself proved his attachment to the principles at the time of a mass riot near Warsaw; when a crowd besieged a police station, Michnik intervened to protect the endangered policemen and to calm the crowd.

Interned together with thousands of others after the proclamation of martial law on December 13, 1981, Michnik spent nearly three years in prison. When offered freedom in exchange for leaving Poland, he refused. His extraordinary discipline allowed him to write two books of essays in his cell (although he had no solitude there). These books reveal him as a literary critic of the first order, and as a historian endowed with a style much more vivid than that of university scholars.

There was a moment in his career when Michnik was a communist-revisionist. He is still a revisionist, but in a different sense. What a title for an author from the left (and he does not renounce the socialist ideal) to give his book published in Paris in 1985: *From the History of Honor in Poland!* For here the forgotten or abandoned notions of true and false, of good and evil, acquire extreme importance, and the history of Poland over the last forty years is interpreted according to the honorable or dishonorable behavior of individuals toward the authorities. And what is perhaps surprising in a man concerned with civic duties, Michnik is an attentive reader of contemporary Polish poetry, finding in it the most expressive voice of freedom. In this he is a legitimate son of a country that, at least in one of its aspects, deserves to be envied by Western writers: poetry is treated there by everyone as a serious affair. The superiority of Michnik over practitioners of professional literary criticism, so well versed in the latest intellectual fashions, consists precisely in his use of the simple criteria of honor and conscience.

And yet Michnik's attitude is not that of an offended moralist. Confronted with a newly acquired moral zeal among libertarian activists, he addresses to their angelic righteousness the following warning, which I quote from his essay of 1979:

> Whatever happens tomorrow, already today I feel I must point out that an angel who requires heroism not only from himself but also from others, who completely refuses to recognize the value of compromises and perceives the world with a Manichaean simplicity, who pours scorn on people who conceive differently their duties towards their fellow citizens—such an angel, even if he admires heaven, has already entered the road leading to hell. No matter whether he justifies his actions by a phraseology of national independence or by a socialist-universalist utopia—he sows the grains of future hatred.

Michnik represents the best tradition of the Polish intelligentsia, that of liberalism and tolerance. He has always worked assiduously against temptations of hatred in himself and his compatriots. His program of international brotherhood embraces not only the immediate neighbors of Poland—the Czechs, the Slovaks, the Lithuanians, the Ukrainians, and the Germans, but also the Russian nation. To the complaints, often repeated by the Poles, of being abandoned by the

West, he opposes the words of gratitude to the West for its interest in the cause represented first by the Committee for the Defense of Workers, and then by Solidarity. Since that active interest was, in the first place, voiced by the people and the authorities of France, he speaks of the debt Polish militants owe to the country of the Rights of Man and Citizen.

As a historian, Michnik expresses in his writings the struggle for independence of his country, which fills the whole of the 19th century and results in the creation of a free Poland—destined, however, to be submerged again in World War II and become a captive in its aftermath. The ancient dilemma reappeared—the choice between collaboration or resistance. Far from being a nationalist, Michnik clings to his idea of the people as a subject of their history and not just an object—a thing impossible where the rulers of a country are not elected democratically but, on the contrary, are imposed from abroad. He quotes Engels, who used to say that "a proletarian international movement is possible only among independent nations."

What is the meaning of such notions in Europe, which pretends to exist while it is no more than a shadow of itself, partitioned as it is as a consequence of Yalta? Choosing a nonviolent resistance, Michnik does not hope to change the map of Europe. He places his hope in a constant pressure on the rulers exerted by the citizens aware of their rights. Rulers are never inclined to grant demands of the population unless they are forced to. It is true that Poland belongs to the Soviet bloc. Yet the Polish People's Republic signed the Helsinki act, and the Civil and Political Rights Covenant, as well as the Convention No. 87 of the International Labor Organization on the freedom of association and the Convention No. 98 on the rights of workers to organize and to negotiate. This fact suffices to define all actions envisioned and initiated by Michnik as perfectly legal, while the means used by the police and judiciary apparatus in Poland are in flagrant violation of international agreements.

In general outline, Michnik's program resembles that of Lech Wałęsa. And it is because of a conference called by Wałęsa that Michnik is serving a three-year prison term. His crime consists in having discussed with his co-prisoners, Bogdan Lis and Władysław Fransyniuk, the possibility of proclaiming a general strike of fifteen minutes. The strike never took place, but the very act of considering it was enough for the authorities to brand them as criminals.

Michnik is a political animal. Everything in him is action-oriented. It is possible that we owe his literary works to the months and years he spent in prison, for there he could not act other than by handling his pen. I confess that for me, deprived as I am of a political temperament, he is a strange phenomenon, precisely because of the combination of energy in motion, of moral purity and high intellectual qualities, a combination almost against the nature of public commitments. We are bound to each other, for he has dedicated penetrating studies to my poetry. Yet before his unbending will, which pushes him to pay with his own person every time he encounters injustice, I feel what probably was felt by an average Hindu confronted by the devotion of Gandhi: admiration mixed with incredulity and hope.

What is, then, the efficacy of nonviolence elevated to the level of principle, and applied to the conditions of our contemporary life? Terrorism seems to correspond to a nihilistic vision in which the only thing that counts is naked force. The terrorism of revolutionaries and the terrorism of the state seem to be two faces of the same coin. Purely peaceful movements—the Prague Spring of 1968 and Solidarity of 1980–81—have been smashed, and the possibility of a dialogue between the population and the government, always advocated by Lech Wałęsa and Adam Michnik, encounters a cynical refusal on the part of those who found their authority on force. What is, then, the use of nonviolence, and what would Mahatma Gandhi have to say on that topic if he were still alive?

It seems to me that habitual notions of links between causes and effects enclose us in simplistic, mechanistic, and desperate dilemmas. The history of the century provides us with a number of proofs to vindicate the role of actions that appear insignificant and likely to fail, yet are potentially fecund. Sometimes we have had the opportunity to marvel at the sight of a huge tree whose growth, from its original form of a little seed, we would never have guessed. Michnik's writings are important to the intellectual history of Poland, and mark a decisive change of mentality. They are also of great importance for Polish poetry—one more reason why I should stress their value. Of course it is perfectly possible to say that changes in orientation among intellectuals are without significance, that literature doesn't weigh much when confronted with armored cars. This is precisely what the government of Warsaw does. And it is also possible, as the government's spokesman did, to reject the appeal addressed to General Jaruzelski by thirty Nobel Laureates, who called for the liberation of Michnik and his colleagues. Yet the scorn one manifests toward international opinion proves sometimes to be quite costly, as the history of the century demonstrates. It opens the chasm of iniquity that threatens to swallow men driven by hubris.

By his actions, always nonviolent, Michnik established the unity of his premises and his conclusions. I would draw your attention to a hypothesis: capable of seeing greatness in the past in people like Gandhi, we may fail to see what takes place in the present. If this hypothesis is correct, Michnik is one of those who bring honor to the last two decades of the twentieth century, even if a film on his life will not be produced soon.

// Introduction

by Jonathan Schell

// Rarer by far than originality in science or art is originality in political action. And rarer still is original political action that enlarges, rather than blights or destroys, human possibilities. The opposition movement in Poland, which remains active four years after the military government of General Wojciech Jaruzelski declared a "state of war" and banned the independent trade-union federation Solidarity, has made, it seems to me, such a contribution to the world. Hitherto, probably the most original invention of our century in the field of politics was, unfortunately, the catastrophic one of totalitarianism, which so hugely expanded the human capacity for organized evil. Now, at last, many decades and tens of millions of lives later, out of the human spirit has been born what has every appearance of being the first entirely fitting response. This response, it is true, may be possible in part because the totalitarian system in question—the Soviet communist one in its Polish version—has moderated considerably since it reached its apogee of brutality, in the days of Joseph Stalin. It is also true, of course, that totalitarian governments have been effectively opposed from without, by other governments—most notably by the Allies in the Second World War, who defeated the Nazi regime militarily and then dissolved it. But now a totalitarian government has summoned forth a powerful antagonist from within its own body politic. The Polish self-limiting revolution, as it has been called—self-limiting because, although it enjoyed the overwhelming support of the Polish public, it held back from attempting to overthrow the government—has many novel features. There is the crucial full-scale and sustained participation of the working class. There is the alliance of the secular opposition and the Catholic Church. There is the dedication to liberty, and the movement's internal democracy. But more important, perhaps, than any of these features has been the discovery of a new style of action—one that contributed greatly to making them all possible. Though schooled in opposition to totalitarian rule, the Polish movement has not grown to resemble its opponent; its answer to totalitarian violence and deception has not been violence and deception with some new twist, some new political coloration. Instead, in a radical break, it has ceded those ageless instruments completely to its governmental foe, and sought its strength in altogether different sources, including, above all, the multitudinous peaceful activities of a normal civic life. In doing so, it has departed not only from totalitarian practices but from the violent practices of most other revolutions. Some people have questioned whether the Polish opposition movement really amounts to a revolution. Inasmuch as it has not overthrown, or even sought to overthrow, the state, it might be said to have fallen short. Yet, as though to make up for that deficiency, it has been all the more thorough in other areas of life—the social, the cultural, the moral, and even the spiritual. In no area, however, has it been more thorough than in the area of its own practices, which constitute nothing less than a new chapter in the history of revolution. In that respect, it is not just a revolution; it is a revolution in revolution. The revolution began, suddenly and spectacularly, in August of 1980; then, in December of 1981, Solidarity, its organized arm, was outlawed and driven underground; since then, the revolution has bubbled up again in many forms, sometimes more vigorously than ever, though without again achieving dramatic organized expression at the national level. The revolution's ultimate achievement for Poland has yet to be revealed, but for the world at large the chapter of political history that has already been written is the record of an abundance of inventions and discoveries in political and moral life which no subsequent events can erase. Poland still paces up and down in its geopolitical cage, but through the bars it has already passed these inestimable gifts to the rest of us.

Among the voices that speak to us from Poland today, the most important may be that of Adam Michnik. He offers a prediction and some advice:

> I . . . believe that the totalitarian dictatorships are doomed. By now, no one gives credence to their mendacious promises. They still have the power to jail and kill, but almost no other power. I say "almost" because (alas) there still remains their ability to infect us with their own hatred and contempt. Such infection must be resisted with our whole strength, for of all the struggles we face this is the most difficult.

Michnik now sits in a jail belonging to the totalitarian regime, yet his first concern—and herein lies one of the keys to his thinking, and, one should add, to his character—is with the quality of his own conduct, which, together with the conduct of other victims of the present situation, will, he is sure, one day set the tone for whatever political system follows the totalitarian debacle. His essays are the most valuable guide we have to the origins of the revolution, and, more particularly, to its innovative practices. Michnik was born in 1946, in Warsaw, to parents whom he has described as "Polish Communists of Jewish origin." In prewar Poland, his father had spent time in prison for political activities. From early adolescence, Adam proved to be an irrepressible political activist—though of a strikingly different bent from his parents'. (By 1977, the father had become enough of a supporter of the son's anti-communist activities to join a hunger strike in a church in support of an appeal for the release of Adam and others from prison.) At fifteen, he founded a political club called the Seekers of Contradictions but known informally to many Poles as the Revisionist Toddlers. (Later, the regime, seeking to give the Toddlers a more fearsome aspect, began to refer to the club as the Commandos.) At eighteen, he was arrested for the first time, for involvement in the writing and disseminating of a letter called "An Open Letter to the Party," which was critical of the regime and was signed by Jacek Kuron and Karol Modzelewski—men in their late twenties who were prominent in the budding opposition movement. Kuron and Modzelewski received sentences of three and three and a half years, respectively; Michnik was detained in prison for two months. Thereafter, his life became a round of political activities alternating with prison terms. In 1964, he enrolled in the History Department of Warsaw University, and in 1966 he was suspended for participating in a discussion in which the philosopher Leszek Kolakowski criticized the regime. In 1968, he helped organize a protest against the closing of the play "Forefathers' Eve," by Adam Mickiewicz, the revered nineteenth-century Polish poet, and was expelled from the university on the order of the minister of Higher Education. Protests against his expulsion were mounted at the university; so was an official campaign, tinged with anti-Semitism, against the protesters. In February of 1969, he was sentenced to three years in prison for belonging to an underground organization that was trying to overthrow the state, although in fact no such organization existed. After serving a year and a half, he was released, and took a job at the Rosa Luxemburg factory, in Warsaw, which produces light bulbs. In 1971, he left his job, and eventually he entered Poznan University as an extension student, and he remained there until 1975, when he received an M.A. in history. In May of 1977, he was arrested again, but this time he was released, along with others, only two months later, following widespread protests in the intellectual community against the arrests. In the late nineteen seventies, he helped to found the Independent Publishing House, and he also helped to found the so-called Flying University, which offered uncensored lectures in people's apartments, among other places. In August of 1980, he and several others were arrested again, and this time the workers in the shipyards in Gdansk made these prisoners' release the final condition of a historic agreement with the government—the agreement under which Solidarity was legalized. After martial law was imposed, he was imprisoned once more (this time without trial), and he was held for more than two and a half years. Six months after his release, he was rearrested, tried, convicted, and given a sentence of three years, which he is now serving.

Michnik is not a political philosopher—and certainly not a "political scientist"—nor is he a proponent of any ideology or system of political thought. His writings, like the Federalist papers of Madison and Hamilton, or the articles and letters of Gandhi, are not only reflections on action but a form of action themselves. With equal justice, one might say that his actions—together with those of countless others in

Poland—are a kind of writing, for action, when it is creative, has a power to disclose new possibilities which is as great as that of any book. Michnik's writings, then, both mirror and help to shape the new possibilities that have been and are being brought into existence by the Polish people. An ability to write about events and to participate in them at the same time is unusual. Writing, by its nature, requires solitude, whereas political action, by its nature, requires perpetual association with others. This dilemma was apparently resolved for Michnik by the authorities when they repeatedly threw him in jail. In his essay "Letter from the Gdansk Prison," written in the spring of 1985, he notes that in his recent six months of liberty he had been unable to write, but when he found himself in jail again literary production resumed immediately and, with characteristic irony and good humor, he offers to the general who had him locked up "gratitude for your thoughtful watch over my steps and for providing proper direction to my meditations." (One of the pleasures of Michnik's essays is that they combine gravity of purpose with lightness of style.) At large, Michnik stirs up so much trouble for the regime that it finds it must lock him up; but once he has been locked up he starts to write, and his letters, smuggled to the outside, are read all over Poland, and abroad, and cause, if anything, even more trouble for the regime. It's one more of the quagmires—and not the least of them, either—that the regime is at a loss to fight clear of.

The Czech writer Milan Kundera has remarked that the best novels do not merely confirm what we already know but uncover new aspects of existence. The same can be said of Michnik's political writing. He is never merely adding decibels to one side or the other of an existing argument, never merely engaging in verbal gunfire from a fixed position. Perhaps as a result of this, his essays, though produced in the midst of political struggle, are models of balance and fairness. He is concerned with deepening his own and others' understanding, and therefore he cannot afford the luxury of distortion for partisan reasons. His literary bent also militates against tendentious renderings. Of a writer whose portrait of the contemporary scene he finds too narrowly politicized, he asserts that the man misses "the whole dramatic aspect of the social and political reality . . . the fascinating panorama of defeat mixed with hope, reason with naïveté, fear with bravado." Once, when

Solidarity was functioning at its peak, an enraged mob in the city of Otwock surrounded a policeman who they believed had severely beaten up two drunks. Michnik, among others, was summoned to the scene, and, introducing himself as an "anti-socialist element," he helped calm the crowd and save the policeman from harm. The same spirit of unwillingness to see injustice done, even to those who are doing injustice to him, permeates his essays. Unwilling to bend before any regime, he is equally unwilling to surrender the independence of his mind or conscience to any rival faction or orthodoxy. In action and in word alike, he reminds us that although liberty can and probably must be guaranteed by institutions human freedom is always ultimately an achievement of the individual spirit.

In 1976, four years before Solidarity came into existence, Michnik wrote a prophetic essay called "A New Evolutionism," wherein he recommended a new direction for the political opposition, which at the time was small and relatively weak. The essay is written against the backdrop of Poland's "obligation to its friends"—one of many euphemisms used in reference to the prime fact of political life in Poland, which is the overwhelming power of the Soviet Army and the often demonstrated resolve of the Soviet Union to use it to keep its Socialist satellites under its political domination. (In no part of the world does the phrase "our friends" have a more ominous ring than in the nations of Eastern Europe.) If this threat were somehow to disappear, it seems safe to say, the Polish Communist government would fall immediately. (In actuality, of course, the disappearance of the threat is about as unlikely as any event could be in our world.) To be sure, domination by a foreign power, and by neighboring Russia in particular, is hardly a new experience for Poland: it was partitioned for more than a century—from 1795 to 1918—between Austria, Prussia, and czarist Russia, and against these military opposition was nearly as hopeless as it is against the Soviet Union now. In our day, a new factor tightens the vise in which Poland finds itself—the presence in the world of nuclear weapons. Poland is at the very heart of that part of the world which is frozen in immobility, militarily and diplomatically, by the nuclear stalemate. In the past, even though rebellion was unavailing, Poland could dream of rescue by foreign armies, or by some drastic realignment of the international order as a result of war; and, in fact,

in our century Poland was twice liberated by war from its oppressors—
first when it achieved independence, in the aftermath of the First World
War, and then when the Nazis were driven from Poland, only to set
the stage, unfortunately, for Soviet domination of the country. Today,
however, Poland has to recognize what all of Europe recognizes: that
in the nuclear age the map of Europe is unlikely ever to be redrawn by
marching armies. The likely alternatives offered by our time are nuclear
stalemate and nuclear annihilation, and in neither is there any hope for
the rescue of Poland. In sum, the Poles are kept in subjugation by a
triple weight: at the local level, the totalitarian regime in Warsaw; at
the national level, the threat of direct Soviet invasion; and, on the
international level, the militarily paralyzing influence of nuclear
weapons, which holds the whole unhappy arrangement firmly in place.

To most postwar observers, this combination of circumstances
meant hopelessness, and they unhesitatingly pronounced any dramatic
improvement in the situation of Poland to be impossible. Because
Poland had no chance of defeating the overwhelming military and
police forces arrayed against it, the argument ran (when anyone even
bothered to spell out something so self-evident), any resistance was
doomed to fail. It was Michnik's genius to separate the two halves of
the proposition, and to accept the first (the impossibility of defeating
the armies and the police forces) and reject the second (the hopelessness
of all resistance). If there is an advantage to be gained from facing
overwhelming adversity, it is the death of illusions: mind and body are
saved from wasting themselves in pursuit of the impossible. Historically, the Poles have been the most romantic of peoples, much given
to the pursuit of the long chance and the distant dream, but not even
the most fevered dreams of military resistance could survive the discour-
agement of nuclear weapons piled on the two hundred divisions of the
Soviet army piled on totalitarian rule. Final acceptance of that verdict
cleared the way for new investigations, and a new kind of thinking.
Abandoning, for the time being, all hope of a jailbreak, the members
of the Polish opposition began to examine more closely the cell in
which, it appeared, it was the country's fate to live for an indefinite
period; that is, realizing that there was no salvation for Poland in our
time in the movements of armies, they began to scrutinize the minutiae
of their local environment. Soviet troops, it was plain, could not be

driven out of Poland; but what if ten people gathered in someone's apartment and listened to an uncensored lecture on Polish history? The Communist party could perhaps not be dislodged from its "leading role" in affairs of state; but what if a group of workers began to publish a newsletter in which factory conditions were truthfully described? And what if millions of people, casting off fear, began to take local action of this sort all over the country? The new ferment, in the words of Irena Grudzinska-Gross in *The Art of Solidarity,* would be "an effort to overstep the limits of the political horizon while remaining inside the same geographical borders."

Perhaps the most acute mind training the lens of its political microscope on these questions was Michnik's. In "A New Evolutionism" he surveys the political scene and proposes a new path of action. He works from the assumption that "to believe in overthrowing the dictatorship of the Party by revolution . . . is both unrealistic and dangerous." He yearns for full independence for Poland but accepts the fact that any project for attaining it in the foreseeable future is hopeless. Nevertheless, he discerns opportunities for action of a kind that he believes can be highly successful. Between the rock of Soviet power and the hard place of contemporary Polish life, he discovers a space. In the conventional view, the interests of the Soviet Union and those of Polish society are unalterably opposed across the board. Michnik arrives at a startlingly different conclusion. "The interests of the Soviet political leadership, the Polish political leadership, and the Polish democratic opposition," he writes, "are basically concurrent." They are concurrent because for all three of them Soviet military intervention would be a disaster: for the Soviet leadership because it would suffer huge and lasting losses in its global political prestige; for the Polish leadership because it would lose the limited sovereignty it now enjoys and, furthermore, might be "dethroned"; and for the Polish opposition because of the bloodshed and the increased rigors of direct Soviet rule. Such an invasion would precipitate "a war that Poland . . . could not win on the battlefield but that the Soviet Union could not win politically." The concurring interests of the three parties, he concludes, define "an area of permissible political maneuver . . . the sphere of possible compromise."

Approaching the question of what can be done, Michnik canvasses past efforts, and it is wholly characteristic of the spirit of his writing that even when his final judgment of one effort or another is negative he gives generous credit for whatever good was achieved. Michnik is anything but a Hegelian dialectician—anything but a believer in blind forces of history acting behind men's backs—but he always keeps an eye on the larger historical story of which any particular initiative is a part, and is keenly aware that the inch of progress made in one decade, though inadequate in itself, and perhaps based on false premises, may make possible the next inch in the next decade. In Poland's recent past he identifies two schools of reform: the revisionists, who sought to soften and liberalize communist rule by invoking the humane aspects of Marxist and other socialist theory; and the so-called neo-positivists, a Catholic group that rejected communism in principle yet sought as a matter of pragmatic policy to moderate it by cooperating with it, even to the extent of participating in the Polish parliament. Revisionism, Michnik writes, was "faithful to the Bible [that is, to Marxism], although it interpreted it in its own way," while neo-positivism "adhered to the Church [that is, the actuality of the communist government], hoping that it would sooner or later disappear." Both were techniques of working within the system—of appealing to "the rational thinking of the Communist Prince"—and for a while both brought limited positive results, often in the form of books and articles and a slightly freer intellectual atmosphere. Yet both schools had to pay the price that is always paid by those who choose to work within the system: they were required, in order to maintain their influence, to renounce ties with people dedicated to changing the system from without. The fatal crisis for each school came, therefore, when protest from without boiled over: for the revisionists in 1968, when the student movement in favor of liberalization of intellectual life arose, and was crushed by the closing of some university departments, the expulsion of students, and reprisals against their parents; and for the neo-positivists in 1976, when workers demonstrated against an announced rise in food prices, and the government took extremely harsh reprisals. At those moments, any opposition that hoped to retain its standing in the society at large had to declare which side it supported—"that of the beaters or that of the beaten"—and because neither reform movement was able to do this both lost the public's confidence.

Michnik's analysis of the failure of the efforts to change the system from within leads him to make a pivotal recommendation: "I believe that what sets today's opposition apart from the proponents of those ideas of reform in the past is the belief that a program for evolution ought to be addressed to independent public opinion, and not to totalitarian power. Such a program would offer advice to the people regarding how to behave, not to the government regarding how to reform itself." The suggestion was simple, but its implications were radical. The change in the venue of action entailed a change in substance. Those who took the route of working with the Prince depended on the decisions and whims of the Prince to achieve any results. But those who took the route of working in and with the society could act directly. Then it was up to the government to *re*act. The first method, based on the belief that the government, by holding a monopoly on the instruments of force, also monopolized political power, viewed cooperation with the government as the only way to share in power. The second method, based on the belief that there were sources of power elsewhere, in public opinion, sought to develop those. And yet Michnik, unlike many people in other times and places who had given up on the government in power and turned to the public for redress, did not seek the overthrow of the government. Rather, he wanted the society immediately and directly to take over its own destiny in certain realms of life, and only then to turn to the government—for negotiation. The eventual result, he hoped, would be a "hybrid," based on a compromise in which the government, while holding on to state power, would acknowledge and accept other, independent institutions in the society. Michnik enumerates the groups in society that he hopes will advance "a new evolutionism." First, and most important, are the workers, whose participation is "a necessary condition for the evolution of public life toward democracy." The key event, he foresees with uncanny accuracy, will be the foundation of independent "institutions representing the interests of workers." Second is the Catholic Church, which has always remained independent but has recently shown an increasing interest in defending the independence and the rights of others, including the workers. In the Church, Michnik notes, "Jeremiads against 'Godless ones' have given way to documents that quote the principles of the Declaration of Human Rights." Third is the intelligentsia, whose duty it is to think through alternative programs while defending fundamental moral and political principles.

Michnik acted on his own advice, and was soon busy organizing and participating in a host of independent groups. One deserves special mention: the Workers' Defense Committee usually known as KOR—the acronym of its Polish name. KOR did not agitate politically, or otherwise address the government. Instead, it set out to render concrete assistance—financial, legal, and medical—to workers and their families who had suffered in one way or another from government repression. Indeed, the committee explicitly declared its purposes to be not political but social, and it restricted its activity to what Jan Józef Lipski, one of its founders, who has written an excellent history of the organization, refers to as "social work." But what in the eyes of KOR might be considered social was considered by the government definitely political, for in a totalitarian system every aspect of collective existence is supposed to originate with the government and be under its management. In this deep reach of totalitarian government into daily life, which is usually seen as a source of its strength, KOR discovered a point of weakness: precisely because totalitarian governments politicize daily life, daily life becomes a vast terrain on which totalitarianism can be opposed. It was here that KOR implicitly pitted itself against the regime. In consequence, the KOR members soon began to suffer the repression against which they sought to defend the workers—loss of employment, arrest, imprisonment, beatings, and, in a few cases, loss of their lives. It was just one of the remarkable qualities of this organization that its members were willing to suffer government reprisal not in the name of some sweeping political program or visionary goal but in order to get some money into the hands of a fatherless family or to arrange for favorable testimony in the trial of a worker. Only great goals might seem to warrant great sacrifices, but the KOR workers were ready to make great sacrifices for modest goals. "In some dissident circles . . . KOR members were sneered at as 'social workers,'" Lipski writes, "but within KOR such a designation by one's colleagues was regarded as an honor."

The adoption of an overall policy of direct action in society entailed the adoption of a number of other policies that were novel in the closed society of Poland. One was the policy of openness. When KOR was founded, in September of 1976, its members wrote a declaration of purpose to which they not only signed their names but also—an act without precedent for an opposition group in Poland—affixed their addresses and telephone numbers. Thereafter, the committee followed as much as possible a policy of open, public action. Closely related to the policy of openness was the policy of truthfulness. In all its statements and publications, KOR strove meticulously for factual accuracy. Characteristically, there was both an idealistic and a pragmatic reason for this policy. The members believed in telling the truth for its own sake, and they also calculated that in a society surfeited with lies an organization that hewed strictly to the truth would win support and gain strength. Another new policy was "autonomy of action." Autonomy was what the opposition wished for Poland as a whole and for every person in Poland. The members of KOR inaugurated it by making it a principle of their own actions. "There was no question of ordering someone by command of the organization to do something he did not want to do," Lipski writes, and he adds, "There was a principle that if what they wanted to do was not contrary to the principles of KOR they should be allowed to pursue their own ideas. And this is why everything that was done was done by people motivated by their own initiative and enthusiasm, and thus produced the best results." It is striking that the activists of the Polish opposition spoke as much of autonomy, which is the capacity of each person for acting freely, as they did of liberty, which is a person's right to do so. (In the West, you might say, we as individuals have great liberty but little autonomy. We have the right to determine the shape of our own future, but we do not bother to avail ourselves of it very much.) Still another policy was that of trust. Ordinarily, we think of the trust we place in someone as more or less a by-product, produced involuntarily in us by the other person's trustworthy actions, and do not think of it as the result of a policy, or even of any intention on our part. But for KOR trust was indeed a policy. One reason for this was the danger of infiltration by undercover police: a decision had to be made regarding what steps, if any, should be taken to guard against this. KOR's decision was to reject suspicion and all the equipment and procedures that go with it, and "to trust everyone within the bounds of common sense."

The policies of openness, truthfulness, autonomy of action, and trust, which together might be described simply as a policy of militant decency, were not elements in any master plan, but they were of a piece. They equipped KOR not so much to do battle with the government as to work around it. Although KOR did not have any designs on state power, it did hope that activity independent of the government would spread by contagion—that there would occur a sort of epidemic of freedom in the closed society. Lipski observes, "The long-range goal of KOR was to stimulate new centers of autonomous activity in a variety of areas and among a variety of social groups independent of KOR. Not only did KOR agree to their independence but it also wanted them to be independent." Its hope was abundantly fulfilled in the years just ahead.

Nothing illuminates the inner spirit of KOR, which strikes me as an exemplary organization for our time, more clearly than its final act. In September of 1981, the members decided that its role was being filled by Solidarity, and voted the KOR organization out of existence. Missing entirely from KOR, apparently, was that compound of personal interest, factional rivalry, and bureaucratic momentum which, acting independently of all external reasons and causes, often supersedes the purposes for which an organization was founded, and transforms it into a dead weight on the world. When KOR's *reason* for existing dissolved, *it* dissolved. To paraphrase George Orwell's comment on Gandhi, "How clean a smell it has managed to leave behind!"

In August of 1980, the stream of KOR flowed into the great river of Solidarity, but had already done much to determine the course of the river's flow. The policies of openness, truthfulness, autonomy of action, and trust were preserved. "The essence" of the movement, as Michnik later wrote from prison, still "lay in the attempt to reconstruct society, to restore social bonds outside official institutions." What ensued was an eruption throughout the society of civic activity of immense diversity, ranging from the trade unions themselves to associations formed to halt pollution and to protect consumers (areas that had been monumentally neglected by the regime). One is reminded of Tocqueville's description of America: "Americans of all ages, all conditions, and all dispositions constantly form associations. They have not only commercial and manufacturing companies, in which all take part, but associations of a thousand other kinds, religious, moral, serious, futile, general or restricted, enormous or diminutive. The Americans make associations to give entertainments, to found seminaries, to build inns, to construct churches, to diffuse books, to send missionaries to the antipodes." (The notable difference, of course, was that whereas the local groups in Tocqueville's America worked more or less in harmony with the national government those in Poland worked in opposition to it.) In this burst of activity, the very ingredients of political life, having been pounded apart by forty years of totalitarian rule, now came together again in new and vital forms. The classic formula for revolution is first to seize state power and then to use that power to do the good things you believe in. In the Polish revolution, the order was reversed. It began to do the good things immediately, and only then turned its attention to the state. In a sort of political and moral version of the hedonist's credo "*Carpe diem,*" the opposition proceeded directly, and without postponement, toward its goals. Its simple but radical guiding principle was to start doing the things you think should be done, and to start being what you think society should become. Do you believe in freedom of speech? Then speak freely. Do you love the truth? Then tell it. Do you believe in an open society? Then act in the open. Do you believe in a decent and humane society? Then behave decently and humanely. In Michnik's words in "A New Evolutionism," "every act of defiance permits us to build right now the framework of democratic socialism, which should be not just a legal and institutional structure but, what is even more important, a real, day-to-day community of free people." And, as he puts it in the same essay, "in their struggle for truth, or—to quote Leszek Kolakowski—'by living in dignity,' the opposition intellectuals are striving not only for the proverbial better tomorrow but also for a better today."

Timothy Garton Ash, the author of "The Polish Revolution: Solidarity," has aptly noted that the opposition's style has been to act "as if" Poland were already a free country. And once those in opposition began to act that way something unexpected happened. As soon as they started to act "as if," the "as if" started to melt away. Then they really *were* defending the worker (and often with success), or giving the lecture, or publishing the book. It wasn't "as if" it were a book, it *was* a book, and soon people were really reading it. Of course, in the country at large the "as if" did not melt away. That became clear when the book was confiscated, or the lecture was broken up by a government goon squad, or the innocent worker was sent off to prison in spite of the opposition's best efforts to defend him. Nevertheless, in the immediate vicinity of the action—and that vicinity expanded steadily as the movement grew—the "as if" was no pretense. There a small realm of liberty was created. And "liberty, when men act in bodies," Burke wrote, "is *power*." Thus a second surprising discovery was made by the opposition—the discovery that merely by fearlessly carrying on the business of daily life it grew powerful. But the power gained was not power that had been wielded by others and had now been wrested from them; it was new power, which had been created where there had been none before. The program, then, was not to seize political power from the state but to build up the society. In 1970, demonstrating workers had been brutalized by the police, whereupon some of them marched to Party Committee buildings—known in Poland simply as Committees—and burned them down. Later, Jacek Kuroń offered a piece of advice that gained renown and foreshadowed the future course of events: "Don't burn down Committees; found your own."

The distinction between "society," which was to be renewed by the movement, and "power," which was to be left to the state, became common currency within the opposition, and was the subject of much discussion. While no one really expected the government to "wither away," as in the old Leninist dream, a certain contemptuous indifference to it did develop among the members of the opposition. This indifference showed itself radiantly in the extraordinary personal courage demonstrated by people at all levels of society, who at times acted as if there were no repressive government in Poland, and it also showed itself, less happily, in the utter failure of the movement to anticipate the imposition of martial law: that took the leadership of Solidarity by surprise almost the way Solidarity had taken the government by surprise sixteen months earlier. Just as society had massed its millions for action without being noticed by the government, so the government now massed its soldiers and police for action without being noticed by society. It may be that the two sides underestimated each other's strength so drastically because they possessed different *kinds* of strength, and each side judged the other on the basis of its own kind:

to the government the opposition looked weak because it lacked military and police power, while to the opposition the government looked weak because it lacked public support. According to the "realistic" laws of the government's existence, the Solidarity movement was an impossibility, but equally, according to the more "idealistic" laws of Solidarity's existence, martial law was impossible. Michnik has characterized the difference memorably:

> The mighty and spontaneous social movement, deprived of examples, changing from one day to the next amid incessant conflicts with the authorities, did not possess a clear vision of piecemeal goals or a well-defined concept of coexistence with the communist regime. It allowed itself to be provoked into fights over minor issues, into inessential conflicts; it was full of disorder, incompetence, unfamiliarity with its enemies and the enemies' methods. Solidarity knew how to strike but not how to be patient; it knew how to attack head-on but not how to retreat; it had overall ideas but not a program for short-term actions. It was a colossus with legs of steel and hands of clay; it was powerful among factory crews but powerless at the negotiating table. Across from it sat its partner, which could not be truthful, run an economy, or keep its word, which could do only one thing: break up social solidarity. This partner had mastered this art in the thirty-seven years of its rule. This partner, the power élite, was a moral and financial bankrupt and was unable, because of its political frailty, to practice any type of politics. . . . The Polish communist system was a colossus with legs of clay and hands of steel.

What was perhaps most surprising about the imposition of martial law was the surprise itself. In less than a year and a half, Solidarity had made its "ideals" enough of a "reality" so that the effectiveness of time-tested tricks of repressive rule like martial law had been all but forgotten by a whole country. Solidarity lived by trust and it died by trust. Certainly this costly inattention to the government's plotting was a failure of the movement, yet it was a failure that had a certain definite grandeur.

In *A Warsaw Diary*, Ryszard Kapuściński writes, "Here everything is based on a certain principle of asymmetrical verification: the system promises to prove itself *later* (announcing a general happiness that exists only in the future), but it demands that you prove yourself now, *today,* by demonstrating your loyalty, consent, and diligence. You commit yourself to everything; the system to nothing." The opposition worked in exactly the opposite way. It proved itself *today,* and let *later* take care of itself. In so doing, it offered a new approach to one of the most intractable problems of all political life: the endemic discrepancy between evil means and good ends in politics—between the brutal and mendacious methods commonly accepted as a necessity of politics and the noble or visionary ends toward which these means are directed. In the direct action in society practiced by the opposition movement in Poland, means and ends were rolled into one. Every means was an end, and vice versa. For example, each of the "means" of KOR—openness, truthfulness, autonomy, and trust—was also an end. A courageous act or a truthful word was a good "end"—in itself, it enriched life, made life better—and a redressed grievance or an improvement in a factory's production was a good "means" to further accomplishment. To reform the adversary might take some time, but in the sphere of one's own actions the just society could be established right away. It followed that evil means could no longer be employed to attain good ends. If the journey and the destination were the same, it made no sense to spoil the conveyance in which one was riding. Here, I believe, is the source of the movement's nonviolence, which was especially striking for being practiced even more rigorously than it was preached—a discrepancy far more attractive and more unusual than the reverse discrepancy. The use of violence, spoiling means and ends at the same time, would have polluted the source of both the movement's virtue and its strength. The elements of the movement's style of action—its direct approach to society and its problems, its local emphasis, its rejection of violence and lying and other base means of striving for noble ends—formed a self-consistent whole. If you wished to act locally, then what could be more local than yourself? And if you wished to produce results *today,* then what area of life was more ready to hand, more thoroughly within your grasp, than your own actions? And if, accordingly, you made yourself and your own actions your starting point for the reform of society, then how could you permit those actions to be degraded by brutality, deception, or any other disfigurement? While this style of action was nonviolent, "nonviolence" seems both too restrictive and too negative a term with which to describe it: too restrictive because, along with being nonviolent, the movement was nondeceptive, nonsecretive, and non many other obnoxious things; and too negative because the deepest source of its strength was not any form of abstinence but, rather, the positive, energetic, open pursuit of a free and just society through incessant public action of the kind advocated by Michnik. The genius of the movement lay in its having seized upon a method of action that did not depend on violence and whose strength would have been undercut by the use of violence. A little violence would probably have been as harmful to Solidarity as a little pacifism would be to an army in the middle of a war.

The opposition movement's nonviolence was almost certainly a precondition for the strong support that the movement received from the Catholic Church—support that, by all accounts, was indispensable to it. Most observers agree that the national spirit that gave rise to Solidarity was born more than a year earlier, in June of 1979, when Pope John Paul II, the first Polish pope, returned for the first time to Poland. Shortly after the visit, Michnik described the crucial inner change in the mood of the public which it brought about:

> Julian Stryjkowski's phrase "Poland's second baptism" keeps coming to mind insistently. Indeed, something odd did happen. The very same people who are ordinarily frustrated and aggressive in the shop lines were metamorphosed into a cheerful and happy collectivity, a people filled with dignity. The police vanished from the main streets of Warsaw and exemplary order reigned everywhere. The people who had been deprived of their real power for so long all of a sudden regained their ability to determine their fate. This is how the social consequences of John Paul II's visit-pilgrimage can be sketched.

A movement born in a "second baptism" must remain faithful to its spiritual origin or lose its strength, and this movement's ability to remain faithful was made possible by the new style of action it had adopted. In modern times, the introduction of spiritual, or even purely moral, purposes into political life has been justifiably regarded with deep suspicion. The City of God and the City of Man, the argument runs, are in essence based on principles so different that for either to adopt the principles of the other will prove ruinous. The danger for the City of God is that by associating itself with the evil means that are supposedly intrinsic and necessary to political life it will be brutalized and lose its spiritual purity. The danger for the City of Man is that by adopting principles of pacifism, or even of mildness, that are embodied in such teachings as the Sermon on the Mount it will be enfeebled, and collapse, or else that in the attempt to wed the evil means of political life to the pure ends of spiritual life the evil means will be given even greater license than usual, and fanaticism and violence will increase. (The course of events in present-day Iran, where otherworldly purity is pursued with this-worldly brutality, shows that the danger is as real in our time as it has been in any other.) In view of these perils, many wise observers have suggested that the two Cities be kept apart; yet separation also has a cost. The moral teachings of religion lose half their field of operation if it must be acknowledged that right at the heart of human affairs there is a realm—the political—to which they have no application. At the same time, political life is set adrift morally if the moral standards that apply to private life are excluded from it. It is always possible to try to frame moral standards that apply to the political world alone, but every time someone makes a really thorough-going attempt—Machiavelli's writings are perhaps the most prominent example—we find that our private standards are violated, and we are repelled. This ancient opposition between the spiritual and the political realms is, at the very least, eased if in the political realm a method of action is adopted that does not cite noble ends as justification for evil means, or even distinguish between means and ends. Then spiritual and moral energies can flow into the political world without necessarily being corrupted. The two Cities then rest on a common foundation; namely, respect for the dignity and worth of the individual person, whose degradation "today" for some noble purpose "in the future" is rejected. This is not to say that political life can henceforth proceed to perfection—that the fulfillment promised by utopian revolutionaries can materialize forthwith—but only that the actors in the political realm invite judgment of their actions by the same standards that everyone accepts in private life. Political life, then, will be no closer to perfect than private life is, but it will no longer be singled out as a realm in which certain evils are in principle necessary and therefore justified.

Ever since Gandhi led India to independence through nonviolent action, it has become something of a cliché to say that nonviolence could succeed only against a parliamentary democracy like England—that it would have failed against a totalitarian power, such as Stalin's Soviet Union or Hitler's Germany. Inasmuch as Poland has not attained its independence—or, for that matter, even aimed at it—this assumption still holds. And it seems only reinforced when one reflects that the regime in Poland today, though brutal, is far more moderate than the regime of either Stalin or Hitler. Nevertheless, it is now a matter of record that by far the most effective resistance movement ever launched against a totalitarian regime was completely nonviolent. Nonviolent action, far from being helpless in the face of totalitarianism, turns out to be especially well suited to fighting it. Hence it would be misleading to suggest that the Poles made a free choice of nonviolence over violence, as though they had been offered an opportunity to overthrow the regime by violence but had turned it down on the ground of moral principle in favor of nonviolence. Rather, from the outset violence was recognized by almost everybody to be completely useless to the movement. Addressing the question of why the movement adopted nonviolent means, Michnik writes, "No one in Poland is able to prove today that violence will help us to dislodge Soviet troops from Poland and to remove communists from power. The U.S.S.R. has such enormous military power that confrontation is simply unthinkable. In other words: we have no guns." The decision against violence, then, was made not so much by the Poles themselves as by their historical situation. The greatness of the Polish movement lies not in a decision to renounce violence—although the self-discipline required to flawlessly maintain a policy of nonviolence in the heat and anger of the struggle deserves great credit—but in its discovery of peaceful means that still offered hope.

Historically, violence has usually been regarded as the ultima ratio—the final arbiter, to which people turn in the last, desperate hour, when all peaceful means have been tried and have failed. "Hallowed are the arms where no hope exists but in them," Livy writes. But when those hallowed arms fail, people have believed, all that remains is the silence either of submission or of death. In Poland, that sequence appears to have been reversed: the futility of violent means—a futility so evident to all that such means did not even have to be tested—was what led to a recourse to nonviolent ones. It was as though beyond the traditional means of last resort new, peaceful ones had been discovered. The government declared a "state of war," and, employing its monopoly of the means of violence against an unarmed society, it "won" the war. (In Michnik's mocking account, "General Jaruzelski has glorified the name of the Polish armed forces by capturing with a flanking movement the building of the Polish Radio and Television, not to mention the telephone exchange.") In the traditional scheme of things, that would be the end of the story; the last resort would have been exhausted, the last card played, and the population would resign itself to defeat. But this has not happened. It seems, Michnik writes, that "the Polish nation does not think it has been defeated." Failing to think it has been defeated, it fails to act as if it had been defeated, and, failing to act defeated, it is not defeated. "What I saw after my release"—on August 4, 1984—"exceeded not just my expectations but even my dreams," Michnik reports. "I found that the people of Solidarity were wise, determined, ready for a long struggle." The government crackdown has taken its toll, but the spirit of opposition is alive. Repression and activism continue side by side. The arrests are made, but people are not intimidated. They live now in what may be the most curious conditions to have developed in Poland so far: autonomy without liberty—freedom together with jail.

Poland's unfinished experiment in nonviolent action is of particular interest in a world in which violence in the form of the weapons of mass destruction threatens the ultimate self-defeat of man. While the Polish revolution may appear to have little to do with the nuclear question, it seems to me that there is an interesting parallel to be drawn between the plight of Poland under Soviet domination and the plight of the world in the nuclear age. For both Poland and the world, sane thinking must begin with the recognition that the use of violence is futile, self-defeating, and thus "unthinkable." (Michnik's use of this word seems significant.) Both Poland and the world are therefore driven to search for nonviolent solutions to their dilemmas. On this point, realism and idealism coincide, and nonviolence, so often regarded exclusively as a choice of idealists, is supremely realistic. And both Poland and the world have been advised by expert opinion that their plights are inescapable, and they should accept the status quo; anything else, both are told, would "destabilize" the existing situation. Yet Poland has, at the very least, found a path to follow, and in this there is hope for the world, too. We are led to wonder whether in the realm of international affairs and diplomacy there may not be a solution as unlikely in the eyes of the experts as Solidarity was—some ultima ratio beyond violence which the world is driven to employ, for reasons both pragmatic and idealistic, precisely because violence, the old ultima ratio, is now useless and bankrupt. If such a solution should be found, and if it should be employed to reunite a divided Europe, then it would be not only a counterpart of the Polish movement but a complement to it. Then Poland and the world would escape from their plights along the same path.

It is tempting to sum up by saying that the Polish revolution practiced a politics based on life, in which political power, assuming the form of public consent and public support, is the natural and spontaneous extension of human beings' ability to act together to build and create, whereas the government practiced a politics of death, in which political power, assuming the form of fear, is an extension of human beings' ability to tear down and destroy—ultimately, to kill one another. But Michnik, it seems to me, might bridle at such a description, finding in it the seeds of what, in his essay "Maggots and Angels," he calls the political sin of Manichaeanism, in which one assigns all evil to one's foe and all good to oneself. Michnik rejects political Manichaeanism wherever he sees it, but he finds it especially inappropriate for Poland. Acknowledging, as he does, that Soviet power is irremovable from the Polish scene for the foreseeable future, he recognizes that everyone, even the most courageous, must accommodate this reality in one way or another. That being so, it is impossible to divide Poland cleanly into two hostile camps, one evil and the other good. Instead, evil and good are distributed widely and subtly. They will be found in one balance in the government official who has to decide whether to be a little more ruthless and ideological in his decisions or to be a little bit more humane and pragmatic, in another balance in the professor who has to decide just how truthful to be in a certain monograph; and in yet another balance in the jailed activist who has to decide whether to sign the "loyalty oath" that the government has put before him as the price of his release. The first may be a largely greedy and self-interested person; the second may be basically decent but frightened; the third may be heroic but wavering. But in all of them good and evil are present, and in each case Michnik would like to see the good prevail—or, at least, advance a little. In this vision of society's betterment, no one can be wholly written off as a "maggot" and no one granted exemption from the human condition as an "angel."

The epithet "maggot" is not Michnik's own but was used originally by the contemporary writer Piotr Wierzbicki, in a satiric essay called "A Treatise on Maggots," in which he lists the various rationalizations that selfish or hypocritical or weak-willed people use to evade their responsibility to oppose the regime. Michnik responds by engaging in a novel exercise. He sorts through Polish history, asking which people, by Wierzbicki's criteria, would have to be called maggots, and concludes that many of the most highly honored figures would at some point in their careers have qualified. Michnik's purpose is not to discredit the heroes of Polish history but, rather, to encourage a more tolerant understanding of the compromises of the present day. History is often consulted by those seeking to assemble a list of grievances or to draw up an indictment. Michnik's intention is just the opposite: he uses history to forgive the present. Central to his argument is a recognition that the need for compromise had its origin in those political situations "where foreign domination of the Polish nation was chronic, while all hope for armed defense of national values was completely illusory; where compromise with a partitioning power became indispensable for saving the very existence of the nation." In such circumstances—which, of course, are also Poland's present ones—arguments for compromise with the regime, or even participation in it, can never be dismissed out of hand. While it is true that "full acceptance of the compromise formula would lead to moral compromise and spiritual capitulation," it is also true that "full rejection of this formula would lead to a more or less heroic isolation." Using historical examples, Michnik shows that different—and even seemingly opposite—stands could all have merits of their own. Those on the inside might

found institutions—a railroad, a university—of real and lasting importance to the country; those rebelling against the regime on the outside
might be defending the country's honor and inoculating it against
occupation at some future time. The eminent figures who made these
choices debated fiercely, and often bitterly (Michnik offers fascinating
accounts of the debates in his historical essays), but now Michnik seeks
what he calls, quoting the writer Antoni Slonimski, "angerless wisdom,"
in which the contributions made by those figures whose choices differed
are acknowledged, and might inspire more tolerance and cooperation
among people who face the same choices today. In this vision, understanding, toleration, and forgiveness are the watchwords for each
person's dealings with others, yet there is still a realm in which exacting
judgment is called for—one's dealings with oneself. Michnik implies
as much in an eloquent passage whose direct point is that no one can
make a moral choice for another.

> Aleksander Wat wrote somewhere that there is only one answer
> to the question of how intellectuals who live in countries ruled by
> Stalin should behave. It is the Shakespearean answer: they should
> die.
>   Perhaps it is the true answer. But I believe that this is an answer
> that one can give only to oneself, a measure that one can apply only
> to oneself, a sacrifice that one can ask only of oneself. Anyone who
> demands an answer to this question from others is arbitrarily giving
> himself the right to decide about others' lives. And this usually ends
> badly.

Michnik does not say that he is ready to die, but then he feels no
need to say it, since he has no advice to offer anyone else on the subject.
In any case, when it comes to sacrifice, actions speak louder than
words. Michnik counsels us to refrain from demanding self-sacrifice
from other people, but frequently he offers that counsel from jail.

Throughout the history of political affairs there flows an unending
stream of human blood. Sometimes it swells to a torrent, bearing all
before it, and sometimes it slows to a trickle, but it has never dried up
completely. In our time, it threatens to overflow its banks once and for
all and sweep away history itself. Some may reluctantly accept

bloodshed as a necessity of political life, some may deplore it, and some may embrace it, but all who enter the political world must come to terms with it in one way or another. The Polish opposition movement, for which and about which Michnik writes, did not add a single drop to this stream, except that which flowed from its own members' veins. And, while the movement has so far been unable to restrain the violence and repression of its antagonists, the positions it has staked out in the fight—fearless readiness to act in support of one's convictions; unwillingness to lower one's standards, in the name of effectiveness, to the level of one's antagonists'; readiness to make unlimited sacrifice in pursuit of limited goals; respect, in practice as well as theory, for the dignity of each person; readiness to die but unwillingness to kill; and unwavering resolve to live one's beliefs in the moment, so that even in supposed defeat something of beauty and value is left behind in the world—are among the most honorable, the most original, and the most fruitful of which the world has record. From within his prison cell, defying his captors, Adam Michnik writes, in words that will sound down the decades:

> To these people, with their lifeless but shifting eyes, with their minds that are dull but skilled in torture, with their defiled souls that yearn for social approval, you are only raw material with which to do anything they please. They have their own particular psychology: they believe that anyone can be talked into anything (in other words, everyone can be either bought or intimidated). To them, it is only a matter of the price to exact or the pain to inflict. Although their actions are routine, your every stumble, your every fall gives meaning to their lives. Your capitulation is no mere professional achievement for them—it is their raison d'être. And so you find yourself engaged in a philosophical debate with them about the meaning of your life, about taking the meaning away from their lives, about giving meaning to every human existence. You are engaged in the argument of Giordano Bruno with the Inquisitor, of the Decembrist with the czarist police superintendent, of Walerian Lukasinski with the czarist angel of annihilation, of Carl von Ossietzky with the blond Gestapo officer, of Osip Mandelstam with a member of the Bolshevik Party dressed in a uniform with the blue

piping of the N.K.V.D.; you are engaged in the never-ending argument about which Henryk Elzberg once said that the value of your achievement cannot be gauged in terms of your idea's chances for victory but rather by the value of the idea itself. In other words, you score a victory not when you win power but when you remain faithful to yourself.

Letters
from
Prison

EDITOR'S NOTE. After the imposition of martial law, on December 13, 1981, the leadership of Solidarity—about ten thousand people—were arrested, and Adam Michnik was among them. He was held in prison for two and a half years, whereupon he was released in an amnesty—only to be rearrested six months later and sentenced to three additional years of prison. All but the last *Letter,* which was written during the current prison term, in this section of the book were written during the first two and a half years of investigative arrest—December 13, 1981–July 21, 1984.

// Why You Are Not Signing . . . : A Letter from Białołęka Internment Camp 1982

My dear friend,

General Jaruzelski has announced that those internees who desist from activities "contrary to the law" will be released. And so freedom is within the reach of one's hand. A few strokes of the pen on the loyalty declaration will suffice. . . .

Friends and relatives are asking, "So what's stopping you from making these few inconsequential gestures?"

It is very easy, indeed, to exchange the barred window, with its clear outline of a barbed wire fence behind, it for "freedom." The steel gates of Białołęka will open up before you, and instead of the prison yards you will see the streets of your hometown, filled with strolling army patrols and rolling tanks. You will see people being asked for identification cards, cars being stopped to have their trunks inspected, the security agent, with his keen eye, fishing out of the crowds individuals suspected of "violating the state of war legislation." You will hear World War II terms that until now you knew only from history books: "roundup," "Volksliste"—words cleansed of the dignifying patina of time and pulsing with new menace. You will hear about new arrests, about people sought by the police or in hiding, about Draconian sentences.

And if you are capable of making self-interested decisions, then

3

the first reason for not signing is: it isn't worth it. Here, no one can put you in "provisional detention"; here, you need not fear anything. It is paradoxical, I know, but if one morning you are awakened by banging on the door you are not going to be afraid of the uniformed guests; it is only your good-humored jailer handing out the morning coffee. Here, you do not panic at the sight of the cynic with his darting eyes—a stool pigeon is not a threat. Białołęka is a moral luxury and an oasis of dignity. It is also a conspicuous symbol of your dissent and your importance. Since you are an internee, the authorities take you seriously.

They will sometimes try to scare you. A friend of mine, a factory worker from Warsaw, was promised fifteen years in jail; another was threatened with trial for espionage; a third was interrogated in Russian; a fourth was marched out of his cell and told that he would be going to the depths of Russia (when he was really being taken for an X-ray). But all this is bearable. I actually believe that it is easier to cope with than the morally and politically complicated situation on the other side of the wire fence. ("Perhaps it is easier to be in prison than to go free," a good friend wrote to me. "Outside, the waters have rushed forth and turned to foam, and an opaque scum is floating on the top.")

The primate of Poland has condemned the practice of coercing people to sign the loyalty declarations. The pope has openly called this violation of human conscience a crime. One cannot but agree with this definition. All condemnation must be directed at those who extort these written declarations—those who employ this cruel means of degrading human dignity. A young woman, the wife of a Solidarity activist, was imprisoned after being dragged away from her sick infant who, she was told, would be placed in an orphanage. She signed the declaration. A friend of mine was taken away from his mother, who lives alone and is dying of cancer, and was told that "not a soul will even make a cup of tea for your little mother." He signed the declaration. There is no point in listing any more cases of the cruelty of some people, the helplessness of others—the tragic dilemmas and the dastardly black-mail. Everyone is familiar with the various reactions of people who are subjected to these pressures. The primate of Poland left open the question of whether to sign, especially for teachers. In his opinion, for them to maintain their dignity and to be able to continue to teach are both important. The choice is always up to the individual—to the voice of his or her conscience and reason: no one can condemn anyone else's choice. Ostracism would play into the hands of the people in power, since this is precisely what they want—to break society's resistance and the solidarity of the people by creating divisions. To tolerate and understand, however, is not to decide that the act of signing the declaration is in itself morally indifferent. It is not. Every loyalty declaration is an evil; and a declaration that has been forced out of you is an evil which you were compelled to commit, although it may, at times, be a lesser evil. So this act sometimes deserves understanding, always compassion, but never praise. There are at least a few reasons for this. First of all, dignity does not allow it.

Impotence in the face of armed evil is probably the worst of human humiliations. When six hulks pin you to the ground, you are helpless. But you do not want to give up your natural right to dignity: you are not going to reach any agreements with the ruffians, you are not going to make any commitments. When they take you from your house, beat you with all their might, burn your eyes with tear gas, break open your front door with a crowbar and wreck your furniture right in front of your family, when in the middle of the night they drive you to the police station in handcuffs and order you to sign statements, then your ordinary instinct for self-preservation and your basic sense of human dignity will make you say NO.

Because even if these people were doing it all in the name of the best and noblest cause they would be destroying that cause with their misdeeds.

At this point you still know little. Only when, a few hours later, they drive you in the direction of Białołęka (you will look around with curiosity, for previously you knew this road only as far as good old Mokotów prison) will you hear on the prison van's radio, as your teeth chatter from the cold (these circumstances will later be called "humane conditions"), that war has been declared on your nation. It was declared by people who on behalf of this nation govern, proclaim, sign international agreements—the same people who publicly held out a conciliatory hand while secretly issuing orders to hunt us in the night.

And then you really know for sure that you will not make a gift of your loyalty declaration to these people, for they are incapable of any loyalty whatsoever.

And you still don't know what this war means; you still don't know by what methods factories and steelworks, shipyards and mines will be assaulted; you still don't know about the "bloody Wednesday" in the Wujek mine;[1] but you do know one thing already: to sign this declaration would be to negate yourself, to wipe out the meaning of your life; to betray the people who have faith in you; to betray your friends who are dispersed in different prisons—who have been sentenced and interned; to betray the friends who are being sought by the police and who are in hiding; to betray all those who will stand up for you—with a flier in Cracow or Gdańsk, a rally in Paris or New York. The face of Zbyszek who is in hiding, of Edek who has been sentenced, of Sewek hurrying down a Parisian boulevard have not yet begun to flash before your eyes. Nothing is fixed yet, the door is still open before you, you still have a choice. But you know already—your instincts are telling you—that to forsake your dignity is not a price worth paying to have the prison gates opened for you. And so here is the second reason: the demands of common sense.

Reaching agreements of any kind with people who treat the very concept of "agreements" completely arbitrarily, who regularly go back on their promises, and for whom lies are their daily bread, is contrary to common sense. After all, you have never known anyone who has had any dealings with the agents of the security services and has not felt cheated. To these people, with their lifeless but shifting eyes, with their minds that are dull but skilled in torture, with their defiled souls that yearn for social approval, you are only raw material to work with. They have their own particular psychology: they believe that anyone can be talked into anything (in other words, everyone can be either bought or intimidated). To them it is only a matter of the price to pay or the pain to inflict. Although they act according to routine, your every

---

1. On December 16, 1981, while breaking the strike in the Wujek mine (Silesia), the armored police units (ZOMO) killed nine miners. It was the most violent episode of the military coup d'état.

stumble, your every fall gives meaning to their lives. Your capitulation is no mere professional achievement for them—it is their *raison d'être*.

And so you find yourself engaged in a philosophical debate with them about the meaning of your life, about the meaninglessness of their lives, about giving meaning to every human existence. You are engaged in the argument of Giordano Bruno with the Inquisitor, of the Decembrist with the tsarist police superintendent, of Walerian Łukasiński with the tsarist angel of annihilation, of Carl von Ossietzky with the blond Gestapo officer, of Osip Mandelstam with a member of the Bolshevik party dressed in a uniform with the blue piping of the NKVD. You are engaged in the never-ending argument about which Henryk Elzberg[2] once said that the value of your participation cannot be gauged in terms of your chances of victory but rather by the value of your idea. In other words, you score a victory not when you win power but when you remain faithful to yourself.

Your common sense also tells you that by signing the loyalty declaration you are placing a whip in the hands of the policemen. They will wave it around and threaten you in order to force you to sign the next declaration, your agreement to collaborate with them. With this, your loyalty declaration will transform itself into your pact with the devil. This is why you should not give these police inquisitors even the tip of your finger: because they will instantly grab your whole arm. Surely you must know someone whose life has been shattered by one moment of moral inattention or weakness of spirit, someone who has been pursued by phone calls, whose home and office are regularly invaded by the police, who is blackmailed every time he or she goes abroad. Such people pay for one moment of unwisdom with years of degradation and fear. If you don't want to be afraid, if you want to respect yourself, your inner voice tells you, don't enter into any agreements with the policemen.

You harbor no hatred toward the policemen, only pity. You know the high incidence of mental illness among them; you know that every one of them is ashamed in front of his children. You know that the sentence of national oblivion will be passed on them (who can remember

---

2. Henryk Elzberg (1887–1967), Polish philosopher and historian.

any more the executioners and informers of bygone days?), that they can win the fame only of Herostrates—like commissar Kajdan in Stefan Żeromski's *Before the Spring* or colonel Rózański from the Polish Stalinist Security Service. And this is the third reason—the argument of memory.

The history of your nation is fixed in your memory. You know that in its history a loyalty declaration signed in jail has always been a disgrace, loyalty to oneself and to the national tradition a virtue. You can remember those who were tortured and jailed for long years but who signed no declarations. And you know that you, too, will not sign them, because you are unable and unwilling to renounce the memory of the others, especially since there are certain people who keep on popping up in your memories: those who lost the battle for dignity in prison. With your mind's eye you can see Andrzej M., the excellent literary critic, your friend, who while in jail wrote a brilliant essay denouncing people—proof of his moral death; Heniek Sz., an ambitious and intelligent man, who let himself be maneuvered into the role of chief informer on his friends; Zygmunt D., a charming companion and intelligent young man who gave in once and then spent years denouncing his friends. So you remember with dread and terror this human debris, these people who have been battered by the police machine, and you will see that your own future, too, is an open question. The choice is yours, but your memory ceaselessly repeats in your ear: you, too, can be like them. No one is born an informer; you forge your fate daily, at the price of your life. At this point you still haven't heard about the loyalty declarations; the infamous interviews, the shameful pronouncements read on the radio. You still don't know how Marian K. from Nowa Huta, an intelligent and courageous Solidarity activist, was cheated when in his declaration he wanted to render unto Caesar the things that are Caesar's and unto God the things that are God's, but ended up giving everything to the police, because he had not imagined that there exist situations when ambiguity turns into explicitness and half-truths become full-fledged lies. You still haven't heard the interview with Stanisław Z., a worker and an activist in Nowa Huta, an artful dodger whom people always distrusted and who is now living up to their suspicions by echoing the government's propaganda. You still haven't read the declaration made by Marek B., the [Solidarity] National

Commission's spokesman, who was a physicist from Gdańsk and Lech's protégé, slandering Solidarity's people. Nor the declaration made by Zygmunt L. of Szczecin, Marian J.'s adviser, who dictated to Marian all that drivel about "the Jews who are in power" and about "setting up gallows for the party leaders," and who today is condemning "extremists." In other words, you still don't know that this time, as always, people will be lied to, cheated (think of Zdzisław R. from Poznań, to whom you talked at the unveiling of the Poznań monument), cowed yet again. You don't know that this time, too, the rats will be the first to run from the sinking ship. But you do know already that all this is nothing new, that you will not feel like explaining to these policemen who are waving your release in front of your nose, in this crowded police station, that it is they who are the slaves and that no release will free them from their slavery. You don't feel like explaining that these people who are crowded into these smoke-filled corridors, and who have only just been torn out of their homes—these worker activists, professors and writers, students and artists, friends and strangers—that they are the very life and substance of liberty and that this is why war has been declared on them. You don't feel like explaining to the policeman who whacked your face with sadistic delight (he was given permission to do it, at last—he had to spend sixteen months restraining himself) the meaning of Vassili Rozanov's[3] essay, which argues that European culture's most fundamental debate is the antagonism between the man who holds the knout and the man who is being flogged with it. And you don't feel like explaining to him that your encounter is the latest incarnation of this antagonism. You will not talk to him at all. You will smile ironically, you will choose not to sign anything (not even your warrant), you will express your regrets, and—you will leave the room.

They will drive you to Białołęka in the company of people who are the pride of every Polish home. You will ride together with a famous philosopher and an eminent historian, a theater director and a professor of economics, a Solidarity leader from Ursus and one from Warsaw University, students, and workers. In Białołęka itself they will not beat you. On the contrary! You are to serve as proof of their liberalism and

---

3. The Russian philosopher (1856–1919).

humanism; for very soon they will be showing you off to the International Red Cross delegation and to Sejm[4] deputies, and even to the primate of Poland. So they will be quite courteous, quite helpful, quite gentle. But every now and then they will make you take a walk between two lines of men in helmets, armed with truncheons and shields, in order to frighten you and to remind you of their power. The only thing that these masquerades will remind you of is that this regime is like the vicious dog that loves to bite even though his teeth have fallen out. Pavel Korchagin's ethos has disappeared;[5] nowadays when someone shouts at a policeman, a flash of fear appears in his pupils. You can detect this fear and uncertainty under his helmet, through his uniform, behind his shield (a Japanese import). And you will realize right away that a policeman's fear means that there is still hope for you. Hope is important. Perhaps more important than anything else.

After all, this is precisely what the battle is being fought over: the policemen want to force out of us a declaration that we are giving up hope. They know that the person who pledges his loyalty to this system of coercion and lies is forsaking hope for a Poland in which lies and coercion will be rejected. These declarations are supposed to make us into lowly and servile people, who will not rise up to fight for freedom and dignity. So by refusing to talk with the policeman, by refusing to collaborate, by rejecting the status of informer, and by choosing to be a political prisoner you are defending hope. Not just hope within yourself and for yourself but also in others and for others. You are casting your declaration of hope out of your prison cell into the world, like a sealed bottle into the ocean. If even one single person finds it, you will have scored a victory.

I know what you are thinking: he is reciting platitudes and banalities, demanding heroism; he is hopelessly romantic. But this is not quite true.

I agree with the first point. Banal truths, if they are to remain

---

4. The Diet, Polish parliament.
5. Pavel Korchagin, hero of Nikolai Ostrovsky's novel *How the Steel was Tempered* (1934) is a symbol of the total devotion to the communist cause.

banal, must be remembered, especially at times when banal behavior requires some courage, whereas relativism—which incidentally does serve a purpose in intellectual activity—can lead people to dilute moral standards and question what should be morally self-evident. But I do not believe that allegiance to these truths is the same as having romantic values.

You know that you are no hero and that you never wanted to be one. You have never wanted to die for your nation, or for freedom, or for anything else, for that matter: the fates of Winkelried and Ordon [legendary heroes who died for their countries, which were overwhelmed by superior enemies] have never tempted you. You have always wanted to be alive, to live like a normal person, to have respect for yourself and for your friends. You have always enjoyed the moral comfort that allows you to take pleasure in your inner freedom, in beautiful women, and in wine. This war surprised you in the company of a pretty woman, not while you were plotting an assault on the Central Committee headquarters.

Nevertheless, they did declare this war on you and over thirty million other people, and so you are forced to recognize that amid the street roundups, the ignoble court sentences, the despicable radio programs, and the distribution of leaflets by underground Solidarity you will not regain the normalcy that was based on respect for yourself. Now you must choose between moral and material stability, because you know that today's "normalcy" will have the bitter taste of self-defeat. And you will not, for the sake of life's enjoyments, give in to the tempting offers of freedom made by the policeman, who seeks to delude you with promises of happiness but really brings suffering and inner hell instead.

No, this is not heroism. It is mere common sense. Bertold Brecht said, "Woe be to nations that must have their heroes." How can one disagree with this? Heroism presupposes exceptionality. Today, Poles need normalcy and ordinariness if they are to resist the rule of the military and the police.

Let me make myself clear: this is not a program of romantic intransigence but rather a strategy for social resistance. It serves no purpose today to bring back the classic conflict in Polish political thought between romantic insurrectionism and realistic organicism, as does Daniel P. in the weekly *Polityka*.[6] Let's take a closer look at his arguments.

P. sees the validity of both sides of the dispute, but he argues for the point of view of the organicists, who have decided to remain on the editorial staff of *Polityka*, and to risk being asked by their children "What did you do when instead of arguments came the soldiers?"—who chose a responsible attitude instead of voluntary withdrawal from public life—so-called internal exile. "There is no point in chasing after lost innocence," P. writes. There is no point in changing from a realist's costume to a fundamentalist's. Spurs and bedroom slippers do not go together," he writes of the *Polityka* editors who rebelled.

In his opinion, "It would not be in the public interest if newspapers stopped being published in Poland, or if their variety were further limited. We must act so as to make the army go back to the barracks. . . . Who else will do it if we take comfortable little jobs as spokesmen for Polish-American private commercial enterprises or as editors of apolitical publications?" Daniel P. uses all the arguments that you know so well—from, for example, the discussions that arose after Piotr Wierzbicki's "A Treatise on Maggots"[7] was published. P. does not preach in Newspeak, he doesn't talk nonsense; he uses serious arguments and clearly formulates the pressing dilemmas of present-day Poles.

His reasoning must be debated on two levels—the concrete and the universal. If both the insurrectionists and the organicists are necessary, then we need people who are organicists in form and insurrectionists in substance. We need people who do not lie publicly, whom we can trust, who reject compromise with the system of government that has been imposed on this nation—yet who do not ask for rash actions, call for terrorism, or organize urban or rural guerrillas. In other

6. The journalist Daniel Passent is deputy-editor of the weekly *Polityka*. Created in 1956, *Polityka* served the party's liberal wing. Its founder and first editor-in-chief Mieczysław Rakowski, deputy-prime minister of the Jaruzelski government, was one of the main architects of the December 13, 1981, coup.

7. See this volume, page 169.

words, the classic dilemma can be described as grass-roots activity versus collaboration, not just as grass-roots activity versus insurrection.

Compromise is necessary for a healthy public life, provided that it is real compromise, both in substance and in the public eye. When a compromise is seen by the public as renunciation of conviction or as flagrant treason, it is no longer a compromise. It becomes a falsehood or a misunderstanding. To side with WRONa[8] today is to take a stand against the nation—we both know this all too well. The loyalty declaration that the policemen are demanding from you and the somewhat different one that Daniel P.'s colleagues in his editorial office have been asked to sign are not a compromise; they are acts of collaboration, and have been conceived exclusively as such. Whoever attempts to save the August "renewal" (I don't like this term, which is used by the party; I prefer the expression "a formula for democracy") with this act is irrevocably bringing about its destruction. So much for the general question. Now for concrete examples. Daniel P. seems to believe that *Polityka* will become—as it did some years ago—an oasis of half-truths in the sea of lies, a paper with a touch of decency. I am of a different opinion. I believe that this idea's time has passed—not on December 13, 1981, and not even on September 1, 1980, with the signing of the Gdańsk accords—but in the middle of the Gierek decade, when *Polityka* was transformed from a relatively liberal and restrained critic of the system into its agile apologist. In June 1976, at the time of the Radom and Ursus workers' strikes, *Polityka* became a typical product of the decadence of the Gierek team and the spokesman for Gierek's disintegrating strategy. In the Solidarity era, it was no longer a credible paper—not for the authorities and not for the people. It was not even an interesting paper, merely an anachronistic one. The political rise of its editor-in-chief coincided with the political death of *Polityka*. Today it is only a caricature of itself. The entire history of *Polityka* is the story of a mirage which a sizable part of the Polish intelligentsia came to believe—an

8. WRON is an acronym of the Military Council for the National Salvation, a temporary military government that ruled Poland during the State of War (December 13, 1981–July 22, 1983). WRON is just one letter short of "wrona," i.e., "crow." Much of the antigovernment propaganda was based on that coincidence.

illusion that the system could be reformed from above if the intellectuals joined in the palace intrigues, if they knowledgeably walked in the corridors of the Central Committee, and if they spent enough time in ministers' waiting rooms. This idea has been killed, and nothing will resuscitate it. Social conflict—and, through it, potential social compromise—can take place only on the factory floor and in the university lecture hall and not in a session of the Sejm or the Central Committee's plenum. However intertwined and complex the history of the relations between the communist rulers and Polish society has been, with this last "war" the party has deprived itself of its mandate to govern, and no one can do anything to change this—not even by pulling the traditional four-cornered military cap by force over the police helmet.

If we are to have any influence on Poland's future, then it must be forged by an organized society exerting incessant pressure on the authorities. To rely on the good will of the WRONa bosses is like waiting for manna to fall from the sky. Yet it is reasonable to rely on their weakness: it is reasonable to believe that those in power can be forced to compromise. This belief is justified by the fact that there is an obvious ideological and programmatic vacuum within the party. The apparatus stands for power and privilege, not for ideas or values. The most obvious manifestation of this is the regime's habitual reliance on the argument of force as a substitute for the force of arguments. Let us travesty Hegel: Minerva's C.R.O.W. flies out at dusk.

You know how profound the feeling of loneliness can be. You think that you are powerless against the police-army machine that was mobilized on that December night. You still don't know what will happen. You still don't know that people will begin to recover from the shock, that underground papers will appear, that Zbyszek B. will lead his Solidarity region from the underground, that in Wrocław they will fail to capture Władek F.; that Gdańsk, Świdnik, and Poznań will again shake up all Poland; that illegal union structures will be formed. You still don't know that the generals' vehicle is sinking in sand, its wheels spinning in place, that the avalanche of repression and calumnies is missing its aim.

But you do know, as you stand alone, handcuffed, with your eyes filled with tear gas, in front of policemen who are shaking their guns at you—you can see it clearly in the dark and starless night, thanks to your favorite poet—that the course of the avalanche depends on the stones over which it rolls. [Czesław Miłosz] And you want to be the stone that will reverse the course of events.

March 25, 1982

// Why You Are Not Emigrating ... : A Letter from Białołęka 1982

Dear friend,

You asked me what I thought about General Jaruzelski's offer of emigration. This act of kindness applies only to internees; those who have already been sentenced, those who are currently in jail, and ordinary citizens who didn't happen to be interned cannot apply for an exit visa.

The answer to your question is really quite simple: I do not plan to emigrate. But the problem of emigration itself is neither simple nor new nor irrelevant to the present situation. As long ago as you can remember, Polish attitudes toward emigration have been ambivalent, combining envy with lack of trust, a feeling of inferiority with megalomania. You can probably remember from your childhood those biting remarks about General Anders,[1] who wanted to return to Poland "riding on a white horse"; the vicious comments about the writers who had "chosen freedom" [decided to stay in the West]; the ironic jokes about the ministers in the London government-in-exile, who had settled down nicely on British soil while grotesquely preserving the institutions

This letter has been signed with one of Adam Michnik's pen names—Andrzej Zagozda.

1. Army General Władysław Anders (1892–1970) commanded Polish troops in World War II. Later he became a symbolic leader of the exiled Polish community in London.

of their prewar state and issuing arrogant advice to their countrymen back home.

Let's honestly admit this much: by encouraging such opinions, the official propaganda machine scored a great success. In our youth, in the 1950s and 1960s, the community of émigrés did not have a good reputation. They were considered something alien. There existed a stereotype of the émigré as someone who turned his back on his country, who placed himself outside his nation, who did not share its good and bad times, who hopelessly yearned for a return to old times and privileges for himself—the émigré who chose easy earnings, security, and prosperity and who, for American money, told lies about Poland on Radio Free Europe.

The dominant view was that in order to speak about the most important Polish issues one had to be here, on the banks of the Vistula, where life is difficult and uncomfortable—not on the Seine or the Thames, where life is comfortable and predictable.

Few people read émigré publications then, and almost no one sought inspiration for political action in them. The "little stabilization" of the sixties was in splendid bloom. People wanted to enjoy some peace after the years of Stalinist terror. And following the years of poverty after the war, they were settling down and looking for satisfaction in professional and family life. This state of affairs was unacceptable to the émigré way of thinking. For the émigrés, the "little stabilization" was not enough. They thought only of independence and democracy. Thus, whatever real substance the émigrés' political message may have had—and I do not want to idealize it—people in Poland would accept no programs involving any major changes in their lives; the émigrés could at most upset their spiritual stability, and give them a guilty conscience for failing to try to broaden their national and human rights. The Poles who were scattered all over the world were viewed as rich relatives from abroad and not as a component of Poland's twentieth-century history. How incredible! To think that such opinions were possible in a country whose culture is irrevocably linked to émigrés; a country that for so many years relied for its spiritual existence on its émigré community—on the writings of the romantics, the music of Chopin, the political activities of the nineteenth-century Great Emigration; a country whose people should by rights understand the reasons for and the significance of emigration better than anyone else! While the Great Emigration was shown respect and taught in schools, its praise recited at anniversary celebrations, the contemporary emigration was ignored and slighted. This continued only until a certain moment. As the official propaganda became increasingly annoying, as the censors' net caught disloyal allusions in newspapers and books with increasing frequency, and as the will to protest and defend oneself grew, the people turned more often and more gladly to the émigré heritage. Customs officials confiscated copies of the Paris *Kultura*[2] from travelers' suitcases; police squads, when they searched apartments, took away books by the émigré writers Miłosz and Gombrowicz, Herling-Grudziński and Mieroszewski, Wierzyński and Hłasko. Masses of people listened to Radio Free Europe, searching not only for information about the parts of the world not covered by the Polish media but also for honest news about their own country—about the follies of censorship and the protests of the intellectuals. The rebellious intelligentsia sought to communicate with Polish society via London and Paris—and they succeeded. Thus, the émigrés, too, found a language they could share with their countrymen; they, too, began to communicate with Poland, again becoming useful, again becoming a part of their nation. This was not—as you will remember—a process without its costs.

It was risky to cooperate with the émigrés, and this was demonstrated by the harsh sentences handed down at a series of trials. But the reconstructed bridge was functioning again. Émigré publications carried more and more material from Poland, and this material became increasingly interesting. The "little stabilization" was over; the "great chaos" of 1968 came.

In First Secretary Władysław Gomułka's famous speech on March 19, 1968, in which he attacked "enemies and troublemakers," he abundantly cited Juliusz Mieroszewski's writings in the Paris *Kultura*,

2. *Kultura*, the most influential émigré publication, is a political and literary monthly. Founded in 1949 and Paris-based, it is published by Jerzy Giedroyc's "Institut Littéraire" together with a historical quarterly *Zeszyty Historyczne*. Close to four hundred books in Polish have been published by Institut Littéraire, with authors such as Arthur Koestler, Alexander Weissberg, Alexandr Solzenitsyn, Czesław Milosz, Witold Gombrowicz, and Boris Pasternak.

searching in them for the causes of the Polish political problems. The majority of students (you were an exception) were unfamiliar with these articles, but Gomułka, or his speechwriter, showed a keen intuition. For it is easy to see in retrospect that it was indeed Mieroszewski who managed to build an intellectual bridge between the impractical maximalism of the émigrés and the excessively practical pessimism of people in Poland. He created a vision for evolutionary change in the system, a vision which later informed the practices of the Polish democratic opposition.

Gomułka also noticed something that was not yet apparent to many people: the effects of the emigration were being felt in Poland. Books were being smuggled back across the Polish border in great quantities, passed from person to person, hidden from the watchful eye of the police. Those who emigrated sent back information about the world and truth about our nation's history, and they sent back masterpieces of contemporary literature, and uncensored reflections on hope and hopelessness in Polish life. And the emigration itself was being enriched by new people and was undergoing an internal transformation. Émigrés were no longer the anonymous contemporaries of our parents and grandparents: they were your friends and mine.

One consequence of the 1968 March events was a reassessment by the Polish intelligentsia of the question of emigration. The state authorities allowed emigration. So the professor who was fired from his university and the student who was expelled were forced to ask themselves: now what?

The eternal Polish question: here or there, real emigration or internal emigration, compromise and grass-roots work or a firm stand and silence, work within the official structures or construction of independent ones? I'm sure that you can remember the scores of discussions on this subject, how the answers varied, how variously the reasons for and against were expressed. But isn't it now clear that *everyone* contributed to the August 1980 breakthrough: those who formed independent organizations—who aided the persecuted, who created the free labor unions, who founded independent publishing houses; those in the official structures who spoke with less candor, but whose voices were more audible, and thereby created the valuable intermediate zone between the illegal and the official; and, finally, those who emigrated and wrote wise books (Leszek Kołakowski, Maria Hirszowicz, etc.), edited *Aneks*—a superb political quarterly—organized material help for people in Poland, and informed the world about what was going on in Poland? All this, however, is clear only today. In 1968 the conflicts were delineated more sharply, and the choices were usually seen as mutually exclusive. I am sure that you can remember the heated arguments and the accusations, the bitterness of friends and the satisfaction of adversaries. You can also remember—for how can we forget—our fury at those who chose to emigrate . . .

Today, we regret our anger but not our choices. We stayed in Poland then, even though it was neither an easy nor a safe decision. The security agents reminded us of it often enough with their unrestrained persecution. Let me repeat: everyone was right then. But if you can remember the fundamental issue of our dispute, it was how best to resist the policies of the communist authorities, who had divided us into "Jews" and "Aryans," and then offered the "Jews" the opportunity to "choose a mother country for themselves." The anger was directed at Gomułka, minister of internal affairs Moczar, and their colleagues, who introduced racist discrimination into our country, but part of that anger was then redirected at our friends who had given in passively to this discrimination.

Why did they leave? For many reasons: because of wounded national pride and trampled personal dignity, to make a living and to have peace and quiet, stability and security, to continue their intellectual work in conditions of freedom, and also to serve the Polish cause. Finally, because they wanted to. And a human being should have the right to do what he wants. Today, no thinking person can say that these people, by leaving, placed themselves outside the nation.

But one must also take into consideration the reactions of unthinking people. After all, to them—and also to the young, the uninformed, the deceived—all this was not so obvious. They saw emigration as running away. For the young and the unwise saw that not everyone was leaving. The activities and intentions of those who left were rendered credible by those who stayed—the scholars, the writers, the student activists. Being here, in Warsaw, Cracow, or Gdańsk, taking your stand, you lent credibility and meaning to the actions of those who were in New York, Paris, London, and Stockholm; you testified to the honesty of their actions and initiatives, of their books and declarations. In other words, by refusing to emigrate, you gave meaning to those who chose to emigrate. When the question "Did today's emigrants' attachment to Poland end when they started being mistreated?" was asked publicly, you—by being there and acting as you did—discredited such blabber. Such questions were not asked only by people who had been trained by agents. That is why these arguments should not be ignored. The young and the unwise must be reminded of the value of emigration, but we must also take into account the emotions of frustration and aggression aroused by emigration. In captive and atomized societies, such emotions often have great popular appeal. They are a product of frustrations built up over the years. An unsuccessful life, a failed career, an overdose of moral compromise—all give rise to frustration. This can bear fruit in the form of aggression toward others— those who have done well, those who have found their place in the sun, those who do not share in our misery and are free of our humiliations. When the authorities know how to manipulate these emotions, you can observe the phenomenon of redirected aggression: the odium of anger descends not on those who are in power but on the oppositionists, and especially those in exile.

These are not new or optimistic or heartening observations but— you will agree with me—they do describe realistically the mechanisms of human anger in this best of all possible worlds.

All this is worth thinking about today when—again thanks to the good graces of the communist powers-that-be—you are confronted with the question of emigration.

This problem has been intensely discussed by the internees and one can hardly be surprised by that. At one time, an execution squad or a long jail term for espionage awaited people like us. Today, we are told that we have a choice: either leave or stay in jail indefinitely.

So you have a choice: jail or exile. Jaruzelski is a humane master. But why, in a country from which it is normally not easy to travel abroad, do the authorities give this option to people they regard as their enemies?

The government's calculation, it appears, is simple. Emigration is supposed to divide Solidarity from within and make the union repulsive to the public; it is supposed to prove the moral baseness of the people who once loudly demanded, "let Poland be Poland," and who, after a few months in jail, exchange Poland for Canada. It will be easy to contrast these people with the "healthy base" who are to create the new state-sponsored labor union that will be free of "politickers" from "the Solidarity extreme."

The government wants to follow the example of the Soviet Union, which, in order to undermine the democratic movement, has, in the last ten years, given some dissidents the opportunity to emigrate. This is the government's reasoning: a worker activist or an opposition intellectual emigrates; then after enjoying the limelight for a short period, he turns into a troublesome acquaintance, a burdensome regular in the waiting rooms of various institutions which want only to get rid of him. He is no longer an authority at home, hence no one listens to him, and he loses his importance in the West.

You are familiar with the West, so you know that such reasoning is not absurd. Émigrés quarrel among themselves, they are condemned to dependence on one another; they are forgotten by the rest of the world.

So often, the migration from jail into exile is a road from hell to nothingness.

But this is not what I wanted to talk about right now. In political terms, each decision to emigrate is a gift to Jaruzelski by which we relinquish our authority, provide him with an excellent argument against Solidarity, and facilitate the pacification of society.

Andrzej Z. wrote in a letter to his fellow internees, ". . . to society we are a symbol of resistance. Not because we are so magnificent but because, by depriving us of freedom, the powers-that-be have cast us in this role in their play entitled *The State of War,* and we are acting in it regardless of our will." So—let me add—*noblesse oblige.* "We are given," wrote Andrzej Z., "the option of emigrating not because every citizen of our country has that right but because (rightly or wrongly) we are considered persons who are 'trusted by society,' and the authorities want to prove us unworthy of this trust. It is one thing to have free choice of the country of one's residence and another to win one's freedom by helping the bandit who has deprived us of that freedom and by harming those who will not be offered this transaction."

You do understand, I hope, why I share Andrzej Z.'s point of view. The emigration offer is a challenge to the Solidarity movement, a challenge that is both political and moral. The interned Solidarity activists who choose exile are committing an act that is both a capitulation and a desertion.

I have put it in strong terms, I know. I can just hear you say that it is not in my character, that I'm abandoning my principle of tolerance, that the decision to emigrate is a very personal one. All this is true. But the decision to be active in Solidarity, to seek society's trust, has also been personal, and it has affected others as well. It is important to keep in mind the existence of those other people. Of many different people: those sentenced for the December strikes that were organized in your defense, those imprisoned for posting notices in your defense, those pursued by the police for organizing actions in your defense. It is worth stopping to think about all these people and their reaction to the news—which will reach them in their hiding places and prison cells—that you are leaving Poland.

And I am not talking about the political dimension of this situation—the fate of the Solidarity movement. Perhaps you no longer want to be involved in it? Perhaps you want to stop hitting your head against the wall and trying to accomplish the impossible? I have in mind ordinary human decency and elementary loyalty. Not only toward those who are fighting but also toward those who have placed their trust in you, and in whom you have lit the flame of selflessness, truth, and dignity in public life: those who bring food for you while you are interned, who pray for you in churches, think of you with faith, hope, and love, and for whom you are—as was all of Solidarity—a symbol of a better Poland, the Poland of tomorrow.

When you remember them, you will easily understand that politics here is inseparably linked with morality and that a political choice is inseparably linked with a moral choice. You must remember this.

Indeed, you do not believe in a quick victory, in the imminent reconstruction of pre-December Solidarity. You know that an arduous journey is ahead of you, that it is marked with the suffering of defeat and the bitter taste of human frailty. But then you did not idealize pre-December Solidarity. You can remember all too well your own concern with the turn events took—with the advancement of the loud-mouths and the trimmers, with the intoxication and daze brought on by sudden promotions, with the creation of a court and of court intrigues. You watched it from close by, so you must have seen the symptoms of a revolution betrayed and the seeds of degeneration sowed. But in those months, which you would exchange for no others in your life, and for which you have always been prepared to pay with years in jail, you also saw people getting up from their knees, people yearning for free and true words, people taking in those words as if they were the communion wafer, people with radiant faces and trusting eyes—and you know that no one will be able to crush all this with tanks. And you know that you are not going to see faces like these on a Parisian boulevard.

I hope that I have expressed my views clearly. From what I have written it should be clear that I have no emigration phobia. It was not phobia that dictated these remarks. And it was not patriotic blindness. And it is not courage that makes me choose prison instead of banish-ment. If anything, I am making this choice out of fear. Out of the fear that by saving my neck I may lose my honor.

March 1982

// The Polish War: A Letter from Białołęka 1982

//   This is an undeclared war. On that Saturday night in December [1981], agents of the Security Service banged on our doors; then—after breaking them open with crowbars, beating us severely, and attacking us with tear gas—they drove us away to prisons and called us internees. We were the first prisoners of war in this war which the communist establishment has declared on its own people. This nighttime action was the first victorious battle for General Jaruzelski, who implemented in a most peculiar way the resolution of the Ninth Congress of the Polish United Workers' party [PUWP] calling for a separation of powers: he became at the same time the minister of national defense, the prime minister, and the first secretary of the party. And now he is the chief of the temporary military government, WRONa [the C.R.O.W.]. He will forever be associated by Poles with that stupid and ugly bird—that caricature of the eagle that symbolizes the Polish state.

The war was declared on the Poles without a moment's notice. In the future, the historian will appreciate the precision of the strike, the excellent timing, the efficiency of the action. The historian will appreciate the consistency with which the enemy's resistance was overcome, and the poet will certainly sing the praises of the brilliant military victories that took place in the streets of Gdańsk and in the yards of Warsaw factories—in steelworks, mines, and shipyards. By capturing with an outflanking movement the Polish radio and television building,

25

not to mention the telephone exchange, General Jaruzelski has covered the Polish armed forces with glory. Indeed, not since Jan Sobieski's siege of Vienna has any of our military leaders been able to claim such a success. Now musicians will compose symphonies, artists will design wreaths, and film directors will make patriotic films—all to honor the generals of that December night. The Council of State will certainly vote a new decoration for participation in the campaign of December 1981. . . .

But let's stop joking. Even though the government propaganda *is* a joke, let us ask ourselves, stunned as we may still be, what the meaning of the Polish events was.

On the night of December 12, a desperate communist elite set out to defend its position as the ruling class, to preserve its power and the privileges tied to it. The position of the power elite—and I will not go into this in detail—was indeed endangered. Not only in Poland but in the entire communist bloc. The armed coup that took place in December was not intended to create a communist utopia; rather, it was a classic antiworking class counterrevolution carried out to defend the conservative interests of the ancien régime. Notwithstanding the claims made by the official propaganda, the coup was not a response to attempts to take over political power. Solidarity had neither a shadow cabinet nor a plan for a coup d'état. The origins of the December coup should be sought in the basically unsolvable conflict between the multimillion-strong social movement that was organized into Solidarity and the totalitarian structures of the communist state. The bone of contention was the very existence of an independent and self-governing institution supported by the people. So it was not power that was at stake but the range of power (in other words, the limits of the party's *nomenklatura*), the style of power (of law and order), the nature of the compromise to be reached by the government and the governed (the degree of pluralism allowed in public life), and the form of the workers' institutions and local self-management. The implementation of a program of reforms that would encompass all these areas of public life subverted the basic principle of communist rule. It was quite clear that the government apparatus would not renounce willingly even a scrap of its power; thus conflicts were inevitable. But we imagined that the confrontations would evolve differently—that the government would not go so far as to resolve a social conflict with military force, substituting the argument of force for the force of arguments.

This is not the first crisis in the history of communist states. But whoever compares the 1956 events to the Prague Spring and to the Polish fifteen months—they are all twelve years apart—will notice the differences between these movements as well as the similarities. They shared the goal of broadening national and civil rights; they differed in their dynamics of social change. In 1956 the impulse for reform came from Moscow—from the hall of the Twentieth Congress of the Communist party of the Soviet Union, where the party bureaucracy tried to eradicate Stalin's still-present shadow and remove the ax being held over its head by the security forces. From there came the inspiration for the activity within the parties which shook up Poland and Hungary. In Poland, the authority of Gomułka, who had only just been released from prison, provided sufficient guarantee both for the Kremlin and the Polish people. For the Kremlin, Gomułka was a rebellious communist with whom they could nonetheless talk; for the Poles, he was a spokesman for their national and democratic aspirations. In Hungary, the resistance of the Stalinist wing of the party to reform left the initiative to rebels in the streets, who dictated the pace of change. The party apparatus collapsed like a house of cards. Soviet intervention was a simple consequence of this collapse.

In Czechoslovakia, the impulse for change came from inside the party, from those circles that realized that without profound reform the communist system would become less and less economically effective, that it would favor waste and backwardness. At the heart of the Czechoslovak conflict lay the attempts of Dubček's liberal and victorious faction—which had the support of the entire population—to implement democratic reforms from above. This was accompanied by reduced dependence on the Soviet central authority. The Czechoslovakian "socialism with a human face" in fact had many faces, ranging from the apparatchiks' desire for moderate reform to the nonconformist journalists' vision of a pluralistic society. But the decisive factor was the Czechoslovak leaders' rejection of the overt Soviet *diktat,* and their appeal to their own people—and not to the Kremlin—for a mandate to govern.

Poland was different. One can hardly speak of "socialism with a human face"; rather, one must speak of "communism whose teeth have been knocked out," communism that could no longer bite and no longer knew how to defend itself under attack from organized society. But this attack did not use force. Despite the hysterical claims that there was "all-out counterrevolution" and "fascist terror in factories," not one person was killed, and not one drop of blood was shed during the Polish revolution. Many observers asked: how is this possible? The origins of the Polish reform movement—otherwise known as the Polish self-limiting revolution—should be sought outside official institutions. For many years now, democratic opposition groups, supported by significant sections of the population and protected by the Catholic Church, have existed and functioned effectively. Taking advantage of the relatively tolerant policies of the Gierek team—tolerant policies that resulted from its relations with the West and its own political weakness rather than from liberalism—these groups promoted social self-help and self-defense, organized independent intellectual activities, and worked outside censorship to fashion programs for the fight for freedom. The essence of the programs put forward by opposition groups (the most widely known group was the Workers' Defense Committee [KOR] founded after the June 1976 strikes) lay in the attempt to reconstruct society, to restore social bonds outside official institutions. The most important question was not "how should the system of government be changed?" but "how should we defend ourselves against this system?" This way of thinking left its mark on the August strikes, on the strikers' demands, and on Solidarity's program, strategy, and actions.

The energetic struggle over the reform of totalitarian structures lasted fifteen months. The outcome of the conflict was as untypical as its course. The official declaration of war against the people gave a new meaning to the conflicts that preceded it. War, wrote Clausewitz, is a continuation of politics by other means. This time, it was a war with an organized society, launched by a state that is the instrument of political forces organized into the Warsaw Pact.

Poles will argue about and analyze Solidarity's mistakes for a long time to come. A nation, like a woman—let us recall Karl Marx's apt saying—cannot be forgiven for the one moment of oblivion when she allows a villain to take possession of her.

This labor union, which was actually a front of national solidarity, had in it all the virtues and vices of the society that gave birth to it: of a society that, for forty years, had lived without democratic institutions, outside the realm of civilized politics; a society which had been continuously cheated, made stupid, and humiliated; a society that is both disobedient and judicious; a society that values honor, liberty, and solidarity above all else and that all too often associated compromise with capitulation and treason.

Solidarity was a working people's democratic movement that functioned in an antidemocratic environment, among the totalitarian structures of a system whose sole source of legitimacy in the eyes of the people lay in the Yalta agreements. No one need remind Poles of the meaning of these agreements, as has been done recently by Henri Nannen [editor of *Stern* magazine], who seems to believe that only people living west of the Elbe deserve human rights, whereas the savages in the east have exclusive right to the knout and barbed wire as instruments that quite properly regulate their public life. The Poles remember Yalta. . . . The problem, however, was to translate the reality of Yalta into today's vocabulary. This was not easy.

The mighty and spontaneous social movement—deprived of examples, changing from one day to the next amid incessant conflicts with the authorities—did not possess a clear vision of specific goals or a well-defined concept of coexistence with the communist regime. It allowed itself to be provoked into fights over minor issues, into inessential conflicts; it was often disorderly and incompetent; it lacked familiarity with its enemy and the enemy's methods. Solidarity knew how to strike but not how to be patient; it knew how to attack head-on but not how to retreat; it had general ideas but not a program for short-term actions. It was a colossus with legs of steel and hands of clay: it was powerful among factory crews but powerless at the negotiating table. Across the table sat a partner who could not be truthful, run an economy, or keep its word—who could do but one thing: break up social solidarity. This partner had mastered that art in its thirty-seven years of rule. This partner—the power elite—was morally and financially bankrupt, and because of its political frailty was unable to practice politics of any type. Solidarity took this political weakness for overall weakness, forgetting that the apparatus of coercion which has not been affected by democratic corrosion can be an effective instrument in the hands of dictatorial power, and especially in the hands of a dictatorship that is being hounded. The Polish communist system was a colossus with legs of clay and hands of steel. In demanding democratic elections to the Sejm and the people's councils, Solidarity's activists seemed to forget that such appeals would sound alarm bells for the rulers, an omen for them that the end was near.

Let us repeat: Solidarity never demanded the removal of the communists from power or control by the union of the ship of state. But the point is that the ruling apparatchiks (never mind whether they were right or wrong) interpreted Solidarity's declarations in this way. They perceived in the union a grass-roots movement for expelling party committees from the factories; they were haunted by the specter of elections to the people's councils; they had nightmares about a national referendum on the form of self-government. Furthermore, ahead of them were drastic price rises. The December coup was their last resort.

Solidarity did not expect a military coup and was taken by surprise. It is not the workers who should bear the responsibility for this failure but all those (the author of this piece, for instance) who were summoned to create a political vision for the union through their intellectual work. The theoretical reflections on systemic change—and this should be noted—lagged behind the events. In fact, apart from a few political slogans that gained popularity, political reflection was virtually nonexistent. Practice preceded theory. Not for the first time in the history of Poland. . . .

The principal debate within Solidarity (though it was never clearly defined) concentrated on the speed and extent of change. At first, the proponents of compromise dominated the discussions. In the course of time, however, it became obvious that the authorities perceived the union's willingness to compromise as weakness. All concessions had to be extracted by strikes or threat of strikes. The perpetual strikes—which were skillfully provoked by the authorities—tired the people, who were already exhausted by the difficulties of everyday life. The apparent absence of tangible improvements in the quality of life led to the polarization of society and made people question the sense of this tactic. Some said: enough of strikes, they serve no purpose; others replied: there have been enough strikes that led nowhere—what we need is a general strike that will force the government to make real concessions. It is difficult to know which group was more numerous, but it is certain that the more radical group could be heard more loudly. It was they—mostly young workers from large factories—who waged radical solutions on Solidarity's leadership, and these were increasingly difficult to block (even though both Wałęsa and Kuroń[1] tried to do so). The government was more and more despised and discredited. Almost no one believed that Polish soldiers could be used against Polish workers; virtually no one believed in the possibility of an armed coup d'état.

All this was the result of naiveté and wishful thinking. But it was difficult to imagine that any attempt could be made to bully the Polish people with the help of the Polish armed forces inasmuch as this had never happened before in Polish history. The months that preceded the coup established in the consciousness of society a view of conflict between state and society which made no allowance for the possibility that brute force would be used. Gallows and black lists existed solely in the unbalanced imaginations of party notables. The union had but one answer to an attack from the authorities: a sit-in strike. The army's assault on factories made this tactic ineffective. The knowledge that peaceful opposition will not work can have disastrous consequences. The blood spilled in the Wujek mine should provide a lesson on what language should be used in talks with the authorities.

What did the communists think of Solidarity?

The August crisis was no surprise to them, but they were astonished by the way the strikes developed—by the maturity of the demands, and the discipline and solidarity of the crews. Gierek's team, which had been carried to power in December 1970 on the wave of the shipyard workers' bloody revolt, adopted as its central dogma the need to avoid armed confrontation with the working class. The government's consent to independent labor unions was an act of despair, mitigated by a belief that the movement could be limited to the coastal region and later

1. Lech Wałęsa was chairman of the Solidarity labor union, while Jacek Kuroń, an adviser to Solidarity's governing body, National Commission, was a longtime opposition leader and a founding member of the Workers' Defense Committee (KOR) (1976–1981).

manipulated and broken up from the inside. But then in September, when the nationwide wave of strikes forced the authorities to allow a single union to operate throughout the country, they could hope only to exhaust the union with provocations and to create an internal split. Solidarity represented a deadly threat to the government, for it challenged the chief principle of communist ideology, which is that the party represents the working class.

The plan to wreck the union by "political" means failed. The continuous conflicts—over political prisoners, Saturdays free of work, registration of the farmers' union—did weaken Solidarity, as did the internal disagreements provoked from without. But this weakening did not improve the party's position. For the government, divided and dominated by power struggles as it was, the party became the main problem.

The party—that is, the aggregate of its members—was altogether absent during the August strikes. This instrument for breaking up society, so effective in times past, this time failed. In its attempt to call up the party yet again, the apparatus opened a Pandora's box. On the one hand, in its search for scapegoats it began to uncover increasingly shocking evidence of corruption in Gierek's leadership; on the other, the rank-and-file members began to give up their party membership cards or—and this was worse still—to organize "horizontal structures," which demanded democratic reform of the party itself and rejection of the Stalinist model, which is predicated on the supremacy of the apparatus. Here lay the basic difference between the events in Poland in 1980 and the 1956 and 1968 crises. Before, the communist leaders Nagy, Gomułka, and Dubček had won their societies' trust, and the proponents of reform from above had society's support. But in Poland in 1980, the entire party lagged behind the changes. The party did not initiate social change; rather a social movement outside the party caused change in the party's own ranks. The party's reform program, in comparison with Solidarity's, was a blatant anachronism.

The reformers within the Polish party were not a unified group. Among those given that name were personalities as different as Andrzej Werblan, one of the ideological dictators of the Gomułka and Gierek eras; Stefan Bratkowski, a well-known journalist, one of the founders of the "Experience and the Future" group,[2] and chairman of the Journalists' Association; Wojciech Lamentowicz, a thirty-six-year-old associate at the party school; and Zbigniew Iwanow, one of the leaders of the August strike in a Toruń factory. All of them, despite their great differences, shared a quandary—one faced, in fact, by all communist reformers, in all parts of the globe. In their attempt to move the totalitarian party in the direction of human freedom and social justice and away from the bureaucratic control that chokes free thought and creativity and favors mediocrity and corruption, the reformers were able to assault the apparatus effectively only as long as they were a group and could form a faction fighting for power. As soon as they formed a faction, however, the reformers not only instantly placed themselves outside the party but were obliged to employ the same methods in their everyday political struggles that they had harshly condemned in their adversaries. The "horizontal structures," associating single party cells that were too weak to win locally, and be accepted by the apparatus, were an attempt to square this circle. They did not survive the mass attack by the conservative structures within the party.

The Polish party reformers of 1980 were a caricature of their ideological fathers and older brothers of the Polish October and the Prague Spring. At first sight, their reforms were less abstract and better grounded in the realities of social life: the discussions about them were focused not on intense disputes over the philosophical thought of young Marx but instead on economic reform. But it was only on first sight that things appeared this way. This movement in fact had no connection with the true tissue of intellectual life. Quite the opposite, it was the final stage in the ideological destruction of the "real" communism. The party reformers were speaking in a normal language, but their ideas were still clenched in the pincers of Marxist-Leninist newspeak. For the party reformers the issue of "how should the party be made more democratic" was central, because this was intended to lead to the democratization of society; but for society the focal issue was how to

2. "Experience and the Future" (DiP), a group of Catholic and party intellectuals, met in 1976 to elaborate proposals for system reforms. In the following four years, two extensive analyses of the Polish crises were produced.

tear the largest possible areas of public life out of the *diktat* of the party *nomenklatura*.[3] The party apparatus accused Solidarity of being a political party instead of a labor union; Solidarity suggested that the party should become a political party that would seek social credibility instead of remaining the labor union for the government and party bureaucracy. As the people saw it, such was the most accurate definition of the social role of the ruling Communist party. And it proved to be correct. The relatively democratic extraordinary ninth congress of the PUWP changed little in this respect; the democratically elected members of the highest body were individuals who had been thoroughly discredited. They included Albin Siwak, made out to be a Polish Stakhanov—a shock worker with the ID card of an employee of the security services in his pocket. With Siwak in the Politburo, the PUWP could not hope for social credibility. The new leadership and the congress' program were stillborn creatures. At this point, the apparatus could only hope for an internal split in Solidarity and on the mediatory role of the Church.

And they did hope for it. The idea for a Front of National Reconciliation that was supposed to rely on the government, the Church, and Solidarity, as symbolized by the meeting between Jaruzelski, Archbishop Glemp, and Wałęsa, was a last attempt to maneuver the union "bloodlessly."

The Catholic Church, Poland's highest moral authority, supported by the prestige of the Polish pope, no doubt leaned toward compromise solutions. It tried to construct bridges of social understanding, to tone down tensions, to moderate both the government and Solidarity. The front was to be a compromise, not Solidarity's abandonment of its principles and goals. The apparat's suggestion of a common list of candidates for the elections to the "people's councils" was precisely an attempt to force Solidarity to give up its objectives. The Church could not and did not want to lend its support to such solutions. This was the turning point. It became clear to the union that conflict could not be avoided; the authorities saw clearly that the limits of compromise had

---

3. *Nomenklatura,* a characteristic feature of the communist political system, is the practice of setting aside numerous important public posts for candidates selected by the Communist party. The list of both the posts and the candidates are secret.

been exhausted. Then came the Radom debates,[4] the session of Solidarity's National Commission,[5] and the armed coup.

The union did expect a conflict. It was to be a conflict not about who was in power but about methods of exercising power. The union believed that the apparatus would lose the battle to retain the *nomenklatura*—an event that was a precondition for any program of democratic reform. It must be acknowledged that the nighttime action in December was conducted effectively, thanks partly to the total absence of scruples among its executors. Solidarity was pacified with tanks and bayonets; the resistance of factory crews was overcome. But this victory for the government may have unexpected consequences, may prove to be a case of political shortsightedness. A bayonet may be used to frighten, to terrorize, to kill, and to win battles against unarmed populations; but no one—Stefan Bratkowski has often cited this saying of Talleyrand's—can sit on a bayonet. And, let me add, no one can use a bayonet to wipe fifteen months of freedom from human memory.

I have already attempted to answer the question of why it was so easy for the government to overcome the people's resistance. Along with the shock caused by the unexpectedness of the coup, and the Polish belief that the spilling of blood is a barrier that must not be crossed, one more factor was decisive: Russia's shadow.

The possibility of Soviet intervention was often discussed. The Kremlin's intentions, confirmed daily by statements in the press, were clear. Solidarity was not popular in the Kremlin. The discussions in Poland were about the direction of the policies of the Soviet Union—of its entanglement in the Afghan conflict, its domestic problems, and of the complex international situation. Our conclusions were unclear. Some of us quietly hoped that it would be possible to elaborate a model for Polish-Soviet relations in which there would be room for Polish autonomy. We also believed that the Soviet leaders would use armed intervention as a last resort, in response to civil war or a seizure of

4. On December 3, 1981, Solidarity's Presidium met in Radom. Parts of the edited tape of that meeting were played on the radio and used as a justification for the military coup.

5. The last session of Solidarity's National Commission was held in Gdańsk on the weekend of December 12–13, 1981. Most of the national leadership was arrested right after the meeting ended, and its participants retired to the hotel.

power. We thought that the authorities were using the Soviet bogey only too willingly, in order to achieve the psychological effects of an intervention without an actual intervention.

Subsequent events proved that this reasoning was correct: the USSR did do everything to camouflage its participation in the December coup d'état. The scenario that was executed was most favorable to them. "It was the Poles themselves who solved their own problems."

The declaration of the state of war must have brought to people's minds memories of Targowica, the shadowy symbol of national disgrace. The specter of Russian invasion—in the event of Jaruzelski's failure—was crucial in determining the attitude of the Polish people. I believe that this fact is yet another demonstration of the amount of common sense and rational thought in this romantic nation. Poles can do more than fight—they can think.

The Poles did not count on help from the West, which made the strong reactions of Western societies and governments a pleasant surprise. This not only gives people heart but may also serve to reduce the level of repression. Expressions of public opinion have an important moral dimension, for they serve as a reminder that democratic values are indivisible, that they have supporters throughout the world, and that they survive being trampled by soldiers' boots. For all of those in prison or on the run, such reactions are an injection of hope, a light at the end of the dark tunnel that is Poland under martial law.

The actions of governments are determined by broad international strategies, in which Poland is a mere episode. We should have no illusions about this. But let us stop and look at one issue within these strategies: economic sanctions. I am not going to attempt to interpret America's policies; I have no idea what has motivated President Reagan. But I doubt that the imposition of sanctions by the United States was inspired by anger that Solidarity did not manage to reinstate capitalism in Poland—as the official propaganda would have it. If this were true, Reagan would be out of his mind, and I do not suspect this of the president of the United States.

I rather think that the sanctions were a relatively predictable response by the West to the armed coup, so accordingly the organizers of the coup bear full responsibility for its consequences. It is Jaruzelski and WRONa, not Reagan and the Pentagon, who are responsible for the disastrous consequences of the sanctions for every Polish family. But it must be stressed that people from the West continue to send food to Poland through channels other than governmental ones, which is no wonder since the government has lost credibility in the West.

It is not difficult to reconstruct the thinking of Western leaders. The communist economies are unable to develop without Western technology and raw materials. Generous credits are not necessarily a factor that speeds up reform; the example of Gierek's government demonstrates this. Likewise, it is impossible to reform an economy with bayonets, denunciations, and policemen. So credits are thrown down the drain. Can one wonder that this hardly encourages the West?

Can one wonder that the West wants to do business with a government that enjoys at least a minimum of credibility among its own people? That further credits are made conditional on the restoration of civil liberties in Poland? Official propaganda has been trying to portray these sanctions as an attack on the very existence of the Polish people, as a hindrance to democratic reforms, as a violation of Poland's sovereignty. I am not in favor of sanctions, but it is simply cowardly for those responsible for them—WRONa—to deny their own responsibility. It is not Reagan who has ruined Poland's economy but rather those who subordinate the spiritual and material fate of the Polish people to their own selfish and narrow interests. How much more has to happen before these people understand that by eliminating independent institutions with the methods of an army-police dictatorship they are necessarily isolating themselves from their own nation and the entire civilized world?

What now? Answers to this question are being sought in every nocturnal Polish discussion, many of which go on despite the curfew. On the night of December 12–13 the ruling communists returned to the position they held in 1945, when they were a minority sect whose power rested on the use of bayonets. Then it was the sect of pro-Soviet Jacobins; today it is the sect of pro-Soviet mandarins. Then they were defending their program; today they are fighting for their privileges. Historical experience brings to mind two models for defusing such crises. Let's call them the Kádár and the Husak models.

János Kádár inaugurated his rule [in Hungary] in 1956 as a Soviet vice-regent brought in on a tank. The first few years of his rule were marked by ferocious repression but were followed by a gradual "untightening of the screws" from above.

Right from the beginning, Gustav Husák [in Czechoslovakia in 1968] announced his determination to maintain the achievements of the Prague Spring. After the Soviet intervention, all the public institutions formed during the Prague Spring continued to operate. But slowly, step by step, they were liquidated. People were forced into humiliating self-criticism, into denouncing their colleagues. "Extremist" elements were eliminated, independent institutions liquidated—all this under the banner of rescuing the last bits of reform. In this way, the Prague Spring was murdered by the hands of its creators.

The Kádár model represents a path from socially destructive repression to paternalistic liberalism. The Husák model is the road from a fictitious preservation of democratic structures to the total sterilization of public life.

For the Polish communists, Kádár is a hero, and they would like to follow in his footsteps: this is why court sentences are accompanied by declarations of renewal and reforms. It is easy to figure out the government's intentions: destroy Solidarity, restore the functioning of the totalitarian institutions, and erase the hope for a dignified life from people's hearts. The aim is to wreck Solidarity with the hands of its activists—making use of those who signed the loyalty declarations, or were otherwise humiliated and defeated. Representatives of WRONa attempted to persuade Wałęsa to accept this plan. This proved ineffective. A Solidarity without Wałęsa, Bujak, or Słowik can only be a dummy that conceals antiworker policies.

The widespread efforts at repression—curbed only by protests in Poland and abroad—has included the "pacification" of factories, jailing of union activists, and a campaign of defamation. All along, the government has been saying that everything is all right, that Poland is becoming normal.

But from church pulpits—the only places where language has not been defiled—true words are being spoken about the nation's condition. There, the repression is openly discussed, as well as aid to its victims. One knows from other sources that resistance exists. Illegal newspapers keep appearing, and independent institutions are being reconstructed. No, this movement will not be subjugated.

Only bits and pieces of news from Poland and the rest of the world reach my new lodgings, which are guarded by armed and uniformed men and enclosed by bars and barbed wire. But here we do at least have plenty of time for thinking things over.

These fifteen months have been a lesson in freedom. Solidarity can be erased from walls but not from human memory. The exemplary character of the Polish experiment has been stressed repeatedly: for absence of violence, for its tactic of restoring social ties outside official structures. This model will continue to function under the new conditions; it may prove useful not only to Poles but to other societies in this geopolitical sphere. We should also remember that the mechanism of the Polish coup d'état may serve as an example as well.

A military elite has never been in power in a communist system. The party apparatus has usually performed that role—and in periods of intensified terror it is the security apparatus that has wielded power. The army has been only an instrument; and when it reached for power it was purged: the fates of the Soviet marshals Tukhachevsky and Zhukov illustrate this thesis. The Polish coup may provide a precedent. It is worth considering the thesis that by striking at Solidarity Jaruzelski also *nolens volens* rendered the power of the party's apparatus fictitious. Until now, it has been the party apparatus that was in power, with the army to back it up; perhaps now it is the army apparatus that rules while the party provides a facade.

An armed coup d'état is a technique of social change, but the form need not determine its contents. An armed coup established a dictatorship in Chile, whereas another one opened the doors for democracy in Portugal. The army—the only body in a communist system which is relatively independent of the party and the security services—can play any number of roles. For instance, the army that is entangled in an unpopular war with the courageous Afghan people, whom Marx called the "Poles of Asia," is capable—in Solzhenitsyn's scenario—of playing a role completely different from the one it plays in Poland, even though, paradoxically, the Polish example may prove useful.

Here, behind bars, each gesture of solidarity is like a breath of fresh air. I offer thanks with all my heart for everyone, on behalf of myself and my companions. Every piece of good news helps us to live. But there are bad moments, too. When a German social democrat

announces—quoting the vice premier of the Polish People's Republic—
that the condition of the internees is satisfactory, I bitterly remember
the fate of the German Social Democrats forty-five years ago and the
assurances of various statesmen that all was OK in Germany—that the
enemies of the rule of order were being kept in humanitarian conditions.
The Polish government's vice premier, who represents himself as an
expert on his imprisoned political opponents, is a grotesque and pitiful
figure, and his German interlocutor is either cynical or naive.

A few words about the internees. We have been jailed without the
public prosecutor's warrant, and every one of us can win his freedom
by signing a loyalty declaration and agreeing to become a police informer. A broken man, our guards reason, will be incapable of defiance.

We—workers, farmers, intellectuals—are hostages. Our fate is to
be a warning to others, our condition a showcase for the world outside
Poland, we ourselves goods for barter. Those who have been sentenced
for striking are worse off. Everyone (ourselves included) has been
placed in a new situation by the Polish-Jaruzelskian war (to use the
term coined in the streets of Warsaw). It is difficult to find a universal
formula. Everyone has to answer in his own conscience the question
of how to counter the evil, how to defend dignity, how to behave in
this strange war that is a new embodiment of the age-old struggle of
truth and lies, of liberty and coercion, of dignity and degradation. Let's
repeat after the philosopher: in this struggle there are no final victories,
but neither are there—and here is a slight reason for optimism—any
final defeats.

The faith that there are no final defeats has led me to write these
remarks. This is my contribution to the war. It may be some time before
I can again express my opinions. And so I wish my good friends,
especially those who are being pursued and who are fighting, much
strength to allow them to cross the empty darkness that stretches between despair and hope. And much patience to allow them to learn the
difficult art of forgiveness.

February 1982

// On Resistance: A Letter from Białołęka 1982

My dear friend,

You have asked me how things look from this vantage point—from Białołęka prison—how I assess the effectiveness of resistance, what my projections are.

Things look different from here; it is easier to avoid getting lost in the details, to see the framework of the situation. But knowledge is limited. The absence of detail deprives you of the flavor of everyday life. After five months of isolation, you lose your feeling for the melody of the streets of Warsaw and the moods of its people, whom you have known for so many years. So you must make allowance for this.

You ask me whether I believe that it is sensible to maintain a political underground. Before I answer this question, let me ask you a question: Do you believe that Solidarity was an event of historic significance, or merely an unimportant episode in Poland's history? Was it a coincidence of events, a unique deformation of the historic process, or the natural, institutionally permanent embodiment of the aspirations of the Polish people? If it was a mere episode, then we can expect the ruling communists to wipe out its traces—and not only off the walls of our cities. But if it was an authentic movement of national rebirth, then no one will manage to replace it with artificial creations, such as the Committees of National Rebirth, that are being founded throughout the country on the orders of the army commissars. If it was authentic, then the communists' scheme is pathetically unrealistic, and even the most energetic activity on the part of WRONa's people—those armed with guns as well as those armed with bugging devices—will fail to exterminate Solidarity.

What Are They Fighting For? Where Are They Going?

The plans of the government are clear-cut. Their aim is to force the Polish population into the straitjacket of totalitarian dictatorship. Again, we are to be deprived of our rights—as individuals, as a society, as a nation. For what else happened on the night of December 12/13? "Factories were taken by force. Workers' organizations were dissolved and decimated with the help of the police. The working class was transformed into an amorphous, apathetic mass devoid of political consciousness. From then on, the government had to deal with individuals and not with organizations. Napoleon was right: it suffices to be stronger at one particular moment." This is not my assessment of the political situation that followed December 13. These are the words used by Bertold Brecht to describe Hitler's takeover of Germany. And if WRONa achieves its goals, this is how future historians will write about Poland in the period after December 13, 1981. I did not call WRONa's goals a program, for those gentlemen have no political program to speak of. Their actions, which they call the "Polish *raison d'état*," are motivated by panic and fear; their ideology, which they call "national accords," consists of eradicating opposition of all kinds; their methods, which they call the "exigencies of martial law," are brutal terror; their dress is the army uniform, which they have stripped of the last remnants of people's respect. They are crude but ineffective, ruthless but ridiculous; they have even managed to make the traditional four-cornered army cap into the Soviet lackey's clown hat.

They have no program; they have no principles; they have no respect; they have only guns and tanks. How much longer will they hold on to them? When will the epidemic of democracy penetrate into the minds of the men in green uniforms? Regardless of what may be written in their newspapers, they know that they did not win this war but only a single battle, in which an army of a few thousand men battled against defenseless workers. But they lost something that every government wants most; they lost their credibility and all hope of credibility. No one believes them now, and no one will believe them in the future. The last hope for communism to take root in Polish society lies buried with the bodies of Wujek miners.

They have not managed to split Solidarity, and I doubt whether they can hope to do so in the future. Society's resistance to WRONa is not the work of a handful of uncompromising extremists but the expression of society's needs. Since these needs are not fulfilled by official institutions, people go elsewhere. It is not surprising that underground Solidarity exists; it would be astonishing if it did not exist.

We are in a completely new situation, different from anything we have known in the past. Never before has the party apparatus been subordinated to the army, never has the army in a communist state exercised direct power over the population. It is difficult to foresee the consequences of this state of affairs; the competition within the power elite between civilians and soldiers may be full of surprises.

Looking Back

Underground organizations have never operated effectively in communist states. Communists have succeeded at little else than breaking up resistance, especially conspiratorial resistance. They have mastered this skill perfectly. This can be seen in the differences between the 1939–41 underground in the General Gouvernement and the underground in the same period under Soviet occupation in the Lvov province; the underground thrived alongside the Gestapo and disappeared under the jurisdiction of the NKVD. Why? It would seem that the Nazis simply wanted to have peace and quiet in the country, under their occupation, so they made sure that people observed their regulations and remained calm. They could not be bothered to create political organizations for the conquered people, whom they wanted to transform into a race of slaves. They made this perfectly clear to the Poles. They promised nothing: their execution squads were accompanied neither by dreams of a better tomorrow nor by servile declarations from Hitler's Polish fans.

The Soviet conquistadores were different. They systematically destroyed all social ties, political and cultural organizations, sports associations, and professional guilds, and abrogated civil rights and confiscated private property. They made people not merely their subjects but turned them into their property. In contrast to the Nazis, the Soviets imposed their own organizational structures on the Poles; they allowed the poor to plunder the property of the wealthy, they publicized declarations of servility, and they concealed executions and banishments. Imitating the spirit of the Crusades, they came to spread the New Faith. They left the door open by allowing everyone—in principle—to choose to convert to the religion of the Progressive System (people who proudly state that Poland never had its Quisling should be reminded of the role of Wanda Wasilewska.[1] The Poles have sufficient grounds for national pride that they do not need to lie about their past).

In his observations about the Soviet occupation, Józef Mackiewicz, a controversial author and not exactly my favorite one, wrote that while the Nazi occupation made heroes out of us, the Soviet occupation broke our moral backbone. It was possible because of the deadly mixture of terror and social promise, because of the revolutionary demagoguery that, at a price of a denunciation, ennobled common robbery by endowing it with ideological meaning, and so destroyed the traditional structures of social organization and opened the doors wide for the Progressive System. These doors were open to anyone who had understood that, owing to history's inescapable laws, the Old World lay in ruins. Victorious communism also promised social advancement, and, to a certain degree, it did fulfill this promise.

The regime was generous! It allowed the people to pillage the property of their exploiters and enemies. The manors of the nobility were wrecked by peasant axes, their libraries burned, the masters' cattle taken from their barns. Shops and workshops were robbed, as were pharmacies and private homes. Yesterday's magnates—who became today's adversaries—were forced into poverty and humiliation. In this way, the system founded on exploitation and private property was being

---

1. Wanda Wasilewska (1905–1964), writer and political figure, was a daughter of an eminent Polish socialist couple and herself a member of the prewar Polish Socialist party (PPS). She joined the communists at the beginning of World War II and played an active role in the creation of the Polish communist government. After the war she remained in the USSR.

eradicated; in this way the communists were implementing the principles of social equality. This reduction to the lowest common denominator brought out in people's souls the worst and lowest instincts and reactions. But it worked.

This was the revenge for the promised but never implemented agrarian reform. This was the revenge for the lack of concern for the wronged and the humiliated. Only in the newspapers and propagandistic speeches were the workers promoted to the role of the ruling class—but one could hardly deny that the road to advancement was cleared for some of them. The party activists of the middle echelons came from the lowest social classes—from areas of poverty and misery (but the party's highest echelons were reserved for the select few)—and became secretaries of party cells, members of people's councils, directors of factories, employees of the security services. These people formed the social base of the Leading System. But it was not they who determined its strength. In this first high-flown pioneering and heroic period of the building of socialism the government's power was based principally on the powerlessness of the society, which had been crippled by the war.

Communism and Society's Resistance

Since those days, much has changed. Wanda Wasilewska's heirs in their four-cornered hats no longer can offer the lowest social classes shops to pillage or jobs. They can no longer blame the bourgeoisie and the large landowners, the London government-in-exile, and the reactionary underground for all ills. Still, in solving the riddles of today it is important to remember those bygone years.

Under the rule of the communist dictators, people constantly looked for new and original forms of opposition, forms that would be effective against the totalitarian force. People looked for the smallest hole in the totalitarian wall, the smallest crack, for every possible way to save the nation from turning into a heap of sand. When the underground that functioned from 1945 through 1947 was finally destroyed and the legal opposition offered by the Polish Peasant party (PSL) was eradicated, a significant part of the intelligentsia chose to withdraw from public life, into "internal emigration." In the context of obsequious declarations and slogans shouted at rallies, silence equaled resistance.

In those years, many unsubmissive people documented their opposition through silence. Others looked for institutional forms of coexistence with the government, taking advantage of the at first extensive, but then constantly shrinking, protective umbrella of the Catholic Church. The milieu of *Tygodnik Powszechny* [Cracow Catholic Weekly] chose to be present in public life in the realms of culture and learning, and it consciously renounced political activity. In those years, however, every article on St. Stanisław or the September 1939 campaign, on tourism or archaeology, had a political dimension. Omissions gave the weekly its political coloring. The more brutal the government's attacks on the Church became, the more the pool of subjects that could pass into the Catholic paper through the censor's sieve shrank. *Tygodnik Powszechny,* edited by Jerzy Turowicz and enriched by the writings of Stomma, Zawieyski, Kisielewski, Woźniakowski, and others provided an escape for the reader, an opportunity to survive, a chance to preserve fundamental values, common sense, and psychological equilibrium in a world that had been taken over by police terror and ideological insanity. The Church provided a true barrier against the totalitarian power. It was an institution that defended the nation's identity, its rights and values. It gave strength to the frail and heart to the persecuted. It was thanks to the Church that the nation's secret resistance persisted, although it should be admitted that mass terror along with large-scale brainwashing and the corruption of conscience was also effective. It is dishonest to deny this.

In the Stalinist era, conspiratorial organizations modeled on the World War II underground were also founded. They were all short-lived and brutally repressed, and news about their existence came mostly from prisons and court records. The episcopate, let us recall, cautioned people against underground resistance.

Dictatorships either disintegrate or evolve. When they disintegrate —as a result of internal or external upheaval—the wave of social revolt brings to the top proponents of total change—"steadfast" oppositionists and imprisoned adversaries. When dictatorships evolve, the power apparatus becomes unsteady on its feet and gives birth to a movement of protest and to antagonists from the inside. The communist system contains protest in its ideological nature. It cannot get away with propagating egalitarian slogans while promoting a network of shops for the elite; it cannot get away with proclaiming ideas about worker power while using police to mercilessly suppress workers' strikes; it cannot get away with calling itself the heir of the tradition of liberty while stamping out by force every sign of freedom. As long as communism was a living ideology that claimed the allegiance of honest people, it was naturally bound to carry within it the seeds of its own heresy and negation—call it revisionism. Revisionism—which has never been defined precisely by either its enemies or its proponents—was an intellectual movement that accompanied the corrosion of the party apparat's iron ideology. In its attempt—in principle—to be a movement aimed at repairing the Leading System, revisionism tried to moderate and restrict the system's totalitarian character, violating—at least unconsciously—the very essence of communist rule.

There is no such thing as a nontotalitarian ruling communism. It either becomes totalitarian or it ceases to be communism. The role of revisionism was to coach the Communist party for its confrontation with the explosions of social anger that followed Stalin's death and for its attempts to introduce elements of everyday reality and traces of the language of morality into internal party discussions. The revisionists demanded liberal political reforms, although revisionism never turned into a political program. In its confrontation with the conservative party apparatus, revisionism had to be defeated. At that point, it had a choice to make: to recognize the apparat's view of social order and identify with the authorities and against society's aspirations or to continue to call for political reform and eventually part ways with the Communist party. In either case, the movement ceased to be revisionism—born of the era of ferment—and was transformed either into an accessory to power or a simple opposition group. What was characteristic of this period was that social protest gained strength while the system lost its oppressiveness. When terror subsides, the people become more courageous. Society's protests from 1953 to 1956 were not led by the revisionists, but neither were they led by those who had maintained relentless resistance since 1945. Those who had resisted since 1945 paid for it with isolation in jail or in internal emigration. The protests in the 1953 to 1956 period emerged from the depths of the disorganized and atomized society, and that society had no political program and could easily be disrupted or manipulated. They were neither social nor political movements (in the classic definition of these terms) but an expression of the exasperation of groups whose poverty had not diminished and who had just enough courage to protest openly.

The story of the 1956 Polish October can be told on two planes: on one, it was a social revolt of workers; on the other, it was ideological opposition from party revisionists. The suppression and pacification of both groups cannot be forgotten. The methods used by Władysław Gomułka to calm the revolt should be analyzed separately. One thing is certain: the Polish October was not repressed by force (even though the police actions against the street demonstration in the autumn of 1957, following the dissolution of *Po prostu,*[2] transformed Warsaw into a city under siege). The October revolt was washed away. The shape of the defeat precluded the creation of any institutionalized opposition movement.

The October movement of renewal was converted into "our little stability," which was accompanied by the tough and consistent resistance of the Church, by some criticism expressed in intellectual circles, and by sporadic manifestations of worker dissatisfaction. But there was no underground conspiracy. Underground conspiracies did not appear on a large scale even following the student revolt of March 1968 or the December 1970 workers' protests. Here and there—but only on the margins of society—plans for creating an underground and starting conspiratorial organizations would spring up, but they played no role of any importance. Illegal attempts to organize became known only when those behind them were put in the dock. Those who wanted to act in opposition to the authorities found other methods, both legal and illegal, but the illegal methods were not underground organizations; rather, they consisted of clandestine distribution of émigré publications and clandestine shipment abroad of materials to be used in these publications, public discussions in the legal Clubs of the Catholic Intelligentsia supplemented by seminars in private homes, and by writings confiscated by the censor's office which were duplicated and passed from hand to hand. All this represented a ferment, a resistance, and a revival of independent ideas.

---

2. *Po prostu* was a periodical that the young liberal party members founded during the 1956 period of reforms. Its closing a year later marked the end of the Polish October.

But an independent Polish political life did not exist. This only began to change in 1976. Then the first programs of social resistance were organized. The principal theme of these ideas and these activities was openness—openness at any price. Some people went as far as to walk voluntarily into a home where an open but illegal lecture of the Flying University[3] was to take place and the secret police had already arrived. "Open but illegal"—in this somewhat paradoxical expression lies the very essence of the tactics of that era. Books and periodicals were printed underground, but the names of their authors and editors were openly disclosed. Openness was a way of fortifying collective courage, of widening the "gray area" between the censor's scissors and the criminal code, of breaking down the barrier of inertia and fear. The chances for success lay in openness, not in conspiracy.

Incidentally, neither the Soviet intervention in Hungary nor the armed "fraternal aid" for Czechoslovakia provoked conspiratorial resistance on any scale. Post-Stalinist communism was also unfamiliar with conspiracy as a large-scale phenomenon. The reasons for this are worth thinking about. The post-Stalinist system was neither a system of total terror for the whole community nor of abstract promises for the under-privileged. It was a system that was able to construct a stable relationship between the powers-that-be and society. The Czech intellectual Antonin Liehm described this stability as a "new social accord" between the power elite and the people. This "accord" was based on the assumption that the authorities would not make life difficult for the people if the people would not make governing difficult for the authorities. So the government did not interfere too brutally in the citizens' private and professional lives, and the citizens did not meddle in the areas reserved for the party *nomenklatura*. Gierek's Poland and Kádár's Hungary were classic examples of this "new social accord," but certain aspects of it could also be seen in other countries, including the USSR.

It should be remembered that in Hungary the Kádár line was preceded by exceptionally brutal repression, which destroyed confidence in direct resistance, whereas in Gierek's Poland liberalism was

---

3. Flying University (TKN) was one of the institutions of democratic opposition that led to the creation of Solidarity. Founded in 1978, it consisted of seminars and classes held in private apartments and devoted to subjects that could not have been taught officially.

the natural consequence of the government's fear of the working class, whose revolt had brought Gierek to power. Liberalism in Poland was also the result of conflicts with Western countries, in which Gierek wanted to maintain a good reputation.

It was characteristic of Husák's Czechoslovakia that the leaders of the "renewal" initiated "normalization." Dubček himself called for an end to social resistance, and thousands of activists of the Prague Spring went into exile. The underground in post-1968 Czechoslovakia has included, and still includes, small groups of déclassé oppositionists whose spiritual atmosphere resembles the first Christian communities hiding in the catacombs more than they resemble an illegal political opposition movement.

The End of the Psychology of Captivity

The communist system in Poland did not collide head-on with a permanently active underground. At first, the absence of such an underground was the result of bloody terror and a skillful social policy; then it was the result of a new social accord, which existed only because of the continued remembrance of Stalinist terror. But at all times the communist dictatorship sought to break down social ties. The power apparatus and its institutions, which served to destroy solidarity among people and to keep society well disciplined, were the only forms of social organization.

As a result, the system created a psychology characteristic of communities subjugated by communism. Long periods of apathy and depolitization were interrupted by sudden political earthquakes. These, however, were not followed by programs of reform or by alternative political plans. They were only protests, not reform movements. Supposed programs of reform were drawn up in government offices but they never reached the factory floors. Independent political thought did not exist in communist states; instead, the only choices left open to an oppositionist were either futile maneuvering or blind violence. At the beginning of this century, Polish thinkers and politicians called this atmosphere the psychology of captivity. Józef Piłsudski, Roman Dmowski, and Edward Abramowski, who represented conflicting political parties and ideologies, agreed on one thing: a slave revolt has little in common with a movement for social or political change. The rebellious slave does free himself for a moment; but his main desire is revenge, which is rarely constructive. The rebellious slave will at best look for a better tsar, but he is incapable of discovering his own subjectivity, for he has been deprived of his community, his ideals, and his language. He is left alone with his hate, which spells helplessness. One needs to understand this psychology of captivity in order to unravel the mechanisms of social apathy under a communist regime. Only the surface events can be seen from the outside: the commemorative celebrations, the parades, the 100 percent turnout in the sham elections, the high party membership in factories and offices. The uprisings, the burning of party headquarters, the dissidents' open letters, and the dissidents' solitude are also visible. But reading between the lines, it is easy to find the common denominator in all of these events—the psychology of slavery.

I believe that the August 1980 workers' revolt and the activities of Solidarity have terminated this psychology. In those fifteen months, people had a taste of freedom; they forged their solidarity and discovered their strength; they again felt themselves to be a civic and national community. I do not want to idealize Solidarity, its actions, or its activists. I know about the demagogy and baseness—residual effects of the captive psychology—that were present in it. But these are inevitable aspects of every mass movement and the unavoidable heritage of years of slavery. Solidarity was the first mass movement in our history that lasted for many months, that struck deep roots in Polish hearts and minds, in work places and private homes. This permits one to believe that the movement of resistance against WRONa has a real base, that the underground has a chance of surviving future police actions. This chance stems from the Solidarity tradition and from the gains won by the pre-August democratic opposition. In addition, the entire body of experience of the nineteenth- and twentieth-century underground activities serves today as a book of knowledge about the values and methods of illegal resistance. This book must be reread, so that we can adapt old examples to new situations.

Many different accusations have been made against the Poles over their stormy history, but no one could ever say that they know nothing about conspiracy.

The Forms of the Underground

Poles know a thing or two about conspiracy, and the authorities are clearly aware of it. Hence in radio and TV programs and in propagandistic articles, a theme has been recurring: fear of the underground. These voices are a sign of a bizarre renaissance of the ideology of the state and of an anxiety about conspiracy that is worthy of the nineteenth-century Cracow conservatives. These voices proclaim that the highest value for the nation is the state, that antistate activities will lead to national catastrophe, that all the people should unite their efforts to support the state, and so on and so forth.

These are the arguments used to manipulate public opinion; to itself, the party speaks openly about fighting counterrevolution. What funny people! It really is overzealous to try to convince the Poles (of all people) who have been fighting for their own state for so many decades, of the worth of having a state. Yet they keep on talking about the people's own state, a sovereign state, a state that belongs to the people, a state that is ruled by the people in the interest of the people. And about a state that derives its value from being founded in law. However, when a state's power has been confiscated by a band of gangsters who impose their ways on the people, then the attitude "loyalty to the state" is simple complicity in crime. Resistance against such a "state" is natural, and civil disobedience is the only attitude worthy of respect.

The stance of the authorities toward human rights is especially important in this context. Tocqueville wrote:

> Thanks to the concept of human rights people have been able to define lawlessness and tyranny. Because of this, every citizen can remain independent without being arbitrary and he can subordinate himself without degrading himself. When a man subordinates himself to coercion, he grovels and debases himself, but when he subordinates himself to the rule of law which he himself has accorded to his neighbor, he in a sense stands above those who govern him. There are no great people without virtue, there are no great nations—and there is even no society—without respect for human rights. For what is the value of a community of thinking and intelligent individuals who are united solely by force?

No nation has ever been given human rights as a present. These rights have to be won through struggle. The question is: How should this struggle be conducted?

I am one of those who in the past ten or so years have criticized the idea of conspiratorial activity. Today I am for organizing an underground. We have no choice. Jaruzelski has made the choice for us.

This is what Polish honor and Polish thinking demand from us today. Honor: because a nation that humbly submits to those who are taking away its liberty does not deserve this liberty. Thinking: because a nation that sees no real chance for the restoration of its liberty and is not prepared to take advantage of such a chance when it arises will never attain freedom. It is difficult to be optimistic today. But who ten years ago could have foreseen the existence of a democratic opposition, an independent press, and finally August 1980 and Solidarity? It is obvious that what happened only once cannot be made into a model, but those events are an invaluable legacy. They are proof of how much can be accomplished by people who want to do something sensible for their country.

Today, the underground is a fait accompli. The forms it should take remain an open question. Let us begin by describing what it should not be. It should not be an underground state with a national government, a parliament, and armed forces. *It cannot be an underground state because it has no national mandate.* Our country needs many things but it does not need self-appointed national rule. It needs democratic representation—not a pseudo-parliament, which is the only thing possible in conspiratorial conditions. An underground state was able to function under the Nazi occupation because there was no middle course and because there was a war. Only a blind person could draw parallels between the General Gouvernement and WRONa, especially when it comes to armed conspiracy and attempts at terrorist action. This must be said clearly: armed actions could be conducted only by misguided people or by provocateurs, and the underground has a responsibility to protect society from such actions. Terrorism leads to nothing but revenge and a spiral of terror—to a strengthening of hatred and cruelty and to the estrangement of the majority of people from the underground.

It is not terrorism that Poland needs today. It is widespread underground activity that will reconstruct society, spreading throughout towns and villages, factories and research institutions, universities and high schools. Underground Solidarity has to encompass all this. The institutional form of this movement should be left open. It must obviously include mechanisms for collecting money, help for those who are threatened by penal repression or by loss of their jobs. It must obviously include an intellectual movement that will offer society a vision of a democratic Poland. It must include publishing enterprises, so that thoughts about Poland and the world, intellectual life in general, and social self-knowledge can flourish. Also needed is an umbrella institution—made up of Solidarity activists—which can deal with the fundamental questions of national existence. The role of such a center is important, so it is no surprise that this issue has caused many quarrels. I would think that the existence of such a center is an indispensable condition for effective action, but it also involves significant risk.

Only concerted pressure, which may go as far as a general strike, can force WRONa to make concessions; this is one side of the coin. On the other side, however, is the fact that a centralized and hierarchical organization, modeled on a Leninist party, which would steer the whole national opposition, is not realistic. Life is always richer than organizational structures, and the power of an underground union organization must lie in its roots in factories and not merely in an apparatus made up of professional conspirators. Also, by its very nature, the organization must be connected to a network that goes beyond the factory, for this is indispensable in maintaining links between different groups in society, in publishing independently, in organizing internal union structures, and in organizing distribution of fliers. But if such an organization is detached from those who are living the everyday life of martial law, it can easily lose touch with reality and become an army of generals without soldiers. One chronic problem is the conflict between the attempt to maintain a mass base for the movement and the need for the underground union's cadre structure to function effectively. This conflict is inevitable in a movement of this kind and can be handled wisely only once it is understood clearly. The self-awareness of activists can play an important role here. For the activists must understand that an underground movement makes sense only when it is able to create forms of action accessible to every single Pole, when it remains an open and tolerant movement, and it always remembers that many roads lead to democracy—that the Polish national anthem can be played on many different pianos. Adoption of this broad and inclusive strategy does not mean that every action conceived as a way of disadvantaging WRONa is sensible. For example, the idea of the "turtle"—that is, the call to "work slowly"—which has been appearing here and there does not seem wise. During the war, this slogan made sense because the Poles then were working for Hitler's armies. Today, it would be unreasonable to claim that all production is being used to harm national interests. The Leninist slogan "the worse, the better" is nonsensical in today's situation, and the Poles could pay a high price one day in the future if they destroy the work ethic today. We must look for ways to develop civil society and not just undertake actions simply in order to be a nuisance to the "junta."

But, above all, we must create a strategy of hope for the people, and show them that their efforts and risks have a future. The underground will not succeed in building a widespread national opposition without such a strategy—without faith in the purpose of action. Otherwise, resistance will amount to nothing more than a moral testimony or an angry reaction. And the movement will cease to be one that is aware of its political goals, that is armed with patience and consistency, and that is capable of winning.

"Instant Change" and the "Long March"

Underground Solidarity's basic goals are obvious: to create an authentic society, a free Poland, and individual freedom in Poland. No political miracle will help the Poles if they do not help themselves. A Polish democratic state will never be born if democratic structures do not exist beforehand in Polish society. And independent of the institutional success of the underground, a base for Polish democracy *is* being created today. It lies in the moral sphere. The importance of this sphere is clear. To paraphrase [the writer] Tadeusz Konwicki [the writer], there is more than just logic in the existence of the underground. There is also a need. Otherwise, we will turn into dwarfs and disappear, losing our national dignity. I know that no generalized moral values can replace concrete political perspectives.

Two strategies deserve to be considered: the strategy of "instant change" and the strategy of the "long march." The former assumes a vehement and spontaneous explosion of society's discontent. Such an explosion, even if it is bloodily suppressed, can lead to polarization within the government and restore the possibility of compromise with Solidarity. The underground must be prepared for both the quake itself and the subsequent negotiations. It must figure out ways of preventing bloodshed and ways of backing rightful demands; it must work out in detail a potential social agreement which includes revocation of martial law, a general amnesty for its victims (those who have been imprisoned, dismissed from work, etc.), and the implementation of social accords. It seems that only a spectacular defeat of WRONa's pacification plans can restore to the agenda the possibility of a genuine compromise between the authorities and the people. Otherwise, the authorities will not budge an inch.

But this does not mean that we should bank on a head-on collision between the underground and the government for the success of our efforts. Today, any confrontation must lead to tragedy, since WRONa is full of determination and will not back down even if it means shedding rivers of blood. A compromise must take into account the realities of power. If it is to be a real compromise, it must formulate clearly the meaning of "the leading role of the party in the state" and of "observance of international pacts." The line that must not be crossed in a compromise is relinquishment of the autonomy of the union. The Independent and Self-governing Labor Union "Solidarity" can choose to reorganize its structure and revise its program but only following the sovereign decision of its congress. Allowing the government to interfere in the internal affairs of Solidarity—that is, accepting the leading role of the PUWP in an independent and self-governing labor union—leads not to compromise but to suppression of the union. The question of the so-called international pacts is also important. Our striving for the truth about the history of Polish-Russian relations must once and for all be distinguished from anti-Soviet political propaganda. Every nation has the right to know the truth about its own history.

An assessment of the current international situation requires a cool appraisal of our aspirations and capabilities, of potential losses and possible gains. A clear evaluation of these problems is important independently of what we do about talks with the PUWP or WRONa; it constitutes the central problem for all Polish strategies, including the "long march" strategy. This strategy is based on the assumption that the ruling elite is almost chronically incapable of learning from its postwar experiences, and that the stationary war between an organized civilian society and the power apparatus will last a long time. In the meantime, significant changes may take place in the USSR—changes that are difficult to predict but also difficult to count on. Regardless of such changes, Poland will remain the political focus of every Russian state. And the Poles will have to figure out what relations to have with any such state. In other words, I agree with the opinion of Stefan Kisielewski [the political writer] that our people must themselves approach the issue of Polish-Russian relations. I agree that today this looks like a fantasy. But if it becomes possible, then the absence of a plan will prove to have been unforgivably shortsighted. There is not room here to discuss the many aspects of this problem. Let us merely remember that as a point of departure for an analysis of Polish-Russian relations we might take another look at the contents of the Yalta agreements, which, while placing Poland in the Soviet sphere of politico-military influence, leave to the Poles the choice of their system of government. The Yalta agreement does not stipulate the rule of the PUWP—that rule is merely a consequence of terror, rigged elections, and Stalin's violation of the agreement.

The "long march" idea must assume the isolation of WRONa and the PUWP or the further discreditation of the existing system of government—also in the eyes of the Soviet Union. What is inconceivable—barring a basic revision of the political map of the world—is that the USSR will simply forsake Poland; what is possible, however, is that the PUWP will become completely untrustworthy, its army unreliable and prone to mutiny, and an armed intervention of Poland politically too costly. The Polish people must be prepared for such an eventuality. But to continuously inflame anti-Soviet passions, at the expense of clear thinking about Polish-Russian relations, is a senseless mistake that can lead straight to a catastrophe. The "long march" strategy requires consistency, realism, and patience. These are not platitudes. They define a program of arduous, risky, and often ineffective activity, in the face of repression and suffering—a vision of work on economic, administrative, legal, and educational reform and on spreading among the public a concept of a "reformist Poland." The level of public awareness will determine the effectiveness of these actions. More than ever before, the principle of elementary national education must form a part of this strategy of resistance. To quote from a patriotic song, "Every household will be a fortress for us." This is why it is absolutely essential that we formulate a program like the one put forward by PPN[4] a few years ago, calling for social education for every child. To put it more broadly: it is essential that a sort of civic catechism be drawn up that will define the basic duties in martial-law Poland. There is only one institution whose recommendations in these matters people will accept: the Catholic Church.

The Church under Martial Law

Much has been written about the Catholic Church in Poland. It ought to be kept in mind that the role of the Church has grown greatly. The Church is both a party to the existing conflict between the authorities and society and a mediator in that conflict. The Church is party to it because it expresses the basic aspirations of society and is the sole officially functioning bastion of society's resistance. But the Church is also the mediator, the builder of bridges of understanding between the rulers and the ruled. Even before December 13, 1981, the philosopher and theologian Father Józef Tischner defined the Church's role on the political stage as that of a "witness," not that of a political institution. If I understood his idea correctly, this witness was to guarantee the genuineness of agreements and of their implementation in the light of the basic Christian values: truth, human dignity, and reconciliation. To this I would add the teaching role. I think that it is a misperception to expect from the Church a political program. However, a sort of civic catechism for the duration of martial law fits perfectly into the sphere of priestly concern for the nation's moral condition. It would be natural if projects for such a catechism came up for public discussion—just as the Primate's Council theses about a national understanding have done.

4. PPN, i.e., Polish League for Independence, was a group of intellectuals who in the late seventies issued analyses of some of the most complicated and important political problems. It was the only opposition group that did not disclose the names of its members.

I believe that this distinction between political and educational activity is important, for there exists the danger of vesting in the Church hopes that it cannot fulfill. People may select out of Church documents those that seem to offer specific political prescriptions, they can imagine that they see potential leadership for political opposition within the episcopate, and finally they might then absolve themselves of responsibility in the belief that the Church's activities would serve as a substitute for their own actions. Let us add that today the Church serves as a teacher for the entire society, and that it would therefore be disastrous for a few activists to attempt to appropriate the Church's authority. It would also be unfortunate if programs and tactics were hidden behind a facade of Catholic faith and symbolism. And there is one more thing: the Church is infallible on questions of religious dogma, but it can make mistakes—as it has in the past—in assessing the condition of society. This may happen all the more frequently with individual priests. Therefore, in this matter, the usual critical spirit applicable to any human opinion on society's life should be maintained.

I find something mistaken in the statement made by a well-known Gdańsk priest that contemporary youth does not need "men of marble" or "men of iron."[5] I believe that we do need films such as these two impressive works of Andrzej Wajda and also need the tough and uncompromising characters Wajda gave to his heroes. It is not people like them whom we should fear today but rather individuals with wooden heads and spines of rubber. I want to make this comment because attempts to separate Solidarity from the values and traditions that are reflected in Wajda's films can serve to divide the resistance movement, to threaten its pluralistic nature. The Church's concrete actions—defense of those who have been wronged and humiliated, assistance to the persecuted and their families, public defense of truth and concern for social peace—are major accomplishments in the life of the nation. Thanks to them, initiatives are again being taken, and new islands of autonomy come into existence among the people. In this way, the nation is rallying after the shock of December. The movement of

5. "Man of Marble" (1978) is the story of a worker who becomes a hero of socialist labor in the Stalinist Poland. "Man of Iron" (1981) shows the worker's son becoming the leader of the opposition movement in Poland of the '70s. Both movies were made by Andrzej Wajda.

resistance, with all its different attitudes and forms, is being reborn. And the Church is spreading again its protective umbrella over this movement.

The Specter of *The Possessed*

The underground will never meet all society's needs for a movement of resistance. It can only be one part of this movement, and the national interest requires us to seek a common denominator for different types of activity, different temperaments, and different models of concern for our motherland. The movement of resistance must teach freedom and democracy. The movement's character will determine the character of Poland as it emerges from the state of war. But the shadow of the "possessed" from Dostoyevski's novel looms over every underground movement. Every conspiracy demoralizes. In its depths flourishes the spirit of a sect that uses a language all its own, that is based on rites of initiation, on tactics to which everything is subordinated, on an instrumental attitude toward truth, and on disregard for any values that are not political. There is a unique type of activist-conspirator, whose characteristics make him as useful in the underground as they are dangerous later on. Such an activist has to make arbitrary decisions, to distrust newcomers and strangers. A spirit of democracy is not one of the virtues required by a conspiracy; pluralism is not the style favored by it. Underground activity isolates people from the taste and smell of everyday life, skews perspectives, gives birth to dangerous absolutism and intolerance. Conspiracy requires disobedience to the enemy and obedience to the underground central command. It proclaims equality but within itself calls for hierarchical subordination. Conspiracy thrives on the spirit of Manichaeism: "He who is not with us is against us." It is created to fight police oppression, but for the police it becomes the ideal field of activity. The police force blossoms in a collision with the underground: it penetrates it, plots provocations. Without an underground, the political police lead a frustrated life, but when conspiracy exists the police become a power, a state within a state. Sometimes the police become a sovereign state within an unsovereign state.

Police activities focused on provocation create a type of antiprovocation hysteria in the underground world. It sometimes happens that the investigation conducted by the underground counterintelligence takes the place of analysis of social processes. A totalitarian regime sees the hand of its underground enemy in every crisis; the antitotalitarian underground begins to discern the involvement of hidden police agents in every one of its failures. These are the dangers that accompany the underground. This is what the political and ideological enemies of conspiracy write about it. This is probably why such remarks are rarely accepted kindly. The conspirator idealizes the underground, which is not surprising, but this is precisely why he must constantly be reminded that it is not police terror that will bring about real defeat but the hostile indifference of society. An underground that is detached from a base is doomed to become degenerate and weak.

These mechanisms, which the enemy notices easily and exploits gladly, are easier to see from the outside. But when I am again in the underground, when I again become preoccupied with avoiding the agent's eye, with organizing that one meeting, with writing that particular flier, I too will forget all this, I will become blind to these perils. I will not have the energy, time, and courage to be aware of them, to analyze and describe them. This is why I am writing about them today, as I sit safely behind bars in Białołęka.

A Pinch of Dignity

The underground must know how to interpret society's needs and find flexible means of satisfying them. It must be attractive to people and it must be essential to them. These are platitudes; to adhere to them, however, we must make it clear to ourselves and to others that it is unrealistic to count on a return to the situation that preceded December 13, 1981, to count on a spectacular victory, with virtue rewarded and vice punished. Underground Solidarity must not seek revenge but rather a democratic alternative. Democracy is neither an easy nor a straightforward solution. It is born in pain, strengthened in conflict; it only shows its virtues after a long time. This is why we should not promise the sky to ourselves and to others, for it is not an instant and definitive solution for Poland's troubles that awaits us but only risk, toil, and disappointment. This is usually the price of freedom.

It seems to me that the underground today does not need the moral principles and organizational structures of an army or a party of the Leninist kind. What it needs is the bond of shared aims and solidarity in action. And respect for individuality. And consent for plurality. It seems to me that the underground should not promise a world devoid of conflict. I think that it should suggest a program of practical activity for reform, a program for social self-defense, contacts with real culture and cultural values, participation in authentic civic and intellectual life. Plus a pinch of dignity, a pinch of fraternity. And a daily breath of truth. Of the truth that every compromise is temporary, that every political solution is illusory. Because, as a philosopher wrote, but for death, all solutions are illusory. This is what I think.

Let me conclude with a personal reflection. Involvement in politics in a totalitarian dictatorship always oscillates between two human motivations: the needs of moral testimony and of political calculation. If involvement loses one of these motivations, it turns into either ineffective moralizing or immoral manipulation. Both are dangerous, but both are, to a certain extent, unavoidable. To go underground one must give up professional stability and family life. One must take into account the possibility of imprisonment and loneliness. One must step outside legality, thereby abandoning tactical and political concerns in favor of a basic moral choice. But to be effective in the underground, one must repeatedly abandon ethical concerns for political ones. *La politique d'abord!* It is difficult to argue with this. This is why I believe that the underground also needs people for whom moral testimony is more valuable than political efficacy, people who do not treat the underground as a school for pretenders to the future power elite, people who understand that their political involvement will end in "normal" times when an underground will no longer be needed, people who declare that "normal" times will require other qualities, other characters, talents different from their own.

These are my thoughts in Białołęka after the first twenty weeks of this strangest of all the Polish wars.

P.S. Some of the voices in the discussion taking place in the underground union press reached me after I wrote this text. The reader will easily notice the similarity of many of my remarks to the theses of those articles. The ones that seem closest to mine, though they differ some-what among themselves, while remaining similar in their main lines of thought, are the thoughts of Zbigniew Bujak, Wiktor Kulerski, and Zbigniew Romaszewski [leaders of the underground].

May 1982

// A Letter to General Kiszczak 1983

From: Adam Michnik, son of Ozjasz
Rakowiecka Street 37, Warsaw;
Under investigative detention.
10 December 1983.

To: The Minister of Internal Affairs
General Czesław Kiszczak,
Warsaw.

I have received your letter, Mr. Rzewuski, and I have deliberated on its meaning for a long time, wondering whether I should reply to it. A decent man, however, does not hide his thoughts, contempt for the vile is his rule, and this is how I will deal with you now, Sir. As a citizen, I am unable to follow your advice, which pretends to be inspired by love of freedom but is colored by many lies and reliant on foreign force. Those who dare—for the sake of their own pride and self-interest—to sell the blood of their compatriots are a disgrace to their nation and traitors to their motherland. This is how I feel toward you, Sir.

(From a letter of Prince Józef Poniatowski to Hetman Seweryn Rzewuski, a member of Targowica.)[1]

1. At the instigation of Russian Empress Catherine the Great, several Polish noblemen created the Confederation of Targowica in 1792. It was followed by the Second Partition of Poland with parts of the country incorporated into Russia and Prussia. Thus the geographical name Targowica became synonymous with national treason.

At the beginning of November, filled with disgust at the behavior of employees of your department, I lodged a complaint with you. In that letter I drew your attention to the meanness of their actions, which included confiscating from my cell books that I had with me by permission of the prosecutor, depriving me of the additional daily walk recommended by my doctors, and threatening me because of some information transmitted by Western radio broadcasts. It is no secret to any prisoner in the Third Investigation Pavilion at Mokotów prison that repressive actions there are carried out under order from the security services. The men's names are also no secret—for example, their local boss is Colonel Tamborski from the Ministry of Internal Affairs. In my letter I invoked the standards of honor that bind all civilized people and forbid the ill treatment of imprisoned and defenseless political adversaries. A few days later I asked one of my visitors to check with your office to find out whether you had received my letter. To my astonishment you told this person that it was beyond your capabilities to restrain the actions of your subordinates. You declared yourself powerless to return my books to me. You did have the power, however, to present me with a somewhat curious choice—that either I spend next Christmas on the Côte d'Azur or else I will be facing trial and many years in jail. You also assured me that after that trial, once "the authorities had bitten that bullet," it would be too late for me to leave the country. I thereby learned that the Polish minister of internal affairs finds it more difficult to restrain the malice of overzealous security agents than to predict the sentence which a military court will pass over me, and that, on top of that, he can even make me the generous offer of a vacation on the Côte d'Azur.

Your soul is as generous as the Ukrainian steppe, General. To repay your favor, allow me to offer you—following Mr. Zagłoba[2]—the throne of the Netherlands. "Monarch of the Netherlands, King Kiszczak I": Do you not find these titles beautiful?

When at the beginning of November I read in the party newspaper *Trybuna Ludu* Jerzy Urban's pronouncement that I could be free if I only left Poland, I reacted as if this was just another one of the jokes

2. Mr. Zagłoba, though a comic character, is one of the heroes of Henryk Sienkiewicz's famous *Trilogy* (1884–1888).

of this gifted columnist who has been so grievously wronged in being appointed the spokesman of the government of the Polish People's Republic. He probably won't do much damage to the government of General Jaruzelski since it would be rather difficult to spoil its reputation any further in Poland or abroad. But he is doing quite a lot of damage to himself by presenting such witticisms from *Szpilki* [the satirical periodical for which Urban worked] as propositions worthy of serious consideration. Less than a month earlier, in October, Jerzy Urban had reassured the public that political prisoners "are being held separately and not together with common criminals." Imagine—in all my naiveté, I took this pronouncement seriously and demanded that I be put in a cell with other political prisoners, since I was being held with criminals. But the chief of the prison, Maj. Andrzej Nowacki, and after him the head of the Warsaw Military Court, Col. Władysław Monarcha, were so good as to explain to me that Urban does not know what he is talking about and is unfamiliar with the regulations. So, ever since that incident I have treated the utterances of General Jaruzelski's spokesman as satirical pieces and as such, I've often found them quite amusing (I would recommend, for instance, as especially comical the spokesman's opinions about Lech Wałęsa). It was also in this spirit that I read his remarks about the possibility of buying one's freedom by leaving the country. Your own offer of a Christmas on the Côte d'Azur, however, has made me reconsider the significance of these peculiar propositions.

I am writing this letter exclusively on my own behalf, but I have reason to believe that thousands of people in Poland would agree with me.

I have reached the conclusion that your proposal to me means that:

1. You admit that I have done nothing that would entitle a law-abiding prosecutor's office to accuse me of "preparing to overthrow the government by force" or "weakening the defensive capacity of the state" or that would entitle a law-abiding court to declare me guilty.

I agree with this.

2. You admit that my sentence has been decided long before the opening of my trial.

I agree with this.

3. You admit that the indictment written by a compliant prosecutor and the sentence pronounced by a compliant jury will be so nonsensical

that no one will be fooled and that they will only bring honor to the convicted and shame to the convictors.

I agree with this.

4. You admit that the purpose of the legal proceedings is not to implement justice but to rid the authorities of embarrassing political adversaries.

I agree with this.

From here on, however, we begin to differ. For I believe that:

1. To admit one's disregard for the law so openly, one would have to be a fool.

2. To offer to a man, who has been held in prison for two years, the Côte d'Azur in exchange for his moral suicide, one would have to be a swine.

3. To believe that I could accept such a proposal is to imagine that everyone is a police collaborator.

I know very well, General why you need our departure: So you can besmirch us in your newspapers with redoubled energy as people who have finally shown their true faces, who first executed foreign orders and then were rewarded with capitalist luxuries. So you can show to the entire world that it is you who are the noble liberals and we the spineless wretches. So you can say to the Polish people: look, even they gave up, even they lost faith in a democratic and free Poland. So that, above all else, you can improve your own image *in your own eyes*; so you can proclaim with relief: after all they are no better than us. Because the very idea that there are people who associate Poland not with a ministerial chair but with a prison cell, people who prefer Christmas under arrest to a vacation in the south of France, unsettles you profoundly.

You cannot believe that such people exist. This is why, in your most recent speech in the Sejm, you, General, in the sliminess of your accusations, sank to the level of that Polish classic in this art form, Stanisław Radkiewicz.[3] This is why, even among yourselves, you call us great con artists (because we supposedly get our instructions and money from U.S. intelligence) or else great fools, "fanatics" (because

---

3. Stanisław Radkiewicz, known for his brutality and ruthlessness, was a minister of public security in Stalinist Poland.

we would rather sit in jail than stroll on Parisian boulevards). Surely, not one of you would hesitate for a second if faced with such a choice.

You are incapable of thinking of us in a different way because, doing so, you would inevitably—if only for a split second—be forced to fathom the truth about yourselves. The truth that you are vindictive, dishonorable swine; the truth that even if there ever was a spark of decency in your hearts, you have long buried this feeling in the brutal and dirty power struggle which you wage among yourselves. This is why, scoundrels that you are, you want to drag us down to your own level.

Well, I am going to deny you that pleasure. I cannot foretell the future and I have no idea whether I will yet live to see the victory of truth over lies and of Solidarity over this present antiworker dictatorship. The point is, General, that for me, the value of our struggle lies not in its chances of victory but rather in the value of the cause. Let my little gesture of denial be a small contribution to the sense of honor and dignity in this country that is being made more miserable every day. For you, traders in other people's freedom, let it be a slap in the face.

For me, General, prison is not such painful punishment. On that December night it was not I who was condemned but freedom; it is not I who am being held prisoner today but Poland.

For me, General, real punishment would be if on your orders I had to spy, wave a truncheon, shoot workers, interrogate prisoners, and issue disgraceful sentences. I am happy to find myself on the right side, among the victims and not among the victimizers. But of course you cannot comprehend this: otherwise you would not be making such foolish and wicked proposals.

In the life of every honorable man there comes a difficult moment, General, when the simple statement *this is black and that is white* requires paying a high price. It may cost one one's life on the slopes of the Citadel, behind the wire fence of Sachsenhausen, behind the bars of Mokotów prison. At such a time, General, a decent man's concern is not the price he will have to pay but the certainty that white *is* white and black *is* black. One needs a conscience to determine this. Paraphrasing the saying of one of the great writers of our continent, I would like to suggest that the first thing you need to know, General, is what it is to have a human conscience. It may come as news to you that there are two things in this world, *evil* and *good*. You may not know that to lie and insult is not good, that to betray is bad, to imprison and murder is even worse. Never mind that such things may be expedient—they are forbidden. Yes, General, *forbidden*. Who forbids them? General, you may be the mighty minister of internal affairs, you may have the backing of a power that extends from the Elbe to Vladivostok and of the entire police force of this country, you may have millions of informers and millions of zlotys with which to buy guns, water cannons, bugging devices, servile collaborators, informers, and journalists; but something invisible, a passerby in the darkness, will appear before you and say: *this you must not do.*

That is conscience.

I am certain that this letter will seem to you yet another proof of my stupidity. You are accustomed to servile begging, to police reports and informers' denunciations. And yet here you have a man who is entirely in your hands, who is being harassed by your prosecutors, who will be sentenced by your judges, and who dares to preach to you about conscience.

What impertinence!

However, you can no longer astonish me. I know that I will have to pay dearly for this letter, that your subordinates will now attempt to enlighten me about the full range of possibilities of the prison system in a country that is in the process of building communism. But I also know that I am bound by truth.

This is why I am asking you no favors. Except one: I ask you to think again. Not about my fate, because I hope to endure whatever new ideas your colonels and majors may come up with.

Please think about yourself. When you are sitting down to your Christmas dinner, take a moment to think that you will be held responsible for your actions. You will have to account for breaking the law. Those who have suffered and been humiliated will present you with a reckoning. It will be a grim moment for you.

I hope that at that moment you will manage to retain your personal dignity; and I wish you courage. Do not try to exonerate yourself, like your colleagues from the governments that preceded yours, with the claim that you knew nothing, because such excuses enlist not our pity but our contempt.

As for myself, I hope that when your life is in danger, I will be able to appear in time to help you as I did in Otwock when I helped save the lives of those few of your subordinates, that I will be able to place myself once again on the side of the victims and not that of the victimizers.[4] Even if, afterward, you should once more wonder at my incorrigible stupidity and decide to lock me back in prison all over again.

Adam Michnik

4. On May 8, 1981, a mob attempting to lynch a policeman and to burn down a police station in Otwock near Warsaw was calmed by Michnik's dramatic intervention. His by now famous opening sentence was: "Listen to me, my name is Adam Michnik and I am an Anti-Socialist Force."

// About the Elections 1984

Adam Michnik, son of Ozjasz
Warsaw, Rakowiecka Street, Investigative Prison
Pavilion 3, section 2, cell no. 11

DECLARATION

Why do the communists need these elections to the People's town councils?

To pick new councilmen? No—for this they would need no elections.

To convince someone that they have won society's mandate for their actions? No. No one—not even their wives—believes this.

To pretend to Moscow and the West that the situation in Poland has stabilized? No. Last May's demonstrations undercut all such plans. Moscow has better channels of information, and the West has not yet been made so completely stupid that it would believe this. So maybe they did it to find out for themselves how many people they have managed to intimidate? No. Not even they can obtain the real data. The results of the voting will already be rigged—they always have been—at the level of the electoral boards. They have another reason for holding these elections. Operation "elections" is the next stage in the cycle

71

called by M. F. Rakowski [the deputy prime minister] "breaking the moral backbone."

Such is also the meaning of the "war of the crosses."[1] A cross that hangs on a wall does not lower productivity rates or violate the balance of power in Europe. So why then does a government incapable of supplying Poles with drugs, socks, or a pork chop find the time and resources for this eccentric war with society (because this is a war with society and not with the clergy) over this symbol of suffering and redemption? They always have the same goal. By depriving the people of the cross, they aim to break, humiliate, and degrade them. Imprisoning those who do not want to be lackeys (the attorney Maciej Bednarkiewicz and writer Marek Nowakowski), searching homes for books that appear underground, dissolving creative associations, attacking honest lawyers, violating Warsaw University's autonomy—all these actions serve this end. And the electoral farce serves to extract a ritual gesture of subservience, which consists of participation in a clearly absurd ceremony.

In a book devoted to the study of animals, Vitus Droescher described the habits of baboons. He described the ritual of showing hierarchic reverence: "The ape showing veneration to his superior inclines not his head but his rear end, which he sometimes moves up to his very nose. This, however, does not mean: you can kiss my ———, but, on the contrary, represents the ultimate subordination, a call for copulation." So we are supposed to be like baboons: whoever goes to the ballot box performs such a servile act. He will say to the general: you can screw me. Even if only this is the reason for not voting, it is enough.

A boycott will serve no purpose. It will not influence the actions of the communists. It will not inform public opinion about the size of the opposition. The communists, for all their limited knowledge, have gained some experience in rigging election results. There is no reason to expect them to change their habits. They had an opportunity to find out what the Poles want during the pope's visit in 1983.

---

1. In December 1983, the government ordered all the crosses taken down from walls of schools, hospitals, and other public institutions. Among the ensuing conflicts the most critical took place in Miętne (near Garwolin), where a high school was closed.

A boycott of the elections, from the point of view of global politics, would be meaningless. In the life of every Pole, however, this will be an important act. Everyone who takes part in it will be saving his dignity.

We gave in to fear long enough, as we hurried to the voting booths and stood slavishly in lines, in response to Bierut's and Gomułka's calls, and to Gierek's and Jaroszewicz's. We have justified this cowardly opportunism with convoluted explanations: that it was for our children's security and welfare. Then it turned out that our children would rather have parents who were less protective and more decent.

Wojciech Jaruzelski said recently that the Polish people are living beyond their means. There is a grain of truth in this. Toleration of the current team's rule does surpass the Poles' means. These people would be capable of bankrupting a country much more prosperous than ours and then calling their actions an economic miracle. The long list of their swindles fits into a terrifyingly logical pattern. It is a list of actions that confirms the nation as a prisoner and themselves as the jailers.

I know all too well the mechanisms involved in the role of prisoner, and I deal with jailers on a daily basis. Moreover, I have a special, personal reason to express my opinion on this question. The communists chose to use me, too, in their election campaign. They decided to free the so-called Solidarity Eleven [eleven Solidarity and opposition leaders]—who had been in jail for two and a half years, on trumped-up charges, if we would sign a declaration pledging to refrain from political activities for the next two and a half years, or if we would emigrate. Beginning on April 19 of this year, by way of intermediaries found by Father Alojzy Orszulik, our jailers organized a series of meetings with the eleven of us in suburban Warsaw villas. For me alone they went as far as to arrange four meetings in my cell with my fellow prisoners.

Since I have not authorized anyone to act as mediator in my dealings with my jailers, since as a prisoner I do not feel entitled to participate in any negotiations, since my liberty cannot be the object of any deals, since I want to be put on trial in order to prove my innocence, I have declined to take part in these talks. The above are no doubt the same reasons that led my fellow prisoners to decline the offer to buy their freedom at the price of a declaration of capitulation.

At that time, the jailers also organized a meeting for us with the

General Secretary of the United Nations; this good man also made us an offer to leave Poland. I am convinced that he wanted to be helpful to us. I—who said no to a meeting with him—was treated to a punishment of two weeks in a dark cell: this was the price I paid for declining a conversation. It was the head of the investigative prison, citizen Major Dejnarek, who meted out this punishment for my unwillingness to talk to the representative of the UN's general secretary. Please: let no one else try to help me this way. Let no one assist General Kiszczak in his attempt to ruin my health in the dark cells of Mokotów prison. My body may not withstand another such product of Major Dejnarek's stupidity and ignominy: cowardly rascal is prepared to finish me off just to win Kiszczak's praise.

My jailers have not stopped trying. A female employee in the Ministry of Foreign Affairs keeps tempting some prisoners with trips abroad; for others Kiszczak continues to organize meetings and more meetings in suburban villas. As for me, he is trying to soften me up with the dark cell.

The pattern of these actions is obvious: this is how the terrorists of this world dictate conditions to their hostages. I am deeply convinced that these bandit tricks will end in a total fiasco. These people's intentions are unusually abominable. While yet another fake trial is organized for Władysław Frasyniuk [Wrocław Solidarity leader] (the sentence he was given for his "crime" in jail deserves close attention, for it is a sign that Soviet models of conducting the class struggle in jail are being copied), while Piotr Bednarz [another Solidarity leader from Wrocław] has been led to attempt suicide, and while others turn to a long hunger strike to gain the rights of political prisoners, we eleven are to serve as proof of the humanitarianism of Jaruzelski and his jailers. I don't know who invented these plans and strategies, but I do know that behind them is concealed the ethical horizon of their authors, the jailers from the security apparatus and their propagandists. I know these ethics well from Jaruzelski's and Rakowski's speeches, from Kiszczak's and Olszowski's interviews, from Urban's press conferences, from *Trybuna Ludu* editorials: it is the ethics of treason. Yes, these people know how to betray; they know how to sell out friends and principles. But for them to judge us by their own moral standards—really, this goes too far. In view of these actions, I am appealing to all decent people to forgo the role of the mediator who relays to us the latest schemes of our overseers. I, at least, do not wish to be the object of such negotiations.

I will also accept no amnesty because I am guilty of nothing. I demand—and will continue to demand—an open trial. I have the patience to wait until a verdict is delivered that declares me innocent—until the criminals in their army uniforms (men such as the head of the court of the Warsaw military district, Col. Władysław Monarcha) stop disgracing the Polish judiciary system.

But my jailers must not count on my silence. I will always say what my conscience and reason tell me to say. Hence my call:

At this sad time, a time of lies and coercion, let us preserve our dignity. We have received this most precious of treasures from our fathers. Let us hand it down to our children. And let us look around us. Let us look into everyone's eyes. Let us fix in memory those who on June 17 [election day] are openly subservient. Because, as the poet said, "those who bow down with their foreheads will also strike your face." [Stanisław Barańczak]

Therefore, in full awareness of the responsibility I incur, I am joining in the appeal issued by the leaders of Solidarity to boycott the elections.

June 1984

// Letter from the Gdańsk Prison 1985

//   Jerzy Urban, the government press spokesman, contends that I wanted very much to be arrested. My imprisonment, he says, would be useful to my Pentagon principals, who would like to spread a false picture of Jaruzelski and his group. My American bosses fervently desire the world to believe, falsely, that Jaruzelski's government maintains internal peace by imprisoning its political opponents. Urban's dialectical reasoning leads one to the irrefutable conclusion that Poland is a perfectly calm place, that its government enjoys great moral authority, and the support of an overwhelming majority of society. Only a few extremist groups, incited by Ronald Reagan, storm the prison gates begging to be arrested.

    This incisive analysis conceals Urban's inherent inability to understand that there are people who won't be deterred by the threat of imprisonment from doing what they believe is right. Still, in my conversations with myself, held during long prison nights, I often wondered why Bogdan Lis, Władysław Frasyniuk, and I had been arrested. I saw in this a proof that the government is afraid of rising social tensions caused by the deteriorating standard of living. I also think that our arrest was motivated by a desire to appease the frustrations of the security apparatus in connection with the Toruń trial.[1] Our arrest, and the show

---

1. The trial of four policemen convicted in the murder case of Rev. Jerzy Popiełuszko.

trial which is now being prepared, are an expression of boundless faith in a social order built on lies and police repression. But they also prove that repression leads the government into a blind alley, at least in today's Poland.

Yes, it is possible to govern in this way. As long as geopolitics is favorable, this system may last for quite some time. But it cannot rid itself of the stigma of an alien, imposed garrison. Repression has lost its effectiveness. Our imprisonment does not frighten anyone, nor will anyone be enslaved by it. This has been the case for the past five years.

But it wasn't always like this. Radicals and exiles typically delude themselves that dictatorships are based exclusively on coercion. This is not true. Long-lived dictatorships engender their own characteristic subculture and their own peculiar normalcy. They create a type of man unused to freedom and truth, ignorant of dignity and autonomy. Rebels are a tiny minority in such dictatorships; they are seen as a handful of desperate men who live like a band of heretics. For every dictatorship, the critical moment arrives with the reappearance of human autonomy and the emergence of social bonds that do not enjoy official sanction. As a rule, such moments are short—temporary tremors marking a crisis in the dictatorial power structure.

In the Leading Social System, such loss of balance never lasted longer than a few months. But in Poland the structures of independent civil society have been functioning for several years—a veritable miracle on the Vistula. So long as these structures exist side by side with totalitarian power, which attempts to destroy all independent institutions, the stream of people flowing to prisons will not cease. Poles will stop going behind bars only when they succeed in their struggle for democratic reform of public life. But if they let their independent institutions be destroyed, the whole country will become a prison.

In Poland, "miracle on the Vistula" refers to an event sixty-five years ago, when the young Polish army, organized in the first days of regained independence, successfully defended Poland, and European democracy with it, against an offensive of the young Bolshevik revolution. The present image of that battle was shaped by Soviet propaganda, which claimed that feudal-bourgeois Poland attempted to strangle the first state of workers and peasants. One does not need an extraordinary imagination to visualize the consequences of Poland's defeat in that battle. If Budenny's Red Army had been able to water its horses in the Seine, not much would be left of European democracy. . . .

Poland was led in those days by Józef Piłsudski, one of the greatest and most complex figures in its modern history. Piłsudski once wrote a memorable sentence: "In Poland prison is a constant, everyday companion of human thought. It is a part of consciousness, political culture, and everyday life."

One must remember these thoughts from the builder of Polish independence in order to understand contemporary Poland, with all its hopes, prospects, and dangers. Foreign observers, even friendly ones, often lack the knowledge and conceptual framework to comprehend the whole unconventionality of Polish fate. With few exceptions, such as Timothy Garton Ash or Martin Malia, Poland appears to them a country of incomprehensible reactions and unfathomable conflicts. This is not surprising; after all, Polish observers understand little of the Irish or the Chilean predicament. Yet I think that this lack of understanding may have costly consequences, and not only for the Poles. Hence this essay.

In the eyes of Western observers, the Polish miracle began in August, 1980 and ended on December 13, 1981. I disagree. I place its beginnings earlier, and I think that the Polish experience acquired a truly universal dimension only *after* December 13.

It will soon be ten years since fifty-nine intellectuals signed a petition demanding that the scope of freedom in Poland be broadened. The petition also spoke of workers' right to independent trade unions. The letter of fifty-nine became a warning. "You cannot govern like this any longer," was its message to Gierek. The only answer from the authorities was to carry out reprisals against the people who signed it. A few months later, Poland was shaken by another, incomparably more dramatic manifestation of crisis. In June 1976 workers in Radom and Ursus went on strike, demonstrating in the streets against enormous price increases. The reaction of the government was typical: the price increases were withdrawn and participants in the protests were forced to walk through gauntlets of truncheon-swinging police (so-called paths of health). They were tried, slandered, and made targets of hate propaganda. A spontaneous movement to help these workers emerged among the intelligentsia, giving birth to the Workers' Defense Committee

(KOR) and the democratic opposition movement—the first links in the long chain of the new "miracle on the Vistula."

The ensuing events may be described as a dramatic wrestling match between the totalitarian power and a society searching for a way to attain autonomy. The period between August 1980 and December 1981 was merely a phase in this struggle. It ended with a setback for the independent society and a disaster for the totalitarian state. For disaster is an appropriate name for a situation in which workers are confronted by tanks instead of debates. This is not the place for a detailed recital of the struggles that have taken place since then. Other people will take up this task; some, like Jan Józef Lipski, in his book about *KOR*, and Jerzy Holzer in *Solidarity*, have already made a beginning. I just want to stress two principal traits of the democratic opposition which were later adopted by Solidarity, namely the renunciation of violence and the politics of truth.

Whence the power, the scope, the numbers, the patience, and the perseverance of this movement? Some explain all this by suggesting that there has always been a tradition of struggle for national independence; others detect the influence of the Catholic Church; still others praise the maturity of the Polish freedom strategy designed by the underground leaders. They are all right. But the principal reason can be found in the very essence of the totalitarian system, which had long ago become an obstacle to the development of creative forces—one that promotes sterility and destroys creativity and the spirit of society. The system exists only to protect the interests and the power of the ruling *nomenklatura*. Since the Soviet Union regards the rule of the *nomenklatura* as a guarantee of its ideological and political stake in Poland, the Polish striving for autonomy threatens not only the power of the generals but also Soviet interests. Is it possible to change this particular definition of Soviet interests in Poland? The future of Polish independence depends on this question. The answer will also determine the nature of peaceful coexistence, because it will demonstrate whether Soviet leaders are willing to accept a new political reality.

Polish political reality is such that forty months after the imposition of martial law there exists a large opposition movement and an even more widespread front of refusal to cooperate with the generals. At the same time, Solidarity has not resorted to terror, assassinations, or kidnappings. These methods belong exclusively to the repertory of the authorities. How can we explain this peculiar contradiction, which the official propagandists call "normalization"? What can we call this unusual situation, in which repression, provocations, and sheer exhaustion—the best ally of any dictatorship—have failed to annihilate Solidarity, the main organization of the civil disobedience movement, or to push it into the blind alley of terrorism? How come our nation has been able to transcend the dilemma typical of defeated societies—the hopeless choice between servility and despair?

It seems that the Polish nation does not think it has been defeated. The answer to the questions we posed can be found in Lenin's old adage, well known to the communists: the regime cannot rule any longer according to the old ways, but it does not know how to change them; the people do not want to live according to the old ways, and they are no longer afraid to try new ones.

What does it mean that they "do not want to live according to the old ways"? Well, it means that people don't want to live like objects, silently accepting their own enslavement. They reject their status as subjects; they wish to master their own fate. And they are not afraid to do so.

But what does it mean "to rule according to the old ways"? It means to hope that the society is or will soon become completely terrorized, and thus wholly molded by the state. Changing these ways means to accept the autonomy of society not as a passing inconvenience but as an integral part of social reality. This is the road to dialogue and compromise.

Is this realistic? Is a compromise between the persecutor and his victim possible? Aren't our "fundamentalists" correct in maintaining that no democratic evolution is possible without prior, total destruction of the communist system, and that the only sensible program of action, therefore, must reject hopes for a future compromise with the ruling group and opt instead for the integral idea of independence—that is, full independence from the Soviet Union and complete removal of communists from power? This is the central dilemma of the Polish opposition movement.

Let us defer consideration of this point for the moment, noting only that our generals' idea of normalization differs substantially from Kádár's or Husák's "normalizations" which, in essence, meant total destruction of all independent institutions. Forty months after the Soviet invasion, Hungary resembled a political cemetery; forty months of normalization in Czechoslovakia transformed it, in Aragon's apt phrase, into the cultural Biafra of Europe. But in Poland, even after official liquidation of independent public institutions (trade unions, artists' associations, youth organizations, editorial boards of various journals, etc.), after forty months of repression and provocation, the independent civil society, although pushed outside the official sphere, has not been annihilated. Under the conditions of the Leading System, this is an unprecedented phenomenon. Instead of resembling a communist system after victorious pacification, this situation resembles a democracy after a military *coup d'etat*. The Poles have traveled a great distance on their journey from totalitarianism to democracy.

I am writing soon after the trial of the murderers of Rev. Jerzy Popiełuszko. For some Western observers, the trial provided a proof of our generals' liberal tendencies. And indeed, the trial was an unprecedented event in the history of the Leading System. Never before have the provocations of the security apparatus been revealed to such an extent, albeit inadvertently; never before has the villainy of those who are lords over the life and death of common people been laid so bare. That was without precedent. But in the last ten years, everything in Poland has been without precedent. The independent information network. Solidarity. The authority and influence of the Church. The Toruń trial was also unprecedented in its attack on the Church. The vile slander of the murdered priest; the charge of collaboration with the Gestapo, made against the widely respected bishop of the Przemyśl diocese, Ignacy Tokarczuk; the accusations that other bishops destroyed marriages and embezzled money—this is the other side of the Toruń trial. Its main element is blackmail: "Look, we will continue doing this unless you cease to resist!" Our generals know perfectly well that they will not break the resistance of society unless they succeed in driving the Church back to the catacombs, or in refashioning it into a collaborationist institution, on the pattern of the Orthodox Church in the Soviet Union.

The Popiełuszko murder was an integral part of this scenario because Rev. Jerzy personified the connection between the Church and Solidarity. His Holy Masses for the Fatherland provided extraordinary, heartening moments for the people of Warsaw. The police could never forgive the shepherd of the Zolibórz church the moments of relief he offered to the tormented, persecuted city.

The abduction of the Rev. Jerzy Popiełuszko [on October 18, 1984] was but one in a long series of kidnappings. The perpetrators freely walk the streets of Polish cities; they need not worry about any criminal proceedings against them. Despite widespread demands, there was no resumption of any proceedings against the murderers of Grzegorz Przemyk.[2] Instead, police captain Piotrowski, the murderer who organized the abduction of Popiełuszko and who was later permitted to switch his role from defendant to the accuser of the Church, became an idol for his pals in the Ministry of Internal Affairs. I heard enough during my own detention and interrogations. Moments after saying good-bye to Lech Wałęsa, when I was being put into the police car, I heard them say: "We still have free space in the trunk for Mr. Michnik. Just like for Popiełuszko." A marvelous little joke. . . . They didn't even try to pretend.

With the generals it's a different matter. They do care about appearances. Evidence to the contrary, they do not want to be held responsible for this cruel killing. This is why the Toruń trial had to take place, and why the defendants tried to outdo one another in declaring that there was no one "issuing orders from the top," that the abduction and murder were merely a guerrilla action undertaken wholly on their own initiative. The only point of contention concerned whether the idea was Captain Piotrowski's or Colonel Pietruszka's, either of whom must have been inspired by goblins from the CIA. The Toruń trial had to take place for the stigma of crime to be lifted from the generals' epaulettes. The trial served as a useful smoke screen, but it did not signify any political about-face. Efforts to destroy the autonomy of society are an essential element of the generals' political course. So they reach for an old, discredited instrument: lawlessness in the guise

2. Nineteen-year-old Warsaw student Grzegorz Przemyk died on May 14, 1983, from injuries suffered during his detention by the police. In the trial the emergency ambulance staff was convicted and the policemen acquitted of all charges.

of law. It is used to detain and sentence Solidarity activists on even the most absurd charges. No sooner had the charge of treason against Bogdan Lis been withdrawn than Andrzej Gwiazda was accused of hooliganism. I was promoted to membership in the Temporary Coordinating Commission of Solidarity (TKK)[3]—a genuine honor, were it not for the fact that I had been nominated by the Gdańsk secret police.

The list of political prisoners has rapidly become longer. On it are such people as Michał Luty, the organizer of educational courses for Silesian workers, and Józef Śreniowski, a sociologist from Łódź and an old friend of mine from KOR. However, if my arrest, together with that of Lis and Frasyniuk, will at least darken the liberal image which the generals have tried to cultivate, and if it illuminates the fate of other political prisoners, then our stay in prison will not be for nothing.

The prison machine has been put in motion. It could not have been otherwise. In the face of economic breakdown (once again, a severe winter surprised the rulers of my country), at a time of yet another blow against the standard of living and the rights of the working people (an eight-hour day and free Saturdays), with rising social tensions portending the next explosion, fear is the only remaining hope of our rulers. Although the abductions have ceased for the moment (this genre of political polemics is temporarily inconvenient), our lot has been to exchange our homes for prison. But none of the basic elements in the Polish equation has thereby changed. Poland continues to be what it was: a country in which the nation strives for freedom and autonomy and the authorities try to force it back into a totalitarian corset.

The immediate reason for our arrest lay in the fact that the authorities were scared of the strike set for February 28 in protest against the announced price increases. We were detained on the thirteenth, during a meeting with Lech Wałęsa. On the fourteenth, Polish cities were blanketed with leaflets calling for the strike. On the fifteenth, we were given a prosecutor's arrest warrant. The decision to strike was made by leaders of Solidarity in the belief that it was the union's duty to stand up against increasing poverty, to say no to the policy of

3. TKK (Temporary Coordination Committee) is the leadership group of underground Solidarity. Established in Spring 1982, it includes representatives from the main regional centers of the underground.

substituting additional bites into family budgets for a structural reform of the economy.

I am not sufficiently familiar with the events that followed our arrest, but the facts speak for themselves. Official "neo-unions" were told to reject all versions of the proposed price hikes while the government announced that it was going to put them in effect on a staggered schedule. This provides the best proof that Solidarity's leadership had had good judgment, had correctly read the mood of society, and had chosen the best moment for the protest. It was not an easy decision, however. The discussions which I witnessed illustrated two dangers facing Solidarity. On the one hand, the decision was criticized for not going far enough: fifteen minutes would be too short; the authorities would not even feel a pinprick. A stronger blow was needed, even a general strike. This is what the radicals wanted. I think that their position contained a substantial element of wishful thinking. To seek a confrontation on such scale implied not only a willingness to risk the existence of underground institutions but also ignored reality. And the reality was this: in January, 1985, when the TKK made its decision to call for a strike, people in the factories had neither the strength nor the will to go through with this confrontation. Radical thinking is peculiarly vulnerable to paper designs and to emotions that block sight of reality. It is an experience familiar to generations of conspirators and émigrés. My opposition to ideas of the radicals did not spring from pessimism; to the contrary, my friends accused me of an excess of enthusiasm. Nevertheless, I tried to constrain my optimism, aware that it tends to generate hopes on which it then feeds itself.

I also noticed that TKK's decision drew considerable criticism from regional activists. They stubbornly repeated: "This cannot succeed, people don't want strikes because they are afraid of reprisals, they are tired, they don't believe a strike will have any impact." I understood the reasons for their view, and at the same time I also perceived a paralyzing fear of a setback, an apprehension that factories would not follow TKK's appeal. I did not share this fear. I did not think that an unsuccessful fifteen-minute strike against price increases would mean an apocalyptic defeat. At worst, it would demonstrate that workers are not at present strong enough to defend their interests by striking. However, had the TKK not called for a strike it would indeed have been a real defeat because it would indicate that Solidarity had ceased to be an independent trade union, ready to fight for workers' interests. A merely verbal protest would not be much different from the declaration by official "neo-unions."

The fear of defeat, I think, may often paralyze more effectively than defeat itself. I believe that the underground society, constantly improvising, created its own mechanisms of institutional ossification— its own routine, and the concomitant aversion to change. This is as understandable as it is dangerous. The thinking of underground activists and all members of Solidarity must be geared to dealing with surprises; they must be prepared for situations when the popular mood drastically changes. This happened, for example, immediately after the abduction of Reverend Popiełuszko. Some conservatism in attitudes or institutions is valuable because it preserves continuity. But conservatism may become a harmful restraint, a set of blinders, if it prevents one from being in touch with a changing reality. Far be it for me to exaggerate these dangers, but one should be well aware of them. Those who say that the struggle for freedom exacts a price are indeed right, as are those who insist on carefully counting the costs in order to minimize losses. It is fortunate that Solidarity makes room for both of these predispositions.

I spent almost three years in prison. The officials in the Ministry of Internal Affairs who offered me a choice between emigrating or declaring my loyalty to the regime—a temptation to buy freedom for a loathsome price—always tried to convince me that Solidarity had long ago ceased to exist, and that I, cut off, continued to live with illusions. Sometimes I even asked myself: "Perhaps they are right after all?"

What I saw after my release[4] exceeded not just my expectations but even my dreams. I found that the people of Solidarity were wise, determined, ready for a long struggle. They possessed clear vision. Solidarity, its associated organizations, the wide scope of Polish autonomy that existed outside the official realm, dozens of excellent journals and wonderful books, the seriousness of purpose coupled with the willingness to take risks—all these things comprise the Polish miracle on the Vistula. I attended seminars for workers and students, I read new high-quality journals published in various cities and circulating in

---

4. As a consequence of the Amnesty Act of July 21, 1984.

various circles. I saw uncensored books printed by the underground publishing houses—books by Popper, Kundera, Besançon, Aron, Orwell, Shestov, Solzhenitsyn, Havel, not to mention Polish writers. I saw uncensored paintings and photographs, as well as new films shown on uncensored videocassettes. I saw churches that served as oases of spiritual independence and provided home for centers of aid to the victims of repression.

Granted, not everything I saw was a source of comfort. I also saw sadness, exhaustion, ugly shrewdness, revolting mendacity, crafty operators pretending to be heroes, and Judases wearing the cloaks of political realists. These are normal things in any movement or society. Only Solidarity did not follow the norm, contradicting commonplace expectations.

I wish to avoid the sin of idealizing my friends. They have faults and shortcomings, like all normal human beings. Yet every time I think of them I am full of admiration. I didn't know how to convey this feeling to them and now I regret my reticence. So, at least in this letter, I would like to express my respect and send greetings to Janek, Konrad, Zbyszek, Bogdan, Tadeusz, Wiktor, and Patryk.

Why did Solidarity renounce violence? This question returned time and again in my conversations with foreign observers. I would like to answer it now. People who claim that the use of force in the struggle for freedom is necessary must first prove that, in a given situation, it will be effective, and that force, when it is used, will not transform the idea of liberty into its opposite.

No one in Poland is able to prove today that violence will help us to dislodge Soviet troops from Poland and to remove the communists from power. The USSR has such enormous military power that confrontation is simply unthinkable. In other words: we have no guns. Napoleon, upon hearing a similar reply, gave up asking further questions. However, Napoleon was above all interested in military victories, and not building democratic, pluralistic societies. We, by contrast, cannot leave it at that.

In our reasoning, pragmatism is inseparably intertwined with idealism. Taught by history, we suspect that by using force to storm the existing Bastilles we shall unwittingly build new ones. It is true that social change is almost always accompanied by force. But it is not true that social change is merely a result of the violent collision of various forces. Above all, social changes follow from a confrontation of different moralities and visions of social order. Before the violence of rulers clashes with the violence of their subjects, values and systems of ethics clash inside human minds. Only when the old ideas of the rulers lose this moral duel will the subjects reach for force—sometimes. This is what happened in the French Revolution and the Russian Revolution— two examples cited in every debate as proof that revolutionary violence is preceded by a moral breakdown of the old regime. But both examples lose their meaning when they are reduced to such compact notions, in which the Encyclopedists are paired with the destruction of the Bastille, and the success of radical ideologies in Russia is paired with the storming of the Winter Palace. An authentic event is reduced to a sterile scheme.

In order to understand the significance of these revolutions, one must remember Jacobin and Bolshevik terror, the guillotines of the sans-culottes, and the guns of the commissars. Without reflection on the mechanisms in victorious revolutions that gave birth to terror, it is impossible to even pose the fundamental dilemma facing contemporary freedom movements. Historical awareness of the possible consequences of revolutionary violence must be etched into any program of struggle for freedom. The experience of being corrupted by terror must be imprinted upon the consciousness of everyone who belongs to a freedom movement. Otherwise, as Simone Weil wrote, freedom will again become a refugee from the camp of the victors.

It is worthwhile looking at freedom movements in the Leading System from this standpoint. In *The Gulag Archipelago,* Solzhenitsyn describes a revolt of prisoners in a Soviet concentration camp and paints a vivid picture of the mechanism of oppression imposed by the new leaders on their erstwhile comrades. Solzhenitsyn's story has the power of great allegory; it is a warning to all of us, the mutinous prisoners of the Leading System. All accounts of the Hungarian revolution mention the cruelty of rebellious mobs lynching the hated functionaries of the security police. Crowd psychology may be understandable in such situations, but it also makes us pause to reflect on this twisting bystreet along the road to freedom.

In October 1956, the situation in Poland was almost the opposite of that in Hungary. The lessons of that episode in our history revealed, more clearly than anything else had, the techniques used by the communists to defuse a social crisis. It was a lesson of defeat, not of a successful strategy for attaining democracy and freedom. Czechoslovakia provided a different lesson: it avoided both revolutionary terror and a washout of the kind that occurred after the Polish October. But the Prague Spring remains the great myth of national concord broken by Soviet invasion. The revolutionary process in Czechoslovakia never reached the level of internal polarization at which the very question of power of the Communist party becomes a point of contention.

Only in today's Poland is there a deliberate struggle to set limits on the power of the communist *nomenklatura* and to create de facto pluralism under conditions imposed by the Brezhnev doctrine. The adoption of these goals has been a determining factor in making revolutionary terror an alien concept for Solidarity.

Solidarity's strategy bore full fruit after December 13, when a massive attack by the army and the police was met with an unconventional form of resistance, aptly labeled by Maciej Poleski as a "silence of the sea." Not only did it minimize losses and save the structure of independent society, it also assured a peculiar "victory in defeat." For even if an unfavorable international situation perpetuates the political enslavement of Poland, no one will be able to tear out from our consciousness all the books and newspapers we have read, the discussions we have held. Thanks to this strategy, the present generation of Poles will never again succumb to the poison of self-enslavement.

Solidarity's program and ethos are inextricably tied to this strategy. Revolutionary terror has always been justified by a vision of an ideal society. In the name of this vision, Jacobin guillotines and Bolshevik execution squads carried out their unceasing, gruesome work. The road to God's Kingdom on Earth led through rivers of blood.

Solidarity has never had a vision of an ideal society. It wants to live and let live. Its ideals are closer to the American Revolution than to the French. Its thinking about goals is similar to that of the resistance against Franco in Spain, or against the "black colonels" in Greece; it is unlike the thinking of those who strive to attain doctrinal goals. The ethics of Solidarity, with its consistent rejection of the use of force, has a lot in common with the idea of nonviolence as espoused by Gandhi and Martin Luther King, Jr. But it is not an ethic representative of pacifist movements. Pacifism as a mass movement aims to avoid suffering; pacifists often say that no cause is worth suffering or dying for. The ethics of Solidarity are based on an opposite premise: that there are causes worth suffering and dying for. Gandhi and King died for the same cause as the miners in Wujek who rejected the belief that it is better to remain a willing slave than to become a victim of murder. In this belief Solidarity activists consciously reject the idea of adhering to doctrinal consistency at all cost. Following the teachings of the Polish pope—and hating war the way he does—they will nevertheless admit the possibility of armed defense of freedom against aggressive despotism. It was no accident that one of the most prominent creators of contemporary Polish culture [Leszek Kolakowski] wrote an essay titled "In Praise of Inconsistency."

Having said this, I should add that Solidarity has not been wholly immune to totalitarian temptations. Organized as a social movement struggling against the totalitarian state, composed of people who grew up in the Leading System and were shaped by its totalitarian structures, Solidarity has always been torn between trying to influence administrative decisions and attempting to restrict the omnipotence of the state. In fact, this conflict was the seed of a dramatic dilemma that faced the movement: whether it should seek to become an alternative to the authorities or instead renounce such aspirations and concentrate on a struggle to limit the scope of their power. Solidarity, and every other freedom movement in the communist system, will have to confront this dilemma in the days to come. The future of post-communist societies will depend on how it is resolved. The struggle for state power must lead to the use of force; yet in the struggle for a Self-Governing Republic, according to the resolution passed at the memorable Solidarity Congress in Gdańsk [September, 1981], the use of force must be renounced.

For me, Solidarity was never an instrument in the struggle for power. But this was by no means an uncontroversial position. Acute tensions give birth to strong temptations. Deep humiliation may spawn proposals for extremely radical solutions. Lack of easy answers and clear prospects is conducive of demagogic bidding contests. The sudden politicization of hundreds of thousands of people who used to be passive, and thus were not familiar with political life, produced a combination of populism and nationalism richly decorated with religious symbols. We all saw this explosive mixture developing during the last three months of 1981. Even though it was a marginal development, its appearance wasn't funny and provoked some sad thoughts. In *Konspira*, Bogdan Borusewicz[5] discussed this issue wisely and honestly. The anarchization of daily life, consciously pursued by the authorities as they prepared for the military coup, made people susceptible to even the worst nonsense. Those were golden times for certain suspect characters out to make a career. I had no difficulty imagining the future Dzierzyńskis[6] among these people. Therefore, I believe that the leading idea of Solidarity is to achieve a Self-Governing Republic and not to seize power; it is this idea that offers us the chance of avoiding, down the road, the guillotines or the execution squads for elimination of future "enemies of the people."

When I remember those weeks, in which everything was heading for the worst, when I try to reconstruct the atmosphere of illusion and the conflicts within Solidarity, it seems to me that the crucial problem did not concern the division between the "radicals" and the "moderates," or the dispute between Wałęsa and Gwiazda,[7] or the polemics about the proper assessment of the role played by KOR. In the most important conflict, the original idea of Solidarity was set against the populist-totalitarian tendency, whose screaming drowned out every proposed strategic initiative. It sprang from poverty, hysteria, and demagoguery; its followers spouted slogans about "true Poles." Did this division correspond to the traditional division between the right and the left? I believed so then. Today, I think otherwise.

5. A book of interviews with underground leaders. Borusewicz was a member of KOR and one of the organizers of free trade unions on the Baltic coast.

6. Feliks Dzierzyński (1877–1926), Polish revolutionary and Bolshevik leader, was a founder and chairman of the All-Russian Extraordinary Commission (Cheka), the first Soviet secret police. Responsible for the Red Terror, he died a strong supporter of Stalin.

7. As the situation became more and more tense, the conflicts inside Solidarity grew. Three weeks before the military coup, Andrzej Gwiazda and fourteen other members of the Gdańsk Solidarity commission resigned in protest against what they believed to be Wałęsa's overly conciliatory position toward the authorities.

Traditional divisions obviously produced varying sensibilities and shaped styles of political thinking. Ancient debates that originated in bygone times returned. They concerned issues such as the status of the Church, the appropriate extent of secularization, and so forth. Nevertheless, I think that in Poland the conflict between the right and the left belongs to the past. It used to divide a society that was torn by struggles for bourgeois freedoms, universal voting rights, land reform, secularization, the eight-hour workday, welfare, universal schooling, or the democratization of culture. A different distinction comes to the fore in the era of totalitarian dictatorships: one between the proponents of an open society and the proponents of a closed society. In the former, social order is based on self-government and collective agreements; in the latter, order is achieved through repression and discipline. In the vision of an open society, the state acts as the guardian of safety for citizens; in the vision of a closed society the state is a master and overseer who determines all modes of society's existence.

The inadequacy of traditional taxonomies has already been pointed out by Vladimir Bukovsky,[8] a few years ago. Shortly after the famous exchange for Corvalan, Bukovsky was asked whether he belonged to the left-wing or the right-wing camp. His answer: "We are neither from the left camp nor from the right camp, we are from the concentration camp." And that is the truth.

I recalled Bukovsky on purpose. His book was printed by several underground publishing houses and became a great success in Poland. This shows that Bukovsky's ethical stand, beautifully expressed in his memoir, closely corresponds to the spiritual outlook of the Polish resistance movement. It also shows that the people of Solidarity see the future not as a chain of explosions of tribal hatred but as a new system of relations between nations, which will be based on principles of freedom and equality. The current inside Solidarity which works for this vision is strong and clear-cut. As evidence, one may cite numerous publications in independent circulation—books by Czechs (particularly by the extremely popular Vaclav Havel), Hungarians, Lithuanians, and

---

8. Vladimir Bukovsky, scientist and author who spent many years in Soviet prisons and psychiatric institutions, was exchanged in 1976 for the imprisoned Chilean Communist party leader Luis Corvalan.

Ukrainians. The problem of future relations with our neighbors has become a subject for reflection by such political writers as Poleski, Podlaski, and Jan Józef Lipski. Of course, there are also other points of view, but this current, both here and in émigré writings, is impossible to ignore.

But ethics cannot substitute for a political program. We must therefore think about the future of Polish-Russian relations. Our thinking about this key question must be open; it should consider many different possibilities. Thus we must not rule out the possibility of a change in Soviet foreign policy that would bring compromise within the realm of the attainable. Let us remember that compromise between the Soviet Union and Finland was preceded by a war between these two countries.

The Soviet state has a new leader; he is a symbol of transition from one generation to the next within the Soviet elite. This change may offer an opportunity, since Mikhail Gorbachev has not yet become a prisoner of his own decisions. No one can rule out the possibility that an impulse for reform will spring from the top of the hierarchy of power. This is exactly what happened in the time of Alexander II and, a hundred years later, under Khrushchev. Reform is always possible, even in the face of resistance by the old apparatus. Leaders of the Kremlin may wish to take on the challenge of modernity; they may begin searching for a new model of relations with Soviet satellites. Polish political thought must be prepared for this contingency. Phobias and anti-Russian emotions provide no substitute.

The popularity of Bukovsky's book demonstrates that such phobias are not inevitable—the democratic camp in Russia has numerous friends in Poland and the Russian democratic movement is a natural ally of the freedom movement in Poland, as are other national liberation movements within the Soviet empire, especially in neighboring Ukraine, which is the most tragic nation in Europe. But these are general observations—even a rough outline of the future of our part of the world is still unclear. While tensions exist, it is uncertain how they may be resolved. This requires caution, avoidance of the risks inherent in rigid dogma, and patience. The restraint so noticeable in the Polish movement was due to these considerations, and not, as some critics claim, to nationalistic blindness.

Nor is it correct to accuse Solidarity of political clericalism. Respect for the Church never involved political subordination of the union. Proposals to build a union movement based on the Catholic Church, which appeared in the last few years, were generally of marginal character. They were rejected by the TKK and by Lech Wałęsa as well.

The immense role of the Catholic Church in Poland, so spectacularly demonstrated during the pope's visit two years ago, provoked many comments, often unfavorable, from foreign observers. These gentlemen should hear the view of an individual (myself) who has never been accused of following Church instructions in his writings: the Church is not, and should not be a political institution. The bishops are not, and should not be, the representatives of the Poles' political aspirations. But the Catholic Church is the only institution in Poland that is simultaneously legal and authentic, independent of the totalitarian power structure and fully accepted by the people. The pope is for the Poles the greatest teacher of human values and obligations. This reality has obvious implications, among them the duty of the clergy to speak out on the matters that are of the greatest importance for the moral life of the people. The issue of violations of human rights cannot be excluded from this obligation. Thus, when the bishops criticize hate campaigns, condemn murders, or plead for dialogue instead of repression, they are expressing the aspirations, including the political aspirations, of an overwhelming majority of Poles.

Some people who are widely thought to have close connections with the Episcopate have on occasion expressed the view that Solidarity does not really exist any more. This provoked understandable protests from Solidarity activists. Let us overlook the question of the propriety or clumsiness of such statements—although they often seemed to me ill timed and out of place. Let us note, however, that from a Catholic bishop's point of view it is quite rational not to tie the long-term interests of the Church to the fate of even the noblest trade union or social movement. The Catholic Church existed in feudal monarchies and bourgeois republics, under foreign occupation and totalitarian dictatorship. In each situation, it searched for a suitable *modus vivendi* with the surrounding reality. It seems that at present we are also witnessing such a quest.

If the above hypothesis is correct—and it seems to be confirmed by the concentrated attacks launched by the official propaganda machine against the Church—then one may surmise that the model of the Church's role created by Cardinal Wyszyński must still provide a frame of reference for the bishops. It is a model that brought Polish Catholicism to a spectacular triumph. Let us note that the essential elements in this model—built on the dialectic whose poles are diplomacy and bearing witness, compromise and resistance—has been the full identification of the Shepherd with his flock. The latter used to be conceived as God's people, both in reference to relations within the Church and to relations between the people and the communist authorities. This was a correct premise in the Stalinist period, because the reign of terror left no openings for independent action. Today, in the Solidarity era, this premise has become completely false. Perhaps the origin of some of the rash comments about Solidarity—comments ascribing para-communist attitudes to some of its activists—should be sought in the imprecision of their authors' diagnoses of the present situation.

But nothing can change the fact that the Catholic Church is a great asset for the Poles. And not only because churches serve as headquarters for committees aiding victims of repression, or because chaplains speak up on behalf of the wronged and the persecuted; not only because church buildings ring with the words of a free Polish literature and the sounds of Polish music, or because their walls are adorned with the works of Polish painters; and not only because the Church has become an asylum for an independent Polish culture. The Church is the most important institution in Poland because it teaches all of us that we may bow only before God.

What will happen next?

Even though it is a necessary question, I can provide only part of the answer. I maintain that the Poles do not expect any help from outside. They do not place their faith in Reagan, or in the Pershing missiles—they have no hopes hanging on the outcome of negotiations in Geneva. Although they are happy to receive every gesture of solidarity made by the outside world, they are perfectly aware (and willing to say this to others) that they must, and will, place their faith only in themselves. They know that no one else can help them through their present ordeal.

No one can be a prophet in his own house. Rationally, it is possible only to say that no source of tensions has yet been eliminated, and that none of the critical problems has been solved. Normalization, in the sense of reaching an understanding, turned out to be an illusion. Normalization as pacification became an unmitigated disaster. So what can now happen?

The "fundamentalists" say: no compromises. Talking about compromise, dialogue, or understanding demobilizes public opinion, pulls the wool over the eyes of the public, spreads illusions. Wałęsa's declarations about readiness for dialogue were often severely criticized from this point of view.

I do not share the fundamentalist point of view. It is true that a compromise cannot be achieved by begging and that it is futile to explain to the communists why a compromise would be a sensible solution. This is why the appeals by "neorealists" are so pitiful and empty; their authors should beware of crossing the thin line that divides political speculation from collaboration. When Wałęsa declares the need for compromise he unmasks the intentions of the authorities; when the same is being said by a neorealist who avoids mentioning the word *Solidarity* like the plague, he sends word to the authorities of his own readiness to take part in murdering our union.

The logic of fundamentalism precludes any attempt to find compromise, even in the future. It harbors not only the belief that communists are ineducable but also a certainty that they are unable to behave rationally, even in critical situations—that, in other words, they are condemned to suicidal obstinacy.

This is not so obvious to me. Historical experience shows that communists were sometimes forced by circumstances to behave rationally and to agree to compromises. Thus the strategy of understanding must not be cast aside. We should not assume that a bloody confrontation is inevitable and, consequently, rule out the possibility of evolutionary, bloodless change. This should be avoided all the more inasmuch as democracy is rarely born from bloody upheavals. We should be clear in our minds about this: the continuing conflict may transform itself into either a dialogue or an explosion. The TKK and Wałęsa are doing everything in their power to make dialogue possible. Their chances of success will be greater if the level of self-organization of independent Polish society increases. For street lynchings, angry crowds are enough; compromise demands an organized society. In our activities we must also carefully watch the political map of the world. Poland's fate, unfortunately, is entwined in the superpower conflict; we have already fallen victim to it on several occasions in the past.

President Roosevelt once called Poland the conscience and the inspiration of the world, but this statement had no effect on American decisions at Yalta. Today, no special significance should be attached to merely verbal declarations. But if we nevertheless see some importance in such pronouncements it is because they seem to portend an important change in the direction of U.S. policies. Communist propaganda accuses President Reagan of ideologizing foreign policy. Indeed. It looks as if the United States, beginning with President Carter, took up this ideological challenge. This response was an expression of a belief that the outcome of the conflict will be determined not only by the principle of force but also by the force of principles. This is the reason for the American rejection of the Soviet interpretation of détente, which can be reduced to a simple philosophy: "When you are in power, I demand freedom for myself on the basis of your own principles; when I am in power, I take freedom away from you because such are my principles."

What is taking place in Poland provides a classic illustration of the communist philosophy of peaceful coexistence. In a way, ever since Yalta, Poland has been a testing ground, a precise litmus paper of Soviet intentions in foreign policy. Would you like to know what the Kremlin's goals are? Do you want to decipher the meaning of its calls for peace? Look at Poland. Our generals speak as frequently about national accord and dialogue with society as their Soviet comrades do about détente and arms-limitation talks. The language of communists has a certain peculiarity—its words are written one way and read quite another. In this language one writes "agreement" and reads "military *coup d'etat.*" These truths, banal for the Poles, are slowly becoming obvious to the Western Sovietologists as well. At any rate, it seems that this reasoning has been accepted by President Reagan and his staff. If this is correct, then our analysis, at bottom, is not based on faith in the conscience of Western politicians but on their wisdom and ability to analyze facts coolly and correctly. If they ignore Polish aspirations for autonomy they will commit not only a moral mistake but a political one as well. This is my understanding of American policy toward Poland.

It is a policy that insists on linking economic ties with respect for human rights. This is what brings communist propagandists to white-hot fury. They constantly repeat that no American moves can have any impact on their policy of imprisoning political opponents. They lie. Even Joseph Stalin was once forced to open the gates of his camps and release Polish prisoners. This is something of which it is worth reminding Jaruzelski, who would like to gain approval for his policy of repression in order to more easily break internal resistance. He wants to unfreeze relations with the West, but on his own terms. If he succeeds it will provide encouragement for the entire communist bloc, for it would send this message: repression of freedom won't cost you a penny. *Vae victis!* [woe to the vanquished].

Jaruzelski is now fighting to impose his version of "normalization" on the Poles, and to have it accepted by the Western governments. To the Poles he says: "You have no chance, we will break you with repression. Better accept my interpretation of conciliation. It means that every one of you, even Lech Wałęsa, will be free to adore and praise me." To the West he says: "If you accept me as I am, maybe I will again declare amnesty."

One should not be misled by appearances, however. Internal peace depends on political moves, not police repression. Periodic arrests and trials of Solidarity activists and Catholic priests followed by amnesties do not herald internal peace and dialogue. They are signs that citizens are treated as hostages in the continuing "civil cold war." Nevertheless, the fight for amnesty is easily explainable and, on a humane level, understandable. Therefore it must continue.

Last July, our generals lost the amnesty battle. And they lost the civil cold war too. This doesn't mean that they will stop warring against us, that they will no longer kidnap, beat, and kill us, that they won't send us to prisons and sentence us as hooligans or subversives. I do not in the least exclude the possibility that General Jaruzelski, with his touching military modesty, and General Kiszczak, in his charming simplicity, won't rob us of another few years of life. They have acquired a certain proficiency in this trade, and I don't think that the image of people behind bars keeps them awake at night (well, possibly with the exception of Colonel Pietruszka and Captain Piotrowski). To the contrary: each successive arrest warrant confirms their sense of duty well done. Every confiscated copy of a book by Miłosz, Herbert, Kołakowski, Gombrowicz, Brandys, and Konwicki improves their appetite. Every person broken by prison is a leaf in their laurel wreaths. And they think that this can continue forever. I would like to assure them that they are mistaken. They are much too confident. They forget the inevitability of surprise in the very nature of the Leading System. Here, on a spring morning, one may wake up in a totally changed country. Here—more than once—Party buildings have burned while the commissars escaped clad only in underwear. Edward Gierek, so beloved by Brezhnev and Helmut Schmidt, so respected by Giscard d'Estaing and Carter, within a week traveled from the heights of power into oblivion. *Sic transit gloria mundi. . . .*

Sitting in their comfortable offices, walking down the bureaucratic corridors, listening to denunciations of the opposition brought in by their lackeys, the generals don't know what the common people are thinking. But we, although prisoners, know very well. That's why, from my perspective, I wish for their sake that the conflict in Poland turns ultimately into dialogue. If it turns into an explosion they will be reduced to looking for Lis or Frasyniuk to protect them from the reach of the flames.

I am not going to write about my own case. At the trial I hope to bare the whole structure of the police provocation that was prepared, bunglingly, by Captain Piotrowski's chums in Gdańsk. I would like, however, to conclude with some personal remarks.

For six months, I couldn't write a single word. My friends joked that I should be put back in prison. Jokingly, I conceded that they were right. And now it has happened: I was locked up, and I have written a political essay. It would be small-minded of me if I did not credit the man who inspired me, the general who ordered my arrest. I am in such good company—with Władysław Frasyniuk and Bogdan Lis. Therefore, dear general, I owe you gratitude for your thoughtful watch over my steps and for providing proper direction for my meditations. I don't know what I would do without your suggestions and fatherly support. So much for thanks.

What more can I say? We live in truly interesting times. We witness the barren twilight of the old world of totalitarian dictatorship.

We, the people of Solidarity, have been put to a difficult trial. But even if it becomes an ordeal by fire, fire cleans and purifies what it cannot consume. I am not afraid of the generals' fire. There is no greatness about them: lies and force are their weapons; their strength stems from their ability to release the darkest and basest instinct in ourselves. I am sure that we shall win. Sooner or later, but I think sooner, we shall leave the prisons and come out of the underground onto the bright square of freedom. But what will we be like then?

I am afraid not of what they will do to us, but of what they can make us into. For people who are outlaws for a long time may feed on their own traumas and emotions which, in turn, strangle their reason and their ability to see reality. Even the best people can be demoralized by years of persecution and the shock of regaining their lost stature. I pray that we do not return like ghosts who hate the world, cannot understand it, and are unable to live in it. I pray that we do not change from prisoners into prison guards.

We know that today we need efforts of many kinds. We need underground structures and we must strive for open action. We must act with consistency and, above all, with patience. One cannot repeat this humble word too often—it is a declaration of an ambitious and persistent people, a declaration of unbending hope.

We live in a strange state of suspension. Nothing has been sealed yet. The grand fate of the nation and the small fates of the people still hang in the balance. We are trapped by the humiliating feeling of helplessness and impotence. Is this right?

In 1942 Czesław Miłosz wrote: "In an historical moment when nothing depends on man, everything depends on him—this paradoxical truth is revealed today with particular force."

And also today . . .

[translated by Jerzy B. Warman]

Solidarity

EDITOR'S NOTE. The texts in this section were written during the legal existence of the Solidarity labor union [August 1980–December 1981]. Their main theme is the search for the compromise between the authorities and society.

// A Time of Hope 1980

//   Everyone knows about these extraordinary August days. This time the media was forced to cover events thoroughly, and although the coverage was far from objective, people were able to form opinions on the situation in Poland.

The signing of the agreements was followed by a flood of reports and commentaries. The newspapers spoke up, using language until then present only in the uncensored press. Everybody turned out to be a moralizer, an oppositionist, or a nonconformist. *Sejm* deputies began to talk in the language of Radio Free Europe, while Central Committee members phrased their speeches as if they were the editors of the Paris *Kultura*.

All the observers stressed the quiet determination of the strikers, the spontaneous discipline that ruled in the striking enterprises, the maturity of the workers' demands.

How can one explain this wisdom and maturity? In my opinion it showed the transformation of the daily sufferings into social and political demands, and revealed a precise and sober assessment of real possibilities. The list of issues presented by the Gdańsk MKS [Interfactory Strike Committee] offered a real change in the system of government but stopped short of the border defined by the Soviet political and military presence in our part of Europe.

The workers were fighting for the rights and interests of the whole society. They fought for social rights and a rise in the standard of living, civil rights and freedom of speech, the right to autonomy of the individual and independent labor unions, moral rights and the liberation of political prisoners.

The evolution of forms of worker protest deserves some attention. The workers who in December 1970 won for themselves actual veto rights and who took advantage of them in June 1976 this time forced the authorities to acknowledge the principle of social accords. The excellent organization of the strike made change possible without bloodshed. The existence of workers' representatives spared party committee buildings all over Poland from burning. Those in power ought to realize that the better organized the opposition movement is, the more it is a movement and the less an impulse, and the greater the chances therefore are of a real compromise between the government and the governed.

The July-August strikes—which astonished all with their scale and organizational level—were no surprise to the democratic opposition. The independent press had been drawing attention to the catastrophic direction the government's policies were taking, while the communiqués of the Workers' Defense Committee (KSS "KOR") frequently warned about their disastrous consequences. There had been many such warnings, coming from intellectuals and writers as well as from members of the party. No one in the power apparatus has the right to excuse himself by claiming that the situation caught him by surprise. Especially not those who in the past few years have been in charge of organizing propaganda and police campaigns against independent institutions and activists of the democratic opposition. It would have sufficed to read the publications and manuscripts that were being confiscated during house searches to know what was going on in Poland. They could also have found out about the activities of the group around the Free Labor Unions of the Coast (WZZ)[1] and the editors of *Robotnik,* with the Charter of Workers' Rights,[2] and so on.

1. The Free Labor Unions of the Coast were organized in April 1978 in Gdańsk by Andrzej Gwiazda, Joanna Duda-Gwiazda, and Bogdan Borusewicz, member of KOR and former 1968 student activist. The small group included, among others, Lech Wałęsa, Anna Walentynowicz, Anna Pieńkowska, and Bogdan Lis.

2. *Robotnik (The Worker),* one of the KOR publications, first appeared in Sep-

Here we should pay homage to the organizers of the Free Labor Unions of the Coast and the editors of *Robotnik*. It was they who worked out and popularized the idea of workers' self-organization and demands, and it is to them, to a large extent, that we owe the implementation of worker demands and the peaceful progress of the strikes. The same must be said about the role played by Jacek Kuroń, who was able to organize a data bank that from the very beginning of July kept the public informed daily about the strike movement throughout Poland. This may sound somewhat paradoxical, but I believe that it was also to the opposition, persecuted and vilified as it was by the authorities, that the authorities owe the peacefulness of the negotiations.

It must also be repeated now, when the memories of the dramatic last days of August are still fresh, that all attempts to violate the August agreements, all attempts to restore the traditional methods of government, employing the style based on cheating, censorship, and coercion, will lead to social explosions that will make the August events appear as an era of peace and stability. All European politicians should be aware of this.

The government must realize that the institutionalization of conflict and compromise is the only way to base public life on the principle of social accord. Otherwise, let us repeat, the only light shed on the true outlines of the state of society will come from burning party committee buildings.

For social accords to function, however, social conscience must have engraved in it the political boundaries that must not be crossed—boundaries which are an integral part of the Gdańsk accords and which must be brought to anyone's mind as soon as they remember Budapest burning and Soviet tanks in the streets of Prague.

I have no intention of trying to frighten anyone with Soviet tanks. I merely want to mention three banal facts—facts that should be obvious. First, the recent events provided concrete proof that the Polish

---

tember 1977. Written for working-class readers, *Robotnik* grew significantly and by the middle of 1978 20,000 copies of its biweekly edition were published. The Free Labor Unions of the Coast had a regional edition called *The Worker of the Coast.* The Charter of Workers Rights was printed in the August 1979 issue of *Robotnik,* one year before the emergence of Solidarity. It was a program for the creation of independent trade unions signed by over one hundred human-rights activists.

people could not and did not want to continue to live under conditions of increasing hypocrisy, captivity, and impoverishment. We should be proud, as a nation, that we were able to reclaim our rights in the wisest of all possible ways.

Second, the Poles' way of life depends not only on their own goals and actions but also on their consignment, at the Yalta conference, to the Soviet sphere of influence, with the acquiescence of the countries of the Atlantic Alliance. One can be indignant about this reality, but one cannot forget it.

A third self-evident observation derives from the first two. The Poles' aspirations to freedom and self-determination must be realized in such a way as to make it more damaging for the Soviets to invade Poland than not to.

No one has a solution for these dilemmas. Certainly, no solution emerges from the calls for moderation and realism coming from activists and journalists who, like Ryszard Wojna, have lost credibility because of their long history of insulting public opinion with their pro-Russian, boot-licking servility and of trying to blackmail the country with the specter of another partition of Poland at the critical moment. These very same people would bring up the threat of tanks and call for reason after any sign of protest, any libertarian reflex, any spontaneous initiative coming from the captive and humiliated people. Hearing it all today, I think: Why didn't these people appeal for moderation and realism from Gierek and Jaroszewicz, when workers were being tortured in Radom and Ursus [in 1976], sentenced on trumped-up charges, when every voice of criticism was labeled a show of antinational posture? I have no intention of settling accounts with anyone for things past, but I would like to appeal to those activists and writers, who are now noisily joining the camp of supporters of the workers' protest and promoters of change in Poland: Could you offer a word or two of explanation about your lying and mudslinging in the past?

The government deserves recognition for its choice of negotiations over coercion. But this does not mean that the authorities should be overly pleased with themselves. This is only a first step on the road to constructing a social agreement. The people are waiting for an accounting of government actions in the past decade, which began with the protests of the workers from the coastal cities and ended with another protest in the coastal cities. The people want a settlement of accounts, not a witch-hunt. Let no one be fooled that the public's attention can be distracted with a few show trials or with tales of the real or imagined villas and yachts owned by Maciej Szczepański [the TV chairman]. The people have a right to the whole truth about themselves and about their condition. Only then can we talk about realism and moderation. There can be no realism without the truth about reality.

And the truth is that this country cannot be ruled without an agreement with the people. And that regardless of the speeches made during commemorative celebrations this country is not independent. And also that the Poles must reckon with the restriction of their sovereignty by the national and ideological interests of the USSR. And finally that communists are the only rulers of Poland to whom the Soviet leaders will agree, and there is no indication that this will change soon.

What conclusions can we draw from this? That any attempt to govern counter to the people's will is bound to lead to disaster; that any attempt to overthrow communist rule in Poland is an attempt against the interests of the USSR. Such is reality. We may not like it, but it must be understood.

Despite what the slanderers on duty at *Trybuna Ludu* and *Zycie Warszawy* [newspapers] may claim, I am not attempting to win cheap publicity and popularity with these remarks. On the contrary, I know that some of my friends will accuse me of abandoning the goals of independence and democracy. To them I reply in all honesty: under present-day geopolitical conditions I think that "going for independence" and parliamentarianism is unrealistic. I do believe, however, that we are able to organize our independence from the inside, that by becoming a better organized, more efficient, more prosperous society that enriches Europe and the rest of the world with new values and cherishes tolerance and humanism, we will move toward independence and democracy. But I refuse to participate in a contest to see whose desire for independence is greater, or in creating the illusion that the impossible has become possible.

So what is possible today? Pluralism in all spheres of public life is possible, the liquidation of preventive censorship is possible, a rational reform of the economy and just social policies are possible, press and television based on the principle of competitiveness and truth are possible, freedom of learning and autonomy for the universities are possible, public control of prices and a movement to defend the consumer are possible, independent courts and police stations where people are not beaten are also possible.

It is possible that we will win all this, just as we have won liberty for the workers from Radom and Ursus, an uncensored press, our own publications, the ability to unmask lawlessness, and just as we have won—thanks to the wisdom and solidarity of the workers of the coast—independent labor unions.

We must wrest all this from the authorities because no nation has ever received its rights as a gift. But as we wrest it, let us make sure that we do not tear into shreds the Polish state—not a sovereign state but a state nonetheless: a state without which our fate would be incomparably more burdensome.

The people in the democratic opposition are going to argue about this assessment. Some will consider this program too moderate, others will consider it too radical. The latter group will have to make a choice: Should they accept the authorities' liberal concessions within the existing official structures, or should they aim for the recognition of independent institutions as a permanent component of Poland's civic life? To choose the first option and to consent to the further elimination from public life of, for instance, the members of KSS "KOR," TKN, or the editors of *Zapis*[3] would be equivalent to befriending the authorities while turning one's back to yesterday's allies. It would also bring the danger of a repetition of the retreat that occurred following October, 1956, and risk the loss of the gains of December, 1970. Fear of provoking the government has always led in practice to capitulation before the government. In this way, the authorities have broken up society's unity several times, forcing people to give up the safeguards inherent in pluralism.

It is difficult to predict how the authorities will react. The government will certainly attempt to tighten the noose once again—this can already be seen in the obstacles being placed in the path of the new independent labor unions, the censorship's information blockade, re-

---

3. *Zapis* (1977–1982) was the first uncensored literary periodical loosely connected with KOR and published quarterly by Warsaw writers.

pressions, the efforts to cow people, the attacks on the so-called antisocialist forces—that is, the centers of social initiative that inconvenience the government. The authorities have much to learn before they understand that a dialogue with society includes neither brandishing a truncheon nor a monologue on the television screen. The only way the government can be taught about real dialogue is through social solidarity, the kind of solidarity that was shown by the workers of the coast.

Mieczysław F. Rakowski, the editor-in-chief of *Polityka,* wrote that the principal task for the authorities right now is to win credibility. I agree with him. But the point is that this credibility will not be won with calls for work and reason but with a demonstration of genuine respect for public aspirations. These aspirations are elementary, realistic, and justified. What else can one call the demand to reveal the whole truth about the massacre of December 1970 and the ill treatment of people following June 1976? Without the fulfillment of these demands, calls for realism and declarations about a dialogue will remain mere claptrap. The situation won't be made any better by playing musical chairs at the top, or by bringing in new Central Committee secretaries, or by appointing new Politburo members and picking new scapegoats. There is no one left who believes in leaders who are saviors, no one who gets excited any more by gossip about the conflicts within the party leadership. There is no one left who believes in changes for the better without institutional reform that would guarantee pluralism. Also, there is no one left who will believe mere words—everyone is waiting for deeds.

The question remains: Is such a system at all viable? Is it not a stage in the dismantling of the communist system and in its evolution toward a multiparty system? The answer is that the communist powers in Poland have learned to coexist with independent bodies—for instance, with the powerful and independent Catholic Church. What is more, they have learned that this coexistence can bring benefits. It would seem that for societies that have experienced historical hardships, viable solutions are dictated by a different logic from that of the textbooks. In August, 1980, the Poles proved to all that they know their strength—as well as its limitations. They gave clear proof of their ambitions, and of their awareness of the restrictions on these ambitions. They did not ask the impossible, but they pushed for realistic demands with such steadfastness and solidarity that they astonished the entire world.

All this allows me to believe in the viability of a hybrid system, in which the state's totalitarian organization could be combined with democratic institutions in the society. This solution would by its very nature be provisional, but nothing is as permanent as the provisional. The equilibrium between society and the state will of course be unsteady and susceptible to change, like any social equilibrium in this best of all possible worlds.

This is my reply regarding the feasibility of such a system. As experience teaches us, it is easiest to be a pessimist. For Poland is a peculiar country, as Antoni Słonimski [the writer] said. In Poland, anything is possible. Even change for the better.

Warsaw, August–September, 1980

// Hope and Danger 1980

// For four months now, Poland has been at the center of the world's attention. Today, in mid-December [1980], I am tempted to make an initial assessment of the situation. The Gdańsk accords were signed on August 31. They are the Great Charter of the Rights of the Polish Nation. They form the basis for new relations between the authorities and society—the only chance to overcome the deep political crisis that has been consuming our country and threatening the future existence of our nation.

What Poland needs is tranquillity and stability—everyone agrees on this. The only thing about which people disagree is the method of attaining that state of peace. To the government the solution is simple: people should stop seeking revenge, stop making demands, and start working. Everyone should rally around the party and its new leadership. A political center should be created, a "front of reason," composed of communists, Catholics, unionists, and all other people of goodwill. Since I believe that the government's diagnosis is false, utopian, and therefore dangerous, I will allow myself to form my own opinion. I believe that the idea for a "center" and a front for national reconciliation are typical products of wishful thinking. I do not believe in the Poles' "moral-political unity." I do believe in a compromise based on the Gdańsk accords. Only these accords can serve as an authentic source of legitimacy for the authorities and, at the same time, provide them with their last chance. And they should realize this. Also, the Soviet leaders should understand that the Poles are perfectly aware of the implications of their geopolitical location and of the conditions and limitations of these. After all, the alternatives to a policy of negotiation and compromise are conflict and confrontation. The Poles have demonstrated many times—to themselves and the world at large—that there is no price they would not be prepared to pay for the defense of their national and human aspirations. It would thus seem that one more armed show of the Poles' desire for unity is in no one's interest.

Everyone is astounded at the peacefulness and determination of the Polish people. No one of any seriousness has been propounding unrealistic goals, no seriously thinking person has questioned international alliances. What is more, no one has been promoting the overthrow of communist power. The aim is to curtail this power and to redefine the rules of exercising it. Yet no one—least of all the party apparatus—is ready to accept and implement these rules.

On August 31, when Premier Jagielski rose from the table in the Gdańsk shipyard after signing the accords, obsessive thoughts started to gnaw at the brains of the party apparatchiks about how to avoid fulfilling these accords, how to transform them into a sham or a caricature, how to restore a situation when it was not necessary to be restrained by the strivings of authentic representatives of the working people. From the very beginning, the government's behavior toward the new unions has been odd. The government failed to see the opportunity that lay for it in Solidarity, instead perceiving the union as a threat to its omnipotence. The government has been trying to disinform the public, to pursue the fiction of the old unions. It has finally managed to provoke a crisis of registration, and this led Poland to the brink of a general strike and definitively buried the remains of social trust in the administration of justice.[1] The arrest of Jan Narozniak[2]—the cause of another

---

1. On October 24, 1980, Solidarity statutes were registered by a Warsaw judge who arbitrarily inserted a clause about the leading role of the party. The ensuing conflict was resolved on November 10 when, under the threat of general strike, the judge removed the clause.

2. A month after the "registration crisis" two volunteer employees of the Warsaw Solidarity office were arrested. Several Warsaw factories went on strike demanding curbs on the activity of the security services, and as a result, two activists were released.

conflict with unforeseeable consequences—again proved the party and state leadership's total ignorance of public moods. This ignorance can also be seen in the attacks on the "antisocialist elements" allegedly concentrated in the Workers' Defense Committee (KOR). This has unintentionally created an image of KOR in the mind of the public as a greater moral and political authority than its capabilities actually warrant. The government's attempts to interfere in the personnel policies of Solidarity serve as an example of its complete inability to think realistically. In actuality, political realism would require both a knowledge of the USSR's interests and an awareness of the moods and ambitions of the Polish people. One can never stress this enough to the powers-that-be. It seems to me that the inability to identify the country's moods and ambitions realistically is the greatest of all the obstacles to stability in Poland. Furthermore, this incapacity also favors disintegration within the party itself—a process whose consequences may be both momentous and dangerous.

Do the "antisocialist forces," about which so much is written in the party press and so much is said by the party leaders, really exist in Poland? Let us answer with another question: Is Poland ruled by a socialist regime? Without getting into a discussion of ideology and doctrine, it is difficult not to notice that no one in Poland is questioning the need for fundamental social reforms, no one is advocating putting mines, steel works, or shipyards on the auction block. But there do exist social forces that have questioned the policies of the party and the very principle of the party's role in society. This questioning resulted in the Polish August and in the Gdańsk accords. These forces, which drew their inspiration from various traditions and spoke in different ways, continue to exist and to play an essential role in Poland's public life. The authorities have either failed to notice them or tried to destroy them through corruption and repression. This was a vain effort and had unexpected consequences: dialogue and compromise have given way to incessant irritation, mounting social tension, and permanent conflict. This road leads nowhere. In a situation in which the government is incapable of living with society and society is incapable of living with the government, the opposition has no choice but to engage in laborious and patient negotiation and dialogue. The Church has always played an important role in this. Its history provides a lesson in the strategy of coexistence of independent Catholic institutions with a state structure. The Church has not only represented its own institutional interests but has stood for the fundamental aspirations of the whole people. The existence of Solidarity is bound to bring a change in this, but the Church will continue to play its important role.

The Western press has frequently remarked on the restraint practiced by the Church hierarchy. There is no doubt that this restraint is a response to the complexity of the circumstances. But Western journalists are making a mistake when they identify the unqualified statements made by some individual representatives of the Church (for example, Father Orszulik's unfriendly pronouncement about KOR) with the position of the entire episcopate. It is no coincidence that the communiqués issued by the Episcopate's Conference are free of this type of political remarks. But what is worse is that the authorities may lap it all up and continue to play their game of appearances, advancing as compromises creatures of the Jerzy Ozdowski type, devoid of authority.[3] This is an example of substituting a policy of promotion of lackeys for a true policy of compromise. None of this enhances the new leadership's credibility. Its credibility is further harmed by the slanderous articles being written by Ignacy Krasicki [the journalist] and by the game of musical chairs being played for the top posts in the power apparatus. People can remember all too well the past of the moth-eaten "renewers" who are being recycled now: Mieczysław Moczar and his sinister role in 1968,[4] Stanisław Kociołek and his actions during the December 1970 events,[5] Walery Namiotkiewicz and his many years as personal secretary to Władysław Gomułka. These people have no social credibility whatsoever. Please understand me: I am not calling for personal attacks or witch-hunts. Anyone can change, even Moczar. But a change of this sort, if it is not to be one more fraud, has to be based on an honest self-examination. The personal history of the man who was responsible

3. In November 1980, Jerzy Ozdowski, a member of a compliant Catholic splinter group "neo-Znak," became a token deputy prime minister.

4. The anti-Semitic purges of 1968 were credited to the secret manipulations of Gen. Mieczysław Moczar, then minister of internal affairs.

5. It was because of the assurances of the party secretary of Gdańsk "voivodship" Stanisław Kociołek that the workers interrupted the 1970 strike. On their way to work they were decimated by machine-gun fire.

for the security services throughout the entire Gomułka period and for the Supreme Chamber of Control (NIK) in the Gierek era, when corruption grew on an unprecedented scale, provides no guarantee for the renewal that he may promote today. On the contrary, it creates the suspicion that the government is trying to subvert social agreements with circus tricks.

A situation in which only a strike or the threat of a strike can incline the government to act reasonably is socially dangerous, for it forces Solidarity activists to use strikes as a weapon. When pressure grows following demands for wage increases or in response to other justifiable issues, the frequent use of the strike weapon may lead to anarchy and disintegration of the state apparatus and then to a conflict which no one will be able to control. How can this be avoided? I see no way but to institutionalize social accords, creating a formal network for negotiation and compromise, and for the existence of independent public opinion. The government must gain credibility—not in its old role of dictator but in that of partner. Let us say it openly: The government will never be trusted by the people if it is not trusted by Solidarity. It will never be trusted by Solidarity unless it reveals the whole truth about past political crises—December, 1970, on the coast and, June, 1976, in Radom and Ursus. Today, the authorities' greatest enemy is not the democratic opposition but the authorities themselves—their inefficiency, their indolence, and their stupidity. For how else can we understand the ban on the film *Workers 1980* [the chronicle of strike negotiations]? It takes blindness to miss the harm that decisions of this kind cause. Not a single one of KOR's publications is capable of harming the government as much as one such thoughtless insult to the people's need for truth and honesty.

Perhaps I can be criticized for minimalism. Indeed, I am advocating neither a struggle for independence nor for parliamentary democracy, although I have always made it known how much I cherish these things, and I have not given them up today. But I do believe that faith in the feasibility of such demands amounts to a break with common sense and responsibility for the nation.

I am advocating a compromise with the government, with a government that I do not like at all—a government whose principles do not appeal to me but which is to us what a plaster cast is to a person with a broken bone: burdensome but indispensable. The new situation requires all of us—those in power and the rest of us—to revise our thinking drastically. It was permissible to think one way when it was only ourselves—our individual freedom—which we were putting at risk. Now that our national "to be or not to be" is at stake, we must think differently. One can dislike the people in power, but they have to be accepted as partners in negotiation. It is not easy for me to write this. Nothing I know about them inspires optimism in me. The new arrests and the daily swindles make a straightforward dialogue impossible. The weakness of the authorities is being concealed by the arrogance of its propaganda, and Newspeak catchwords are replacing an objective analysis of the situation. Party Secretary Stanisław Kania reminds me of the captain of a sunken ship who is sitting on a raft but is convinced that he still commands a great transoceanic vessel. His attacks on Jacek Kuroń are proof either that he does not understand Kuroń's rather clear political writing or that he is being misled—seemingly a common occurrence among first secretaries. I do not know which is worse. Nonetheless, I am in favor of compromise because we are all floating on the same raft. And we may all sink with it. But I believe that we will not sink. I believe that with wisdom and courage we will construct an order based on compromise. One thing is certain: there is no going back to the status quo before August 31.

On our raft the captain's orders will not suffice. On our raft the people's solidarity is vital.

Warsaw, December, 1980

// Darkness on the Horizon 1981

// The extraordinary Ninth Congress of the Polish United Workers party was without doubt a political event of international significance. Like everything that has been happening in Poland in the past few years, the congress was unprecedented, even though both its domestic and international effects are still hard to assess. It was certainly the most democratic congress in the history of the communist movement. Its democratic character lay not only in the freedom of speech enjoyed by the delegates and in the unheard-of openness of the discussions but also in the representative character of its delegates. Indeed, it is probable that all the political factions in the PUWP were represented. This appraisal need not be changed in light of the letter from the Central Committee of the Communist party of the Soviet Union to the Central Committee of the Polish party,[1] which weighed heavily on the deliberations of the majority of the voivodship electoral conferences. The letter was a reminder of realities—of the fact that Poland does not lie on the moon.

The secret vote for First Secretary of the party was a true revelation. It must have shocked even the leaders of Western Europe's Eurocommunist parties. But the frontal attack on the upper echelons of the party

---

1. The letter, cautioning and threatening the Polish party leadership, was leaked to the press in September 1981, right after the First Solidarity Congress.

apparatus was the most notable event in the elections to the Central Committee. In this election most of the members of the old leadership were voted out of office—both those who belonged to the hardliners' faction (such as Grabski, Żabiński, Kurowski, and Kociołek) and to the "renewers" (such as Fiszbach and Dąbrowa). A dozen or so members of the old party-state leadership, however, were reelected, assuring continuity and perhaps providing a minimum of assurance for the leaders of the Communist parties of the Warsaw Pact. These delegates were members of the armed forces, and the Ministries of Internal Affairs, Foreign Affairs, and Agriculture.

One might call the congress an authentic revolt of the lowest echelons of the party. The central party authorities have been aware of this danger for several months now, as can be seen in their complicated attitude toward the so-called horizontal structures.[2] The sharp attack on these structures showed the fear of a revolt by the party base. The ideology of the rebellious base has been labeled revisionist and "social-democratic," mostly on the basis of statements made by the leader of Toruń horizontal structure, Zbigniew Iwanow. The diagnosis was correct in that the rebellion did exist, but it was false in appraising its ideology. A careful reading of documents concerning the party's rank and file revealed the group's ideological diversity. Side by side with expressions of democratic ideals, those documents presented expressions of a longing for a retrospective utopia of the "Stalinist-egalitarian" type, and the tendency to criticize with equal severity the power mechanisms within the party and the villas of party notables.

With this background in mind, the mystery of the success—so astonishing to the liberal intelligentsia—of Albin Siwak, the man who has broken all records for demagogy and boorishness, can be fully unraveled. Why did Siwak, who made compromising statements at the Central Committee plenum, in his television programs, in interviews for the Czechoslovak press, and in his attacks on Lech Wałęsa and Stefan Bratkowski,[3] emerge triumphant at the party congress? Because

2. In the Communist parties all contacts between party cells have to go through the center. "Horizontal structures," i.e., direct collaboration between single party organizations, went against this dogma.

3. Stefan Bratkowski, a party reformer and one of the leaders of "Experience and

he had three qualities with great appeal to the provincial delegates. First, he had not been discredited by any functions within the central apparatus of the former ruling team, and so was not suspected of belonging to "that gang who stole Poland bit by bit." Second, he attacked corruption, weakness, and inconsistency in the party leadership, including the first secretary, using vocabulary that could be well understood by the simplest party members. Third, he created the illusion that he was a genuine worker activist, a trustworthy rival for the working-class leaders of Solidarity. Another factor that may have played a role in his success was the party's concern to have a "scarecrow" like him to use against Solidarity. But in essence Siwak represents the party's efforts to distance the working masses from Solidarity and pull them over to its own side. Party activists such as Jagielski or Kania, Barcikowski or Rakowski, could represent the authorities in negotiations with striking workers. Siwak is there to give the party hope that it will be able to win the souls of factory crews—or at least to succeed in dividing these crews against one another. To the members of the new Central Committee, he also represents hope of winning credibility. Not only among workers but also among the "allies." Siwak stands for the kind of verbal opposition that the allies view with the greatest sympathy, seeing in it—and rightly so—a tool for combating the camp of Polish democracy. Siwak's election is to serve as a sign to the allies that things are returning to normal in the Polish party, that the newly elected Central Committee is at least as trustworthy for the allies as its predecessor.

The election of Albin Siwak, a man of mediocre talent, should therefore be considered as the truest declaration of the intentions of the party's highest forum. This does not bode well for the future. Siwak's election cannot serve as a substitute for a program of political and economic reform. It foretells neither normalization of conditions inside the party nor sensible policies toward Solidarity. And no one should be deceived that Siwak's election will appease the allies. From their point of view, the very character of the congress is unacceptable. The pluralistic discussion, the relatively free elections of delegates and members

---

Future" (DiP) group, was also the newly elected president of the Polish Journalists Association.

of the Central Committee—all shatter the classic model of a ruling Communist party and are equivalent to a challenge to the party apparatus. The criticism, by the public and from within the party, of the party activists who built their own villas is a violation of one of the ruling caste's essential privileges. Previously, such criticism was made only when the party's leadership ordered them. The removal from the party of Gierek, Jaroszewicz, and a few other members of the highest party-state authority is a brutal reminder to the allied notables that they, too, are politically mortal. All this is bound to provoke hostility among the communist elites of Eastern Europe toward the Polish experiment.

The very existence of Solidarity has played a decisive role in Polish affairs, not just because of one or two actions but because it is a mighty and independent organization of the working people. Solidarity's constant presence as an organized society on the political stage has been, is, and will continue to be a constant source of tension, and no one in Poland should doubt this for a minute.

As before, Poland's only hope today lies in making the allies aware that a return to the pre-August situation is possible only through a violent solution—in other words, with an explosion on a European scale. Stabilization can be attained only with a system of social compromise. But here again no one should deceive himself. Stabilization represents quite different things to the apparatus and to organized society. Even those party activists who are considered to be among the most enlightened define a program for stability in fairly unrealistic terms. For instance, Tadeusz Fiszbach [Gdańsk secretary], in his pronouncement at the Ninth Congress of the PUWP, said that "the unions ought to be assured of the right to participate in strategic decision making—to define social goals, while recognizing that their basic function consists of protecting the interest of the working people. The control of strategic decisions by the unions should be intermediary, via their representatives in the elective organs of state, in enterprises, and in the regional self-governing units, as well as through the actions undertaken within the framework of the formal procedures of decision making. This must be accompanied by the labor unions' relinquishment of direct interference in the state's ruling functions during the implementation of decisions that have already been made."

This quotation could be used as a point of departure for a realistic political discussion if one could define the mechanism of appointments and principles of functioning of the representative and self-governing institutions, the extent of their independence, and so on. The discussion would encompass the basic principles of political reform and the implementation of the Gdańsk "social accords." Solidarity must be thoroughly prepared for this. It will not be easy. The current situation of the Independent and Self-governing Labor Union "Solidarity" does not augur an easy future. Problem number one is the food situation. Poland will soon face not merely supply problems but hunger protests. The government is solely responsible for this. Rumors are circulating that it is purposely manipulating food supplies and consciously "starving out" the people. Is this true? No one knows, but no one believes the government's assurances. "They always lie, so why should they be telling the truth this time?" the people ask.

A price hike for staple foods cannot be avoided, but Solidarity has made its consent conditional on a complex reform program. The government has put off addressing this issue for a year, and now the popular consensus is that reform is possible only as a result of a growing grass-roots movement for workers' self-government. The authorities interpret this movement—not without justification—as a strike at the party's *nomenklatura* (the nominations of enterprise managers) and—nonsensically—as an "attempt to take over state power." The official propaganda has asserted repeatedly that politickers of radical proclivities have infiltrated Solidarity, while the people expect more decisive and more effective actions from the union leadership. It is significant that all of the union's recent protest initiatives have originated outside the National Coordinating Commission (KKP). By dividing the unionists into extremists and moderates, the authorities are using the tactic—already classic in the history of ruling communism—of trying to split up the independent social movement. Although one can hardly deny the government's successes (for example, the elimination from the leadership of Gdańsk Solidarity of Mrs. Anna Walentynowicz),[4] in the long term this tactic is as futile as it is perilous. It is futile because the

4. The firing of Anna Walentynowicz, crane operator at the Gdańsk shipyard, started the strike that led to the creation of Solidarity. Later on she became critical of the policies of Lech Wałęsa.

movement has been growing up from the grass roots in response to real needs—so personnel reshuffles will achieve little. It is perilous because antagonizing radical elements outside the union may easily result in the destruction of society's discipline, which has astounded the whole world. So far—let us remember—this discipline has been based on a willingness to endure sacrifices.

The power apparatus is not uniform, and there is no reason to believe that it will become uniform anytime soon. The party congress did not eliminate differences within the party and did not purge its factions. Voivodship party committees are still headed by people who are known to openly oppose Solidarity (Kociołek, Zabiński), and this makes local conflicts likely. The party is still going to be divided between, on the one hand, the supporters of the Katowice Forum and the Patriotic Association "Grunwald"[5] and, on the other, the promoters of the horizontal structures. The party leadership will continue to be torn by personal conflicts. None of this simplifies the picture.

The government's policy of supposedly solving conflicts by peaceful means has so far amounted to seeking an agreement with Wałęsa and his circle. The government cannot rely on Wałęsa's undisputed authority forever. Not just because specific agreements with Wałęsa and his advisers cannot replace permanent institutions based on social accords but because what is needed is a broad vision of reform of the institutions of worker and regional self-management, reform of the people's councils and the Diet, reform of censorship and the mass media.

Such a reform is contingent on Solidarity's political realism in appraising its chances and capabilities. This appraisal must take into account Poland's international position and must weigh the USSR's interests in our part of the world. Such are the ABCs of Poland's politics today.

But this assessment must also take into account that every compromise is the result of the action of different forces, for no power has

---

5. Katowice Forum, a group of younger party hard-liners, attacked the party policies of negotiating with Solidarity. The Patriotic Association "Grunwald" emerged in March 1981, with a ceremony celebrating "the victims of Zionist persecution in Poland."

ever abandoned its privileges without a struggle. Only policies based on Solidarity's consistency and strength can form a solid base for an understanding. The union will obtain a favorable compromise only when the power apparatus and the allies themselves realize that this compromise favors them too. "Covenants without the sword are but words and of no strength to secure a man at all," wrote Hobbes in his *Leviathan*. And he was right.

August 1981

// A Year Has Passed 1981

// The Promise of a Civil Society

On the last day of August 1980 the deputy premier of the government of the Polish People's Republic, Mieczysław Jagielski, and the chairman of the Interfactory Strike Committee, Lech Wałęsa, signed an agreement on the grounds of the Lenin shipyard in Gdańsk; it was clear to all that a new chapter had opened in Poland's history. Much was said at the time about this being a "social agreement," although it was only a preliminary one, merely a compromise that could temporarily satisfy both the government and the people. For the first time organized authority was signing an accord with an organized society. The agreement marked the creation of labor unions independent of the state which vowed not to attempt to take over political power.

The essence of the spontaneously growing Independent and Self-governing Labor Union Solidarity lay in the restoration of social ties, self-organization aimed at guaranteeing the defense of labor, civil, and national rights. For the first time in the history of communist rule in Poland "civil society" was being restored, and it was reaching a compromise with the state.

Compromise or a Marriage of Convenience

For both sides this compromise was a marriage of convenience, not of love. The authorities did not for a minute abandon their attempts

124

to minimize the importance of the union, and society did not lose its justified distrust of the government. From the very beginning attempts were made to block out information, create informational confusion, cow the provincial unionists.

Later, the authorities tried to introduce new clauses into the union's statute. Their policy was guided by the desire to preserve the status quo. And yet public pressure was so powerful, the pressure of the working masses so great, that within two months a multimillion-strong labor union independent of the state was registered. The origins of these events were obvious: they lay in society's long resistance, that was marked by the tragic dates of spurts of national revolt. These dates— 1956, 1968, 1970, 1976, which today are being engraved on monuments of national memory, are the dates of the stations of the Polish Via Dolorosa. The Church's opposition to atheistic policies, the villages' resistance to collectivization, the intelligentsia's defiance of censorship—all made up the "Polish syndrome" that bore fruit in the form of the August strikes and Solidarity. The actions of the intellectual groups that organized aid to the participants of the June 1976 strikes played a special role. It was then that a common denominator for the activities of different social groups, especially the intelligentsia and the workers, was successfully created.

The Originality of the Polish August

In contrasting the Polish events with the Budapest Rising or the Prague Spring, two essential differences, which define the originality of the Polish experiment need to be stressed. The first regards the direction of the changes; the second, their reach. The Hungarian case was characterized by the actual disintegration of the party apparatus and assumption of political initiative by the rebellious people in the streets.

In Poland the conflict took place inside factories that were being controlled by the workers' strike guard.

The Prague Spring occurred because of an impulse for change that came from above, from among the activists of the party apparatus. In Czechoslovakia a part of the communist power elite undertook to emancipate itself from Soviet tutelage. In Poland the centers that initiated the democratic movement lay outside the party and outside the power apparatus. The current claims by party notables that a guiding current within the party existed prior to August can only be considered the boasting of the propaganda machine. As a result, the Communist party was automatically driven into being the conservative defender of the existing institutions of power. This position has given it some credibility in the eyes of the Kremlin's leaders, though hardly any in the eyes of the Polish people.

Conflict and Coexistence

This past year saw a perpetual conflict between the government and organized society, with the Church serving as mediator. It is also possible to see in this conflict the testing of various strategies for coexistence which are being formulated by either the authorities or Solidarity. They did have something in common: the authorities have not contested the existence of Solidarity. They have, however, contended that Solidarity is undertaking actions that lie outside its statute by interfering in politics, denouncing certain high-ranking officials, demanding that certain discredited politicians be recalled from their posts, calling for law and order, and seeking access to the mass media. The authorities have attacked the uncensored union press, the occupations of administration buildings, street demonstrations, and Solidarity's tactics for extorting concessions.

Solidarity has accused the government of not fulfilling agreements, of holding on for dear life to yesterday's realities, of creating a personnel merry-go-round, and of being completely deaf to all the public's demands that are not backed by the threat of strikes. It has been the conflict of two worlds, in which the ancien régime has found itself under the constant pressure of an awakened society. The pressure has been so spontaneous, the authorities so unadapted to the new situation, that their only response has been to attempt to break up the union from the inside. They started to attack the so-called antisocialist forces, to divide the union's activists into radicals and moderates. The purpose of this tactic has been transparent, its connection with reality rather loose, since it has been the young workers in the large factories who are the most radical. From them comes the greatest pressure for demands and change.

Members of the MKZ [Interfactory Founding Committee][1] by their very nature have been more moderate, more susceptible to the arguments of their fellow negotiators from the government and—what is more important—to the voice of the Church, which has been toning things down.

The Reactions of the Church

The primate of Poland, Cardinal Stefan Wyszyński, has from the very beginning declared himself in favor of seeking compromise solutions. Such was the meaning of his homily on Jasna Góra in August, and later of his appeasement of the most drastic conflicts in Bielsko Biała, in Bydgoszcz, and in the case of rural Solidarity. His tactic was not always well understood by the public, and it revealed the differently accented approaches of individual representatives of the Church hierarchy. In the changed social situation cracks began to appear in the former unity of the clergy. The episcopate's documents provided a clamp for holding it together, but individual bishops stressed differently the needs for decisive action and for restraint.

Changes in the Power Apparatus and
Movement in the Party

The decomposition of the power apparatus and movement within the party are among the most interesting sociological phenomena. There, from the beginning, "operation scapegoat" has been conducted, throwing out more and more members of the elite to appease public opinion. Members of the party and state leaderships have become the target of brutal attacks, and have been accused of incompetence, lack of education, muzzling the people, and theft; they have been publicly abused, their villas and their not very properly obtained university diplomas written about with delight. When this whole scandalous spectacle did not bring the expected results, the quarrel about methods of defusing the crisis started. Some (Kania, Jaruzelski, Barcikowski,

---

1. The committee that in August 1980 negotiated with the authorities for the legal existence of Solidarity. Lech Wałęsa was its chairman.

Rakowski) stressed the need to play for time and to conduct stationary warfare based on tolerating Solidarity; others (Olszowski, Grabski, Kociołek, Zabiński) defined Solidarity's actions as counterrevolutionary and demanded decisive action, pushing for confrontation by repeatedly organizing trouble that would erupt into conflicts. But no one formulated a program for emerging from the crisis. Then the lowest echelons of the party became active, demanding an immediate extraordinary party congress. This led the party apparatus to panic and launch a sudden attack on the horizontal structures—that is, the practice of establishing contacts between party organizations outside the existing party channels. These initiatives originated in the party organizations in Toruń, and especially from the secretary of the factory party committee in Towimor, Zbigniew Iwanow. The defeat of the horizontal structures, symbolized by the expulsion of Iwanow from the party, foreordained that the extraordinary congress, for all its stupefying democracy (secret voting for the delegates and members of the Central Committee, and even the first secretary), would bring the party no credibility among the people. For all the declarations about the pursuit of policies of "understanding," the election of Albin Siwak to the Politburo represented the highest party forum's homage to the idea of post-Stalinist populism, which defeated concepts of democratization. The social accords were understood as a tribute to exigencies of the moment, while the election of Siwak testified to the party's ideological orientation. Of course, the participants in the Katowice Party Forum and the Association Grunwald who support Siwak compose a tiny social margin, but in the party that is condemned to the specific form of communist Newspeak, this line can count on a certain popularity that grows with rank. But above all it represents the thinking of an apparatus that has been removed from power or is threatened with removal—it is from these circles that will originate the political intiatives of the Polish Bilaks.[2]

Movement in the party—the deformed reflection of activity throughout society—should be viewed against the background of the political revival of other institutions and organizations of the establishment. When we analyze the personnel and programmatic changes in

---

2. Vassili Bilak, a longtime Slovak party activist, was one of the signatories of the letter inviting the Warsaw Pact armies to end the Prague Spring.

SD [Democratic party], ZSL [United Peasant party], or even PAX [Catholic Association] it becomes clear that they are all searching for new institutional forms, although until now they had been content with purely decorative roles. The Diet debates also serve as proof that even this institution may take on a new meaning in the new situation.

What Is Solidarity?

And yet it is Solidarity that has been playing the key role. In order to understand the meaning of this, it is worth recalling the contents and the reach of the Gdańsk accords, guaranteed in the eyes of the people by the existence of Solidarity. Claims that this labor union has gone outside the limits of its statute are ridiculous. Equally ridiculous were the assertions made by the official propagandists a year ago that the very idea of independent labor unions had been forced on the striking workers by antisocialist elements. Rather, this is an example of how the foul vocabulary used in propaganda clouds the picture of reality; instead of presenting the world as is, propaganda attempts to form it. Hence the dispute over language—the essence of the controversy over Judge Kościelniak's changes in Solidarity's statute—played an important role in Solidarity's strategy. To accept the wording used in the propaganda would have meant to acquiesce in lies in public life. The union had to speak a language that the people, whose trust is its strength and its weapon, could understand and agree with. It is also for this reason that the union has to fulfill public expectations, as broad as they are. And so the Solidarity union is everything at the same time: a labor union that defends the rights of the working people in their places of employment; an office that prosecutes lawbreakers in the power apparatus; a defender of political prisoners, law and order, and an independent culture—a true representative of the people in dealings with the authorities. But one thing it has not been: a political party aiming to take over power, even though it has been accused of precisely this.

Solidarity, a social movement with many functions, has for a year now been the guarantor of the growing Polish democracy. But it is still too soon to draw up a balance sheet of its bright and dark sides. It is still too soon to give a sociological profile of this movement—a movement that knows how to win but not how to retreat; that combines demands for market reform with the ethos of egalitarianism; that uses the language of national solidarity to formulate the traditionally leftist idea of social self-government; that is a cross between contradictory elements and a mélange of matter; that combines the cult of its leader with a democracy that reaches pathological proportions; and that joins an astounding wisdom with a rare naiveté. It is a democratic movement in the midst of antidemocracy, a movement of great hope—of self-limiting Polish revolution: a movement that strictly observes geopolitical realities but is forced to defend itself from the attacks of the press of neighboring countries.

Indeed, for the allies [Warsaw Pact] the very existence of Solidarity is proof that "something is rotten in the state of Denmark." Let us not go into complex and hypothetical reflection on the subject of a possible military intervention in Poland. The absence of basic information forces one to believe in prophecies. But one thing is certain: the Poles' determined stance shows that the consequences of such an intervention would be incalculable. And not just for Poland.

Which Way to Democracy?

The history of the past twelve months again poses the question of whether the communist system can be reformed. Five years ago I had the opportunity to express the opinion that the experiences of the Spanish road to democracy might be applicable to Poland: a road of peace, which does not mean a road with no potholes. Today, one could say that those experiences, taking into account all the social, political, and geographic differences, have proved useful.

If dark clouds hang over Poland today, if the public mood is determined with increasing frequency by food shortages and not by a broad realm of freedom of speech, it is because the problem of a universal reform of the state, based on the implementation of the "social accords" and on a system of public compromise, has not been put on the agenda. Some voices in the official press seem to be starting to discuss these problems, but it is merely a beginning of a new stage.

The task that faces the Polish nation is to work out a plan for a realistic system of political democracy, even while consciously restraining ourselves in order not to impinge on the state interests of our powerful neighbor. I therefore declare myself for a compromise solution. Such is the demand of the moment. No reasonable person can promote a general confrontation today. Solidarity has a different perspective before it, a perspective of searching for solutions that lie—as it has been formulated in the independent press—between collaboration and evolution. The Bastille can be assaulted by an amorphous mob armed only with emotions and courage; a long-term policy of democratic evolution can only be conducted by a movement that is well-organized, that is aware of its goals, and that acts in solidarity.

August 1981

The
Democratic
Opposition

EDITOR'S NOTE. The essays in this part were written between 1976 and 1979, when Michnik and others were formulating the plan and vocabulary that led to the radical changes of the years 1980 to 1981.

// A New Evolutionism 1976

//   The historic events that we call the Polish October [1956] were a source of hope that the communist system could evolve. This hope was grounded in two visions, two concepts of evolution. I will label them "revisionist" and "neopositivist."

The revisionist concept was based on a specific intraparty perspective. It was never formulated into a political program. It assumed that the system of power could be humanized and democratized and that the official Marxist doctrine was capable of assimilating contemporary arts and social sciences. The revisionists wanted to act within the framework of the Communist party and Marxist doctrine. They wanted to transform "from within" the doctrine and the party in the direction of democratic reform and common sense. In the long term, the actions of the revisionists seek to allow enlightened people with progressive ideas to take over the party. Władysław Bieńkowski, one of the most typical representatives of this group, defined these ideas as enlightened socialist despotism.

Stanisław Stomma, a leading exponent of the second type of evolutionist vision, called his orientation "neopositivist." In that vision, the strategy chosen by Roman Dmowski,[1] at the turn of the century,

---

1. Roman Dmowski (1864–1939) was the spiritual father and political leader of the National Democratic party (SN-Endecja) and an antagonist of Józef Piłsudski.

was to be applied to today's historical and political conditions. Stomma considered himself a Catholic and recognized Catholicism as a permanent component of Polish public life. As head of the Catholic Znak group, he wanted to repeat the maneuver of the leader and ideologue of the national democratic camp and, like Dmowski when he joined the tsarist Duma in 1906, Stomma and his colleagues entered the Sejm of the Polish People's Republic in January 1957. The group of Catholic activists around Stomma, who based his thinking on analysis of the geopolitical situation, aimed at creating a political movement that, at the right moment, could lead the Polish nation. For Dmowski, that moment came with the outbreak of World War I; for Stomma, it could possibly come with the decomposition of the Soviet bloc.

From 1956 to 1959, Stomma's ideas had the partial support of the episcopate, owing to the concessions granted the Catholic Church by Władysław Gomułka's ruling group. Stomma's evolutionist concept differed fundamentally from the revisionist idea. First of all, neopositivism took for granted Poland's loyalty to the USSR while at the same time rejecting Marxist doctrine and socialist ideology. Revisionists, by contrast, tended toward anti-Soviet rather than anti-Marxist sentiments, as was the case in Hungary. To use a metaphoric comparison, if one considers the state organization of the Soviet Union as the Church and the Marxist ideological doctrine as the Bible, then revisionism was faithful to the Bible while developing its own interpretations, whereas neopositivism adhered to the Church but with the hope that the Church would sooner or later disappear.

The two concepts shared the conviction that change would come from above. Both the revisionists and neopositivists counted on positive evolution in the party, to be caused by the rational policies of wise leaders, not by incessant public pressure. They both counted on the rational thinking of the communist prince, not on independent institutions that would gain control of the power apparatus. Most probably without making these assumptions, neither the neopositivists nor the revisionists would have been able to conduct their public activities, although, as it turned out, adoption of these assumptions inevitably led to political and intellectual defeat. Both the Church's revisionist critics and the neopositivist opponents of the Bible's principles were defeated.

The revisionist orientation definitely had some positive characteristics alongside its negative ones. We should remember both the intellectual fruits of the revisionism of that era and the political activity of important groups of the intelligentsia who were inspired by revisionism. The former are obvious: it is enough to recall the outstanding books written by Leszek Kołakowski, Oskar Lange, Edward Lipiński, Maria Hirszowicz, Włodzimierz Brus, Krzysztof Pomian, Bronisław Baczko, and Witold Kula. Revisionism, in its broadest conception, was manifested on the literary front in the works of Kazimierz Brandys, Adam Wazyk, Wiktor Woroszylski, and Jacek Bocheński. All these books, whatever their scientific or artistic value, popularized the ideas of truth and humanism, which were under attack in the official propaganda. The publication of each of these books rapidly turned into a political event.

In addition to positively influencing Polish learning and culture, revisionism inspired political activity among the citizens. By opposing passivity and internal exile, revisionism laid the basis for independent participation in public life. Faith in one's ability to exert influence on the fate of society is an absolute prerequisite for political activity. In the case of the revisionists, this faith depended on a belief that the party could be reformed. We can see clearly today that their faith was based on delusions; still, civic activity and open demonstrations of opposition were its real and positive results in the years from 1956 to 1968. The majority of oppositionist initiatives during that period originated in these circles, not among steadfast and consistent anticommunists. It is important to remember this fact in weighing the responsibility for the Stalinist beliefs of Poland's leftist intelligentsia. It was the revisionist ex-Stalinists who originated and disseminated dissenting points of view among the intelligentsia—points of view which would later help to revive civil life in Poland in the midst of its difficult reality.

And yet revisionism had been tainted at its very source by the belief that the strivings and goals of the "liberal" wing in the party apparatus were identical to the demands of the revisionist intelligentsia. I think that the revisionists' greatest sin lay not in their defeat in the intraparty struggle for power (where they could not win) but in the character of that defeat. It was the defeat of individuals being eliminated from positions of power and influence, not a setback for a broadly based leftist and democratic political platform. The revisionists never created such a platform.

Revisionism was terminated by the events of March 1968. In that month the umbilical cord connecting the revisionist intelligentsia to the party was severed. After March 1968 the idea that a progressive and democratic wing existed in the party's leadership was never to regain wide currency. One of the few people who continued to cherish this political hope was Władysław Bieńkowski,[2] although his formulations were generally considered as protective coloring and not genuine reasoning. In fact, by popularizing his work, Bieńkowski created a completely new style of political activity. Previously, "staying inside the party"— that is, appealing for support only to party members—was an unwritten law of revisionism. Bieńkowski gave new substance to the old formulas; revisionism, conceived by him as a belief in the existence of a wise party leadership, was transformed into merciless and unceasing criticism of current leaders and their stupidity. On the one hand, he propagated ideas clearly hostile to the authorities and a program that was explicitly oppositional; but on the other hand, his program was addressed to the authorities and not to the public. Those of Bieńkowski's readers who were not party members could not learn from his writings how to live, how to act, and what to do to further democratic change.

Also in 1968, the year revisionism died, the demonstrating students chanted: "All Poland is waiting for its Dubček." For a while, the leader of Czech and Slovak communists became the symbol of hope. To this very day, the myth of Dubček and the Prague Spring has played an important role in Poland, and the meaning of this myth is far from simple. It serves to justify both radiant optimism and the darkest pessimism; it provides a defense for attitudes of conformism as well as for gestures of heroism. Why?

In October 1956 the threat of Soviet intervention in Poland made a national hero out of Władysław Gomułka—a man who would walk off the political stage covered with infamy and contempt fourteen years later.[3] His example reveals the basic ambiguity in the whole myth of the heroic party leader. There are reasons to believe that even if there

2. Władysław Bieńkowski wrote several books critical of the communist regime. Formerly he was an activist of the Polish Communist party and a close associate of Władysław Gomułka.

3. Władysław Gomułka is credited with winning in 1956 the trust of Nikita Khrushchev and other Soviet leaders and thus preventing a Soviet invasion.

had been no armed intervention the extreme polarization and open conflict between the progressive wing of the party and the extraparty opposition KAN (club of the Non-party Engagés movement) were bound to surface in Czechoslovakia. It is difficult to predict the future, but I would venture that more than one "Dubčekite" would quickly have been transformed into a tamer of the turbulent opposition.

The myth of the "good" party leader is necessarily ambiguous. Many of those who joined the PUWP defended their decision in the following manner: "This way I will be able to serve the cause of Polish democracy, because in this way alone I will be able to lend effective support to the Polish Dubček when he appears." So far, this service to the cause of democracy has amounted to service to the totalitarian powers. Those who did not join the PUWP and who declared themselves to be totally anticommunist also use the example of Czechoslovakia to justify their decision to shun all oppositional behavior. These people call oppositionists "political troublemakers," and view the fate of Czechoslovakia and Dubček as proof that "there is no way anything is going to change here."

For me, the lesson of Czechoslovakia is that change is possible and that it has its limits. Czechoslovakia is an example of the fragility of totalitarian stability, and also of the desperation and ruthlessness of an empire under threat. The lesson of Czechoslovakia is that evolution has its limits and that it is possible.

The experiences of the neopositivists should also be closely examined. There is no doubt that their actions had the positive effect of helping to create an independent public opinion and of popularizing a way of thinking that differed completely from the obligatory official style of party propaganda.

As I have already mentioned, a starting point for the ideas of the Znak movement in 1956 was geopolitical realism and a rejection of the Poles' supposed predisposition to revolt—a lesson learned from the tragedy of the 1944 Warsaw Uprising. In return for backing Władysław Gomułka's new party leadership, the Znak movement received significant concessions from the authorities. Several Clubs of the Catholic Intelligentsia were formed, and *Tygodnik Powszechny*, the *Znak* [Sign] monthly, and the Znak publishing house were reactivated. The Znak movement gained the right to express its own opinions and to formulate its own model of national culture. One cannot overestimate the importance of the assimilation of contemporary Christian thought by Polish intellectual life. It would be equally difficult to overestimate the role of books written by Stefan Kisielewski, Hanna Malewska, Jerzy Turowicz, Jerzy Zawieyski, Stanisław Stomma, Antoni Gołubiew, or Jacek Woźniakowski. Because of the works by these authors, a broad base for a culture independent of official norms and molds came into existence in Poland. Thanks to speeches made in the Sejm by Stefan Kisielewski, Jerzy Zawieyski, and Stanisław Stomma, young Poles were given an opportunity to become familiar with an ersatz political pluralism. By its very definition, the small group of Znak deputies was destined to fulfill the role of a realistic, pragmatic, and Catholic "opposition to Your Royal-socialist Majesty."

The *Więź* group of the Polish Catholic left occupied a different niche, combining revisionist hopes with the political strategy of Znak's neopositivists. The innovative ideas of Tadeusz Mazowiecki, Anna Morawska, and other essayists published in *Więź* brought its editors into conflict with the episcopate; but these ideas also made possible an ideological dialogue with the lay intelligentsia. As paradoxical as this may sound, it was the *Więź* group which enabled the leftist intelligentsia to revise traditional stereotypes of Christianity and the Church.

The support lent to Gomułka by Znak and *Więź* was limited to a specific political objective—to expand the domain of civil liberties. An important component of this goal was normalization of relations between Church and State—for example, by freeing of the [then imprisoned] Primate of Poland, by relinquishing administrative harassment, by legalizing religious instruction, and so on. In these circumstances, the Znak movement confined its activities to loyal, albeit restrained and dignified, support of the authorities' policies. Much like the revisionists, the Catholic politicians believed in having concessions and rights "granted" from above rather than in organizing pressure from below. They sought harmony, not conflict; they cared for order, seeking agreement with the party, and sought to avoid imputations of oppositional attitudes.

Even though the leaders of Znak never committed the fundamental mistake of the revisionists—instead, they always stressed their ideological and political separateness—the history of their movement inspires critical thoughts about the line of action chosen by the Catholic neopositivists.

A policy of conciliation makes sense only if both sides take it seriously. In relation to communist power, whose political vocabulary lacks the word *conciliation,* such a policy has meaning only if it is conducted from a position of strength. Otherwise, conciliation turns into capitulation, and the policy of conciliation into a march toward political self-annihilation. This is how the Znak group of deputies evolved.

Agreement to a succession of personnel changes in the Znak group of deputies dictated by the authorities led to an increasing conformity of the movement's political line with the official line. Abandonment of its principles led the Znak deputies to lose their authority in the eyes of the people, who, even though they themselves were powerless, respected courage and consistency. The deputies followed a path that proceeded from compromise to loss of credibility. I am using strong language, yet it is difficult to find other words to describe the votes of the Znak deputies (except for those of Stanisław Stomma) in favor of the government amendments to the Constitution of the PPR [1976]— for amendments that were opposed by independent public opinion in Poland.[4] This was the last stage and the final product of their abandonment of principle in exchange for immediate but illusory gains. It is one of the many paradoxes of Polish history that Stanisław Stomma, a politician whose eyes were fixed on the example of Alexander the Great and his policy of realpolitik, ended his political career in the Polish People's Republic with a romantic gesture worthy of Rejtan.[5]

The ideas of the revisionists and the neopositivists contained two basic answers to the political dilemmas of the years 1957 to 1964—a period of social normalization and political thaw, increasing prosperity among the people, and relative expansion of civil liberties. Both groups reflected to a great degree the atmosphere of political peace and sociopsychological stability.

4. The protests against the changes in the Constitution were the beginning of the self-organization of the opposition in Poland.

5. Tadeusz Rejtan (1746–1780), a deputy from Nowogródek to the 1773 Diet, tore his clothes and threw himself on the floor begging other envoys to reject the partition of Poland.

The fragility of both revisionism and neopositivism surfaced when social conflict became more acute, in the late sixties and seventies. The student and intellectual movement in March, 1968, the workers' explosion in June, 1976—both spontaneous public manifestations led to the downfall of the revisionists and neopositivists. The uselessness of both abstract formulas adopted from the history of philosophy and the tactical programs that resulted from these formulas was bared in the clash with real social processes. The conflicts between the public and the authorities showed the illusory character of the hopes held by both the revisionists and the neopositivists, and placed them in a situation in which they had to make a dramatic choice. When there is open conflict, one must clearly state a position and declare whose side one is on—that of those being beaten up or that of those doing the beating. Where the conflict is open, consistent revisionism as well as consistent neopositivism both inevitably lead to unity with the powers-that-be and assumption of their point of view. To offer solidarity with striking workers, with students holding a mass meeting, or with protesting intellectuals is to challenge the intraparty strategy of the revisionist and neopositivist policies of compromise. Social solidarity undermines the fundamental component of both strategies: acceptance of the government as the basic point of reference.

The dilemma of nineteenth-century leftist movements—"reform or revolution"—is not the dilemma of the Polish opposition. To believe in overthrowing the dictatorship of the party by revolution and to consciously organize actions in pursuit of this goal is both unrealistic and dangerous. As the political structure of the USSR remains unchanged, it is unrealistic to count on subverting the party in Poland. It is dangerous to plan conspiratorial activities. Given the absence of an authentic political culture or any standards of democratic collective life, the existence of an underground would only worsen these illnesses and change little. Revolutionary theories and conspiratorial practices can only serve the police, making mass hysteria and police provocation more likely.

In my opinion, an unceasing struggle for reform and evolution that seeks an expansion of civil liberties and human rights is the only course East European dissidents can take. The Polish example demonstrates that real concessions can be won by applying steady public pressure on the government. To draw a parallel with events at the other end of our continent, one could say that the ideas of the Polish democratic opposition resemble the Spanish rather than the Portuguese model. This is based on gradual and piecemeal change, not violent upheaval and forceful destruction of the existing system.

The Soviet military and political presence in Poland is the factor that determines the limits of possible evolution, and this is unlikely to change for some time. The desire to resist has been paralyzed by the specter of Soviet military intervention and Soviet tanks in the streets of Warsaw. The memory of Budapest and Prague has led many people to believe that the Soviet leaders will not allow any changes whatsoever. But on closer examination, the matter seems much more complicated.

Let us recall: Władysław Gomułka owed his enormous popularity in 1956 to his skillful definition of the "Soviet question." Every competent party leader can win obedience and allegiance by cleverly juggling fear and the public's desire for security. Mieczysław Moczar tried to strike the right note, and Franciszek Szlachcic appealed to these popular sentiments with a phrase that made the rounds in Warsaw: "Polish-Soviet friendship should be like good tea: strong, hot, but not too sweet." These two politicians [and security service officials] started their march to power by seeking greater popularity, and though they did not succeed, the Soviet question remains a showy stage for political exploitation.

When one analyzes the complexity of Polish-Soviet relations, it must be noted first of all that the interests of the Soviet political leadership, the Polish political leadership, and the Polish democratic opposition are basically concurrent. For all three parties, a Soviet military intervention in Poland would be a political disaster. For the Polish leadership, such an intervention would signify dethronement or the reduction of its position of leader of a nation of thirty-four million, with limited sovereignty, to that of policeman acting on behalf of the Soviet imperium. The Soviet leaders, however, certainly remember the international repercussions of their interventions in Hungary and Czechoslovakia, as well as the resolve of the Polish workers in December 1970 and June 1976. If we include also the traditional anti-Russian sentiments of the Poles, and their propensity to fight out of sheer desperation (as demonstrated, for instance, in the Warsaw Uprising of 1944), then we can conclude that a decision by Soviet leaders to intervene militarily in Poland would be equivalent to opting for war with Poland. It would be a war that Poland would lose on the battlefield but that the Soviet Union would lose politically. A victorious Soviet war with Poland would mean a national massacre for the Poles, but for the Soviets it would be a political catastrophe. This is why I believe the Soviet leaders, as well as the leadership of the PUWP, will go far to avoid such a conflict. This reluctance delineates the area of permissible political maneuver; this alignment of interests defines the sphere of possible compromise.

I am not contending that Soviet intervention in Poland is impossible. On the contrary, I believe that it may be unavoidable if the Moscow and Warsaw authorities on the one hand, and the Polish public on the other, lose their common sense and a sense of reality and moderation. The opposition must learn that in Poland change can only come— at least in its first stages—within the framework of the "Brezhnev doctrine."

The revisionists and neopositivists also believed that evolutionary change should be planned within the parameters of the "Brezhnev doctrine." I believe that what sets today's opposition apart from the proponents of those ideas is the belief that a program for evolution ought to be addressed to an independent public, not to totalitarian power. Such a program should give directives to the people on how to behave, not to the powers on how to reform themselves. Nothing instructs the authorities better than pressure from below.

"New evolutionism" is based on faith in the power of the working class, which, with a steady and unyielding stand, has on several occasions forced the government to make spectacular concessions. It is difficult to foresee developments in the working class, but there is no question that the power elite fears this social group most. Pressure from the working classes is a necessary condition for the evolution of public life toward a democracy.

This evolution is not easy to chart; it requires that fear be constantly overcome and that a new political consciousness be developed. Factors that retard this process include the absence of authentic workers' institutions and of models and traditions for political resistance. The day the first independent organization for workers' self-defense was founded, when the strike committees in the shipyards of Szczecin and Gdańsk were formed, a new stage in worker consciousness began. It is hard to tell when and how other, more permanent institutions representing the interests of workers will be created and what form they will have. Will they be workers' committees following the Spanish model, or independent labor unions, or mutual aid societies? But when such institutions emerge, the vision of a new evolutionism will become more than just a creation of a mind in search of hope.

The role of the Catholic Church is a crucial element in Poland's situation. The majority of the Polish people feel close to the Church, and many Catholic priests have strong political influence. The evolution of the Polish episcopate's program of action should be carefully analyzed. This evolution can be observed easily in official Church documents. The Church hierarchy's consistently and specifically anticommunist position, in which all social and political changes that have taken place since 1945 were rejected, has been evolving into a more broadly antitotalitarian stance. Jeremiads against "godless ones" have given way to documents quoting the principles of the Declaration of Human Rights; in pastoral letters, Polish bishops have been defending the right to truth and standing up for human freedom and dignity. Most important, they have been defending the civil liberties of the working people, and particularly their right to strike and to form independent labor unions.

The Catholic Church, which consistently resists pressure from the government and defends Christian principles as well as the principles of the Declaration of Human Rights, has necessarily become a place where attitudes of nonconformity and dignity among the people can mingle. It is therefore a key source of encouragement for those who seek to broaden civil liberties.

The new evolutionism aims at gradual and slow change. But this does not mean that the movement for change will always be peaceful—that it will not require sacrifices and casualties. In the past, this movement partially consisted of mass actions by workers and students—and this may continue into the future. Such actions are usually followed by disputes in the power elite. Therefore, we should ask whether forces within the party and its leadership exist which are capable of adopting a program of reform, and whether revisionism might reappear within the party. Can the democratic opposition find an ally in one of the party coteries?

Revisionism is a movement of intraparty renewal which came into being in the fifties and is now an outdated phenomenon. It is difficult to imagine a movement that would use Marxist-Leninist doctrine, or even any of its elements, to enforce reforms in Poland today, since this doctrine is a dead creature, an empty gesture, an official ritual. It no longer stimulates discussion or fires up emotions. It is incapable of causing internal tension and division.

I believe nevertheless that change within the party is inevitable. Among the hundreds of thousands of party members who have no interest whatsoever in dialectical materialism, there are many for whom membership in the PUWP is simply a necessary precondition for participation in public life. Among them are many believers in realpolitik, pragmatism and economic reform. Their political beliefs and decisions are shaped by the pressure of public opinion and by forces within the national economy. Pragmatism causes these people to let narrow ideological criteria be overridden by the need for the development of education, stronger scientific-technical cooperation with capitalist countries, and increased competition. This obviously does not mean that these individuals are striving for democracy. A party "pragmatist" has no reason to aim for democratic change—for pluralism and authentic self-government. But he does have reason to understand the effectiveness of compromising with forces favoring plurality instead of brutally suppressing them. For he knows very well that repression solves nothing and instead prepares the ground for the next explosion of social discontent, the consequences of which are impossible to foresee.

The party pragmatist will therefore do his best to avoid such situations. This is why he can be a partner of the democratic opposition, with whom it will be possible to reach a political compromise. But he will never be a political ally. I think that this distinction is important. If the people of the democratic opposition fail to distinguish the various trends that exist within the power apparatus, I believe they may ignore reality, become fanatical maximalists, and go astray into political adventurism. Identifying their own goals with those of the pragmatic wing of the party, however, could lead them to repeat the mistakes of the revisionists, to form false alliances and lose their ideological identity. The people of the democratic opposition should not place excessive hope in "reasonable" party leaders, or give in to arguments that "one should not make things more difficult for the current party leadership because the next one may be worse." The democratic opposition must formulate its own political goals and only then, with those goals in hand, reach political compromises. Take, for example, a situation in which the workers revolt and the government declares that it wants to "consult with the working class" instead of organizing a bloody massacre. The people of the democratic opposition should treat this reaction neither as a sufficient concession ("but they are not shooting") nor as a meaningless fiction. On the contrary, the democratic opposition must be constantly and incessantly visible in public life, must create political facts by organizing mass actions, must formulate alternative programs. Everything else is an illusion.

The intelligentsia's duty is to formulate alternative programs and defend the basic principles. More precisely, I refer to those small groups of intellectuals who believe in continuing the traditions of the "insubordinate" intelligentsia of the early 1900s—the traditions of writers such as Stanisław Brzozowski, Stanisław Wyspiański, Stefan Zeromski, and Zofia Nałkowska. I feel solidarity with those traditions and those people, although I am the last person to overestimate the importance of their actions. But those voices, albeit weak and sporadic, are nonetheless authentic: they form an independent public opinion, with nonconformist attitudes and oppositional thought. This course is being followed by people from various traditions and social strata: former revisionists (including the author of this article), former neopositivists, and those who became ideologically aware after the events of 1968.

The direction the ideological thinking of the young generation will take—as well as the drift of political change in Poland and in other countries of Eastern Europe—will depend on the convergence of these groups with the activities of the working class. When a free press and independent organizations do not exist, the moral and political responsibility of these groups is much greater than at any other time. The people of the opposition should renounce material profit and official esteem in order to fulfill this exceptional responsibility, so that we can expect the truth from them.

In searching for truth, or, to quote Leszek Kołakowski, "by living in dignity," opposition intellectuals are striving not so much for a better tomorrow as for a better today. Every act of defiance helps us build the framework of democratic socialism, which should not be merely or primarily a legal institutional structure but a real, day-to-day community of free people.

Paris, October 1976

// Some Remarks on the Opposition and the General Situation in Poland 1979

(Written jointly with Jan Józef Lipski)

EDITOR'S NOTE. This article, signed by two KOR members—Michnik and Jan Józef Lipski—was a reply to an article published in the underground three months earlier by another KOR member, Jacek Kuroń. Kuroń considered the prevention of a social explosion the most urgent task of the opposition and advocated the creation of a nonoppositional "movement of demands." That movement would channel social discontent into practical pressure on the authorities in matters of economy and social organization. The underlying question was that of the possibility and desirability of collaboration between the opposition movement and the authorities. Both articles marked an important point in the political discussion leading to the creation of Solidarity.

// Because of both its content and its author, Jacek Kuroń's article "The Situation in Poland and the Opposition's Program," which appeared this year in issue no. 3 of *Biuletyn Informacyjny*, constitutes an important event in independent publishing. Kuroń tackles fundamental problems that require an honest and subtle analysis. Our remarks will merely be a sort of glossary for discussion, an attempt to define several points which we consider important.

Kuroń ties his reflections to the possibility of a sudden explosion of public anger. We fully share his concern about the potential consequences of such an explosion. But we believe that the issue of how a democratic opposition should function in our society is broader and that it is partly unrelated to the possibility of an imminent outburst. An explosion may result when normal channels for social pressure on the authorities become blocked; but the people have always defended themselves from totalitarian power by channeling such pressure through approved organizations, even at times when tensions were less acute than they are at present. Therefore, it may seem misleading to simply counterpose the political opposition with "the movement of demands."

In Kuroń's thinking the movement for independent institutions can be classified as political opposition. In our opinion these independent institutions form a part of the broad movement of demands for civil rights, a movement aiming to make our society democratic and autonomous. There is no point in listing the other components of this movement here since everyone is familiar with them, beginning with the role of the Catholic Church. It is obvious that independent institutions could not function at all if it were not for the existence of a middle ground between the open opposition and the institutions of coercion—between, for example, the Workers' Defense Committee (the KOR) and the Politburo of the Central Committee of the PUWP. This area is full of ideological color and varying attitudes; the majority of our people live and function in it. The relationships between independent institutions and initiatives undertaken in this zone are of utmost importance for the present and future. They require a plurality of attitudes and a mutually respectful understanding of the need for various forms of resistance and action. Otherwise we, as a society, may lose our common language, and the atmosphere of the opposition's actions may become poisoned with the spirit of political sectarianism. In presenting his thoughts, Jacek Kuroń sidestepped this aspect of the problem.

Kuroń's formulations on the relations between "the movement of demands" and the political opposition, on the one hand, and various groupings, factions, or coteries within the power apparatus, on the other, seem premature. This is because—thus far—we have no concrete knowledge concerning any ideological conflicts within the party; therefore, all speculation about such conflicts must remain purely theoretical. Kuroń is right to dismiss those arguments that favor abandoning political activity in deference to supposed factional struggles. He is also right in warning opposition groups against identifying with the potential reform program of any of those factions that might emerge in the future. Let us repeat: these are purely hypothetical theses, but they are worth considering in order to analyze the historical experience of the Polish October and the Prague Spring. The conclusion to be drawn is that in formulating its basic values, the opposition must remain independent and distinct. The only sensible way of supporting the liberal-reformist" faction in the party is to exert pressure on the authorities as a whole. Kuroń is right again of course in saying that pressure must be based on a concrete plan of demands, not on general ideals and slogans, however beautiful they may sound. Support for a faction by no means removes the possibility of conflict; it merely moves it elsewhere. In the past, the government—or certain of its bodies—has attempted to appeal to the people. It would be absurd to think that on such occasions in the future the opposition could avoid taking a political stand. It would be further-more ridiculous to claim that such a stand could disregard our country's complex geopolitical situation or our common responsibility for the fate of our nation. By deciding that the dispute over reforming the state was merely a sham quarrel among communists, the opposition would risk its own isolation. It is simply not true that the people will never profit from any change issuing from groups within the party. It is true, however, that such changes will never be sufficient.

Therefore the question of the relationship between the movement of independent institutions (which has been in existence since 1976) and the program of social demands within official institutions (which are largely part of the system contested by that independent opposition) calls not for argument but rather for definition and commentary. This issue has already caused much confusion and misunderstanding. People are wondering whether Kuroń's article advocates an end to the creation of independent public institutions in deference to activities within offi-cial institutions (which have for the most part been taken over by the Communist party); whether he is forsaking the gains made to date by the independent opposition in favor of a policy of entering into relations and agreements with organizations controlled by the authorities, that is, officially accepted institutions.

This is a grossly simplistic but typical misunderstanding. The publication of uncensored books and periodicals is the most frequently cited product of the opposition's tactic of creating independent institu-tions. The uncensored press is not just free from censorship, but it has virtually no contacts with the official system. I [*sic*] write "virtually" because it often happens that these publications are read by people who are connected with the system. And there is another point of contact: the police take every opportunity they can to confiscate copies of these publications. This is how the independent press can and should function under today's conditions. Labor unions and student organizations, in contrast, must operate somewhat differently. A labor union that vows never to deal with the government is no labor union. One of the duties of a free labor union is to force the authorities to talk, to negotiate; it should make demands and discuss their implementation, threaten and if necessary carry out those threats, and even make compromises. Whether labor unions are formed alongside official unions or whether they *are* official ones taken over by workers—they provide a means of concerted action with the authorities and, should they become even temporary partners, could gradually force the totalitarian power to make concessions. For example, were the discussion to involve an issue like the purification of air in the factory halls, a labor union activist who claimed that he refused to tarnish his good name by talking to the authorities would be better off doing something else.

These functions could easily be fulfilled by an official labor union that has been taken over by the workers themselves. If workers' councils today obey the party and the management and not their electorate, this results from the passivity, lack of courage, and general absence of social consciousness on the part of the workers as a whole. And this will have to change.

The attempt to revive committees that could assist prisoners, undertaken a while ago by Father Jan Zieja, is another example of how independent institutions can be created. In this case, the security police prevented the organization of this much-needed institution. It was clear, however, that such relief committees—which would resemble KOR— would not have been able to fulfill their role if they could not reach the prisons. Perhaps a time will soon come when the government will have to sanction them. But let us be honest about this: such an institution, which the people need, would have to conduct endless negotiations with the public prosecutor's office, the militia, the criminal courts, the Ministry of Justice, and with prison authorities on a daily basis. There are countless similar examples.

Should people act by creating independent institutions unrecognized by the authorities or by struggling inside official institutions with the aim of winning them over? This question resembles the classic problem, "Should I wash my hands or my feet?" Both!

The opposition acts and struggles primarily among people who have not yet chosen to fight by our methods since those methods seem to involve too many risks for the fighters and since victory over totalitarianism seems distant and uncertain. This frame of mind will change gradually, in some situations radically. But today things are the way they are. There are so many groups between the declared opposition and the now-substantial number of people who believe the maintenance of a monoparty to be in their interest that one could say a continuum exists. It can be dangerous when important distinctions in views and goals are obliterated. But it would be even more dangerous if the groups fighting for change were to detach themselves completely from the passive population. This would spell disaster and death to the opposition. The opposition's successes and its very existence remain possible only because those who decide to take the gravest risks do not separate themselves with insurmountable barriers from those who may help them actively from time to time, from people who pass on uncensored newspapers after they read them, from those who agree to make irregular monetary contributions, or from those who are cautiously and quietly sympathetic. Or even from those who may yet be won over. Their cautious—and sometimes cowardly—reserve often irritates those who risk everything. Still, it is better that things be this way than that a wall exist cutting the active opposition off from those latent social energies which sooner or later will be released.

Fortunately, one can already today begin listing organizations acting officially with such a degree of independence that it is more appropriate to speak of "limitations on their freedom" rather than of their subordination. And their numbers will grow. They in no way threaten the opposition. On the contrary, they broaden and strengthen it. What is more, we should not smile contemptuously when we are told that an engineer or a doctor speaks of his professional work as a battlefront similar to the opposition's, only that there the battle is fought differently. We all know how much hypocrisy is often contained in such words, but there is also much heroism. As usual, the truth generally lies somewhere in between. It is understandable that a man who a year or two ago lost all chance for advancement in his career or even lost his job altogether because he chose to actively participate in the opposition will listen with distrust to stories about the struggle waged in another institution by someone more cautious than he; his distrust is often justified. Still, he should not persist in such a negative attitude. Many of those who today believe in limited and careful resistance are our cautious allies, and tomorrow they will participate in the open fight for democracy.

We should not naively imagine that the PUWP regime, which as a last resort can always lean on the military potential of the USSR, will disappear any month now. We have reason to be optimistic in the long run, but still we must count on acting alongside the governing monoparty. In these circumstances, it does matter what type of policy triumphs in this party and what reforms the party will be forced to choose under public pressure. The spectrum of possibilities is broad. Whatever the situation, the opposition will have to guard its identity carefully. But it should not insist that it will never, under any circumstances, enter into discussions on any specific topic should it become possible to broaden civil liberties in Poland.

Warsaw, September–October 1979

// The Prague Spring Ten Years Later 1978

// I observed the events of the Prague Spring with anxiety and hope from behind the bars of Mokotów prison in Warsaw. I had been jailed for organizing the student demonstrations in March 1968. My sole source of information about what was happening south of the border was our press. The newspapers were filled with abusive condemnations of "revisionists," "Zionists," and other "troublemakers" in Poland, but the reports about Czechoslovakia were like a breath of fresh air. They helped preserve hope. The increasingly nervous tone of the commentaries in *Trybuna Ludu* [the official newspaper], which I read with growing apprehension, indicated the enormity of the changes that were occurring; the attacks in the Soviet press hinted at the direction these changes were taking. The open interference of Moscow's *Pravda* enabled us to surmise that behind-the-scenes pressure was having no effect. I must admit that I did not believe an armed intervention would take place.

The investigation of my case was concluded that summer, at the same time that Soviet and Czechoslovak leaders were meeting in Černa. Passions subsided—both the major international ones and my own private ones, as the anguish of the extensive and tiresome interrogations came to an end. In the rooms where the interrogations had taken place, the March prisoners could now sit and read the dossiers of their cases under the supervision of officers from the security services. My guardians got so bored reading the daily press that they'd stop from time to time. They would put aside their papers and I the voluminous dossiers and we would begin a conversation, a peculiar dialogue of the executioner with his victim. "You won't get out of this one so easily— you'll be in for at least six years," the investigating officer would reassure me cordially. "Don't be so sure, Sir. Your colleagues in Czechoslovakia felt as splendid as you do now just a year ago, and today they are committing suicide," I would reply with a radiant smile. Following this exchange, my "guardian" would let me read the paper and I would point out to him the more interesting parts of the records of my case. The days floated by lazily and without surprises. The bright August sun kept us company from behind the barred windows. August 21st was just like any other day. The day's schedule was the same as usual: reveille, cleanup of cells, assembly, breakfast, walk, the jailer escorting me to the room where I read the records. The officer of the security police was already waiting for me. I sat down to read. When I took a break and looked up, I noticed an unusual tension in the officer's face. The newspaper he had finished reading, which normally lay casually on the table, had been quietly slipped into his briefcase. Something must have happened. Confused, I went down to my cell for lunch. Immediately after lunch, the guard distributed newspapers among the prisoners. I grabbed one and, unable to believe my own eyes, I read *about the invasion of Czechoslovakia by the armies of five states of the Warsaw Pact.*

I froze. Never before and never since then has an item in the paper had such a staggering effect on me. "Poles are strangling the movement for freedom in Czechoslovakia," I thought. And for the first time in my life I felt the bitter taste of national disgrace.

So much for my memories. I will sum up the lessons of Czechoslovakia in a few points, even though there would be enough of them to fill a large volume.

It has become clear that the people of Eastern Europe who are ruled by totalitarian governments are capable of acting to influence their fates, and that despite what pessimists might say, war is not a condition for internal democratic change. It has also become clear that change need not coincide with changes inside the Soviet Union, as happened in Poland and Hungary in 1956. Societies in which hope is kindled—as was the case with the Czechs and Slovaks in the winter of 1968—transform themselves rapidly and radically. The apathy and stagnation of the Antonin Novotny era can give way to a wave of vigor and creativity. In a society that demands its rights, a society that transforms itself from object to subject, different sociological mechanisms come into play.

Although it was the absence of stimulus from Moscow that made the Prague Spring different from the Polish October, one important similarity lay in the intraparty inspiration for the "movement of renewal." In both cases the strengths and the weaknesses of the movement were determined by the character of this inspiration. Its strength was due to the system's splitting from within—the plague was bred in the very heart of Granada, so to speak, sparing neither the top layers of the party's apparatus, the security apparatus, nor the army. But such a movement was unable to perceive its true historic identity or correctly to define its goals, and that was the source of its weakness. Its leaders used the general term *democratization* in such a manner that its connotations were almost purely negative; the term hardly had any positive meaning, and even then a different one for different people. The leaders themselves, in their call to the people for realism and moderation, failed to appreciate the geopolitical situation (Czechoslovakia) and the real aspirations of the people (Poland); they restored the monoparty system whose human face smiled only at party notables. In both cases, the result was confusion. Why?

To this day the leaders of the Prague Spring contend that socialism was in no danger in Czechoslovakia, that no "peaceful counterrevolution" existed, and that therefore a military intervention was unjustified. I think that this is not true. In Soviet semantics the word *socialism* means the total domination of the Communist party, whereas the word *counterrevolution* denotes all actions that subvert the totality of this domination. Therefore, the Soviet leaders understood developments correctly: the totalitarian system in Czechoslovakia was beginning to burst at its seams. The viewpoint of the leaders of the Prague Spring can thus be accepted only if one assumes that the word *socialism* is fundamentally ambiguous. Actually, the ambiguity went beyond semantics. Without entering into an academic historical discourse, let us put it briefly: this ambiguity contaminated the mentality of the majority of the "first generation" of communists, people who had opted for communism and had chosen ideology at a time when this choice implied the risk of a life of hardship, and not the appanages of power. It was these same people who made up the social base of the phenomenon called "revisionism." Revisionism stemmed from the confrontation of humanistic slogans with totalitarian practices. Communist totalitarianism that wore the mask of humanistic phraseology fell victim to its own hypocrisy. The origin of revisionism (in its Polish, Dubčekian, or any other version) contained its very ambiguity. The word *socialism*, to the Czech, Polish, and Hungarian pupils of Russian communism, somehow meant both the Soviet political practice and the universal idea of the fraternity of working people. Having matured on the soil of the Comintern, these people represented the "revolt of the flower against it roots" (as Stanisław Brzozowski might have put it). Whoever fails to understand this will never understand East European revisionism.

This paradigm belongs to history, however, and it will never repeat itself. This is why all those who believe in the democratic evolution of the countries of Eastern Europe and who are waiting for another Twentieth Congress of the CPSU or for another January plenum of the Central Committee of the Czechoslovak Communist party are deluding themselves. I have in mind especially the Italian and French Eurocommunists, who are waiting, once again, for the inspiration of a democratization process to come from the upper strata of the party apparatus. They are wrong because these days joining a ruling Communist party is the choice of opportunists. Those who believe in the ideals of liberty, equality, and the freedom of labor can be found only in the ranks of the antitotalitarian opposition. It is from them that the impulse for democratic actions must now arise. Such actions are unique in that they do not aim to win power but to help society organize itself through the gradual emancipation of groups and individuals from the grip of the all-powerful apparatus. The people have to look after their own interests, the independent flow of information, free learning and culture. Society must transform itself from a "sack of potatoes" (we owe this apt metaphor to Marx) into the executor of its own interests and aspirations. Only such a society can effectively oppose totalitarianism and become a real partner in power.

This course alone can yield results, when one takes into account the external factor of Soviet policies. It seems that the Soviet leaders invariably intervene militarily in their satellite states whenever power slips out of the hands of the local Communist party. It is unlikely, however, that they would reply with tanks to the activities of the Workers' Defense Committee, to a publication that appears outside censorship, to the Flying University. An intervention is also less likely when it is certain that it will encounter active mass resistance. The Soviet leaders could be sure of this in 1956 in the Polish case; they could be even more certain of it after the events in the Polish coastal cities in December 1970 and after Radom and Ursus in June 1976. When they made their decision in August 1968, they had no reason to think in a similar fashion.

In trying to foresee the future of Eastern Europe one must certainly add that this social process is unlike any other: No one has yet witnessed a society with nationalized property, a planned economy, and a democratic and pluralistic political structure. "The past sheds no light on the future," wrote Tocqueville. "The mind marches ahead in darkness."

August 1978

// A Lesson in Dignity 1979

// The pope is gone. The government has heaved a sigh of relief.

It will be a long time before anyone fully comprehends the ramifications of his nine-day visit. The phrase of the writer Julian Stryjkowski—"Poland's second baptism"—keeps coming to mind. Indeed, something odd did happen. Those very people who are ordinarily frustrated and aggressive in the shop lines were metamorphosed into a cheerful and happy collectivity, a people filled with dignity. The police vanished from the main streets of Warsaw and exemplary order reigned everywhere. The people who had been repressed for so long suddenly regained an ability to determine their own fate. This is how the social consequences of John Paul II's visit and pilgrimage can be sketched.

The visit constituted the great triumph, second to none, of the episcopate's policies over the last thirty years, the principal architect of which has been the primate of Poland, Cardinal Stefan Wyszyński. The distance traveled by this primate from his imprisonment in Komańcza [from September 1953 to October 1956] to the symbolic scene of the airport welcoming ceremony was obvious to all present. The Church's demeanor had been molded by him through his staunch resistance to the government's attempts at Sovietization and also through his realism in assessing the situation; such demeanor left room for heroism and steadfastness as well as for wise compromise. This attitude allowed the Polish Catholic Church to show the world its true face. The traditional image of this Church, sunk in ignorance and fanaticism, was radically changed. What is more, it became clear to all that the Church is a force against which power cannot be exercised in Poland.

Some fear this as a new variation of the alliance between altar and throne. I do not share such concerns. There is no evidence that the Church has abandoned its practice of oscillating between "diplomacy" and "bearing witness." Especially now, the momentous value of bearing witness is obvious.

John Paul II's pilgrimage to Poland bestowed a new meaning on the Vatican's *Ostpolitik*. To understand this, one must reexamine the Polish primate's prior policies. When in 1950 news of the accord between the government and the episcopate[1] reached the Holy See, one of the Vatican politicians is said to have exclaimed: "I am in despair!" This person considered the agreement an undesirable concession, given the conditions of open and total conflict. Later, however, following the Vatican's "opening to the East," the policies of the primate and of the entire episcopate seemed too hard-line to the Vatican's diplomats. This line, however, for all its many nuances and transformations, had remained essentially constant. The Polish Church sought to safeguard the principles of the gospel and—without losing touch with reality—to wrest the rights it deserved by imposing the practice of dialogue and small-scale compromise in the relationship between Church and state, to reshape reality by creating faits accomplis.

In this context the pope's entire line of action and certain of his initiatives toward the authorities become understandable and perfectly clear.

During the pope's visit the authorities' behavior proved relatively reasonable. The television coverage of the religious services was downright scandalous (in the words of a friend of mine, a French journalist, the coverage resembled the broadcast of a soccer match in which the cameras show you everything but the ball). And although people in Warsaw had to tune in to stations beaming from the Vatican or Munich for radio reports from Częstochowa or Gniezno, some information was

---

1. On April 14, 1950, after more than a year of negotiations, Cardinal Wyszyński and the Polish government signed an agreement. It was the first such agreement ever signed by the Catholic episcopate and the ruling communists.

made officially available (two Masses were broadcast on national television, others on local channels), and the press did publish the texts of the pope's sermons and speeches with minimal interference from the censors. Although here and there nonsensical sanctions were imposed, the militia and the security forces did not behave provocatively. Although Jacek Kuroń did spend those days under virtual house arrest (he had more guards than the pope himself), this time no preventive mass arrests of people from the democratic opposition were undertaken.

The best the authorities could and did do was to grin and bear it. They made believe that those millions of people with radiant faces crowding around John Paul II did not constitute proof of the total fiasco of their thirty-year rule, that they did not constitute proof of the utter collapse of their moral claim to power.

But the fact remains that no serious disruptions occurred; this lay in everyone's interest, although for different reasons. Some—for example, Radio Free Europe—became overly cautious. That radio station simply stopped giving information about arrests of members of the democratic opposition, who in turn became disgusted by this censorship.*

The democratic opposition fully respected the religious character of the pope's visit and did not try to take advantage of it to further any political goals. This is not to say that the visit/pilgrimage did not also have a political dimension. For some time before the arrival, the Western European press occasionally compared the pope's upcoming pilgrimage to Khomeini's return to Iran and his struggle with the Shah. This analogy was intended to suggest a parallel sense of the conflict between a dictatorial power, with its modernizing tendencies, and a social movement of protest which articulated itself through anachronistic ideas and retrospective utopias. But one can hardly imagine a greater misconception. The body of values and attitudes represented by the papal homilies and speeches had nothing to do with the spirit of integrality, or a desire to return to an era when the Church had "means of wealth" at its disposal and used those more than anything else. The

---

*I am not attempting to disavow the radio or calling for a fundamental change in its policies. We can understand all the reasons for its moderation. But we believe that this should still not lead it to censor information about repression. [Author's note]

pope said clearly, "There is no imperialism in the Church. There is only public service." It was also clearly stated that the Church wants to pursue its goals through nonpolitical means. In the popular perception, the pope's pilgrimage gave Poles the opportunity to express their true aspirations and aims; it was a national plebiscite. But it was not simply a question of choosing between Catholicism and atheism. I saw Catholics grinding their teeth as they listened to the pope. I saw atheists, meanwhile, deeply touched by the pope's words. "What are you in favor of?" we were all asked. "Of conformist consent to totalitarian coercion or of the inviolable right in God's and man's order of things for human beings to live in freedom and dignity?" An overwhelming majority of Poles chose the latter.

John Paul II's words touched us deeply. Any reconstruction of the ideas behind them risks reducing and skewing their meaning, especially when it is done by someone who is not and never has been a Catholic. It is probably not I who should be writing about them. But if I still attempt to do so—intimidated as I am—it is with the conviction that Pope John Paul II spoke to all of us and to each one of us individually. To me, too. So I will try to relate what I heard, what I understood, what I am applying to myself.

The Polish historical experience is a special one, as is the experience of Polish Catholicism. "When native state structures were missing," said John Paul II, "this overwhelmingly Catholic people found support in the hierarchical order of the Church. This support helped it to survive the eras of partitions and occupations, and to retain and deepen the awareness of its identity. . . . Today, Poland's episcopate is in a special way the heir and expression of this truth." For again after 1945, "The Church's organization became not only the focal point of its own pastoral mission but also a very important support for the life of society, for the existence of a nation aware of its rights which—being an overwhelmingly Catholic nation—looks for this support in the Church's hierarchic structures."

The relationship between the Church and society is superior to that between the Church and the state. The latter must be normalized on the basis of "fundamental human rights, including the freedom to worship, which has an undeniable, basic and central meaning. The normalization of relations between the state and the Church is proof of the practical respect for this right and for its consequences in the life of the political community."

The cult of Stanislaus [the Polish saint], who for the Polish bishops sets "a model of fearless and unbroken courage in conveying and defending the sacred deposit of faith," should be seen in this context. It also offers proof of how deeply Christianity is inscribed in Poland's fate. "It is impossible to understand this nation's contribution without Christ. It is impossible to understand this nation, whose past is so glorious and also so terribly difficult, without Christ."

What do these words mean to me, one who stands outside the Church?

I believe that when we try to account for history by limiting ourselves to the various social and economic factors which condition human fate, none of these factors can answer the question of why Father Maksymilian Kolbe[2] or Janusz Korczak[3] chose to die; or why in turn we surround their actions with such deep reverence.

Two nineteenth-century rebels, Jarosław Dąbrowski[4] and Romuald Traugutt,[5] who differed fundamentally in their ideas about ideological and political choices, nevertheless agreed on one thing: both were ready to bear witness to the highest national and human values—with their own blood. This readiness has shaped a particular ethos in the Polish tradition, the ethos of sacrifice, in whose name our grandfathers and fathers never stopped fighting for national and human dignity. And this ethos cannot be understood without acknowledging the constant presence of Christ in Polish spiritual life.

But this is not all. Also present in Polish culture there has existed the ethos of a multinational commonwealth constituted on the basis of tolerance and equality of nations. And even though in reality these ideals of equality and tolerance did not always prevail, still they always

2. Father Maksymilian Kolbe (1894–1943) volunteered to enter the starvation bunker at Auschwitz in lieu of another camp inmate.
3. On August 8, 1942, Janusz Korczak was deported to the Treblinka death camp together with the children of the Warsaw ghetto orphanage. He refused many offers of safe conduct.
4. Jarosław Dąbrowski (1836–1871), Polish national hero, died in battle while he was commander-in-chief of the forces of the Paris Commune.
5. Romuald Traugutt (1825–1864), political leader and military commander of the January Uprising, was hanged by the Russians on August 5, 1864.

remained the dream of the best sons of this earth. When he addressed warm words to Polish Christians of other denominations, the pope was, I think, recalling this very ethos of Polish tolerance.

Such is also my understanding of John Paul II's remarks about the specific experience of all of Eastern Europe, an experience that is both dramatic and instructive for all the countries of this continent, an unshakable contribution to the common cultural heritage and to the "spiritual unity of Christian Europe which is made up of two great traditions: the Western and the Eastern."

Much can be said about the meaning and nature of this historical experience. Here, let us recall just one aspect of it: the Eastern European societies have been subjected to experiments in "modernization" under conditions of totalitarian coercion. Rapid industrialization, which for many years served as the principal argument for the system, was undertaken at the same time as the fundamental rights of working people were being trampled, along with their dignity and the dignity of work itself. The pope recalled this history in his sermon at Częstochowa and, more emphatically, in his homily at Mogiła. In retelling the history of Nowa Huta and the story of the battle for the cross in there,[6] John Paul II said that "the history of Nowa Huta has also been written by the Cross," the symbol of Good Hope as well as the symbol of suffering.

The workers' fight for the Cross, to build a church in Nowa Huta, was a struggle for dignity and identity and proof that "man does not live by bread alone," especially when there is barely enough bread. For "the contemporary problem of human labor . . . in the final analysis, comes down . . . not to technology . . . and economics, but to the basic category of the dignity of labor and the dignity of man. . . . Christ," said John Paul II, "will never countenance the view of man as a mere production tool. [He will not permit] man to be assessed, gauged, valued only by this method. . . . This is why Christ lay down on his cross . . . to protest any sort of degradation of man, including degradation through work. . . . The employee and the employer, the system of work and of wages, the state, the nation, and the Church, must all take account of this."

---

6. Nowa Huta, a huge steel mill, was a pet project of Stalinist Poland. Against the wishes of the authorities, the workers built a church there. The church is now an important center of religious and social activity.

The problem of the liberation of labor currently lies at the center of many disputes in Western Europe. It is into these very disputes that the pope from the East is making a special contribution, offering his knowledge of the experience that has molded the features of this "other face of Europe," to quote Tadeusz Mazowiecki. The pope "has come to the whole Church, to Europe, and to the world to speak about these often forgotten nations and peoples. He has come to issue the great appeal." What does this mean? I venture to say it means that the vision of a wounded and divided Europe, a Europe whose Warsaw and Cracow, Budapest and Prague, Vilna and Lvov have all been amputated, a vision created by the powers of this world at the Yalta conference as a result of military actions, is today coming into question. It is being questioned with great force by a man who forsakes force, following the teachings of a Christ who is God to some and to others a symbol of the most important values of European culture, and to everyone the source of moral norms and the light of hope.

So if today anyone were to repeat the question once asked by Joseph Stalin, "How many divisions does the pope have?" such a question would be the equivalent of condoning this totalitarian order founded on "the denial of faith—faith in God and faith in man—and on a radical trampling not just of love but of all the characteristics of humanity, mankind," an order based on "hate and contempt for man in the name of a mad ideology."

By recalling the tragedy of the 1944 Warsaw uprising, a rising that was abandoned by its allies, by saying that "there can be no just Europe without an independent Poland on its map," John Paul II is rejecting the categories of "national egotism" and the reduction of politics to a calculation of forces. He therefore introduces into politics an ethical factor; without this factor many countries have been able to become superpowers, but without it all nations inevitably turn into dwarfs. Our century has not spared us proof of this.

The pope's words spoken in Auschwitz in front of the Hebrew and Russian inscriptions were a logical consequence of his universal order of values, a message to his compatriots: "Never should a nation develop at the cost of another nation, at the price of another's enslavement, exploitation, and death." John Paul II expressed anew the thoughts of John XXIII and Paul VI, both as their successor and also as "the son of a nation which in both distant and recent history has experienced much torment from many sides." "But allow me," continued the pope, "not to name them. . . . We are standing in a place where we want to try to consider every nation and every man as a brother."

This "Golgotha of our time" naturally brought to mind memories of the victims of these systems of hate, of friends and relatives who had been gassed in the crematoria or turned into glass in Siberian camps. Right there, of all places, we were being asked to affirm belief in fraternity and unity rather than in hate and vengeance, justified though those feelings might be. We were told: "I speak in the name of those, all over the world, whose rights are forgotten and violated. I speak because I am obligated—we are all obligated—to the truth."

I am able to express this incomplete and clumsy reconstruction of a few of the threads linking the pope's homilies and speeches in the only language accessible to me, a secular language. It is also in this language that I raise other questions: Wasn't the cult of St. Stanislaus once abused for ends that had little to do with the defense of faith and much to do with the Church's worldly ambitions? Is the Church's hierarchical structure not threatened by its special role in the life of the nation? Did the Holy See always, with equal clarity, express its views on the political systems that created extermination and labor camps? I am asking these questions because I know that others who have been deeply affected by what John Paul II said are asking them as well.

What I found to be most moving—and most difficult to define—in the pope's sermons was the way he addressed each one of his listeners at the most personal level. Once one accepts the saying that "in our time Poland has become a land of unusually responsible testimony," one must ask whether we can really handle these "enormous tasks and obligations." Or more precisely: Can I handle them?

I was told: "Man is a rational and free being, he is conscious, autonomous, and responsible, he can and should seek the truth. He can and should make choices. . . . This historic process of man's awareness and choices is closely connected with the living traditions of his nation, in which the words of Christ, the testimony of the gospel, Christian culture, and customs founded on faith, hope, and love have had broad repercussions through generations. . . . Can one push away all of this? Can one say no? Can one reject Christ and all that he has contributed to mankind's history? Of course one can. Man is free. Man . . . can say no to Christ. But the fundamental question then is this: Is one allowed to? And 'allowed to' in the name of what? What argument of reason, what value of will and of the heart can one use with oneself and with those one is close to, with one's fellow-Poles, and with the nation . . . to say no to all that by which we have been living for a thousand years?" Therefore: Am I allowed to reject this culture based on Christian values, on faith, love, and hope?

Anyone's reply to this most important question of a man's life risks sounding a little false. Everyone should answer it for himself and to himself. Because I believe that this system of values is rejected not only by those who continually violate human rights because of their positions, or by those who permit them to do so by remaining silent and following in Pontius Pilate's footsteps, but also by those who declare solidarity with these values, but defend them by way of dishonorable methods.

I will not here make a list of those methods. Let me just say that when I listened to John Paul II's homily in Cracow, I had a strange feeling. When the pope asked the faithful Catholics "never to forsake Him," he was also addressing me: a pagan.

He was urging me to avoid those dishonorable methods.

June, 1979

// Maggots and Angels 1979

//   When I finished reading Piotr Wierzbicki's essay, my first reactions were both enchantment and envy—envy in particular because it was not I who had written the "Treatise on Maggots."[1] How many times have I sharpened my pen, issued threats, and launched fiery tirades, driven to despair by the "maggoty" behavior of my fellow men. But each time I ended up writing nothing. Not only because I did not have enough talent for it but also because as soon as my ardor left me, I would feel a certain falseness behind these emotions. It was only after reading Wierzbicki's essay that I began to understand the nature of this falseness and became capable of framing my own opinion on it.

Wierzbicki writes: "We will leave it to the historians to discover the forebears of maggots from past eras." Since I feel that I have certain connections with the historian's profession, I will allow myself to supplement his essay with a few remarks.

The genealogy of the "maggot" phenomenon should be sought in political situations in which foreign domination over the Polish nation had become a chronic reality, when all hope for armed defense of national values had become completely illusory, and compromise of

---

1. Piotr Wierzbicki's the "Treatise on Maggots," published together with Michnik's reply in the September 1979 issue of the uncensored quarterly *Zapis*, was an attack on the conformity of Polish intellectuals.

some sort with the partitioning power had become indispensable for preserving the very existence of the nation. The issue of what the permissible limits of a compromise were became a daily subject for discussions among people who wanted to live and act properly within the conquered country. Full acceptance of the compromise formula was seen to result in moral and spiritual capitulation. Full rejection of this formula, on the other hand, would only lead to a more or less heroic isolation. In the period of partitions, compromises and difficult choices were our daily bread. Let us list just a few of them as examples.

There was Hugo Kołłątaj, a man whom we venerate today, with full justification. He was one of the authors of the May 3 [1791] Constitution, a leading ideologue of the Camp of the Reform, an ardent patriot, and virtually a symbol of the Poles' undefeatable striving for sovereignty, one of the organizers of the Kościuszko insurrection, for which he was to pay with eight years in an Austrian jail after the insurrection was defeated.

Some fragments of Kołłątaj's biography, however, allow the historian to classify this author of *Anonymous Letters* as belonging among the maggot's ancestors. When in the course of the Russo-Polish war (1791–1792), victory for Russia began to seem inevitable, Kołłątaj not only succeeded in convincing King Stanisław August to sign the Targowica Confederacy, but he also joined in doing so himself. Although he did emigrate two days later and immediately began to organize a patriots' conspiracy, although his gesture had no practical influence and Targowica cost him his estates as well as his benefices, no one can remove the fact of his having signed the Targowica document from the pages of history. Many people, among them Walerian Kalinka, judged Kołłątaj severely. In his *Genealogy of Today,* Aleksander Świętochowski wrote that Kołłątaj "cared above all for his position, his estates, and his profits. When these were endangered, he secretly joined Targowica, leaving the country in the hope that he would manage to deceive his friends, win over his adversaries, and regain his properties." Świętochowski further cites the Russian ambassador's opinion of Kołłątaj: "He left for Cracow and is attempting to join our party. Anyone can buy him." Kołłątaj himself responded to all this in a letter to a friend in September 1792: "I am not ashamed that I wanted to join Targowica, because I wanted to do it as a free man, without any constraints, because I wanted to do it with a completely different goal in mind, in order to save many good things, not the way it is being presented today. So as the future learns more about it, it will of course become obvious that I was not so blind, so enamored of my own ideas, that I would not come to the rescue of the Motherland and serve her, even at such a critical juncture."

Thus Kołłątaj was trying to save "what could be saved," to salvage a remnant of the reforms, even if this involved cooperation with characters such as Szczęsny Potocki. From a historical perspective the illusory nature of Kołłątaj's calculations is striking. I personally believe, however—as did Wacław Tokarz—that Kołłątaj's mistake lay elsewhere—in that he failed to understand that "a man of his stature is not allowed to walk along roads where, at best, second-rate diplomats tread." I also agree, however, with Tokarz when he says that "Kołłątaj . . . should be judged from the point of view of those conditions in which he was forced to act. These included the fall of the Commonwealth . . . and the resulting tightening of the already suffocating foreign dog-collar . . . and the temporary weakening of the national character. . . . In such a situation," Tokarz concluded, "the practical politician, if he really does aim to save the nation, cannot be expected to walk the straightest path."

There was Stanisław Staszic. He was the author of the famous *Remarks on the Life of Jan Zamoyski* and *Warnings for Poland,* and for many years he was president of the Society of the Friends of Learning and made great contributions to our science and culture. We are right to keep alive his memory and to quote his motto about work: "Not for today but for the benefit and use of future generations." But this venerated Staszic fits perfectly into this species of the ancestors of the maggots. He favored the radical program of reform in the era of the Four-year Semj (he saw in it a chance for defending Poland's sovereignty), but in the period of the Congress Kingdom of Poland he lost hope of defeating Russia. He became a forerunner of the program of organic work[2] and acted within the limits marked by the kingdom's

---

2. In partitioned Poland "organic" and "insurrectionist" were the two extremes of the political choice available. "Organic" work consisted of steadily and responsibly strengthening and building up Polish industry and agriculture, and avoiding any insurrectional acts.

political and legal status. He believed that the resolutions of the Congress of Vienna served the Polish national interest best, and he viewed the risking of the status quo obtained from that Congress by various young conspirators as extreme recklessness.

One night in 1818 the public booed the Great Prince Constantine's favorite during a play. Constantine, enraged, prohibited booing during theater performances. The public saw this as a violation of the Constitution, and the press vehemently criticized the decree. In response the prince imposed censorship on the press. This act was signed by none other than the then Deputy Secretary of State Stanisław Staszic. The public was infuriated by Staszic's deed. The opposition deputies demanded that he be taken to court for violating the Constitution. Staszic bitterly complained to Koźmian: "They take us to court, we who have been making sacrifices for our country and for their sons, who have been putting a barrier before unbridled pens and tongues and are thereby saving our country from all the misery that would otherwise be brought on by carelessness and stupidity. No, a nation that uses lessons from the past in this way, that does not understand the difference between liberty and licentiousness, a nation that is so much in love with anarchy, that appreciates merit in this fashion and persecutes persons of merit— such a nation cannot long exist, for it is jeopardizing and will destroy its fate, its constitution, its freedom, and the future of its children."

I have no intention of standing up for Staszic. On the contrary, I side with his critics, the deputies of the "Kalisz opposition." But I emphatically want to make the reader aware that Staszic's conflict with the Kalisz group members (who would themselves soon be accused by radical youths of compromising too much) was not necessarily a quarrel between the maggot and the nonmaggot, that both sides were right in some respects, and that both sides included people of great merit in the history of our nation amongst their ranks, people who are much respected today.

Indeed, the Kalisz group was right to declare that the imposition of censorship was glaringly and inadmissibly unconstitutional. But Staszic was right, too, when he tried to explain that some kind of a compromise with Prince Constantine was a necessary precondition for continuing work "for the benefit and use of future generations" and that the ban on booing the prince's favorite was, after all, not the harshest limitation on civil rights, worth brandishing the sword against Russia.

And finally Maurycy Mochnacki was also partly right when, a few years later, he explained to both the followers of Staszic and of the Kalisz group simultaneously: "Even if we were to lose this Poland as we have it today, it would be better to execute her than to send to the scaffold the very intention of rebuilding her whole and independent."

The disagreements were violent and the differences fundamental between those who favored and those who opposed accommodation, between legalists and conspirators, between organicists and insurrectionists. In the heat of discussion those who advocated radical actions always obliterated the difference between betrayal of nation, accommodation, and organic activity, showing a tendency to reduce all these different types of behavior to a common denominator: greed. Only time would smooth out the edges and permit an evaluation of the effectiveness of various forms of resistance against the misery of foreign domination. It also became possible with time to see the complementary nature of some of these opposites.

To state it more clearly: there existed different ways of fighting for the Polish cause, and they varied in their effectiveness. Those who took part in the armed insurrections were not the only ones fighting for the nation's existence. At times it was accommodation which brought good results, at other times legal opposition; still other times the people were virtually condemned to organic work. If at the time of Kościuszko or of the Polish legions in the Napoleonic wars, or of the "November night" [November 23, 1830], the tactic of rising up made sense (and I believe that it did, even though this is still questioned even today), it is nevertheless likewise certain that the insurrectionist conspiracies in the kingdom of Poland during the era of Governor Paskevich were in all probability political nonsense. We identify most closely with the tradition of uprisings. And no wonder. Without this tradition we would be a different nation today—a more submissive one, far easier to subjugate. It makes sense, then, that the Poles' spiritual self-image is based on personages such as Kościuszko, Prądzyński, Traugutt, and Piłsudski. But what would our national consciousness look like without all the other people who sought out different roads? Without Staszic and Stanisław Potocki, without the Hôtel Lambert and the Galician conservatives, without Świętochowski and Spasowicz?

The profiles of the insurrectionists stimulate the imagination and emotions much more. An attack from the battle of Samosierra is more photogenic than the tedious organization of education or the modernization of agriculture, not to mention the construction of a network of sanitary facilities. But let us remember that we would not have been able to organize our statehood had it not been for the work done in the spirit of "organicism" and "accommodation," especially in Galicia. And let us also remember that our grandfathers often had to pay a high price for their decision to undertake these tasks, risking moral reproach from their antagonists.

My historical supplement would not be complete if I failed to mention the ancestors of the current maggots in the era of the Second Republic (1918–1939). The attitudes discussed by Wierzbicki always result from compromising between conscience and service to an imposed authority. But these authorities do not need to be foreign and do not necessarily need to be imposed from the outside. Was not Thomas Mann's letter to Walter von Mole, written in September 1945, a fiery accusation of German maggots? And Solzhenitsyn's remarks about *obrazovanshchina?*[3] And, finally, Antoni Słonimski's open letter to Wacław Sieroszewski and Julian Kaden about the question of Brześć?[4]

Słonimski wrote: "I did not believe, and I had the right not to believe, the rumors about ill treatment and torture of the imprisoned political adversaries. . . . The accounts given in the questions asked in parliament surpassed anything that one might have imagined. . . . I therefore believe that writers who have tied and still tie their activities to the ruling camp . . . should stand up and condemn in public these despicable and base acts. . . . Wacław Sieroszewski and Kaden-Bandrowski occupy leading positions in our professional associations. Therefore, the public has its eyes turned in their direction. I believe

3. Alexandr Solzhenitsyn attacked the new Soviet intelligentsia—"the schooled" stratum of the Soviet society—as semieducated, servile "smatterers" (in *From under the Rubble,* 1974).
4. In September 1930, at Józef Piłsudski's orders, many leaders of the Center-Left Coalition, among them some of the most prominent Polish parliamentarians, were arrested. They were held in military prison in the Brześć fortress and severely mistreated.

that it was the duty of these very writers, since they are trusted both by the government and by the public, to take an open and decisive stand on this issue that is so important and painful to us all. . . . A writer on social issues, a leading writer of the victorious political camp, who remains silent on the issue of Brześć, alarms me so much that I feel justified in challenging him here and now."

Słonimski's letter speaks volumes for the shock experienced by the majority of the population, especially those democratic circles that backed the Piłsudski camp, following the Brześć affair. These circles found it almost impossible to believe the stories that were emerging from behind the prison's walls. When these stories were confirmed, they found themselves facing a dramatic choice.

We must try to understand their position. These people had spent years firmly believing in the correctness of the political path chosen by the chief architect of national sovereignty, Józef Piłsudski. It is not easy to revise such staunch beliefs overnight. After all it was none other than Antoni Słonimski who had initially attacked the opposition's press campaign against the imprisonment of their leaders in Brześć. And even after the letter to Kaden and Sieroszewski (which I have just quoted) was written, even after Słonimski had become deeply involved in a conflict with those who had organized the Brześć operation, his feuilleton in *Wiadomości Literackie,* proof of his first impulsive reaction, remains on the pages of Polish intellectual history. I have often talked about this subject with Słonimski. He would tell me about the drama of those days, about the great respect that his friends and associates had for Piłsudski's people, about the difficult partings with old friends (Matuszewski, Beck, and, most important, Wieniawa). And Słonimski would explain to me that although he himself broke off relations with the *sanacja*[5] regime, not all those who favored it were scoundrels or conformists. Many of the regime's followers served Poland, made sacrifices, and did what they honestly considered to be for its good. Indeed, can one so easily and unequivocally dismiss all those who in that period defended the government and justified its—admittedly disgraceful—actions? Among those who did so were Tadeusz Hołówko

---

5. Sanacja is the post-1926-coup regime in Poland whose name comes from the intended "cure" (sanatio) of the rotting political atmosphere of parliamentary democracy.

and Walery Sławek, Jan Lechoń and Kazimierz Wierzyński, Eugeniusz Kwiatkowski and Stefan Starzyński. All these people have unquestionably rendered such great services that they deserve in-depth consideration and not simplistic invective.

Nevertheless, it was only many years later that Słonimski shared this "angerless wisdom" with me. At that time people used quite a different tone to formulate their opinions. We can read for instance in Wincenty Witos's memoirs that "Mr. Beck is a traitor on the payroll of Hitler's Germany, while Mościcki is an ordinary character who abuses his official position for his personal ends. The ruling clique is robbing the people and the nation of everything, pushing them into the abyss of poverty and degradation, while drowning themselves in pleasure and immorality. If these pests," Witos concluded, "do not change or resign, it is the duty and the right of the conscious society to use force; otherwise, it, too, will become an accomplice."

Can people who acquiesced to such a system of government thus not be considered the forerunners of maggots?

One of the reasons why I have brought up those distant times is that it makes it easier, I think, to overcome emotion and reflect calmly.

We should note, then, that reality is viewed in one way by the active oppositionist, in another by the intellectual who is giving an account of it, and still differently by the moralist who is judging the "visible world." Each of these points of view has its light and dark side. The oppositionist's view, for example, is inevitably tainted by one-sidedness; this helps him to reshape the world but prevents him from perceiving its many different dimensions. Moralism enables the individual to notice the ethical traps that lie in wait for anyone who takes on active responsibility, but it also favors an exaggerated cult of "clean hands." The spectator's view more easily encompasses an understanding of the complexity of the human condition but clouds the search for solutions to such questions as "What should be done?" and "What is good and what is evil?"

One's view of the world depends on whether one wants to change the world, understand it, or pass moral judgment upon it. I know that I am not going to alter this situation by writing this article; indeed, I cherish no such ambition. But I do want my adversary Piotr Wierzbicki to understand that if he completely gives in to thinking in moralistic or oppositional terms (which boil down to the same thing), he is bound to lose sight of an important segment of reality.

I believe that it is one thing to evaluate a given political system and another to judge individuals involved in it and their actions. One can render a negative balance sheet for the sanacja regime but at the same time appreciate the importance of the construction of the Gdynia port, a feat accomplished not by gnomes but by some members of the sanacja camp. People can be judged according to their achievement or by their intentions. When one judges by intentions, it is impossible to do so solely on the basis of a fragment of biography. Indeed, Stefan Starzyński's motivations, when he accepted the political program of OZON, appear different from his moral personality as seen through the prism of the heroic defense of Warsaw [in 1939] and his martyr's death.[6]

Or let us consider Eugeniusz Kwiatkowski. He was a politician who accepted the realities that were being challenged by those who opposed the sanacja camp. Why did he do it? One may suppose that Kwiatkowski often faced a difficult moral dilemma: he had to accept Brześć and the rigged elections if he wanted the Gdynia harbor or the Central Industrial Region to be built, if he wanted to have an effective influence on Poland's economic policies. And it may well be that he asked himself the question: Which is more important, to demonstrate for moral-political reasons against the lawlessness of Brześć or to build the port? And it may have been difficult for him to arrive at an answer.

I have to mention all these rather banal truths so that I can recall yet another platitude: one can take the side of Kwiatkowski's adversaries, of the anti-sanacja opposition, of Witos and Puzak for political and moral reasons, but one cannot fail to see the complexity of the whole picture. And when one touches on the delicate issue of judging people's intentions and motives, one must exercise great caution. I am deeply convinced that such an assessment should assume goodwill. That is, one should believe what people say about their own motivations and excuse the bad effects of good intentions rather than search for base motives. And, above all, one should understand the many different

6. Stefan Starzyński (1893–1943), last prewar mayor of Warsaw, executed by the Germans in a concentration camp. OZON, a Sanacja-sponsored Camp of National Unity, was a strongly progovernmental organization.

sides of the human condition and of human nature; one should remember that at times we are all inconsistent and pusillanimous. In such cases, one should attempt to understand why this happens.

It is important to remember these embarrassingly simple observations when one endeavors to discuss the intelligentsia's attitudes under the rule of the Leading System. The picture painted by Wierzbicki is clear-cut and unambiguous. According to him, Poland was ruled by Stalinist-Bierutist officials, and troops acting on behalf of the party and the Union of Polish Youth were smothering Polish learning. And that's it. In this schema, the whole dramatic aspect of the social and political reality is lost, and with it the fascinating panorama of defeat mixed with hope, reason with naiveté, fear with bravado, the dynamism of society with behind-the-scenes intrigues of Soviet advisers. As if in reply to the Stalinist primers which we were once force-fed, we now have here a primer à rebours, in which the colors are equally dense and bright and the worldview equally infantile.

Whoever is interested in the truth about that exceptional era—the truth about captive minds and devastated souls, the truth about the heroic nonconformity of some and the inquisitional ardor of others, and the Wallenrodian cunning[7] and apathy of still others—should not look for it in Wierzbicki's essay. How untrue is its picture of that epoch when one compares it with Kisiel's [Stefan Kisielewski] feuilletons or the stories of Jan Józef Szczepański, with Adolf Rudnicki's Clearances or Marian Brandys's Sons and Comrades, with the essays of Witold Kula and Czesław Miłosz or the prose of Maria Dąbrowska and Hanna Malewska. Wierzbicki writes that he drew his knowledge about maggots from his own book, The Circus (I admit that that is an excellent caricature of the Country That Loves the Country That Loves Peace). For me the most instructive book that has appeared in the past year is Kazimierz Brandys's Irreality. It is the fascinating story of a Polish intellectual whose initiation into adulthood consisted of being hit over

---

7. Konrad Wallenrod, the hero of an epic poem by Adam Mickiewicz, led to defeat the Teutonic troops of which he was commander to avenge their persecution of his native Lithuania. "Wallenrodism" is synonymous with trying to undermine the system from within.

the head by a member of an ONR[8] fighting squad on the grounds of his own university, and it paints a suggestive picture of the complexity of Polish history. Brandys describes a situation in which the narrator is summoned to the security office because of his activity in the resistance movement at the same time as he is becoming familiar with the text of a decree on land reform. Is this peculiar entanglement of events the invention of maggots, another prevarication of "maggoty" intellect that loves to repeat the refrain that the truth lies somewhere in the middle?

Since I am writing principally about those people who have entered into compromise agreements with coercion I should mention in passing other people who at some point allowed themselves to be seduced by rightist or leftist totalitarian ideologies. I want to reassure potential polemicists that I am drawn to neither totalitarian ideologies nor to totalitarian practices. But I try to keep in mind that the Polish followers of totalitarian, quasi-fascist nationalism paid such a high price in blood during World War II that their intentions and motives need to be viewed in a different light. I am thinking of Stanisław Piasecki, Gajcy, Trzebiński, and Pietrzak. I am also thinking about Adam Doboszyński, who during his trial revealed the Stalinist methods of investigation and who even after his interrogation (which included torture) maintained an unusual dignity in the courtroom. He was murdered in accordance with the sentence passed by a Polish communist court in 1949, having been falsely and disgracefully accused of collaborating with the Nazis, and he has not been rehabilitated to this day.

I am also thinking of one of my professors, a prewar activist of the ONR-Falanga, who reached out to me at a difficult moment and spent long hours explaining to me the complicated story of his generation and his associates. This did not bring me any closer to fascist ideology, but it made me understand the roots of its popularity.

I have also tried to understand those people who, seduced by the totalitarian power's leftist rhetoric, became tools in the hands of the directors and the mass-production manipulators of "socialism's great construction sites." We know from their writings, in which they tried

8. ONR (National Radical Camp) was an extreme nationalist and fascist party in prewar Poland.

to make amends, that they lived through a tragedy. Their fate, a fragment of the spiritual biography of the Polish intelligentsia, should serve as a lesson and a warning. These people fell victim to deceit and self-deceit. Were they the first? Or the last?

Let us look at a fragment of one such text that endeavors to settle accounts:

> We harassed our people. Your office harassed our Motherland. . . . We continued to march on in lawlessness. . . . We told our brothers to rejoice or to grieve, to love or to hate, often without ourselves feeling the pain or joy that we were summoning. The number of those calling was so great that it multiplied the summons, which were often contradictory. . . . We, who were issuing the calls, faithless as we were, unable to bear the solitude in which we confronted ourselves and which revealed our own nothingness to ourselves, attacked our brothers. We inflicted suffering on them. . . . We deprived our brothers of the last freedom, respected by all tyrannies, the freedom of silence. . . . Because anyone who disagreed with us in any way at any time, who did not serve as our echo, was declared a rebel. We imposed the saddest of rules. . . . We began to resemble a pack of wolves. We preferred to stay in Koło and reign in it as if it were an inherited village—even though the villagers were slaves—and to be masters at any cost.

"Koło" is not the name of a Communist party cell and the author of this text was not a disillusioned communist. These words were written by Adam Mickiewicz after he broke off with the Koło of the followers of Andrzej Towiański.[9]

> They lived by the aurora
> and gave darkness.
> They lived by the idea
> and parted with the people.
> They lived by their dreams
> and lies became their daily bread.

9. Andrzej Towiański, mystic prophet, exerted considerable influence on Adam Mickiewicz in his later years.

And this was not written by one of Towiański's followers. The above is a quotation from Adam Ważyk's "Critique of Poem for Adults."[10]

Why do I bring up these texts, juxtaposing them in such a peculiar manner? Because I am overcome with dread when I think of the intellectual shallowness of opinions about the past, of judgments that are disconcertingly popular and yet pathetically stereotyped, that are a mixture of primitivism, ignorance, and ill will. I am not applying this characterization to Wierzbicki so much as to all those who see his "Treatise on Maggots" as the Bible of moral norms and the encyclopedia of knowledge about contemporary Poland.

In my opinion the reality of the early post-World War II years was incomparably more complex than one would think on the basis of his extremely simplistic formulas about the "reds" and their intellectual servants, the maggots.

That period is among the most painful and mendacious in our history. Perhaps it was painful precisely because it was so mendacious. I will set aside for another occasion a much-needed analysis of the period and limit myself to only a few fragmentary remarks here.

Poland had been bled weak and the war had been resolved at the Yalta conference. The postwar reality was determined by the international balance of power and not by the amount of blood spilled or the heroism of antifascist resistance. The Western Allies had abandoned Poland. What courses of action were left to the population?

I have often pondered this dilemma. I have tried many times to locate in recent history the exact point at which an error or a wrong choice in Polish policy foredoomed the nation to its subsequent misery. And I cannot find it. As I've examined the wartime and postwar history of the Polish cause, I've had the feeling that Clio, the muse of history, must have turned her back on Poland, as if she didn't even give it the slightest chance of interrupting the stream of misery or of finding ways to emerge from its national oppression. All the different trends in Polish politics lost.

10. Publication of Adam Ważyk's *Poem for Adults* in July 1955 opened the new phase in post-Stalinist liberalization of Poland.

I have great respect for the achievements of the postwar emigration, for the people who did not return to their native country in order to be able to remind the world about the fate of captive Poland; for the people who spent years living out of suitcases, waiting for their turn at armed action, and then made a gigantic effort to create that great framework of national culture that is so important today for the young generation in Poland. Emigration, however, could not be made into a political program for the entire nation, and the short-term political diagnoses and prognoses of the émigrés proved false.

It was possible to be totally "steadfast" only in exile. The leaders of the underground in Poland, centered in the Council of National Unity (RJN), decided in early 1945 to accept the Yalta agreement. Sixteen underground leaders—including the government-in-exile's delegate to Poland, the chairman of RJN, and the commander of the Home Army—went to negotiate with representatives of the Soviet government. All of them were kidnapped and imprisoned in Lubyanka prison. As a direct consequence of this treacherous attitude of the Soviet government toward the Polish underground, the conspiratorial organization "Freedom and Independence" (WiN) was formed. I have great respect for the WiN people who already in 1945 took up the hard task of organizing an independent resistance movement, an effort to form a conspiracy aiming toward independence despite the changed circumstances that had become so much more difficult. They put their own freedom on the line, and often their lives, so as to bear witness to the continuing Polish longing for independence. I have the greatest admiration for the steadfast and heroic stand that Józef Rybicki took during the trial of the WiN leadership in January 1947. I know that with his every word he risked his life. But I have also attempted to understand those who acted differently and to respect their choices.

The "steadfast" émigrés wrote many bitter and critical words concerning the return to Poland of Karol Popiel, the leader of the Labor party. For many of the steadfast ones, to break off relations with the government-in-exile was tantamount to betraying Poland. Despite the far-reaching compromise that Mikołajczyk and Popiel chose, the Poles in Poland accepted the return of these émigrés with enthusiasm. That compromise consisted of recognizing the validity of a provisional government that included the communists, thereby cutting off the institutional continuity [of the Polish state], and of accepting the new territorial shape of the country. One of the leaders of the socialist movement, Zygmunt Zuławski, agreed to a similar policy. These people attempted to rescue whatever they could from the new reality, paying for it with compromise. They were accused of having taken up the struggle within boundaries dictated by their adversary—but no other boundaries existed. We should recall that the episcopate took a similar stand.

Mikołajczyk, together with the entire Peasant party, lost the battle for democracy because the battle could not be won against police force and harsh Soviet *diktat*. The Peasant party's struggle, which lasted several years and for which its members paid in blood, will remain their glory and their historic achievement. But this does not change the fact that their political hopes for help from the West proved illusory.

The defense of "that which can be saved" was also the goal of the majority of the so-called licensed Polish Socialist party (PPS). Those who attempted to preserve the authenticity of self-management and of the cooperative movement were also defeated. Before this had transpired, they'd made many compromises and allowed their old fellow party members to be excommunicated; these included Puzak, Zaremba, Ciołkosz, and Żuławski. The tragedy and the perfidy of this system lay in precisely in how it pushed people whose honesty could not be questioned into behaving in morally ambiguous ways.

Everyone who became active in public life—intellectuals, artists, and social activists—witnessed some of these situations. Among such people were many who rendered services that are today questioned by no one. Let us remember that those who chose an active presence over internal emigration included Tadeusz Kotarbiński, Kazimierz Ajdukiewicz, Tadeusz Manteuffel, Kazimierz Wyka, Maria and Stanisław Ossowski, Maria Dąbrowska, Leon Schiller, Antoni Słonimski, and Jerzy Zawieyski. And I repeat that they all attempted to maintain a presence in the nation's life and to defend what seemed defensible.

Time passed and the Stalinist noose tightened increasingly around the neck of a nation already laid to waste and drained of its blood. Everyone had to answer the question: What is the limit of permissible compromise? How high a price may one pay for being allowed to continue lecturing, publishing, or practicing one's profession? For in totalitarian systems a price must always be paid for public presence, and here the price was going up. The conditions that were being dictated were accompanied by more or less veiled threats and blackmail.

I myself do not remember those times, but I know about them from various reports and documents. Today, after so many years, it is difficult to evaluate the particular choices made during that period, to find moral criteria that correspond to the reality of those times. I envy whoever knows of such moral criteria, but except for the proven and conscious harming of other persons, any other criterion seems shaky to me. How can one evaluate the attitude of Professor Manteuffel, the director of the Institute of History during the Stalinist period? Or the attitude of Professor Wyka? Or Maria Dąbrowska's, when one takes into account the obituary she wrote for Stalin? If Nadezhda Mandelstam is right in saying that silence face-to-face with totalitarian coercion is "a real crime against human kind," then nearly everyone was guilty of that crime. Even the noblest people were condemned to passivity and silence. Only the inhabitants of prisons and camps were excluded. "Blessed prisons!" wrote Solzhenitsyn. Only within them could a person become free of complicity with this damned criminal machine.

Aleksander Wat once wrote that there is only one answer to the question of how intellectuals who live in countries ruled by Stalin should behave. It is the Shakespearean answer: "They should die."

Perhaps it is the correct answer. But I believe that this is an answer that one can only give for oneself, a measure that one can apply only to oneself, a sacrifice one can ask only of oneself. Anyone who demands such an answer to this question from others is arbitrarily giving himself the right to determine the fates of others. This usually ends badly.

What I have just written can lead to the conclusion that I do not favor excessive moral rigor. I also do not like the practice of judging intellectuals who became involved in Stalinism, because this practice does not take into account earlier or later parts of their biographies. Let us imagine what would happen if one of these moralists assessed Andrzej Kmicic[11] exclusively on the basis of that period of his life when

11. Jacek Bocheński replied in *Zapis* 2 (1977), to the sociologist Jan Szczepański's article "The Faith of Intellectuals" (*Kultura*, February 20, 1977), in which the sociologist criticized the tendency of the intellectuals to judge and protest the decisions of those in power.

he served the Radziwiłłs and was thereby causing harm to the Common-wealth whether he liked it or not. Or imagine the moralist who insists on recalling that Adam Czartoryski was the Russian emperor's minister and omits such details as his later membership in the rebels' government or as one of the leaders of the Great Emigration.

Natalia Kicka, the general's wife, recorded in her diaries the story of Stanisław Sołtyk, which is worth retelling. At the time of the Confed-eration of Bar [1768], the Russian ambassador Repnin organized the kidnapping of Polish senators (including Bishop Kajetan Sołtyk) and contrived a ruse toward this end. He went to Stanisław Sołtyk, the bishop's nephew, and "with words smooth as silk obtained an affidavit to the effect that the bishop suffered attacks of dangerous madness. The bishop had reprimanded his nephew for his crazy pranks, and so the nephew avenged himself by signing the document that Repnin gave him. And when Bishop Sołtyk asked the Muscovites who came to imprison him the justification for his loss of liberty, they replied by referring to the public good and showed him his nephew's affidavit. 'Let the hand that signed this wither away,' exclaimed the bishop. And the man's hand did indeed wither away."

But then events took a different turn. The fainthearted nephew became an ardent patriot, one of the leaders—along with Walerian Łukasiński—of the conspiracy for independence during the era of the Congress Kingdom of Poland. He was jailed along with other con-spirators. "In prison," wrote Kicka, "Stanisław Sołtyk suffered greatly, both morally and physically, because of his palsied hand."

So much for the general's wife. We know from other writings that many of Sołtyk's sympathetic contemporaries did not spare the jailed conspirator biting remarks about his youthful sins.

When I read the newspapers that came out immediately after the war, filled with reproaches about people's ugly *prewar* past, intended to discredit those who proved their metamorphoses with their own blood; when I read the aggressive attacks on people who were involved in Stalinism and who then spent years being harassed and persecuted in order to prove the earnestness of their ideological transformation—I remember the story of Sołtyk, who is rightly venerated on the pages of historical monographs. I think about this with sadness: Will we always be capable of rehabilitating people only after they die?

Of course, there were other people who became involved in Stalinism, mere careerists and lowly informers as well as cruel torturers who tormented the innocent. We will gain the fullest knowledge about such matters when the political police open their archives to the public. Wierzbicki paints a picture of that future time, saying that "one day a great crowd will march out into the streets and everyone will have to give an account of what he has done for Poland." I must admit that Wierzbicki's vision does not appeal to me. I would not like it if on the first day of freedom a huge mob were to come out into the streets to settle accounts with everyone for what they have and have not done for Poland. It smells like lynching to me. A crowd all excited about its newly regained liberty is capable of lynching but not capable of an honest settling of accounts. Anyone who encourages such a crowd in its desire to settle accounts can only sew the seeds of hatred. So it is better to leave accounts to historians.

Regardless of what may be written in "A Treatise on Maggots," neither university presidents nor editors, externally servile but in their hearts "pro-Western" or "counterrevolutionary," led easy lives during the Stalinist era. They were closely watched, continuously suspected of lingering "bourgeois consciousness." Overzealous propagandists viewed them as disguised defenders of the past. Such agitators saw the world in very simple terms: The capitalist system, the cradle of fascism, was the number one enemy of mankind's happiness. Anyone who chose the slightest compromise with the rotten culture of the capitalist West was by definition the enemy.

This simplistic view of the world, the ease with which these agitators passed judgments, their political fanaticism brimming over with intolerance, at one point in those years inspired a young but already widely published author to write the following: "For the bourgeois writers, settling accounts with German fascism became an escape from political commitment, and worse, [their antifascism] turned into a cover for imperialist ideology! . . . We should reconsider the value of those works that in the years of nationalistic deviation we labeled 'antifascist' or 'moralizing,' thinking that these labels would suffice forever. We should dismantle this overused platform on which Stefan Żołkiewski [a communist] and Jerzy Żawieyski [a conservative Catholic] embraced."

This was from Tadeusz Borowski's pamphlet about maggots.

Stefan Kisielewski reacted with a letter that should be quoted here. "I believe," he wrote to Borowski, "that you are a writer of great talent and of equally great ignorance. Your worldview was shaped by occupied Warsaw, by the hell of Auschwitz, by wretched occupied Germany. This is frighteningly little. You remind me of the Malaysian girl in one of Conrad's novels: she reads the only local paper that reprints dispatches from the European dailies and comes to the conclusion that Europe must all be a great slaughterhouse. . . . But I doubt whether I will be able to stop your descent of the intellectual slope down which you have been sliding. I do, however, want to have a clean conscience: I warned you."

It would be mere demagoguery to claim that Wierzbicki has been repeating the same accusations against the same people who were once attacked by the fanatical proponents of the Stalinist line. I am capable of distinguishing between a text that serves the rulers of this world from one that ardently protests against conformity and hypocrisy. I also have no intention of simplistically showing up Tadeusz Borowski, who paid for his choice of Stalinist ideology first by squandering his talent and then by committing suicide. I only want to convince any potential fans of "A Treatise on Maggots" that abandoning a worldview that encompasses the complexity of human obligations and achievements and replacing it with a crystal-clear picture can lead to simplistic judgments and harmful verdicts. I don't know if I will succeed in persuading them, but I can repeat Kisiel's words: I warned you.

Please believe me: I can really understand Wierzbicki's anger and protest against the processes Miłosz has labeled "moral decay" and "Pétainism." But I can also understand the bitterness of those who spent years clenching their teeth and suffering humiliations and yet created a piece of our intellectual reality, preserving and restoring old values, building new ones—only today to be dismissed as maggots.

It is nonsensical to ask the satirist to render cautious and balanced judgments. The very idea of a satire assumes radical opinions. I hold no grudge against Wierzbicki for using the term *maggot* and thereby sharpening the contours of reality but only for his inability to identify those contours due to his antimaggot passion.

One wouldn't gather as much from reading Wierzbicki's text, but Poland's reality differs fundamentally from the realities of our neighboring countries, and we are less susceptible to the processes of Sovietization. Why?

There are various factors that make us different: historical tradition, the Catholic Church and the courageous albeit realistic policies of the episcopate, the countryside which has withstood collectivization, and finally the incessant pressure of the people. This pressure has manifested itself at times in violent explosion (Poznań–1956, March 1968, December 1970, Radom–1976) but more frequently through silent, dogged, daily resistance. This resistance is exemplified, for instance, in the refusal to make a denunciation. It permeates the mental atmosphere of a good part of our intellectual life: lectures and seminars at universities, doctoral research and publication of learned treatises, novels, volumes of poetry, essays, meetings of the Union of Writers or the PEN-Club, films and plays, museums, concerts, and art openings. All this is usually the work of people who do not sign protest letters or make spectacular gestures of opposition. But it is also thanks to them that we in Poland have been breathing a different spiritual air. This spiritual air—this tissue of culture and national consciousness that is growing daily, invisibly—is not simply the result of reading *Zapis* or *Biuletyn Informacyjny* or publishing in the Independent Publishing House (NOWa) but is the outcome of *the totality* of Polish accomplishments.

This totality causes envy in citizens of the other states of the "camp" who visit Poland. They are envious not only of KOR and TKN and the uncensored publications but also of our official ones (not only *Tygodnik Powszechny* or *Więź* but also *Twórczość, Pamiętnik Literacki,* and even *Polityka*); they are envious of our full churches and efficiently run centers of religious instruction, Dejmek's theater productions, Wajda's films, the appearance of our streets with their well-dressed women. It is due to all these factors that we have maintained our identity and our ability to oppose the process of Sovietization.

I would be the last one to say that our situation is satisfactory and our aspirations fulfilled. The uncensored press constantly stresses the distance we have yet to travel. But we should sometimes consider our situation, our infirmities and our miseries from the perspective of dangers and not solely from the perspective of demands and goals. These dangers include the national fates of our neighbors to the east—Lithuanians, Byelorussians, Ukrainians. These peoples must fight at the most elementary levels for the continued existence of their languages, religions, and national cultural monuments. We must appreciate these differences, and appreciate the various alternative fates of nations under communist regimes. We should also consider the circumstances that determine the most fundamental difference between the situations of the Russian and the Polish defenders of human rights. To put it briefly: although the police manage to poison our lives, we in Poland feel strong and are strong because we enjoy the moral and material support of a broad strata of our society. We enjoy the support of people whose temperaments make them neither politicians nor heroes, people who do not want to give up their careers or relatively stable family lives, who rarely choose to sign a protest letter, but who, I am convinced, determined the success of actions in defense of workers in Radom and Ursus. Were it not for such people, it would be difficult to conceive of independent publishing.

I have a different attitude toward these people "between the government and the opposition." When a learned professor of sociology, in reaction to the intellectuals' protests against the tortures in Radom, writes a sophisticated theoretical study in which he disparages the protests of these intellectuals, I am infuriated just as much as the author of "A Treatise on Maggots," and I read with great satisfaction Jacek Bocheński's penetrating reply to such lucubrations.[12] But if this professor, instead of practicing a comparative historical psychoanalysis on the protesting intellectuals, were to have taken advantage of his parliamentary immunity and gone to Radom to attend one of the trials in order to learn firsthand about the functioning of the courts, and then prepared a report for the government about what he had seen there without joining in the protest action, would Wierzbicki still call his behavior "maggoty"? I would not. Instead, I would be happy that rational outlooks are surfacing in the power elite, that the ruling groups are learning how to define their own interests correctly, that I can find among my adversaries even this one trace of political culture. So far there have been very few such indications. But let us remember that if we give up

---

12. Andrzej Kmicic, hero of Henryk Sienkiewicz's *Trilogy*, became a true patriot by going through a long series of trials and errors.

hope for such an evolution, the alternative scenario can only encompass new violent confrontations between the government and the people. Every such confrontation has the potential to become a national tragedy. It is our collective duty to avoid such situations, because they could mean that the whole nation, all Poles including the authorities, might be forced to pay an inordinately high price for their lack of responsibility on these matters.*

The above arguments should, of course, by no means be interpreted as encouraging anyone to participate in intraparty contests; I share Wierzbicki's skepticism on this matter. But it is worth remembering that we live in a society where hundreds of thousands of active people belong to the Communist party. Often, this is the price paid for participating in public life, holding managerial jobs, and so on. Wierzbicki is allowed to believe that this price is too high, that it is not worth paying and ought not to be paid, and indeed I share this belief. But we live and will live among people who think otherwise. We must learn to live with them and teach them to live with us. We must learn the difficult art of compromise, without which authentic pluralism will not be possible. We must also observe the norms of political culture vis-à-vis the government, even if the government itself does not observe them. Only then will we manage to confront totalitarian pressure with dignity.

Wierzbicki describes a conversation between an oppositionist and a maggot about signing a protest letter. He mocks a whole list of "maggoty" excuses and hoaxes. I read his arguments with mixed emotions. I have watched such scenes more than once and I must admit that Wierzbicki's description is masterful. But . . . I myself have ad-

---

*I have expressed a similar opinion on several occasions, including in the article "A New Evolutionism." That article evoked a polemical reply from Professor Jan Drewnowski, who in the Paris *Kultura* accused me of seeking an agreement with the communist authorities. In another article [in *Zeszyty Historyczne*] Professor Drewnowski developed this idea into an argument that the Soviets already intervened in Poland in 1944–45, and that another intervention would change nothing. Would a new Soviet armed intervention in Poland really change nothing? I am leaving this question to the readers. For my part I would simply express the opinion that the interventions by Soviet armies in Hungary in 1956 and Czechoslovakia in 1968 did indeed change much. Terribly much . . . [Author's note]

vised several people against signing such letters because I believed that certain persons and institutions of public life must be preserved.

Wierzbicki does not have to convince me that this type of argument—the preservation of an institution—is misused too often. Instead, let him convince me that Marian Brandys's signature on a petition is worth more than his epic about light cavalrymen finding its way onto the shelves of bookstores and libraries, or that the signatures of Dejmek or Wajda are more important than their plays and films. Bless those times when one can sign protest letters *as well as* publish books or direct films. But we know that often one has to choose. And I have no easy formula for such choices. I envy anyone who knows such a formula. But I am a little bit afraid of them as well. I myself have taken part in organizing several protest letters. I can appreciate their importance. The intellectuals who signed them accomplished an extraordinary thing. Risking their professional stability, the possibility of being published, and so on, they raised their voices to defend imponderables, to defend a national culture in the process of being destroyed, to defend people who had been hurt and humiliated. Those petitions were proof of the awakening of the national consciousness, of the rebirth among the intelligentsia of a sense of responsibility for the shape of Polish aspirations. They articulated these aspirations.

But such letters only constituted the tip of the iceberg of Polish ambitions, which then—as now—have taken many different forms. This is why it is sectarian nonsense to throw all those who think and act differently into that capacious sack labeled "maggots." It can be done only by someone who believes that he has discovered the sole moral and correct road to sovereignty and democracy. I well know this type of "truth bearer" from history. And that is why I am afraid.

I share Wierzbicki's negative attitude toward the dangerously popular idea that most oppositional actions are in fact provocations by the police. This is not to say, however, that the police never use provocation. Recently, fliers signed by the group "Self-defense of Faith" were distributed in a church in Łódź. In these fliers, alongside patriotic and religious declarations, one could read a bitter attack on churchmen fond of new ideas, such as Cardinal Wojtyła and Archbishop Gulbinowicz, who were accused of popularizing pornography and cooperating with "cosmopolitan" institutions such as KOR. Does one have to be a maggot to ask about the origins of those peculiar fliers?

Wierzbicki makes fun of the frequent argument that "now is a completely inappropriate moment to start this particular action." I have heard dozens of such excuses. But I would admit that if today (December 6, 1978) someone came up to me asking me to sign a petition demanding that the Soviet armies leave Poland, I would refuse to sign it, even though I like this demand, and even though I would risk being called a maggot. It is in fact not the appropriate time.

I learned from the "Treatise" that maggots dislike "nationalism" and have even been infected with this dislike by some oppositionists. The swift dispatch with which Wierzbicki resolves this whole problem I suppose means that any quibbles as to which group of opinions and emotions he calls "nationalism" would simply be in bad taste. But, risking audacity in polite society, let me inquire: Is striving for independence equivalent to nationalism? If so, then the dispute is only a matter of definition. But "nationalism" can also be the name of a specific political doctrine or—occasionally—a line of thought that establishes its values from the standpoint of so-called national egotism. The fact that communists attempt to fight nationalism, albeit less and less frequently, does not necessarily mean that it is the duty of the oppositionist and the partisan of sovereignty to adhere to a specific political doctrine or—further—to an ideology of hatred or contempt toward other nations.*

Striving for independence in Georgia, Latvia, or Estonia is by no means equivalent to nationalism, but in Georgia or the Ukraine nationalism can tend toward a dumb obscurantism, a disease whose source can be easily understood but which poisons the circulation of the nation's spiritual life. One can understand the obsessive hatred of the Crimean Tartar toward all that is Russian: the language, Russian literature and music, and finally all Russians. It is difficult, however, not to see this attitude as a symptom of the sad disease of captivity.

---

*Let me note that Wierzbicki's comments that Husak was imprisoned by the communists for "Slovak nationalism" are a total fantasy. Husak was persecuted for defending Slovak national aspirations and the tradition of the Slovak uprising—which he did phrase in communist terminology. [Author's note]

In the many discussions about "A Treatise on Maggots," I heard, in response to critical voices, the remark that Wierzbicki is simply continuing the tradition of the great romantics, of Juliusz Słowacki who in his "Agamemnon's Grave" stigmatizes the weakness and faint-heartedness of Poles and not the oppression of the partitioning powers. This is an apt remark. "Flinging abuse at one's own nation is a moldy and dignified privilege of Polish literature," Jan Błoński has pertinently remarked. Indeed. Słowacki wrote about the "peacock and the parrot" and about the "unhappy land of the helots," but he also wrote:

> Although I know that these words will not resound long
> in the heart—where a thought does not stay even an hour . . .

He wrote in an apostrophe addressed to Poland:

> Curse, but my soul will chase you away
> Life a Fury—with whips made of snakes,
> For you are Prometheus's only son:
> The vulture is eating not your heart but your brains.

This is the gist of the matter. I am all for "slander" and "fouling," I am for lampoons and mockery—this is not where I differ with Wierzbicki. I am merely annoyed with the direction of his attack. I am annoyed that he brands intellectuals not for lack of thinking but for lack of gesture. This Polish—arch-Polish—adoration of gesture! "There is nothing that the Pole will lay down as eagerly on the Motherland's altar," wrote Brzozowski, "as his spiritual work. When it is necessary to show contempt and disrespect for the greatest intellectual dilemmas, 'civic conscience' speaks up inside us very loudly. When it comes to intellectual questions and the demands of intellectual honesty, the average Pole has more than courage, he has civic *cheek*."

How appropriate to our day. . . . I am afraid that one reaction to our captivity may consist in our becoming *slaves to gesture* and thereby scorning any artistic and intellectual values that cannot be directly translated into the language of politics. I am not talking about Piotr Wierzbicki here, who probably remains at a safe distance from these dangers. But he may inadvertently have created with his "Treatise" an ideology for all those whose "brains and not hearts are being eaten by the vulture." Oppositionists, who are being sought by the police and tormented with house searches, may learn from this text a contempt for those people to whom convictions, temperament, or merely fear dictate another life-style and a different way of serving the common cause. This is a danger that frequently appears in the histories of subjugated nations, and also in the history of Poland. For if the everyday life of the Pole who lived at the time of the partitions was—necessarily—filled with compromise, the didacticism and moralistic heroism of Polish literature were reactions to that condition. So the Pole had imprinted on his mentality a peculiar duality. The Polish people, ready to compromise in their everyday lives, when the call came could become courageous to the point of folly. At such times, literature would reign absolutely in their lives. "Politicians," writes Jan Błoński, "usually abandoned politicking or else turned into martyrs. . . . Martyrdom would become an alibi for baseness, the meanness of fathers would provoke in their sons a willingness to make sacrifices and vice versa."

The cult of martyrdom, of heroic sacrifice, created in the Polish tradition a beautiful but dangerous ethos. For the conspirator who had been formed by this ethos, jail was a daily reality, a part of the price to be paid for his entire uncommonly heroic life. The conspirator had to be prepared at all times to die heroically. This readiness, in conjunction with the romantic ethos, distorted his view of the world, favoring self-idealization. The conspirator who perceived conformists as resembling slaves found in himself and his friends the pathos and tragedy of the romantic heroes. Seeing maggots in the cowed population, he "angelized" himself and his friends, fighters for a sovereign and just Poland. The "angelic" character of the picture he had of himself led him—often subconsciously—to assign himself special rights.

The memoir written by Henryk Kamieński about Edward Dembowski illuminates this phenomenon. The castellan's radical son, a born conspirator, a man of great mind and fantastic courage, employed questionable methods in his attempts to create a national insurrection; he manipulated others, indulged in moral blackmail, and lied. He was granted the right to act in this way by his own sacrifice and his sacred goal: the radiant future. With this goal in mind, different generations of conspirators came to judge the world in a Manichean fashion: whatever served their goal was good; whatever obstructed it was evil; whoever did not take his place among the ranks of fighters for the right cause deserved disdain. Manicheanism has been the faith of saints and inquisitors . . . Manicheanism has also been the curse of captive peoples.

One needed to be part saint and part inquisitor to stab Józef Miniszewski with a stiletto during the January Uprising because he had served Aleksander Wielopolski with his pen. One needed to deem oneself an angel to be able to shoot Teodor Bujnicki in Vilna in 1944 for the poems that he wrote—poems which were admittedly rather sordid—in honor of the occupying Soviet forces.

I am not hurling reckless accusations; the people who committed these murders were undoubtedly irreproachably honest and had heroic backgrounds. But the point is that they had no brakes; their Manichean view of human obligations would not allow them to abandon these actions. They were consistent. Frighteningly consistent. Their goal justified everything.

In 1914 once again young boys from the intelligentsia put away their books and notebooks and seized their guns to "save the Motherland." They were treated coolly and with distrust. They replied to this coolness with a song:

> We don't need your approbation
> Or your hearts, or your tears,
> The time when we appealed
> To your purses has passed. May a dog f—— you.

In this song there is a dangerous note of contempt, the mentality of people who, by "placing their lives at the stake" for an ideal Poland dreamt up by the bards and conspirators, feel they've earned the right to heap contempt upon the real Poland, the Poland of ordinary people. This mentality bore fruit in the extreme courage and the magnificent armed achievements of the legions. But it also bore fruit in an utter disregard for the safety of other people and their aspirations. This is why, when we listen to this song today, we hear in it that very disquieting tone in which, a dozen years later, the orders to imprison the opposition members of parliament in Brześć were to be issued. One group of legionaries took to persecuting another group. Scorn toward others, whatever its cause, can have horrible consequences.

All those who know the history of the communist movement know this well. It is enough to recall Broniewski's poem "Magnitogorsk, or a Conversation with Jan" to find oneself immediately in that circle of the "victim" and the "radiant future." The furnaces of Magnitogorsk, a symbol of the industrialization and of that future, were to redeem the anguish of nights and days spent in a prison cell. They were also intended to redeem other torments, ones which Broniewski omitted but of which he must have been aware. That vision of redemption in the communist paradise of the future sustained the personal sacrifice of many communists who spent years in jails, just as that vision led inexorably to the exploits of the interrogators in a ministry of internal affairs which was run by communists who had been political prisoners before the war and were now fallen angels. The victim was transformed into the executioner, the saint into the inquisitor.

The fate of the "underground people" and of the "legionaries," of the heroes of Broniewski's poems—comrade Jan and tailor Izaak Gutkind—is a strict warning to those who would act in disregard for the law. Let today's angels remember that the public respect they enjoy imposes on them a special duty of moral sensitivity. Otherwise, base contempt for those whose happiness they would serve may easily become intertwined with their heroic sacrifices.

It is not easy to write about angels. It is not easy to write such things when one recalls how their everyday lives were sapped by tedious and often futile effort, when one remembers that already today they are paying for their choices with expulsion from work and police persecution, whereas tomorrow . . . ?

Regardless of what tomorrow may bring, I feel today that it is my duty to say that the angel who demands heroism not only of himself but of others, who denies the value of compromise, who perceives the world with a Manichean simplicity and despises those who have a different concept of obligations toward others—this angel, loving heaven as he may, has already started on the path that leads to hell.

Never mind that he may justify his actions with the jargon of independence or by a socialist-universalist utopia—he is already sowing the seeds of future hatred.

I am no insane aesthete. I don't believe that all people can be well disposed toward one another all the time. But I do believe in the creative power of our actions. I do believe that we are capable of enhancing or diminishing the amount of hatred and intolerance in our public life. Finally, I believe that the form of an independent and democratic Poland is being shaped today. I would like that Poland to be based on tolerance and political culture, although I know that long years of work will be necessary to popularize these values. This is why they should start being popularized already, not through verbal declarations but in daily action.

This is also why I fear that Wierzbicki's essay might be interpreted in a certain way. "A Treatise on Maggots," with its passion for revealing the major underlying illnesses of Polish intellectual and civic life, is rich in suggestiveness. It is a continuation of that great tradition of the Polish social lampoon. Wierzbicki does not flatter his reader; he accuses and perturbs him. Such an attitude on the part of an author deserves respect.

But unless this "Treatise" is complemented with a "Treatise on Angels," it will serve not as a pail of cold water splashed across the easy enthusiasm of the intelligentsia but rather as a primer good only for heartening the spirits of the dissidents. Because in our country angels are destined to be criticized by third-class journalists whom they scorn. And the angel who is not criticized, the angel who is convinced of his angelic character, may metamorphose into the devil. You don't believe me? Read a book about the noblest and most courageous people in Russia, the book that I spent years hating but to which I keep returning like a drug addict to his cocaine, the book that is a distorting mirror in which every angel will see his face reflected back repulsively deformed, a book that is off-putting and piercing to the point of cruelty. Read *The Possessed.*

I know that every maggot who wants to justify his "maggothood" takes Dostoyevski's leather-bound book off the shelf, sits down in his deep armchair, and reads out loud to his interlocutor the most appropriate passages. But I also know that unless the Polish democratic opposition thinks through and absorbs the experience of *The Possessed*, it will be threatened by Stavrogins and Verkhovenskys *à la polonaise* more profoundly than by the secret policemen with their creased faces and stone eyes.

Because a movement that does not honor a society's constant values is not sufficiently mature to undertake the reshaping of that society.

Historical
Essays

// Shadows of Forgotten Ancestors 1973

//   It is not easy to write about oneself. But this text has to be about me because reams of paper have already been covered with words about him. Since I have done no background research, there is little that I could add to the study conducted with Benedictine diligence by [the historian] Władysław Pobóg-Malinowski. I also don't want to write a biographical essay: others who are better prepared will certainly do that. So what is this intended to be? It will be a text about him as he figures in my own spiritual biography, about why this person is so important—to me. I cannot generalize about the experiences of my generation; I don't know how, in the case of my contemporaries, family traditions collided with what they were told in school, how the tales recounted by their relatives and friends corresponded to the propaganda they were getting elsewhere. This is why I am writing in the first person singular. This will be the testimony of an individual—perhaps, even, an atypical one.

Attempts to capture control of the human mind are a fundamental feature of the regime under which I live. Such attempts begin in grade school when a spiritual world in which everything is clear, unambiguous, and "defined to the last detail" is systematically constructed. But as far as the powers-that-be are concerned, "defining things down to

---

This essay was entered under the pen name Bartłomiej in a competition entitled "Józef Piłsudski in the eyes of young generations of Poles," organized in 1973 by the Józef Piłsudski Institute in London. It was awarded first prize.

the last detail" is not limited merely to shaping a vision of the present. It also involves remolding that of the past. No wonder: those who can succeed in reigning over perceptions of the past will also be able to manipulate thoughts about the present and the future. This is especially the case in a country where history has often served as a pretext for disputes about the present. Uncovering lies about the past frequently allows us to discover our own identity. A key to the past can unlock many of the myths being created today. This is what happened with me.

It was not an easy route. I was born after the war and I treated the reality that surrounded me as natural, as a world based on truth and justice. Most certainly I was atypical. Others had different experiences. In 1945 a large portion of the Polish intelligentsia had been remanded into the hellish dungeons run by the security services or forced into internal or external emigration. Others had been compelled to collaborate with an enemy they detested and despised. Very few were able to believe that a new opportunity was opening up through which Poland was going to be able to slide onto the track of a new civilization characterized by social progress, democracy, and humanism. The communists were in that last group. My parents had been communists before the war. To be more explicit, they were Polish communists of Jewish origin.

At home no one assured me that I was living in the best of all possible worlds, but neither was anyone reminiscing in my presence about how good things had been before the war. Because not everyone had it so good in those days. There were many poor people who were constantly humiliated, hurt, and persecuted in that independent Poland. They became communists not for money or for government jobs but in order to live in dignity. This may be one reason why I have never juxtaposed a bad postwar Poland with a good prewar Poland. And I am not about to do so today.

In those days my vision of prewar Poland was formed under the giant shadow of the man who had governed it: Józef Piłsudski, the dictator responsible for Brześć and Bereza,[1] the author of a fascist constitution, an enemy of progress.

1. Bereza was a concentration camp set up by the Polish government in 1934. Political opponents of the regime, especially Ukrainian nationalists and communists, were confined therein.

I began to criticize Polish reality as I became aware that official ideas clashed with everyday practice. I quickly came to the conclusion that the revolution had been betrayed, socialism's ideas were being neglected, and that political and social democracy existed only on paper. But when I looked back to the interwar period, it was only to contrast the magnificent personage of Wera Kostrzewa [the communist leader] with the gloomy, cynical, and dictatorial rulers of my own time.

I considered the so-called national question as solved, and I could not understand the emotions that flared up when Zbigniew Załuski's book was published. I saw the author of *The Seven Sins*[2] . . . as a nationalist (and I was not mistaken), and I tended to explain away the ensuing emotions as one basic component of the mentality of a conquered nation. To me the Poland of A.D. 1963 had been sovereign since the Polish October [1956] (and I was profoundly and fundamentally wrong on this count).

The events of 1968 therefore came as a shock to me. To this day no one has yet written a monograph on the March events. I would advise whoever writes one in the future to consider this question: Which traditions of Polish political culture were reborn at that time? An analysis of the press, which in certain respects enjoyed more freedom then than at any other time, might be instructive. After all, even in the immediate aftermath of the breakthrough of October 1956, the censorship office confiscated articles that were openly anti-Semitic. Systemic crises always uncover real social consciousness. The crisis of 1956 revealed the outlines of Polish democratic thought. The crisis of 1968 highlighted those aspects of Polish thought which are backward, stupid, chauvinistic, and xenophobic. Władysław Bieńkowski aptly dubbed it the "obscurantist revolution."

One could of course continue to claim that it was not the people but only those horrible communists, those monstrous rulers, who with their many voices roared, "We want blood!" just as they had done in the era of the Stalinist trials. But I believe that to adhere to this idea is to mistake a hopeful illusion for reality: The fundamental difference

2. Zbigniew Załuski's controversial book was first published in 1963. It is a procommunist, yet extremely conservative defense of traditional Polish values, especially of the integrity of the Polish soldier. The book was a harbinger of the anti-Semitic and anti-intellectual purge of 1968.

between the years 1952, for example, and 1968 is that in 1968 the anti-intelligentsia and anti-Semitic pogrom was conducted with the active consent of a significant segment of the population. In Poland communism had created its own subculture, whose essence consisted in a traditionalist nationalism. This element could not be exploited to its limit because of the Big Brother's presence. But allusions in the press and the widespread gossip were enough to allow many people to momentarily see that thug of a secret policeman as a national hero, a patriot, and a fighter for independence. Which Poles could believe this? Did there exist in Poland a tradition that justified these convictions? Did the knights from the Kingdom of Darkness and Ignorance who believed themselves to be the only Poles worthy of that name have a tradition to claim? Had there been others in Poland before them who used their participation in anti-Semitic pogroms as a source of national pride?

Anyone who once believed that October 1956 had made Poland independent, or who drew reckless conclusions from the Albanian or Romanian cases (as I did), was cured of such illusions by the subsequent lesson of Czechoslovakia. At that time the true cards were revealed in this game of political poker. As the Polish heroes of the anti-Semitic witchhunt were marching at the head of armies bringing "fraternal help to the peasants and workers of Czechoslovakia who are moaning in the fetters of West German revisionism," it then became clear that sovereign Poland was in fact being ruled by Big Brother.

Unfortunately, irony is completely out of place here. Only those who did not talk with people of different social groups in Warsaw immediately after the intervention will find themselves smiling at it. When I recounted such conversations to my friends who had spent August 1968 in jail,[3] they did not believe me. But I wasn't making it up! A large number of people in the street heartily approved of the participation of Polish troops in the destruction of freedom in the country of our southern neighbors, for this plague could spread to Poland. I asked myself again: Was there ever anyone in the prior history of our country who would have been prepared to ally himself with the

---

3. Adam Michnik was in prison that August (see the essay *The Prague Spring Ten Years Later*). This fragment was meant to mislead the police.

Russian state in order to stamp out a revolutionary plague? Who would have called cooperation with Europe's gendarme patriotism?

Searching for analogies is a weakness of man's mind. In the encounter with totalitarian reality we are helpless, powerless; we look for situations that can show us how others behaved when faced with dilemmas similar to ours. It was then—in 1968—that I happened to read an account of a meeting between Dmowski and Witte in 1905, and at once from beyond the shadows emerged the faces of those actors who took part in those remarkable events, people who were fated to experience in a single lifetime utter hopelessness and then to witness the red-and-white flag going up atop the Royal Castle in Warsaw. National independence brought with it a new perspective on the direction politics had taken over the preceding twenty years. One could see more clearly which actions had brought that independence closer and which ones had pushed it farther away. The essence of the dispute about the form of this independence also became clearer.

So what was it that caught my attention in that Dmowski-Witte conversation? It was the Polish politician's statement to the Russian premier that revolutionary movements in Poland were the work of Jews who'd come from Russia and that the only way to remedy this situation was to hand the Warsaw government back over to Poles, who would themselves put an end to the activities of the socialist fighting squads.

The man who headed these squads, Józef Piłsudski, was the object of abuse and contempt to the National Democratic journalists. He was held to be a tool in the hands of Russo-Jewish agitators without whom it would never have occurred to the Poles to fight for independence and social reforms.

Piłsudski had emerged from out of the darkness that had fallen over the Kingdom of Poland following the defeat of the January Uprising [1863]. It seemed important to me to analyze that darkness, to scrutinize it closely in order to learn how people thought and acted in those days.

The tactics most frequently employed were those of silence and internal emigration. This choice was understandable and logical immediately following the defeat; but some time later it became ambiguous. Preserving the national language, customs, and traditions in the solitude of one's home, defending national culture inside the four walls of one's house and during occasional meetings with neighbors and cousins—all this gave rise to a certain type of patriotism and a unique sort of patriot. This patriot manifested his Polish heritage by eating the traditional borscht and singing carols at a time when others were already preparing conspiracies. He did not plot. For him conspiracies were the creation of Muscovites and of reckless demagogues who would expose their nation to new repressive massacres.

The preservation of "national substance" by reducing it to language and customs made people forget the reasons for the conflicts between the Poles and tsarist Russia. The Russian schools aimed at Russifying spirits, corrupting minds, teaching people to live in lies and slavery. The defenders of "national substance" were preserving merely the form of Polishness and forsaking its indispensable content. We would say today that they were national in form and Russian in content.

The "Russians"—how tactless this sounds today, when being anti-Russian is a mask for conservative attitudes and for ordinary conformism. In those days anti-Russian sentiment allowed National Democrats to call on Polish students to boycott freedom demonstrations run by Russian academics. Today, anti-Russianism allows people to acquiesce in the abuse of Solzhenitsyn ("the reactionary Slavophile") by Polish hacks. After all, he is a Russian!

I once heard a present-day defender of "national substance" say: "Let's beware of Solzhenitsyn!" Someone answered: "I'm more afraid of Brezhnev, even though he may not be a Slavophile." The second person was right. Polish chauvinism, imbued with anti-Russianism (only one form of xenophobia), may lead to servility. Mieczysław Moczar and Bolesław Piasecki[4] are a clinical, pure expression of this attitude.

Was Piłsudski anti-Russian?

Yes, Piłsudski was anti-Russian. But his revolt was not merely a revolt against Russia. It was a revolt against a large part of Polish society. It was a revolt against conformism, intellectual and moral sloth, against the backwardness of his compatriots. Piłsudski understood

---

4. Bolesław Piasecki (1914–1979) was a leader of the fascist ONR-Falanga before World War II. After the war he was allowed to establish PAX, a lay Catholic organization, which has been instrumental in undermining the Catholic Church.

perfectly that the defeat of Russia would hardly restore national sovereignty; the Poles themselves would have to want this sovereignty. The Polish Socialist party [PPS], which he led, sought to train Poles in the spirit of independence. How was this done? By the newspaper. By the free, independent, uncensored printed word. A society in captivity must produce an illegal literature because it must know the truth about itself, see an unfalsified picture of itself, hear its own genuine voice. The existence of illegal literature is a prerequisite for the fight against captivity of the spirit.

As the editor of the illegal newspaper *Robotnik,* Piłsudski realized this perfectly well. In his beautiful tale about illegal publications—where he drew a profile of the *samizdat* of his day—he stressed the importance of the fight for the human mind, for genuine feelings, for truth. The tale included not only the adventures of the purveyors of the free word but also instructions: What should be done and how? How could pamphlets be printed in Poland? How could books be smuggled in from abroad? Piłsudski never accepted the absurd stance of people living in exile who placed themselves outside the Polish community. He had been an exile himself for some time, and he knew that for a conquered nation emigration is a priceless treasure, an eye and an ear on the world, a mouth that can speak freely and breathe fresh air, absorbing it into the nation's body.

And what about us? We can remember the trial of the "mountain climbers" [in 1970]. They were accused of smuggling into Poland [through the Tatra mountains] books published abroad, written by Witold Gombrowicz, Kazimierz Wierzyński, Gustaw Herling-Grudziński, and others. They received prison sentences. But it was not their sentences, albeit draconian, which shocked me. What shocked me were the reactions of some of the smart alecks sitting around in Warsaw's cafés. "This is what all these conspiratorial games lead to," muttered the intellectuals who peddled their articles to shameful weeklies and always condemned collaboration with émigré monthlies. Why? Because the emigration is too right-wing (or too left-wing), too radical (or too unradical), but really only because fear and internal subjugation forced them to put a gag over their own mouths and deny themselves their basic professional duty, *the duty to speak the truth.*

Leszek Kołakowski's article "The Polish Question" made me think of Piłsudski. Who could understand better than Piłsudski that a nation unable and unwilling to fight for its freedom does not deserve freedom. Such a nation forgets about life in freedom.

A nation living in captivity cannot be made up solely of heroic conspirators. It must also have its "organicists," constructors of factories and bridges, schoolteachers, doctors, even administrators who will make concessions toward the foreign rulers. But woe to the nation that calls its conspirators unbalanced youths or demagogues devoid of national character, that sees foreign inspiration or a stranger's purse behind its best sons and that surrenders the struggle for hearts and minds to the eminently reasonable conformists who identify Polish interests with their own. Woe to that nation, for such a nation must disintegrate.

What is realistic is rarely good; "realistic" thinking in politics often misses material realities.

I don't know if I can really understand the dilemmas those people faced, but I can sympathize with Piłsudski's anger when he saw baseness renamed "realism." Who ended up being the realist? Was it Roman Dmowski, who opted for cooperation with tsarist Russia? This most logical of Polish political thinkers, a skillful player and a cool realist, failed to observe and understand the dynamics of the social processes in the Russian empire. Accepting—"realistically"—the indefinite) presence in Warsaw of the Russian colonels, he concentrated on educating the public according to his ideology of the "modern Pole." The "modern Pole" was to obey the Russian governor-general, break the windows of Jewish-owned shops, and wait for a change in the international balance of power. All Polish territories might then be united under the Russian tsar. Not only Warsaw but also Poznań and Cracow would then lie within the reach of the Cossack whip. Dmowski thought the "modern Pole" should open up a discussion of principles with assorted radicals who, in his view, were mostly Jews. And in 1905 he did open up such a discussion, with the assistance of National Democratic fighting squads, armed with brass knuckles and guns, who helped Russian soldiers exterminate the revolutionary plague.

Piłsudski was not as modern as this. He condemned the direction of nationalistic feelings into anti-Semitism whose outcome was pro-Russian, since he correctly saw in this an emulation of the Russian Black Hundreds. He viewed the substitution of the struggle against tsardom with the plundering of Jewish shops as shameful and stupid;

he called cooperation with the police in breaking up workers' strikes by its proper name: treason.

Realism, realism . . . Would there have been a Poland without those socialist romantics who raised their hands against the colossus (which later turned out to have legs of clay)? Would the Poles have won independence had it not been for those who continuously talked about the need for independence? Did the gallows on which Montwiłł-Mirecki perished, a comrade of Piłsudski's in the socialist fighting squads, not become a challenge to new activists? Can a nation exist without imponderabilia?

A nation that lives without the essentials, that forgoes the defense of things that are sometimes elusive and indefinable, thereby renounces its own culture, retreating to the level of a tribe. Realism and readiness to make concessions can be virtues in a politician, but they are virtues that must be closely watched. They are the virtues of Wallenrodism—pretending to be someone that one is not, masking one's real face and one's real objectives. It often happens, especially nowadays, that the mask on a person's face becomes his face. The instrument used to fulfill values becomes a value in and for itself. Such realism bears fruit in the form of the Bolesław Piaseckis who conceal their villainy under the cloak of patriotic tradition. "Wallenrodism becomes degradation," concluded Stanisław Witkiewicz [the writer] in 1904. Piłsudski, too, was aware of this when he rehabilitated the tradition of resistance and called for resistance. He explained it to Grabiec-Dąbrowski: "Every generation must with their own blood be reminded that Poland lives and will not become reconciled to captivity."

To our ears this sounds like a message from the afterworld. Having been fed the pulp of "realism," we could recognize our own "Wallenrods," who after 1956 split themselves in half. They entered the power apparatus, soon forgot what had motivated them to plug into reality," and quickly learned to consider their part in power as an independent and paramount value.

Piłsudski attempted to explain their shared duty toward the nation. But these were not the only motives for his behavior. In a letter to Feliks Perl immediately before the action of Bezdany,[5] he wrote:

5. Józef Piłsudski raised funds for conspiratorial activities by various methods, including train robbery (in April of 1908 at Bezdany, near Wilno).

I am fighting and I will die only because I am unable to live in this outhouse that is our life, for it humiliates me—do you hear me!—it humiliates me, as it would any man who has dignity which is not a slave's. Let others play gardeners, tending flowers or socialism or Polishness or anything else in the atmosphere of an outhouse (not even of a lavatory)—I cannot do it! This is not sniveling sentimentality; it is simple humanity. I want to win. But without a struggle, a violent struggle, I will not even be a wrestler but a mere beast beaten with a stick or a whip.

This letter was reprinted by the Paris journal *Kultura* in 1968. The date was no accident. Never before had my generation breathed in that atmosphere of dung which now poured incessantly, daily, in a wide stream out of the newspaper columns. Piłsudski's voice sixty years earlier was salvation for me. Someone had finally restored the right proportions to things. Issues I could not understand, which could not be explained in traditional terms, now made sense: an outhouse is an outhouse and this needs no explanation.

Equally important—his is not simply a national but also a very human perspective. It is not patriotic and political concerns but my own concerns, my own good that inspire me to fight. This will rescue me from sinking into the anonymous, shapeless mass of the depraved, captive, and obedient.

There is something profoundly alarming in the popularity as well as the topicality of Stanisław Wyspiański's *The Wedding* [1901]. Its topicality lies not in its cheap allusions ("The Chinese are going strong") but in the issues it raises. It is testimony to the ineptitude of the Polish intelligentsia, to the deep split between the intelligentsia and the people.

Andrzej Wajda's film adaptation of *The Wedding,* shown soon after December 1970 when March 1968 was still in vivid memory, revived this central dilemma of Polish history and of the Polish reality. Piłsudski attempted to overcome this cleavage with action. He assessed the Polish intelligentsia in very strict terms: "They are like hysterical young women who cannot bear hearing glass scratched but who put up with having their faces slapped." He wrote about a "society that has become infantile in its cowardice, that is incapable of fighting on its own behalf, that retreats from the whip which hits its face." What behavior did he recommend to the intelligentsia? The intellectual was to stop going to cafés and to start publishing illegal brochures and editing illegal newspapers. He should give illegal lectures at illegal universities. Through this he could overcome his self-isolation to become a builder and a brain of the workers' movement. He was to be society's tutor.

In what direction did Piłsudski want to educate society? How did he propose to do it? It was to be "an education for national independence." If the Poles are dishonored and depraved, he believed, they will neither want nor be able to fight for sovereignty. Thus it is necessary to educate the nation, to popularize programs for social change. There must be a program for struggle against Russia, a struggle in harmony with other nations that have been conquered by Russia. There must be a program for a future Poland.

Piłsudski educated with newspapers, books, and above all by action. Acquiescence to servitude, he told us, must never be permitted. We are not allowed to remain silent when our fundamental values are being violated. To give up those imponderables is to give up cultural identity, to consent to cultural annihilation.

No one was more vehemently denounced by Piłsudski than the politicians of compromise who welcomed Tsar Nicholas II to Warsaw. In the appeal distributed on that occasion by the Central Workers' Committee of the Polish Socialist party, comrade "Wiktor" (Piłsudski's pseudonym) wrote:

> This is the first time that the tsar is to be met by a Warsaw which is not a rebel menacingly shaking its chains but a docile slave lying submissively at her master's feet.
>
> Or at least this is what is predicted by those who have lost the remains of human dignity and who hope to exchange humility for rubles, medals, and jobs. By force they wish to make everyone drown out in celebrative shouts the moans coming from underneath the soil drenched with the blood of heroes; and with festive attire [they wish] to brighten up the executioner's gloomy face. . . . But this ignominy will not touch us; it will remain the deed of those who have always sought the authorities' support for their selfish actions. They do not want Poland to be free, because for their shady deeds

they need the darkness that captivity creates. The wealth won with our blood and sweat they turn into incense for their idol; and in return for the triumphant welcome they have prepared for the tsar, they are assured new gains and rewards, such as the continuation of rule over us with the aid of the police, gendarmes, and the army. Once again, at the sacrifice of the working people, the proprietary classes are entering into an agreement with the invader. . . . We must be mute witnesses to these demonstrations of welcome and servility by those who will crowd around the tsar to show him how loyal they are. As we watch this exhibition of ignominy in all its colors and shades, the best we can do is to proudly show our red flag which has not been touched by the grime of conciliation.

The truth about the "grime of conciliation," finally articulated, had a cleansing effect. The conquered and captive nation was regaining its real voice and dignity.

Piłsudski was heir to the romantic tradition. He grew up with the poetry of the great national poets, and he loved the works of Adam Mickiewicz and Juliusz Słowacki. For this reason his attitude on the plan to build a statue of Mickiewicz in Warsaw was exceptionally interesting. This action was initiated by a group of conciliatory politicians.

Comrade "Wiktor" clearly expressed his point of view:

An odd thing has happened. Here, in a country where the most repulsive captivity and repression have become widespread, a statue is being built of the man who used word, song, and action to burst the fetters binding the motherland. In a city where children are punished for speaking Polish, the greatest Polish poet is being honored by officialdom! Have the ropes that bind us fallen off? No! We owe this odd phenomenon to the political juggling of the merchants of patriotism. For the government it is . . . a peaceful celebration because it reconciles Polish patriotism with Muscovite captivity.

This fragment of an illegal leaflet deserves close attention. Piłsudski noticed the way in which the great poet's mighty shadow could be used to mask the dirty deeds of the conciliators. We should remember it today: the white-and-amaranthine flag, the crowned eagle, the Royal Castle in Warsaw—all can serve as tools of Sovietization and spiritual denaturalization. They can be used to legitimize the end of the struggle for freedom. They can be used as a gag for those who think differently.

The socialists were often accused of being foreigners in the nation: of being "Russian seeds," "Jewish tools," "servants of the German enemies of the Poles," and so on. Piłsudski rejected these charges with contempt. He thought that to argue with such ideas, which were National Democratic at heart, was pointless and degrading. And this too should be remembered today: When they insult you, ill treat you, accuse you of being traitors to the nation, watch carefully the actions of those patriots armed with a knout.

Piłsudski was not a nationalist. He did not think it either proper or healthy to organize a national consciousness around the hatred of other nations. He was formed by the special climate of the Vilna province, the common motherland of peoples from different nations, cultures, and religions, a multilingual mixture where the Lithuanian lived next to the Byelorussian, the Jew to the Tartar, and the Pole next to the Karaite. Familiarity with other customs and hatred of xenophobia were much more common among people in those areas (as among the population of the eastern borderlands) than in central Poland. Piłsudski saw Poland as the motherland of many nations, a commonwealth of many cultures; he wanted it to be a state in which not only Poles but also Lithuanians, Ukrainians, and Jews could live in solidarity. (Antoni Gołubiew wrote a beautiful essay entitled "Local People" on this subject in *Znak,* but it passed largely unnoticed.) Piłsudski, this "socialist from Zułów," contrasted the idea of a Russian empire with the concept of a commonwealth of nations. He wanted Russia, the "prison-house of nations" and "gendarme of Europe" (these were Lenin's terms), to be torn up by the irredentist revolutionary movements of conquered nations. An alternative solution to the political problems of this part of Europe would have been a Polish-Lithuanian-Ukrainian federation. If it were to be attractive to non-Poles as well, such a state would have no room for national or religious discrimination, for the bench ghetto, anti-Jewish pogroms, or anti-Ukrainian pacification.

Piłsudski later had to abandon his ideas about a federation largely because of chauvinistic National Democratic propaganda. Today, we hardly associate idyllic relations between Poles and Ukrainians or Poles and Jews with the period of the Second Republic. Following World War II, Poland became a nationally uniform country, where people who speak other languages form a microscopic minority. So what is left to us of the old dreams of comrade "Wiktor"?

I don't believe all of them have been lost. What is important are not simply the proposals for solutions to real social problems but also the manner of thinking about society in general. The National Democratic mode of thought adopted by the ruling communists commands pride in national uniformity. A friend of mine called this the substitution of a multicolored, multiflowered meadow with a uniform pile of sand in which each grain looks like every other. The virtue of these grains is the cultivation of uniformity, the animosity toward anything different or strange, and a susceptibility to National Democratic modes of thought. It is not true that National Democratic anti-Semitism was only a response to the otherwise unsolvable Jewish question. Anti-Semitism was the way in which the world was understood by these sand grains, a way that [in 1968] allowed massive anti-Jewish sentiments to develop in a country with practically no Jews.

Piłsudski's system of thought was airtight, impermeable to the germs of chauvinistic demagoguery. Today, when even the most stupid and backward government can toy at will with feelings of animosity toward neighbors (Ukrainians, Czechs, Russians, Germans); when brief press campaigns can reawaken passions, deaden mental faculties with xenophobia, or corrupt people with hatred toward those who are different—we should remember the utopia of that nobleman from the Vilna province who faced the slander and calumnies of his "native" Polish enemies for daring to have such dreams.

In Poland talking about the problem of anti-Semitism is one of the most difficult and risky undertakings. This stems from a complex sequence of cause and effect, which Władysław Bieńkowski has subjected to an interesting analysis in his book, *Motors and Brakes of Socialism.* Bieńkowski's analysis is particularly interesting because, although explicitly condemning the racist practices, he was able to understand the issue in its complexity. This does not happen often in Poland. Toward the end of the Second Republic, following the extreme polarization of public opinion over the "bench ghetto"[6] issue, a situation arose in which every critic of the Jewish community or its representatives, or even of Poles of Jewish origin, was susceptible to being called an anti-Semite. This phenomenon recurred more forcefully after 1968. The poet Arnold Słucki, who died in exile, explained his decision to leave Poland as his unwillingness to live in a society made up uniquely of philo-Semites and anti-Semites.

Piłsudski was not a philo-Semite. In his articles he frequently criticized the philo-Russian politics of the Bund, the Jewish socialist party. The Bund, which was active among the Jewish proletariat, popularized Russian literature and thus also Russian culture. There would have been nothing wrong in this, except that the orientation coincided with the invader's policies of Russification, and in such circumstances encouraged large groups of the population to lean toward Russia. Piłsudski critically assessed the indifferent or negative attitude of the Bund toward Polish aspirations for independence. But his criticism had nothing to do with anti-Semitism because it never led to the inflaming of national hatred. Piłsudski never viewed the Jews as intruders in this land which they had inhabited for hundreds of years. He never used Aryan criteria in his choice of friends and collaborators.

When bombast replaces reflection, and accusations of anti-Semitism abound (even Antoni Słonimski was not spared this charge), one should remember that common sense is not the same as philo-Semitism. Poignant declarations against anti-Semitism can be no substitute for sober analyses of the roots of this frightening illness. The cause does not lie only in the faults of the Polish people. It is also necessary to recognize negative phenomena on the Jewish side as well, a task which by no stretch of the imagination can be interpreted as racism. [The writers] Prus, Żeromski, Dąbrowska, and Słonimski were not racists when they wrote about this subject.

It would be improper to accuse all Poles of anti-Semitism. This accusation is as absurd as it is convenient to the communist power elite, whose characteristics are thus projected onto the nation.

---

6. Since the mid-thirties Jewish students at Polish universities were forced by their anti-Semitic colleagues to stand up during lectures.

Some thirty years ago Ksawery Pruszyński, who was educated in the Eastern territories, wrote the following:

> We grew up with the conviction that we were the heirs of the great motherland . . . which, although defeated, still stretched from sea to sea. . . . Were we told that Gdańsk is not Polish, we would have been terribly surprised. Were we told that Kiev is not Polish, our surprise would have been greater. But had we been told that our motherland is nationally uniform—that it covers the area around the Vistula from the Carpathians to the sea, but that there is room in it neither for Ruthenian peasants nor for Russian Orthodox churches, or even for old Mrs. Szomstein—we would certainly have been most surprised of all. Our generation is probably the last to have grown up with the ideals of the 1863 insurrection, of Poland-Lithuania-Ruthenia. We had all heard of the pre-insurrection funeral of five rebels, at which representatives of three religions marched at its head. . . . After all these years, I'm unable to say what has stayed with me from that childhood. . . . First of all, probably a certain sense of the history of Poland, an idea of Poland as a multinational imperium. Not repulsion toward other peoples but, on the contrary, an attraction. Treating national minorities not as a necessary evil but as valuable constituents that broaden my motherland and enrich our shared house. . . . One of the reasons I am writing these memoirs is because there will never again be childhoods like mine in Poland. Today's world will have hundreds of opportunities to describe its cradles. Mine will not. Still, I believe that as mankind's nationalistic insanities cool out, and as Poles reflect on how to build a home for their nation that will not be wiped out by every one of history's storms, Polish thought will then reach out. Young Polish thought will then seek guidance from the distant and not-so-distant past. It will try to uncover from the rubble the knowledge of how such a great building, which gave centuries of peace and liberty to so many generations, was erected. It will try to learn how this structure managed to join so firmly such different bricks, stones, oak beams. . . . Sooner or later, Polish thought, heedful and concentrated, will march toward those trails and those eras. It will walk on the great routes of the black trail which today are being swept by history's blizzard. It will walk in this blizzard, over the potholes, with a faint oil lamp, stumbling and getting stuck—and searching. . . . Until it gets there.

Today, we are marching in fog. We don't know what the future will bring, how long the current balance of political power will last, or how much longer the USSR's proprietary status will remain untouched. One thing, however, seems certain: we will have to coexist with other nations. It is up to us to find some reasonable formula of coexistence or to become submerged in the throes of tribal hatred. But if we try to rediscover a formula for tolerance and harmony, the patron of our quest will be the older editor of *Robotnik,* the leader of the socialist fighting squads, the partisan with the Nietzschean face: none other than Józef Piłsudski.

Poland has been condemned by its geography and history to be a neighbor of Russia. What was Piłsudski's attitude toward Russia? He considered it the most dangerous of the partitioning powers. He feared and hated it. He detested the imperium's system of government. "Muscovite slavery," he wrote:

> differs from all other kinds in that, apart from the coercion and repression, the captive nation must bear constant humiliation. Tsarist rule, in the style of all Eastern despots, cherishes the outward signs of subjection and humility. It demands the degradation of the slave's human dignity. It is not enough for this ruler to use the whip, he also wants the whipped person to kiss the tool of torture. It is not enough to bring his adversary down, he also feels a need to slap the defeated in the face. . . . The shameless mockery of human feelings constitutes a part of this system of rule, because only those whose dignity has been trampled out of existence can bear the repulsive tsarist captivity.

Of the essence of the Russian state, he wrote:

> All absolute rulers eliminate social control over legislative activity. Therefore, it is natural that all administrative measures, including law making, are shielded by a thick cloak of secrecy. Information about this or that part of the state, reports on the activities of officials, reform projects, legal findings, debates of legislative bodies—all this is diligently hidden from the eyes of those who do not belong to the caste of officialdom.

Piłsudski believed that the social and legal structures of Russia were ideally suited to the state's slavish organization. He saw no chance for democratic evolution. He was also critical of internal Russian opposition. He distrusted Russian liberals. He was contemptuous of their procrastination and conciliatory tendencies and warned against their tendency toward Great Russian nationalism.

In his writings about the Russian revolutionary camp he stressed its weakness, its intolerance, and its misgivings (characteristic of doctrinaire movements) toward the liberation movements of the conquered nations in the tsarist empire. He drew attention to the revolutionaries' paradoxical acceptance of the perceptions of the conquered nations that had been formed by the Slavophilic right. Thus, the idea that the 1863 insurrection was the work of the reactionary nobility and Catholic priests made its way into the Russian revolutionary press.

Piłsudski explicitly expressed his viewpoint in his article "On Pushkin's Anniversary":

> All tribal and national hatred is foreign to us. Fighters for freedom of all countries and nations are our brothers. We are capable of paying homage to all thoughts, regardless of the language in which they are expressed. We are capable of honoring any poet or thinker, regardless of his nationality. But in this case we are not dealing with a poet who invested his words with the spirit of liberty, and who thereby became dear to all who are repressed and exploited. Pushkin had nothing to do with the struggle against slavery; he actually sometimes praised that slavery. It is thus natural that no aware Polish worker can participate in the celebrations of Pushkin.

From today's perspective, this assessment of Pushkin may seem inordinately one-sided and narrowly political. But at the time this was not a matter of literature or a celebration of poetic genius. It was a purely political affair—a question of paying homage to the invader, of strengthening his rule, of oppressing Polish culture yet again.

Piłsudski felt that only a weak Russia, a nonimperial Russia, could be a democratic state. He did not support the Russian counterrevolutionary forces against the Bolsheviks because he doubted the strength of the Bolsheviks and the permanence of their power. While determined to save Poland from being bolshevized, he was not for stopping the bolshevization of Russia. (He was strongly reproached for this by Marian Zdziechowski, who was one of the first to understand the essence of the bolshevik system.)

Piłsudski did not permit Poland to be bolshevized. The "miracle on the Vistula"[7] was a symbol of this. Much water flowed in the Vistula before I understood the importance of this event. For many years I reasoned thus: The Russian revolution began to rot with Lenin's death. Stalinism should be judged most harshly, but not from an anticommunist stance. The Russo-Polish war was a war between the international revolution and bourgeois Poland. In analyzing this conflict, I see no reason to believe that kinship is thicker than class. Polish workers were fighting for socialism, and the Red Army was helping them. On the Polish side, it was not a war for national freedom, but for capitalistic statehood.

When pressed, I was willing to accept the analogy of the Spanish peasant defending his feudal motherland from Napoleon's armies which sought to impose reform by bayonet. But now I see the matter differently: To the 1920 victory over the Bolsheviks we owe twenty years of independent Polish thought, which has been nourishing new generations to this day. Present-day opposition to Sovietization is possible in large measure because of the cultural heritage of the Second Republic, which existed thanks to Piłsudski's military victory over Budënny. Who knows? Had the Red Army won the battle of Radzymin and Poland been ruled by the Provisional Revolutionary Committee, perhaps I would be living in Kołyma or Birobidzhan and not speak Polish at all. Perhaps successive generations of the Polish intellectuals would have been feeding polar bears in Siberia. Perhaps Polish culture would not have escaped the destruction that Russian culture suffered under the Stalinist empire.

It is from today's perspective that the twenty interwar years—and I have no intention of idealizing that period—were years of a *peredyshka,* a free gasp of air, which was used to build a new framework of national culture. We must not forget this even when we are told that victory over the Bolsheviks meant abandoning land reform and other

---

7. This is a reference to the Polish victory in the battle of Warsaw in August 1920, during the Polish-Russian war.

social reforms. Those in particular who should not forget this are the representatives of leftist thought, those people (including the author of these reflections), who claim as theirs the tradition of the left wing of the workers' movement, a tradition that also gave birth to the Provisional Revolutionary Committee of Dzierzyński and Marchlewski.

Piłsudski's anti-Soviet policies were to some degree a continuation of his old political line. As always, he did not trust any Russian rule, be it tsarist, liberal, or revolutionary. In our changed situation today, should we reason differently? We must certainly be aware of the determinants and traditions of Russian political thought. We should critically decipher both official and opposition thought. But the superficiality, falsehoods, and myths of Russian thought should not be countered with Polish chauvinism. Even though I may be jolted by certain formulations or motifs in Solzhenitsyn's work, I believe that dismissing this twentieth-century saint by labeling him a "Muscovite" is frightening evidence of spiritual captivity. Today, we look to Russia not only with hatred but also with hope, not only with anger but also with admiration. It is difficult to overestimate the importance of the activities of Solzhenitsyn, Sakharov, or Amalrik to the Polish cause.

The alternatives open to Piłsudski were to count on the Russian opposition or to count on the irredentism of the empire's conquered nations. This was the central dilemma of those working for Polish independence. Today, the Polish intellectual has no such choice. But he does face another dilemma: to follow Western fashions; to chew on pseudopatriotic pulp à la Zbigniew Załuski; or to watch closely the Russian underground culture, Czech and Slovak literature, Hungarian films, and the intellectual output of the Lithuanians, Byelorussians, and Ukrainians. It is not yet a question of concrete political action, although the time for that will probably come. What is important today is an intellectual attitude, intellectual priorities, a type of national education. It is important for the Polish intelligentsia to evince a readiness to coexist with our neighboring nations and to understand the cultures of other nations.

It is clear from my remarks that I prefer the "early," independence-minded, socialist Piłsudski. The actions of the legions which brought Poland independence were a logical consequence of this "early" period.

Independence was won by people who had been brought up in the Polish Socialist party, the Union of Active Struggle, and the Legions; advocates of republican and democratic ideas enshrined in the constitution of March 1921. It was all made possible, of course, by the international situation: the World War and the Russian Revolution. But without the subjective element which Poles contributed to the international balance of power, the great powers would have seen no reason to become involved in the "Polish question." One cannot but see, after all these years, the great contribution of the legionaries and their commander to Polish culture and to Poland.

Yet it is also clear that, even then, the adverse effects due to Piłsudski "getting off the red tramway at the stop called 'Independence,'" were already in motion. At first, this entailed shifting the weight of action onto the military sector. In the period of the Union of Active Struggle, Piłsudski wrote almost exclusively about military matters. He attempted over time to reform the Polish Socialist party into an independence-minded paramilitary organization. He implemented a policy of secret meetings which would later lead to the formation of the legionaries' clique and to a dangerous veteran's mythology. (Moczar thus had a model when, in the 1960s, he formed his own political team inside ZBOWiD [the Union of Fighters for Freedom and Democracy, veterans' organization].) These actions were opposed by a group of socialist activists led by Feliks Perl, a former coeditor of *Robotnik*. Thus began Piłsudski's conflict with Polish socialism in independent Poland.

This conflict lasted until his death, going through different phases of varying intensity. My sympathies in this dispute lie with the Marshal's antagonists.

I did not write, and did not intend to write, a congratulatory scroll for Józef Piłsudski. For my generation, which has heard so many lies, truth is of the utmost importance. I have tried to write the truth about the events that took place at the beginning of this century because I consider them to be of the utmost importance. It is from those experiences that independence arose. But I am writing my own, rather personal view of Piłsudski and his role, and I would not like to forget the dark side as well. Thus, the May 1926 coup was a violation of the

Constitution. His conflicts with the Sejm paved the way for the ignominy of Brześć. Brześć, this manner of fighting an opposition which had few precedents in our history, was one factor in the destruction of our nation's political culture. Bereza grew out of the spirit of Brześć, as did Ozon and the perilous habit of the power elite to treat the state and nation as if they were its private property.

Brześć, Bereza, and Ozon serve today as models for the enemies of democracy in Poland, and not for those who fight for liberty. By creating a mythology out of these actions, by treating all the periods and aspects of the Marshal's activity as sacred, no one is doing the "Polish cause" a favor. Refusal to face the truth invariably serves the enemies of freedom.

Piłsudski died in 1935. In his last years many former comrades distanced themselves from him, while an unsavory mob of "adulators and rascals" grew to surround him. And yet the leaders of the Polish Socialist party, perhaps even recent prisoners of Brześć, marched in his funeral procession. Why did they take part in this farewell? No doubt they were saying good-bye to their youth, to a segment of their lives. But surely it was not this alone. They were bidding farewell to a man who had given Poland and the Poles a sense of dignity, which is as essential to the health of a nation as oxygen is to the human body.

This is why Piłsudski remains to this day a personal problem for Polish intellectuals who lived during his times. The subject surfaces in the novels of Igor Newerly and Kazimierz Brandys, in the essays of Stefan Kisielewski and Juliusz Mieroszewski, in Jan Lechoń's *Diaries,* and in Antoni Słonimski's *Alphabet of Memories.*

If only it could find its way more often into the consciences and long nocturnal disputes of my contemporaries! If only we, following his example, were able to live with dignity!

Warsaw 1973

// The Dispute over Organic Work*

//   After the defeat of the January Uprising [1863], disputes about the meaning and form of "organic work" came to the forefront of Polish intellectual life both at home and in exile. These discussions often started out with an assessment of the policies of Aleksander Wielopoiski and their unexpected fruition, the armed insurrection. Why were the ideas of the count Wielopolski defeated? The variety of answers to this question concealed the essential dispute about the meaning of Polish history.

To the author of these reflections, the following ideas seem to lie closest to the truth.

1. Wielopolski's attempt to reach an understanding with the tsar, to form a Polish-Russian alliance based on conservative principles and the mutual recognition of the social status of the proprietary classes in the Kingdom of Poland and in Russia, indicated that the count accepted the system of tsarist autocracy. The implementation of these policies therefore led to the consolidation in the Kingdom of Poland of the social and political principles that prevailed in the despotically ruled country of the tsars. This program was contrary to the beliefs of the Polish public.

2. In any event, the count made no attempt to gain the concur-

*This article appeared under the pseudonym Andrzej Zagozda.

rence of Polish public opinion. He was a reformer with the mentality of a reactionary who preferred to use methods of dictators and policemen. Even progressive reforms Wielopolski implemented with reactionary methods, using coercion and repressions which evoked terror. In his merciless struggle with political adversaries he did not hesitate to ask for help from the invader.

3. Besides the fact that the count sought foreign assistance, it is equally important that his program of reforms was reactionary and anachronistic even for his time. For example, the demand to enfranchise the peasants—by one means or another—was a component of all political programs of that era, but it was not to be found in Wielopolski's program; for him the Napoleonic Code was sufficient. His proposed social policies ignored the aspirations of the people in the Kingdom of Poland who had been deprived of their property.

4. Wielopolski's declarations addressed to the Russian monarch, in which he went so far as to align Polish interests with the tsar's policies fully and forever were also contrary to Polish aspirations. The public would have approved of some compromise with the invader, but it would hardly abandon the idea of sovereignty. Wielopolski's policies, which were backed with great force, did not allow the Polish nation to evolve modern and progressive institutions in public life. Instead, they were structured to achieve a lawfully governed (although the law was created by the despotic monarch) and efficiently administered (although this efficiency only enhanced the hardships of his subjects) province of the tsarist imperium.

The count believed the people's opposition to his policies to be a function of the reckless and anarchic character of the Poles, but the truth certainly lay elsewhere. This opposition signified the entrance onto the political stage of a new social strata whose aspirations were being violated by Wielopolski's antidemocratic and socially conservative policies. The opposition expressed an awakening of new strivings, a typical process in the development of a society. Deprecating and ignoring these changes in the nation's structure were bound to lead to open conflict. Thus, the opinion with which I concur was voiced by Józef Szujski, who—following the defeat of the insurrection [1864], replied to Paweł Popiel, an admirer of the count's policies: "There would have been no uprising had it not been for the new betrayers . . . it would not have been organized had it not been for those who today are shouting the loudest . . . who irritated [the people], spitting at them instead of entering into an agreement with them" (Józef Szujski, "About Mr. Paweł Popiel's Brochure," *Works,* Vol. 1).

This point of view was shared by nearly all the émigrés engaged in a dispute about the "organic work." Such must also have been the opinion of the Great Emigration as it tried to formulate the "vital truths" after the November Uprising [1830].

The situation was somewhat more complex for the émigrés after the 1863 Uprising. One of the chief disagreements of this period was the difference in the diagnoses of the present and the programs for the future made in Poland and in exile. A definite majority of the public at home demanded "turning swords into plowshares": rejecting insurrectionist ideology in favor of the principles of legalism, conciliation, and organic work, as well as giving up the thought of a sovereign state for an indefinite period of time. A definite majority of the émigrés continued the ideals of the uprising and the declaration of the Insurrection's national government of 1863. Such ideas can be found in articles in *Ojczyzna, Głos wolny,* and *Wytrwałość,* in appeals of the Union of Polish Emigrés or the Democratic Society.

In *Ojczyzna (The Fatherland)* edited by Agaton Giller, a former member of the national government, we read:

> Political emigration is a necessity for a country which remains under the rule of its invaders, which is deprived of the ability to defend its interests, tortured and persecuted for any display of national spirit and every attempt at independence. As long as the emigration exists, the enemy will not fully triumph over the nation because the emigration is a living protest against the nation's rape, a representative of the nation's rights and of its needs for freedom and independence. A political emigration is essential for a conquered and brutally enslaved nation. (*Ojczyzna,* no. 61, 7/30/1865)

In the spirit of this declaration the emigrants discussed the problems that could not be discussed in the press back home: the problems of sovereignty. Much space and attention were given to justifying the historical need for an independent Poland. The arguments went in many different directions. First of all, Poles want national sovereignty and that settles the matter, argued the émigrés. In accordance with the Spring of Nations of 1848 and the "principle of nationhood," the Poles have as much right to live in a united motherland as the Italians or Germans do. This was the moral argument. To Europeans the Polish émigrés explained that Europe absolutely needed an independent Poland—any kind of Europe, whether Catholic, legitimistic, bourgeois-democratic, or revolutionary and socialist.

The arguments of the émigrés differed significantly from the ideas proposed in the press in Poland. In Poland there were also legitimists, ultramontanes, democrats and socialists, but the politicians in Poland, regardless of their ideological coloring, did not believe that national sovereignty was a prerequisite for the continued national existence of the Poles. The protection of the essence of the nation, of the national substance, self-government, autonomy, or supranational universal ideals were offered instead.

Next to the various insurrectionist and "diplomatic" concepts, a current appeared among the émigrés favoring the idea of "organic work." Behind this term different, often contradictory programs were concealed. For some it meant straightforward economic and educational activity; for others, peacetime preparations for a new uprising; for still others, a break with the nobility's idea of sovereignty. Sometimes "organic work" meant the abandonment of the very idea of national sovereignty and the total condemnation of all political conspiracy. A former commissioner of the national government in the Prussian-ruled part of Poland, Julian Łukaszewski, immediately after the failure of the uprising wrote a brochure entitled "The Government and National Organization" in which he expressed his ideas about the new situation. He proposed the retention of the government and the National Organization, which he saw as indispensable instruments for the internal organization of Polish society. But he demanded profound changes in these instruments, since the "organizational forms that arose during the insurrection have by now mostly deteriorated and become exhausted. The various seals and offices should disappear altogether. The point is to impose the economic principles proposed by the National Government which the nation accepted as its own during the struggle" (Julian Łukaszewski, "The Government and National Organization," *Bendlikon* [1864], pp. 66–67). The political aspects were now to become secondary. The economic tasks were much more important because the situation was disastrous.

> The most important reason for this pitiful state is the strangled political life and abnormal social relations, and also the fact that we have not developed among ourselves a sense of order and unity, an understanding of our own interests, and an economic talent that would have as its attribute a love of work and a sober understanding of our condition. . . . Our great poets—Mickiewicz, Krasiński, Zaleski—have contributed to this by directing people's minds to golden dreams, prophecies and supernatural phenomena, tearing them away from reality. The latest uprising has taught us a great lesson; we have had a difficult education. The noose, conflagration, Siberia, the general repression at home and exile abroad ought to sober us up completely and bring it home to us that it is not in poetry and clairvoyance or in higher missions that political calculations lie, but in the awareness of actual conditions in our country, in its wealth and resources which await future great deeds. But we don't even have the elementary conditions to start to develop our national economy on a large scale. Where is the work force? Where is the necessary capital? Where are the communication routes on land and water? Where are the credit institutions, banks, trade companies? Where are the industrial, joint-stock, and insurance companies? Where are the regulations for social relations? Where is the spirit of enterprise? Where, finally, are the people with professional education, the technicians, machinists and manufacturers to skillfully run the industries? All this must be extracted from the governments that have invaded us. (Ibid., pp. 42–44)

An essential precondition for the implementation of such a program lay in the transformation of the nation's social structure. Łukaszewski's program had an antinobility edge to it. ("After Poland was partitioned," wrote Łukaszewski, "the nobility gave the government of our country over to the invaders; it thereby relinquished its influence and its political rights" [ibid., p. 27].) He placed hopes for a better future in the bourgeoisie.

> Faith in one's own abilities makes the craftsmen and manufacturers into a mobile and independent element; they are progressive

and homogenous. . . . The larger the middle class in a nation, the greater the progress in that nation's economy, the greater the external might and independence of that nation. (Ibid., pp. 50–51)

In formulating his program for "organic activities," Łukaszewski was hardly condemning the tradition of uprisings or approving the idea of political conciliation with Russia. He called those who favored conciliation "vultures" who want to "strangle the nation and give it over to the tsar for prey" ("On Panslavism," *Bendlikon* [1865], p. 9). With its polemical edge, his defense of the insurrectionist tradition struck at the Polish camp of conciliation, which also favored slogans about organic work. For Łukaszewski, unlike the conciliators, the call for organic work was not a departure from the struggle for independence. Rather, it was a continuation of irredentist policies in a new situation. The emphasis on economic activity was in no way to supplant political goals. Łukaszewski even allowed for the existence of plots and conspiracies, something that was offensive to the conciliators since the condemnation of the principle of *liberum conspiro* was a cornerstone of their political philosophy. In the conclusion of his "On Panslavism," Łukaszewski expressed this clearly:

> Conspiracy is an evil, but a necessary evil. It will exist as long as the majority of the people do not show practically and morally that they need no artificial stimulation to strive for independence.

He further explained this thought in the following fashion:

> When we become powerful because of our nation's prosperity, industry and education, let us courageously look in the eye of our enemy and openly demand liberty. If it is not granted, we will not need to conspire because the resources for a revolution will be ready and the entire nation . . . will expel the invader from our land. (Ibid., pp. 55–56)

Łukaszewski expressed his opinions in debate with that pillar of Galician conciliation, Józef Szujski, whom he reproached for "shivering at the very memory of revolution and conspiracy; for chasing after 'normal organic work' in the midst of the abnormal and destructive situation of foreign occupation. His effort will be in vain if he does not set a clear goal: the independence of the whole nation" (*Niepodległość*, 2/20/1867, no. 21, p. 7, cited in Jerzy W. Borejsza, *The Polish Emigration After the January Uprising* [Warsaw, 1966], p. 223).* Łukaszewski admitted that

> The enfranchisement of the peasants has been achieved, but the masses still have no idea about their new civic duties. They must be enlightened, led, and refined. Will Moscow allow this? What is left? We must conspire a little bit in that direction. (Ibid.)

In Łukaszewski's opinion, an explicit formulation of the political goal—the independence of the whole nation—was essential because of the concern for the morality and civic awareness of the Poles and for counteracting their spiritual depravation. From this perspective the Galician policies of conciliation met with criticism of this émigré irredentist-organicist.

> Austria has been sucking the most vital juices out of Galicia, and what it cannot swallow it poisons with the venom of obscurantism or tribal hatred. Even so, the elders of the Galician fatherland reek of servility. They traffic in the dignity of the whole country for a few pennies; they give the treasures of their own land over to the lust of the Habsburgs. No wonder that out of this adultery the bastards of conservatism are born. (Julian Łukaszewski, *Diaries 1862–64* [Warsaw, 1973], p. 221)

Things were different in the Kingdom of Poland, where conciliation did not rule souls: "Way over there, from distant Lithuania, Father Piotrowicz's voice of mighty faith can be heard, bewildering the whole world" (ibid.).

Admiration and respect for Father Piotrowicz were by no means equivalent to sympathy for the ultramontane stance. On the contrary. Łukaszewski called the Polish ultramontanes (members of the Community of the Resurrection) a "band of bigots, who have as their master

---

*I must add here that I have learned much from Jerzy W. Borejsza's excellent book. I also wish to thank the author for his friendly advice. [Author's note]

the cunning Father Kajsiewicz and as their flag the repulsive *Tygodnik Katolicki (Catholic Weekly)*" (ibid., p. 212).

It should be remembered that Father Stanisław Piotrowicz, "on March 25, 1870, publicly burned the Russian prayer book imposed on the pulpit by the authorities and damned those who used it" (ibid., notes by Prof. Stefan Kieniewicz, p. 253). The members of the Community of the Resurrection, a prime example of ultramontane beliefs, demanded a complete renunciation of political resistance and advocated dependence on the policies of the Holy See. Father Piotrowicz's action had a completely different meaning, just as it differed essentially from the—poorly understood—pragmatism of the organicists in Poland. It was an act intended in defense of the essentials, in defense of the nation's moral substance. It must be stressed that Łukaszewski believed that the defense of the national moral essence should be a constant and immovable component part of the program of "organic work."

It seemed necessary to discuss in detail Łukaszewski's program because he stood midway between the conciliators inside Poland and the "steadfast" living in exile. Łukaszewski shared with the conciliators the emphasis on economic activity, as well as for jettisoning the mentality of heroism and sacrifice formed under the romantic concept of "Poland, the Christ of Nations." Together with the "steadfast" émigrés, he stood by the flag of national independence for the Poles. Mieczysław Paszkowski expressed his views differently:

> The enemy aims to disown Polish proprietors. Whoever has managed to save one inch of Polish soil from him has worked in an organic way and has done the nation a great favor. The enemy aims to eradicate the national language, national memories, traditions, customs. Whoever has taught a single child or himself the pure Polish language. . . . Whoever has enlarged his own estate with the goal of using it to serve the national cause, has been an organicist. (An annex to *Niepodległość*, 1/20/1867, quoted by Borejsza, *The Polish Emigration*, p. 223)

Paszkowski identified Poland's interest with the interests of the propertied classes and especially with the interests of the nobility. In his schema resistance against the invader was reduced to simple survival. It meant "waiting out" the bad state of affairs and preserving traditional customs, some of which were rooted in anachronistic social relations. In practice this attitude implied passivity, which distinguished it from the activist conclusions drawn by Łukaszewski.

Perceiving the Russian state as the principal enemy and gradually losing faith in the possibility of effective aid from Western European countries, the politicians in Hôtel Lambert[1] leaned increasingly toward a pro-Austrian orientation. They viewed the Austrian monarchy as the only partitioning power that could guarantee the Poles relatively favorable conditions for national survival. Speculating on a potential Austro-Russian conflict, the Hôtel Lambert politicians saw a possibility for turning Galicia into a Polish Piedmont, that is, a center that in the future would gather Polish irredentist tendencies and unify the territories of the former commonwealth. The programs formulated by the émigré conservatives concerned Poland. The Rev. Władysław Czartoryski, in a speech delivered on May 3, 1865, summarized his demands into two ideas: "calm and work." The historian Jerzy Zdrada summed up Czartoryski's speech: "Recommending organic work, realizing that no legal party could possibly be formed in the Kingdom of Poland . . . he recommended that people hold on to the institution of the church, and with its help wield an influence on the peasant masses" (Jerzy Zdrada, *The Twilight of the Czartoryskis* [Warsaw, 1969], pp. 92–93).

Other Polish ultramontanes could also subscribe to such ideas. Walerian Kalinka, once closely involved in Czartoryski's politics and later a priest and member of the Community of the Resurrection, also accepted the formula of organic work. From his perspective this idea could not be reduced to economic activity.

> Economic activity is only half the organic work; it demands a complement if it is not to lead to the ugliest, most disorganizing results. It is half, and the less important half, not always and not absolutely necessary. For everyone knows that there have been nations in history that were poor but important; yet there is no example of a rich but immoral nation capable of defending itself from its neighbors. Together with the body, or rather before the body, the

---

1. Hôtel Lambert was the Paris residence of Prince Adam Czartoryski, the "uncrowned King of Poland" and the leader of the post-1831 emigration.

soul must be nourished. Therefore, the Church is the most important to organic work, for it is the soul of the national body.* (Walerian Kalinka, *France's Defeat and the Future of Europe.* [Cracow, 1871])

The essence of the differences between the ultramontanes and the circles around Hôtel Lambert lay in the fact that for the former the only point of reference was the political interest of the Holy See, whereas the latter continued to raise the "Polish cause" in an attempt to create an anti-Russian coalition in Europe. The ultramontanes believed that the Poles should relinquish all foreign policy, while the Hôtel Lambert politicians perceived foreign politics as an area of constant flux: they saw hope for a better tomorrow in the transformation of the diplomatic stage. Czartoryski viewed the attempt by the Poles to create a political alliance with the Austrian monarchy as a logical consequence of the requirements of organic work.

The ideas of organic work, especially in their conservative version, were rejected by the consistent pro-independence politicians, the followers of the traditions of 1863 (such as, Zygmunt Miłkowski or Agaton Giller). The representatives of the emigration's extreme left, connected with European socialism, were also hostile to organicism.

In April 1867 an article entitled "Organic Work" appeared in *Niepodległość* (Independence). In the article—which, in the opinion of Jerzy W. Borejsza, was written by Miłkowski—we read: "Recently, a formula was invented which serves as a lock for shutting mouths. If anyone expresses a more definite demand, if anyone states that there is a need for serious work, for work with a goal, they are immediately told: 'organic work.'" The author declared himself a proponent of organic work "in the fields of politics, learning, literature, arts, trade, industry, farming." To him organic work was to be "permeated through and through with a striving for the liberation of the motherland" (*Niepodległość*, 4/30/1887, cited in W. Borejsza, *The Polish Emigra-*

---

*Kalinka's ideas related mostly to the part of Poland ruled by Prussia, where the brutal anti-Polish political course was related to the anti-Catholic *Kulturkampf*. These problems, in all their complexity, are discussed by Lech Trzeciakowski in his book *In the Territories Annexed by Prussia: 1850–1918*. I will discuss these issues in another article.

tion, pp. 224–225). Uprisings were to be an unavoidable necessity. The article's final words—"work as the means, Poland's sovereignty as an end"—were close to the ideas of Łukaszewski discussed above. The differences lay in emphasis; Miłkowski stressed the need to prepare a new insurrection, whereas Łukaszewski was concerned with making his program more concrete and anticonciliatory, postponing plans for an uprising until an unspecified later date.

The journalists of the émigré left questioned the organic program even more aggressively. Włodzimierz Rożałowski, criticizing the pro-Austrian orientation among Poles, wrote:

> We seem to be convinced that if today we dream of alliances—in the official, diplomatic definition of this word—we are preparing a future uprising. But with whom are we to align ourselves? Who will want to enter into alliances with us? Maybe Austria. But against whom? Perhaps against ourselves.

He presented his own program thus:

> It is up to us to take the initiative at once for a future national movement, to go to the people with words of knowledge used in ways that they will understand best, to present them with the goals and the mission, to extract from them a sense of civic dignity and duty by eradicating ignorance and fanaticism. In open associations or secret conspiracies we must create a broad popular collusion, which, once it matures, can undertake an effective war on foreign invaders and domestic enemies alike. (Włodzimierz Rożałowski, "To the People at Home," *Zmowa,* no. 1/1870, quoted in *Polish Radical Democrats,* a selection of writings edited by Felicja Romaniukowa [Warsaw, 1960], pp. 36–38)

Walery Wróblewski's views were expressed in a similar tone:

> In a country that has faltered under the burden of the horrible yoke of foreign force, I cannot understand work that is called organic, that is legal, that is compromising, that is in the spirit of Targowica. I can only see one path for Poland to take, a steep, exhausting path which is covered in blood from top to bottom: the

missionary's path of the spoken and written word, of deeds among the people, through the mediation of conspiring youth. (*Niepodległość*, 2/10/1869, cited by J. W. Borejsza, *The Polish Emigration*, p. 225)

One should not conclude from these quotations that anyone, even Wróblewski with his radical words, questioned the need to develop industry or to spread knowledge. These people only questioned the ideology of organicism, defined in contrast to the principle of sovereignty, as a substitute for ideology, and not as a supplement to purely political programs. This is an important distinction: it was not the idea of "work at the grass roots" but the resignation of national ambitions in favor of "grass-roots work" that characterized the disagreement between Poland and the emigration.

There was a basic difference between the cognitive perspectives of the émigré and of the Pole at home. The Pole back home, as Jerzy Jedlicki aptly observed,

was accustomed to resignation and was not a maximalist. When . . . hope and enthusiasm were revived, he rose up and fought to emancipate the peasant, to liberate the motherland. When those hopes did not exist, he wanted to pull his country out—if not from captivity, then at least from under the rubble. Unable to win independence, he at least wanted to strive for modernity; unable to free his nation from foreign domination, he at least wanted to free it from backwardness.

The émigré was different. "The homeless wanderer," continues Jedlicki, "had to be a maximalist: he dreamed of being the soldier returning to Poland as it liberated itself. Everything that made this mirage more distant, everything that distracted people from this main goal, seemed harmful" (Jerzy Jedlicki, "Polish Ideological Currents and the West, 1790–1863," in *Homeliness and Strangeness* [Warsaw, 1973], pp. 227–288).

Jedlicki cut right to the point. The émigré, almost by definition, felt close to the standpoint of Cato. He was not likely to forgive weakness in the face of the invader. All too often he would identify compromise with treason, and conformism equally often seemed to him apostasy. This can be understood on a psychological plane. Every one of the exiles waited for his imminent return to the motherland, for radical and instantaneous resistance to the invader, because this alone justified his status of exile. Compromise with the invader in a sense took away his *raison d'être,* made him dispensable. The average émigré had to reject all forms of accord, even if these were concluded for important reasons. To the banal thesis that "Poland has been bled white," he would respond: "Our country has no forces. But it was with our hands that the Caucasus was conquered for the Muscovites, with our blood that the unity of Germany was assured; it is our bones that are strewn in Algeria, throughout Europe, and even in Santo Domingo" (A. W[ernicki], "About National Forces," *Głos wolny,* 3/28/1867, cited by J. W. Borejsza, *The Polish Emigration,* p. 247).

Programs of compromise, formulated by the centers of political thought back home, would be called "debasement" by the émigré who remained faithful to the banner of insurrection. The Pole back home attached greater importance to concrete things. If only for this reason, the seemingly identical ideas formulated by the émigré and by the Pole at home had to be different.

Soon after the insurrection was defeated, the idea of reaching an agreement with the Austrian monarchy gained popularity among the Hôtel Lambert politicians. Similar tendencies appeared also in Galicia, and they were expressed by Paweł Popiel, among others. Popiel, one of the most prominent Galician conservatives, wrote an open letter to another conservative politician, the Rev. Jerzy Lubomirski. In this letter he expressed his views on the current situation and on the conditions for an agreement with Austria. He condemned insurrectionist traditions and conspiracies for independence and instead promoted an honest and loyal attitude of obedience to the policies of the Vienna government in exchange for territorial self-government and broad cultural autonomy.

> If we have a right to make demands on this government, to embark on the path of justice and true equality in regard to our country, then this government has the right to ask us for some guarantees. If it is to give us our language, learning and self-govern-ment, it must have some base of support in our country. Vienna must know that we will not use all this against it, that it will not become a tool in the hand of revolution. . . . There is no point in talking about the future in politics. The future lies in the hands of

God. No honest man can renounce the future, no conscientious man will prejudge the future. But what is certain is that only those peoples who have spiritual values, reason, unity and wealth, will have a future. And this cannot be attained without an agreement with the rulers because the rulers are always an organic tool in society. The nation that will always live antagonistically with its rulers will not develop that most important condition for mankind: respect for authority. . . . I must therefore condemn loudly all attempts to regain a political existence when it is still too early for it, before the necessary internal forces and external means and circumstances are present. . . . With our sickly predisposition, with suffering plaguing us from all sides, every single internal or external change or complexity awakens our great hopes. But if today we cherish dreams of antagonism among the great European powers, or of the consolidation of the western—as opposed to eastern—Slavs, or of making a point of Archimedes out of Galicia, we will gain nothing from it. Rather, we will impede the creation of natural, organic conditions for real freedom in the whole country. We should not take a separate stand or defend constitutionalism, which has brought us nothing good, but rather take advantage of legal institutions and gain for ourselves all the freedoms that the current ministry, in accordance with its principles, is obliged to grant to all provinces of the Austrian state. . . . Let us ignore the great politics that have nothing to do with the real concerns of our country, which is in a state of social atomization and immorality. We are standing at a crossroads: either we will, under the influence of secret forces, dissipate in aimless struggle the remainder of our energies, or on the lawful and open road we will win for ourselves conditions for a life that, even if it is not our ultimate ideal, will guarantee us a normal education and basic social forms and principles." (Paweł Popiel, *Writings,* 1:69–74)

It is easy to find in this and other statements by Popiel motifs that evolved into the components of Polish conservative thought. These are loyalty toward the monarch (even if it is the monarch of a partitioning power), condemnation of conspiracy, concern with preserving language and customs, and affirmation of social hierarchy, with the monarchy thought of as the guarantor of this hierarchy. Also typical was his radically negative attitude toward the 1863 Uprising, allegedly caused by "foreign inspiration, partially for foreign ends" (ibid., p. 18), as well as his demand for the elimination from public life of all those who directly or indirectly took part in insurrectionist actions. Even Józef Szujski, a close friend of Popiel's and a prominent journalist of the younger generation of Galician conservatives, entered into a debate with Popiel.

While accepting a large part of Popiel's reasoning, Szujski sharply attacked the proposition that ex-insurgents should be ostracized. "Do not," exclaimed Szujski, "listen to such false prophets as Mr. Paweł Popiel! . . . One has no right to resort to ostracism . . . or to say that whoever does not fit into the narrow framework of our political credo is against us and will be destroyed. For our credo ought to be a broad one in which there will be room for all people of ability and good will" (J. Szujski, "About Mr. Paweł Popiel's Brochure," p. 236). Without defending the insurrection itself and rejecting the option of new attempts at armed risings, Szujski wrote: "Our wounds are honest, and the reasons for our unhappiness great and noble" (ibid., p. 212). Józef Ignacy Kraszewski replied to Popiel in a similar vein:

> Probably no one will stand up for revolution, and no one will deny that advantage should be taken of certain opportunities that present themselves. But that does not require denying the past or completely trusting that the present will deliver what it promises. Healthy politics entails utilizing opportunities, but only insofar as virtue and kind-heartedness permit. (Józef Ignacy Kraszewski, "An Open Letter to Prince Jerzy Lubomirski," cited in Wincenty Danek, *Writings of J. I. Kraszewski 1859–1872* [Wrocław, 1957])

Kraszewski, himself an organicist of the consistently independence-oriented school, pointed out the limits of conciliation and the dividing line between compromise and renegation. In examining Paweł Popiel's political proposals one cannot say for certain whether this doyen of Galician conservatism crossed that line. Yet it seems indisputable that people who believed not merely in conciliation but in capitulation found in Popiel's writings the ideological justification for their behavior. This can also be said for the politics of all those who considered the different interests of the Polish nation and the Austrian monarchy to be the same. Popiel, without prejudging the future, decisively rejected any form of political activity *here and now* that would supersede Vienna's immediate interests and make Galicia a "Polish Piedmont" (this was the meaning of the remark about "the point of Archimedes"). And this was where the difference between Popiel and the Hôtel Lambert lay. Those who reasoned along the same lines as Popiel, wrote Ludwik Bystrzonowski, Czartoryski's close collaborator, "do not understand their position. They are Galicians and not Poles" (quoted in J. Zdrada, *Twilight of the Czartoryskis,* p. 100). About others, it might be said that, even more than Galicians, they were subjects of the Austrian monarch. A classic example of such a legitimist and Austrian patriot was Count Kazimierz Starzeński, formerly a colonel of the Austrian army. In 1849 Starzeński took part in suppressing the Hungarian uprising, and fifteen years later he was honored with a message from Emperor Franz Joseph for his show of loyalty during the 1863 Uprising. During the Italian-Austrian conflict Starzeński made a public offer to form volunteer detachments of "Cracovians" in Galicia to fight alongside the Austrian army.

In reference to Starzeński's initiative Władysław Czartoryski presented Hôtel Lambert's viewpoint. To the émigrés he recommended caution, restraint, and patience in expecting changes in the political situation. He wrote: "No, there is no room for the Polish flag in Europe's battle array today. The emigration, which, be what may, always guards the interests of all Poland, will not and cannot yet link itself with any one of the sides in the war and, regardless of the direction in which it may lean, must wait patiently and calmly." This advice to the émigrés was a veiled polemic against the radical faction of the emigration, which was planning to form Polish legions on the Italian side. Czartoryski carefully drew a distinction between the duties of the émigré Poles and those of the Galician Poles:

> Volunteer divisions in Galicia are a different matter because only in Galicia are neither faith nor nationality threatened by the government. Rather, Galicia has been endowed with institutions that promise it a fuller national life. . . . If I were a citizen of Galicia, I would do everything possible to maintain the existing system. The Galician politicians today are carrying the Polish province . . . and thereby preserving a base for the most cherished hopes for the future.

This is the most important thing that can be done at the moment for the national cause. (*Czas*, 5/31/1866, quoted in J. Zdrada, *Twilight of the Czartoryskis,* p. 117)

In expressing his program of support for the Austrian monarchy, the leader of Hôtel Lambert by no means identified unconditionally with the Galician policy of conciliation. The phrase "the most cherished hopes for the future" was blatantly at odds with Paweł Popiel's remarks about "the point of Archimedes." In turn, unconditional support for the Viennese status quo was definitely at variance with the thinking of the liberal wing of the Galician conciliators led by Franciszek Smolka. Smolka favored the reshaping of the monarchy from a dual one (Austro-Hungarian) into a federal one, as well as an alliance between Poland and the other conquered nations in the name of the universal values of the motto "For your freedom and ours." Smolka was an anti-insurrectionist, but he did not renounce either the tradition or the ideology of sovereignty. On this issue he was in agreement with Hôtel Lambert. But he differed from them in his belief that abandoning the readiness to fight for more autonomy, all for the sake of an illusory vision of harmonious cooperation with Vienna, would lead to defeatism. Smolka believed that it was only by pressuring the central government— together with the pressure of all nationalities—that the Poles would be able to obtain a favorable compromise. He did not believe in the generous and gracious aid of Austrian diplomats in return for Polish loyalty to their monarch. "In politics, no one is guided by sentiments," wrote the newspaper of the democratic-conciliators, *Gazeta Narodowa* in Cracow. "Prince Czartoryski may believe in the effectiveness of sentimentality, but we know of no such diplomacy" (*Gazeta Narodowa,* 5/31/1866, cited in J. Zdrada, *Twilight of the Czartoryskis,* p. 118). The émigré irredentists reasoned in a similar fashion. For them, as for Smolka, an alliance with the nations ruled by Austria was more important than the alliance with the imperial bureaucracy in Vienna.

Smolka and Popiel differed on many issues. Apart from the ones that have already been mentioned, they also held different social beliefs. Smolka was a democrat and Popiel a radical conservative. But they did agree on one question: both accepted the idea of organic work. This idea was also shared by conservatives of the younger generation, who had previously favored an insurrection and who were known as "Stańczycy." Józef Szujski, one of the leaders of this faction, wrote:

> Today, after the enfranchisement has been completed, we have a situation where conspiracy is completely wrong, while the strategy of organic work is completely right! . . . The road of normal organic national development, the road of introducing social order following the enfranchisement and equal rights, is absolutely right. In the political, social, and economic spheres we should openly and publicly begin to utilize all the new forces at our disposal, to make ourselves into a group of public people honored with the trust of the nation. Parliament, public institutions, public associations: these make up our open, legal framework which should embody all our public activity, and these organs themselves should not engage in activities beyond the sphere of what is allowed them.

Szujski justified support for Austria in geopolitical categories: "Whoever today opposes the direction taken by the Poles in Austria, the direction of organic work for the foreseeable future, is siding directly with Moscow whether he likes it or not" (Józef Szujski, *About Mr. Paweł Popiel's Brochure*, pp. 281–284).

Over time, nongeopolitical arguments proved more important, for the Galician conservatives also approved of cooperation with the partitioning power in the Kingdom of Poland. They justified this by their concern for "conserving" social order. For this reason—and others— Szujski's essay, "A Few Truths about Our History," met with harsh criticism from the émigrés. The conservative publicist was accused of backwardness and readiness to compromise. His critics came from many political factions: next to Tokarzewicz, Julian Łukaszewski; next to Agaton Giller, Józef Ignacy Kraszewski. Among Szujski's antagonists were those who believed in organic work, but understood it in completely different ways.

The essence of the difference between these basically dissimilar programs was aptly captured by one émigré publicist, who wrote that the organicist in Poland "wants the work to be done within the limits drawn by the law with a nebulous goal in mind," whereas the émigré organicist-irredentist "wants the work to be done with an immediate goal in mind. . . . We suggest that long-lasting organic work be conducted in such a way so that the next uprising encounter not obstacles and difficulties, but moral and material reserves" (*Niepodległość*, 4/20/ 1867, cited in J. W. Borejsza, *The Polish Emigration*, pp. 225–226).

This stated a fundamental difference: What are the possibilities of action, and what are its limits? And also: What are the goals of organic work? According to Szujski, the limits were marked by the actual laws and regulations. Polish politicians ought to act within the confines of the law, since all other activities might summon the ominous specter of political conspiracy. The harmfulness of *liberum conspiro* was, for Szujski, far greater than the harmfulness of an exaggerated readiness to compromise and excessive loyalty toward the monarch of the partitioning country. The author of "A Few Truths . . ." feared illegal groups of self-education run by students more than the initiatives of Count Starzeński, whose "legion" was placed above the legions of Henryk Dąbrowski in articles in *Czas* (the paper of the "old" conservatives). Szujski favored a pro-Austrian orientation for reasons similar to those that determined the politics of the Hôtel Lambert circle; that is, he justified his choice with a particular concept of anti-Russian policies. But he did not clearly and explicitly conclude that sovereignty for the Poles was the goal of the actions he favored. Neither he nor the other "Stańczycy" tried to convince the Poles that they were striving for independent Polish statehood; instead they formulated unclear ideas about an Austrian-Polish solution. This was to serve as a remedy for the menaced national existence. Over time, the Stańczycy became loyal to three powers. In reaction to this evolution of the "Cracow group," Agaton Giller, who was far from a radical, attacked them vigorously:

> As long as we faithfully adhere to the banner of independence, freedom, and unity of Poland, our cause will be powerful and significant to the nation and the world. . . . It is possible to defend the Polish nation only under the banner of politics and state—without it, the defense will not succeed. (Agaton Giller, "About Servility and Flunkies" [Brussels, 1879], p. 122)

Giller wrote thus about the politics of the Stańczycy:

> Servility is like the plague. Once it has penetrated a man's soul, it can no longer be extracted. It eats through his moral organism and

destroys in his heart all sense of truth, dignity, and nobility. . . .
He who lets the plague into his soul can only be a lackey or a
policeman. He will be a lackey to the mighty, even as he wears the
nobleman's robe and fur hat and carries the curved sword inherited
from his senatorial forebears; he will be a policeman over the weak,
even as he wears the outfit of an editor or an academic's gown!
Servility is the disease of debasement to which whole nations succumb. This disease is especially dangerous for captive nations ruled
by foreign powers. The influence of servility is capable of clear-
ing the way for the invaders to morally annex Poland. (Ibid., pp.
143–144)

All organicists/exiles reasoned basically along the same lines as
Giller. They treated the concept of "work at the grass roots" as an evil
necessitated by the concrete internal situation (the ravages of the defeated uprising) as well as by the external situation (the absence of
favorable international circumstances). Organicism was to be a form of
activity that would lead to independence. Thus the organicist/émigré
could not accept legalism, since what was legal had been declared such
by the legislation of the invader and matched the interests of the invading
power. The main criterion should be not legalism but reality. To put it
more succinctly: the actions to be stipulated and favored were those
that had as their point of reference not the law formulated by the invader
in accordance with the invader's reason of state, but rather the needs
of the Poles for an independent existence. Actions should also be
determined according to the conditions for realistic activity, even if they
contradicted the Austrian, Russian, or Prussian penal codes. As long
as he wanted to remain in the least bit faithful to his role as émigré, no
exile could renounce the idea of national independence in return for an
eternal union—in whatever form—with any partitioning power, no
matter how liberal and tolerant toward the Poles that power might be.
The motto "Polonia irredenta" had to figure on the banner of all émigrés;
this ideal had to be formulated anew, restated and explained over and
over again.

Of the émigré publicists I have cited, Agaton Giller was a classic
case of the "stalwart" émigré who consistently upheld the tradition of
sovereignty and insurrection. It was not by accident: only the stalwart
émigrés cultivated this basic canon of thought on Poland's future and

movement for independence. The canon included (and I am naturally simplifying the issue): the glorification of Polish history; a vision of prepartition Poland as an oasis of freedom, justice, and tolerance; the acceptance of the leading role of the nobility; and the total affirmation of all irredentist activities: conspiracy, plots, and uprisings. Another important ingredient of this canon was the model, formed by romantic literature, of the heroic mentality of the Polish patriot.

One can observe a certain revisionism in the attitudes of the post-January Uprising émigrés in regard to the schema of traditions conceived in this way. The revisions were conducted from three ideological viewpoints, which for the sake of brevity can be called conservative, bourgeois, and plebeian. The conservatives, grouped around Hôtel Lambert, viewed the entire Polish tradition of insurrection critically, seeing aspects of "social revolution" in each effort at an uprising. According to them the 1863 Uprising "was essentially a social blow, and not a national struggle" (J. Zdrada, *Twilight of the Czartoryskis,* p. 53). All activities that in the past had led to insurrections, as well as the nature of the Polish moral code that demanded participation in insurrections, deserved to be judged harshly. Walerian Kalinka, who parted with the Czartoryskis' political ideas and shared the ultramontanism of the Community of the Resurrection, went even farther in his assessment of Poland's past. He wrote in a letter to Władysław Czartoryski:

> A nation that is hard on itself evokes respect in observers, but when it sows illusions they mock it. We have been accusing our enemies for a hundred years of causing the fall of Poland. What have we gained by it? We have only managed to deceive ourselves. We ourselves are the cause of Poland's fall; only we can raise it up if, with repentance in our hearts, we admit our mistakes. (J. Zdrada, *Twilight of the Czartoryskis,* pp. 48–49)

Kalinka, in his extremely negative and critical view of Poland's past, matched the radical opinions of the émigré left.

An example of this radicalism was an article entitled "300 Years Ago," published in *Le Peuple Polonais,* a periodical closely associated with the Democratic Society and Ludwik Mierosławski. It criticized celebrations of the anniversary of the Union of Lublin [1569] both in Poland and abroad.

Józef Hodi-Tokarzewicz, a proponent of the principles of social radicalism, was one of the opponents of this article. Since Hodi advanced a quasi-socialist and federalist version of the Jagiellonian tradition, he had to reject the negative assessment of this vitally important event in the history of Polish-Lithuanian relations. This is not to say that Tokarzewicz idealized Poland's past. In an article published in *Gmina* and entitled "Poland's Past and Future," he wrote:

> Isn't Poland's domestic history an uninterrupted sequence of the most dull decadence and the ugliest anarchy of the nobility on the one hand, and the most horrific captivity and darkest misery of the peasantry on the other? Surely, it is impossible to see in it the pale flicker of fraternity which might prevent the rulers from pushing the ruled into the ranks of beasts and objects. . . . The nobility's past is a great tomb; in fanaticism and madness the people desecrate this tomb and let the wind blow away the ashes from the graves of their oppressors. Our nobility and people have been flowing in two separate streams, heading in different directions for nine centuries now. (*Gmina*, no. 1/1866, quoted in *Polish Radical Democrats*, pp. 48–49)

Similar ideas can be found in the writings of another radical émigré, an outstanding activist of the Polish Republican Hearth, Ludwik Bulewski. He wrote:

> Two roads lead to the two worlds in which Poland can find a place for itself. The old road is full of treachery, quarrels, tricks, wilderness and delusions: the new road is straight, light, wide, and surrounded by clear, fresh, and healthy air. On the old road there is nothing for Poland other than distaste, hatred, and indifference; on the new road, fraternal embraces await it. . . . Inspired by its selfish instinct of self-preservation, the old world has allowed Poland to be erased from the map, in the belief that by crossing out its name, it will destroy its rights and its mission. (*Rzeczpospolita Polska*, no. 2/1869, quoted in ibid., pp. 128–129)

Tokarzewicz's idealization of the past—under the influence of Lelewel's ideas on communal property—was limited to the early Middle Ages. Bulewski's ideas were similar:

> The original institution of our society knew no monarchism, no inheritance, no class hierarchy, no privileges; it was republican in the full meaning of this word, based on the principle of equality in solidarity, and from it flowed the moral goals of the nation. This solidarity, enhanced by education, is transformed into a truly familial solidarity of love for the motherland. . . . And so the true, native Pole who has not allowed himself to be denationalized loves Poland not in one caste but in all its sons, regardless of their family, social origin, class or faith. (Cited in ibid., pp. 165–166)

Bulewski concluded his arguments thus:

> Let's stop playing with words and put an end to the overused and bloody irony: that "we all want Poland!" Because all Polish renegades beginning with Targowica and its king and ending with the Czartoryskis and Wielopolskis have also cried out and are still crying out that they want Poland! It is they who have led us to Poland along their own roads, through the Petersburgs, Parises, Romes and Istanbuls, and today they want to rescue Poland via Vienna. Let us firmly push aside these national Pharisees because the road that leads to Poland goes through Poland only, along Polish routes. (Quoted in ibid., p. 186)

Interpreting the nation's history in this fashion, Bulewski struck at the aristocratic-diplomatic faction. Striving for Polish self-reliance placed Bulewski close to the ideas of émigré organicists such as Julian Łukaszewski. One can easily see the strong antinobility and antiromantic accents in Łukaszewski's texts which I have already quoted. The idea that the way to rescue the nation from captivity lay not only in conspiracy and insurrection but also in industrial and educational activity can be found in his criticism of the mentality influenced by romantic poetry. Karol Swidziński, who in his radicalism was close to Jarosław Dąbrowski, reasoned along similar lines.

Łukaszewski and Swidziński rejected the romantic models of patriotism and the romantic mentality; in this they converged with conservative critics of romanticism, while in criticism of the nobility they resembled the émigré radicals. But it is worth recalling their basic differences here: for the conservatives the artistocracy and nobility were in principle the most important social classes; for Łukaszewski and Swidziński it was the bourgeoisie; the revolutionary democrats, meanwhile, saw the "working people of the towns and villages" as the core of the nation.

The practice of "organic work"—interpreted in whatever manner—gradually became a necessity for the Poles. After the defeat of France in 1871, when hopes for an improvement in the international situation were finally abandoned, Polish public opinion, including the emigration, came out heavily in favor of "work at the grass roots." This was implemented in various ways. Julian Łukaszewski, who had been condemned to exile, "in the 1870s and 1880s continued to attach importance to patriotic activity among the many Polish workers and craftsmen in Romania," according to Jerzy W. Borejsza (*The Polish Emigration,* p. 226). It was also there that he created his masterpiece, the Polish Library, which would later be given over to the Upper Silesian Literary Society in Bytom. The people around the Hôtel Lambert gradually joined in the activities of the Galician conciliatory-conservative camp and practiced the model of organic work formulated by Szujski in "A Few Truths . . . ." After Sedan, using the pens of Prince Czartoryski's former agents who later became the Stańczycy (Wodzicki, Tarnowski, Koźmian), they accepted the politics of triple loyalism and thereby abandoned Prince Adam Czartoryski's political line that had been pursued consistently for many years with shifting fortunes. They lost interest in Polish participation in the diplomatic game and in transforming the European political stage. When they did take part in international politics it was as subjects of the Austrian monarch.

The people around Jarosław Dąbrowski (for instance, Karol Swidziński) also often embraced the principle of organic work. After 1871, Swidziński, together with Pelagia Dąbrowska (the wife of Jarosław), returned to Galicia and there engaged in grass-roots work. But it should be stressed that in his political actions Swidziński was closer to Franciszek Smolka than to the Galician conservatives. The evolution that Karol

Swidziński and his friends underwent illustrates the split that must have taken place in the emigration's left wing. Returning to Poland Swidziński chose to accept reality and abandon the instant implementation of radical social slogans for concrete welfare actions. Others who chose the fate of exile continued to move to the left, in time allying themselves and cooperating with the International. Walery Wróblewski was a typical example of the latter group. In 1874 he defined his credo in the following words:

> Today, every Polish émigré who does not feel tied to the working class and does not realize that the cause of this class is his own cause is either a Jesuit or an ignoramus. In either case he deserves contempt, in either case he is an offender against his own nation.

In an attempt to answer the question: Who is an ally of the "Polish cause"? Wróblewski wrote:

> In Germany there exists one single party that honestly sympathizes with the Polish cause and is prepared to support it: the workers' party. In Austria . . . only the social-democratic party is capable of bringing about harmony among the Slavic nations united under Austrian rule. . . . In France, where anarchy reigns among the old political parties, the workers' party is the only party of hope. . . . Only this party can be our ally. Our former policies were useful in disillusioning us with all the French parties with which we had entered into alliances: they all cheated us. The Poles who will now stand under the banner of social democracy can fully count on the French workers' party, which will not be dishonest with them because of our shared goals. As for Russia, we must openly admit that the only party of any importance to us is the social-revolutionary party; we must work together with it in order to speed up the overthrow vital to the Polish and Russian nations. . . . We do not have great power, but the ideals of socialism written on our flag are brighter and broader than the old ideals of liberal democracy. The Polish cause was one with the socialist cause, and not with the exchange of one king for another. . . . As for myself, while I pay homage to our fathers, I will personally follow their example as long as I live. Without paying attention to the deserters who, like un-

natural sons, have walked away from the aquiline personages of the
past, the soldiers of the social revolution will march forward.

The above reflections are phrased in the language of the revolutionary socialists whom the former radical democrat Walery Wróblewski joined. In this evolution the universal ideals of the brotherhood
of nations were replaced by a concrete internationalist program of
cooperation among workers' parties. The idea of a national uprising
was transformed into the principle of "social revolution"; the idea of
national sovereignty was lodged in the more general slogan of creating
socialist communes. Wróblewski's new program broke off completely
with the classic canon of Polish irredentism, but it did not renounce the
idea of sovereignty.

The three directions of Polish historical revisionism were simply
three ways of thinking within the confines of national futurology. Once
again an old truth was confirmed: thinking about history is simply part
of reflections about the present and the future.

Irredentism that was limited to planning for insurrections and that
on principle rejected organic work was tantamount to adventurism.
Irredentism that lacked a program of social change, a program for the
education of the peasants and urban poor, had no chance of working
effectively for independence. Programs for social struggle which departed from the need to build factories and modernize agriculture, to
develop schools and health services, were neglecting important and
essential realities and making the struggle for social ideals more difficult
to win.

But a program of organic work that abandoned the struggle for an
independent Poland and for reform of social relations served as justification for the passivity of conformism. Organicism that limited itself
to economic activity or administrative service turned into the ideology
of egotistical careerists, who couched their loyalty toward the partitioning power in the cloak of a pseudopatriotic philosophy of history.

Warsaw, 1975

// 1863: Poland in Russian Eyes

// Following the defeat of the January Uprising [1863] against Russian rule, the tsarist policy toward the Poles was a function of two contradictory tendencies in the Russian power elite: conservative and radical-Slavophile. The conservatives, among them the governor of the Kingdom of Poland, Fëdr Berg, aimed at destroying the irredentist movement by tying the Polish propertied classes to the Russian imperium. This alliance against "social revolution" and for the defense of legitimistic "order" was to guarantee calm in the kingdom. For the Russian legitimists, the intellectual heirs of the tradition of the "Holy Alliance," the January Uprising was the particular Polish variant of social upheaval.

Mikhail Nikolayerich Muravyev, the "Hangman," who served as the governor general of Vilna, in his diaries blames the court clique of the conservatives-legitimists for lack of consistency and liberalism in their treatment of the rebellious Poles. However difficult it might be to call Muravyev a Slavophile (he was quite simply a dense and cruel gendarme ruled by primitivism and xenophobia), it must be said that on solutions to the Polish question he was in complete agreement with the Polish Kingdom's Administrative Committee, which was run by Slavophiles. Muravyev wrote this about his adversaries, the Petersburg conservatives:

It is well known that the majority of the Russian aristocracy, brought up on European ideas and having no respect for the Russian religion or the motherland, have always acted without conviction and in accordance with the direction dominant in the West. For them Russia and the Orthodox religion do not exist; they are cosmopolitan, colorless, and insensitive to what is good for their country; what matters most to them is their own interest and their own persons. Such were the dignitaries of the government with whom I had to conduct battle to implement my system of action.

According to Muravyev,

The leading government activists wanted to lead His Highness into a new system of general amnesty. . . . Improvidence, or rather the blindness, of the people in the emperor's entourage was so great, and their attachment to hostile European ideals so surpassed their feeling of love for the motherland . . . that they decided to try their hardest to restore to the northwestern lands all their former privileges of government, so as to enable Polish propaganda to function freely, and to allow the Polish nation to grow stronger. In their blindness they did not recognize that country as Russian and strived to . . . give it absolute autonomy, in accordance with the intentions of Wielopolski.

Valuyev, the minister of the interior, is described by Muravyev as "a man not without talents, but a cosmopolitan given to one single thought and desire: to win fame and recognition from Europe, even to the detriment of Russia." Dolgorukov, head of the gendarmerie, "is an upright and good man, devoted to the monarch, but, because of his weak character and small intellect, he is overpowered by the cosmopolitan idea." Gorchakov, the foreign minister, would "give into Europe when it was time to act," and he "basically adhered to Valuyev's system." In addition, Tolstoy, the minister of postal services, even though he "had no influence on matters of state, would in his private conversations with the tsar hurt the Russian cause by trying to maintain a system that favored the Poles."

Muravyev labeled all these politicians as "cosmopolitans" and as "the Polish party" at the Russian court. Their cosmopolitanism consisted of taking into consideration—albeit cautiously—the opinions of the West, while their pro-Polish orientation lay in supporting for a while the program of Count Wielopolski, who proposed a policy of conciliation with the Russians in exchange for limited autonomy for Poland. After all, the conservative circles considered the possibility of creating some compromise version of the count's conciliatory program even after the insurrection, but all this remained in the sphere of undefined plans. Another tendency, radically Slavophile, came to dominate, whose exponents—Milyutin, Cherkasski, and Samarin—were the directors of the Administrative Committee.

The following occurrence aptly illustrates the essence of the difference between the two tendencies. Yuri Samarin was (from 1845 to 1848) a member of a special government commission called upon to examine the social and national relations in the Baltic countries conquered by Russia. Samarin's mission bore literary fruit in the form of his *Letters from Riga,* whose imperial and nationalist ideology struck at the ruling aristocracy, the German feudal lords. Samarin accused the administration of those states of abandoning the policy of Russification vis-à-vis the Germans and of failing to protect the Estonian and Latvian peasants, who were being exploited by the German lords. The close alliance of the Russian administration and the German aristocracy, Samarin claimed, led to the abandonment of the national assimilation of the peasants. Samarin's theses angered the governor of Riga, and the author was jailed. The issue went to the emperor himself. In his conversation with Samarin, Nicholas I said, among other things:

> You have awakened the Germans' animosity toward the Russians, Sir, you have set them at variance with each other when you ought to have brought them closer together. You have attacked whole classes that have served us faithfully: beginning with Pahlen, I could list a hundred and fifty generals. You want to use force to make Russians out of Germans, with a sword in your hand, as if you were Muhammad; but we should not be doing this, precisely because we are Christians. . . . You have aimed directly at the government: you wanted to say that from the times of Emperor Peter I we have all

been surrounded by Germans and that we ourselves have become Germanized. You must understand what you had done: you have mobilized the public against the government, and this was leading to a repetition of the events of December 14. [The "Decembrist" revolt of 1825]

The historian Andrzej Walicki accurately describes the above controversy as the "encounter of nationalistic conservatism with traditional legitimistic conservatism." For the traditional conservatives the aristocracy and nobility served as guarantor of the social order; social position was more important than national origin or creed. The Slavophiles believed that the social class that guaranteed order was the Russian, Orthodox peasantry that had not been spoiled by European civilization. This conflict sharpened when means of solving the peasant question in the empire were under discussion. The Slavophiles—including Milyutin and Samarin—tried to persuade Tsar Alexander II to embrace the radical ideas of emancipation and enfranchisement. The conservatives, including Valuyev, favored a policy of moderation. The disputes over a policy toward the Poles were a reflection of earlier differences. The conservatives aimed to destroy the revolutionary elements; the elements the Slavophiles wanted to eradicate were Polish.

The Slavophile tendency was supported by the pen of the writer Mikhail Nikiforovich Katkov, a former occidentalist and Anglophile, who now was a convert to tsarist absolutism. It was also backed by the actions of Mikhail Nikolayevich Muravyev, who had little interest in political theories but was well known for his political practices. The Slavophiles Katkov and Muravyev shared a decidedly negative attitude on all attempts at a compromise resolution of the conflict with the Poles. The Polish insurrection, however, was understood in many different ways. To the publicists of the Slavophile camp, the Polish-Russian conflict was, in the deepest sense, a conflict between Russia and Europe. It was an antagonism not only of two contradictory political arguments but of two civilizations, for Poland had throughout its history been the avant-garde of Latin-Catholic civilization. It was for this reason, they thought, that the European press would side with the Poles.

Katkov reasoned differently. He wrote:

The Polish question has always been a Russian question. Already a long time ago history placed the fatal question of life and death between these two nations of the same race. . . . The question that had to be solved was not who was to lead or who was to be more powerful, but who was to exist. An independent Poland could not exist next to a self-contained Russia. Compromises were impossible: one of the two had to renounce political sovereignty. . . . It is not enough for the Pole to be Polish, he wants the Russian to turn into a Pole or else to move out behind the Urals. . . . Our struggle with Poland is a struggle of two nations. To give in to the fulfillment of Polish patriotism is equivalent to passing a death sentence on the Russian nation.

According to Katkov, "the Polish rising is not at all a national insurrection! It was not the nation but the nobility and the clergy that rose up." It was an "intrigue of the nobility and the Jesuits." Katkov explained:

This intrigue had begun a long time before the armed insurrection in Poland. It was able to grab into its hands and organize for its ends all that was unclean, rotten, and insane in our society. Our pitiful revolutionaries, consciously or not, became a tool in its hands. Our absurd materialism, atheism, and all kinds of emancipations . . . found active support in this intrigue. . . . More than one liberal teacher who propagated cosmopolitanism or atheism became an indirect instrument of the Jesuit intrigue and of that particular nationality which burrowed underground, and in the darkness undermined, all the roots of Russian public life.

A definite disparity existed between Katkov's ideas and the opinions of the Slavophiles, although it had no influence on policies. In Katkov's opinion French and Belgian journalists defended the Poles not in the name of the values of Western civilization (as the Slavophiles claimed) but simply because the Poles had bribed them. Jan Kucharzewski commented on this difference thus:

The Slavophiles saw the nest of the intrigue in Rome and considered Poland to be the unfortunate tool of Catholic Rome and of its Jesuit agents. In their opinion, only a Poland cleansed of Catholicism and of Western civilization could live in peace with Russia. Katkov believes that Poland in itself is the origin of evil, Russia's archenemy, and that in this Catholicism and Western civilization do not play a decisive role. . . . The Slavophiles saw Poland as the vanguard of Rome; their program lay in breaking off Poland's ties with the West, and especially in tearing Poland away from Catholicism. Katkov considered Catholic activity as harmful to Russia because under the influence of Polish priests it stood up to defend the Polish cause. There, Poland was a tool of Catholicism; here, Catholicism is a tool of Poland.

But none of these differences had any influence on the form of the proposed political solutions to the Polish question. On this issue Katkov fully supported the policies of the Slavophile Administrative Committee. He viewed it as an effective tool for definitively liquidating the Polish nation. "The common people in Poland," according to Katkov, "do not want their own independence and prefer to be dependent on any other nation, be it Slavic or German, as long as they do not have to march together with their masters. . . . Polish patriotism is a specter rising from its grave. . . . The forces which once joined the Polish nation into one have disappeared. . . ." Katkov argued that the task for Russian policy was to finally settle accounts with those "vegetating debris" of Polish national consciousness.

The Slavophiles understood their mission somewhat differently; for them the fight with the Polish insurrection was above all an ideological war. Their opinions on this were presented by Samarin in his article "The Contemporary Importance of the Polish Question." In his summary of that article Andrzej Walicki extracts three points in Samarin's attitude: "(1) the Polish nation, i.e., the Polish masses, which has all the characteristics of a distinct Slavic nationality; (2) the Polish state, always an invader in its relationship with its eastern neighbors; and (3) 'Polonism,' a cultural force closely related to Catholicism, represented by the Polish nobility and clergy." "Polonism" had transformed Poland into a "sharp wedge driven by Latin culture into the very heart of the Slavic world, with the aim of breaking it into splinters." It was Polonism that in Poland destroyed the Slavic rural community and created a feudal aristocracy that does not exist in other Slavic countries, making the Polish state into an enemy of all things Slavic as well as Europe's faithful vassal. Still, Poland has remained a Slavic nation; the nobility's and clergy's "Latin soul" has not managed to kill the "Slavic soul" of the Polish people. The Russian government should seek support among the Polish people and declare—in the name of the "Slavic character"—an uncompromising war on Polonism. Samarin wrote: "The future of Poland—if it has a future—is lodged in the Slavic world . . . and not in a subservient position in the Latin world."

Such was the credo of Milyutin's Administrative Committee. At the time he was sent on a mission to the Kingdom of Poland, Milyutin was out of favor as a proponent of radical land reform in Russia. But in the Polish situation his radical ideas took on a new dimension. The policies aimed at economic and political destruction of the nobility, and the consistent fight with the Catholic Church combined with enfranchising reforms for the peasantry, were to achieve a final split between the Polish peasant and the Polish nobleman. This would threaten the very roots of Polishness. The Poles' cultural identity was to be destroyed and the Polish peasant was to adore his liberators, the Russian dictators/state officials.

Milyutin and Samarin declared that the ongoing struggle was a confrontation between Russian, Slavic progressive forces and the backward Polish nobility and clergy. This phraseology made it easy for earlier oppositionists, renegades of the liberal and revolutionary movement, to gather under their banners and to wrap in pseudoprogressive ideology Milyutin's cruel repressions and the policies of Russification in the Kingdom of Poland. The progressive slogans and the radical agrarian reform took on a sinister meaning that revealed itself in the way the village communities were organized by the Administrative Committee. Milyutin's reform, admittedly, was more favorable to the peasants than the reform instituted in Russia and even the insurgents' decree of January 22, 1863. The nobility's property was ruthlessly destroyed. The power of landowners over villages was liquidated with equal ruthlessness. "The tsarist government," wrote Stefan Kieniewicz, "made a radical cut: it excluded the landowner from all influence in the village community, subjecting him instead to the community leadership elected by the peasants. This move was not dictated by concern for the good of the peasant but by the interests of tsarist policies. When the reform was implemented the village self-government found itself in the hands of the scribes appointed in practice by the district authorities. The peasant, liberated from the patrimonial suzerainty of the landowner, found himself under the strict tutelage of the tsarist bureaucracy." The emancipation proved to be a means of subordinating the peasant to the dictatorial partitioning power.

This was also the reason for supporting the peasantry's demands against the nobility. The Polish peasant was emancipated by the decrees of Russian bureaucrats against Polish noblemen. The goal of this operation was to destroy the Polish national collectivity.

The policies of the Administrative Committee evoked horror in Polish conservatives, who called them "Greek Orthodox socialism." The Petersburg conservatives and Berg were also displeased, and the latter gradually forced Milyutin's team to become more moderate. This opposition was perfectly understandable. The Russian conservatives had little understanding of the ideological goals of these policies, but their practical effects were bound to cause them distress. The violation of the principle of social hierarchy, the infringement on the principle of private property, the legalization and support of the peasantry's demands—all these moves were unacceptable to politicians who trusted the force of tradition and therefore could not believe in the possibility of liquidating a nation with a thousand-year-old culture by administrative means. They could not approve of policies that revolutionized social relations and aimed at expropriating the Polish upper classes. They greatly feared that these social experiments would be transferred into the Russian state.

The conservatives' arguments were presented by Aleksandr Koshelov, the dictator of finances in the Kingdom during the Milyutin period, who checked somewhat the doctrinaire enthusiasm of his Slavophile colleagues. The policy of enfranchisement in the kingdom, wrote Koshelov in his memoirs,

> did not contradict my beliefs. However, since I knew Prince Cher-
> kasski and Milyutin rather well, I feared that the decree would be

not only the final wartime method to suppress the unrest . . . but also the beginning and the source of other undertakings that would aim to inconvenience and annihilate the nobility. I was, of course, by no means sympathetic to the nobles, but I considered them in these times an irreplaceable element that, if only for this reason, ought to be tolerated and protected.

In a memorandum to the tsar Koshelov explained:

We should not concentrate all power in the hands of the peasantry and rely only on them. To do so, we would have to betray all our traditions and change our whole regime, because it is impossible to act in one part of the empire in the spirit of radical democracy, and elsewhere to hold onto other, healthier principles. . . . This type of bureaucratic mob rule in one area of our country would have disastrous consequences in other areas; it would mean infecting Russia with a disease, implanting into its healthy body a venom that would poison its forces and lead to its downfall.

The author of these words was not a conservative in the legitimistic spirit. Rather, he was linked to the Slavophile camp, leaned toward moderately liberal solutions, and, in discussions during the "thaw" after the battle of Sevastopol, favored a peculiar form of constitutionalism. Koshelov and the Slavophiles were striving to enfranchise the peasantry, but his lack of faith in the omnipotence of the bureaucratic apparatus brought him closer, in this specific situation, to the traditional conservatives. This gives an indication of the fluidity of political and ideological divisions in the Russia of that day. Still, regardless of the difference between Milyutin and Valuyev or between Koshelov and Muravyev, it must be said that no pro-Polish "party" existed in Russia at the time, if we judge the matter on its merits, disregarding comments to that effect in Muravyev's diaries. The programs of Valuyev, Berg, and others were by no means pro-Polish; at most, they made Russia's presence in Poland less burdensome to the Polish propertied classes. Those who recently had been liberals were also not pro-Polish: they agreed on the total denial of Polish irredentist ambitions. On the "Polish question" the Russian liberals supported the Russian monarch.

Jan Kucharzewski uses Fieoktistov to demonstrate the intellectual evolution of a Russian liberal of that era. Let us recall Kucharzewski's excellent reasoning. Yevgeny Fieoktistov was a progressive, a constitutionalist, an opponent of despotic governments and a proponent of freedom of the press. Together with other publicists he edited the liberal biweekly *Russkaya Rech'*, and with others he supported the anti-Polish policies of Tsar Alexander II. He explained his motivations in a letter to the Russian writer, countess Elizaveta Sailhas (Evgenia Tur), when she was in Switzerland.

Replying to her letter, which was pro-Polish and in the spirit of Herzen's *Kolokol,* Fieoktistov explained that he had not changed his liberal beliefs but that the situation in Russia had changed. Public opinion had appeared, a new and positive phenomenon in Russia. In Fieoktistov's opinion this was the beginning of a new era in which the monarch and the government would have to reckon with the ideas of the so-called enlightened classes. This state of affairs would soon lead to the creation of parliamentary-constitutional institutions in Russia. On the Polish question Russian public opinion is in agreement: everyone is convinced that the Poles' irredentist efforts must be suppressed. Fieoktistov agrees with this, which is not to say that he has departed from his liberal ideals. On the contrary: he wants for the Poles "all possible happiness and the greatest political and civil liberty . . . full religious tolerance, and unrestrained development in all spheres of civic life." This can be achieved along with a liberal constitution for the empire. But if the Poles choose the path of struggle for sovereignty, they are condemning themselves to a continued, inevitable conflict with the Russian nation. Herzen is wrong in his belief that the Poles are only fighting the Russian government. They are fighting the entire Russian nation, striking at its most fundamental interests. "Katkov is only saying," writes Fieoktistov, "*à peu près* what the whole Russian public is thinking. . . . If tomorrow, by some miracle, a revolution took place in Petersburg thanks to which, instead of Aleksandr Nikolayevich, Bakunin sat on the throne, the Poles would still be our worst enemy." The implementation of the Poles' irredentist goals would mean a catastrophe for Russia. The separation of Poland could have the effect of an avalanche. Finland, Courland, Lithuania, and the Ukraine could also detach themselves, as could Khazan and Astrakhan, or even Siberia. Next to Russia would be established a state antagonistic by its very nature, separating Russia from Europe, dangerous as a tool in the hands of French or English politicians.

This reasoning seems to represent a typical ideological justification of the anti-Polish attitude of yesterday's liberals. It revealed the whole weakness of Russian liberalism—its internal division and lack of consistency. But to reduce the attitude of the Russian "liberal party" on the Polish insurrection to these elements would be an oversimplification. It seems that the inconsistency in the liberals' stand on the Polish question lay at the very core of liberal thinking: the combination of attempts to modernize and democratize the Russian state and a constant concern with its imperial status. Liberalism was primarily a plan for making the Russian state more efficient and only secondarily a repository of ideological values. This thesis can also be illustrated by the interesting memoirs of the outstanding Russian lawyer, Anatol F. Koni, well known for his liberal and occidental views. Koni paid for his nonconformity by frequently being attacked in the nationalistic press, especially by its arch-priest and prophet, Mikhail Katkov. In one of his feuilletons, Katkov went so far as to write obvious untruths. Koni considered taking Katkov to court for slander, "but I remembered," recalls the famous lawyer, "my student years, the impression Katkov's articles had made in 1863 [the year of the January Uprising], their role in awakening the national awareness of the Russians: they helped to cement the unity of Russia, and for the first time created a situation worthy of the pen of a serious publicist. In view of these doubtless achievements of Katkov's, I found myself unable to raise my hand—or rather my pen. . . ." This emotion did not stop the illustrious lawyer from condemning, a few dozen pages earlier, Muravyev's repressions in Lithuania, for which Katkov had served as an apologist in 1863.

The views of Nikolay Turgenev offer another example of the attitudes of the Russian liberal. His views deserve even more attention because they were not restrained by tsarist censorship: the ex-Decembrist Turgenev was an émigré. He made statements on the Polish issue on many occasions; his opinions evolved markedly over a dozen or so years. At first (in 1847) he favored a program of independence for

Poland and believed that this was the key to freedom for Russia. Then, he changed his mind and replaced the slogan of independence with autonomy. He sharply condemned the oppression of Poles, but justified his position with the argument that such a policy was harmful to the Russian monarchy. Turgenev considered the January Uprising a "serious mistake" of the Poles since it spoiled the accord between the Poles and the Russians on which Aleksander Wielopolski had been working. Turgenev saw Wielopolski's program as the only possible plan for resolving the "Polish question": the integration of the Kingdom of Poland with Russia was to resemble the union between Galicia and Austria or between Ireland and England. Therefore, as befitted a liberal, Turgenev did not propose the full Russification of the Polish territories (this was to apply solely to the so-called annexed lands), but he suggested that a Territorial Council be convened and a place reserved therein for the Poles. The émigré liberal did not restrict himself to theoretical reflection. Discussing the Polish uprising he stated that "the Polish insurrectionists have murdered three or four times more peaceful people in the cities, and especially in the villages, than have Russian court-martials and proconsuls."

But it is only fair to note that among Russian émigrés Turgenev stood alone in his opinions. Other Russian émigrés took a definite pro-Polish stand. Among them was Prince Pyotr Dolgorukov, a descendant of the famous aristocratic family, an adversary of the Romanov dynasty, and an opponent of the absolutist system of tsarist rule. He favored an independent Polish state with the borders of 1815. On the remaining territories that had belonged to the Polish Commonwealth prior to 1772 a referendum was to be conducted. The population of those lands—Lithuanians and Ukrainians—would decide whether they wanted to belong to Russia or to the newly reborn Poland. Dolgorukov did not picture a self-governing Lithuania or Ukraine; in this he was in agreement with the Polish independence-oriented publicists. The émigré "lame prince" reasoned that Russia, governed as it was by a stupid, ineffective, and corrupt bureaucracy, could bring the Polish nation nothing but captivity. "We, the Russians," he wrote, "should be absolutely convinced that as long as Poland does not regain its liberty by whatever means, we are going to remain slaves. . . . The liberation of Poland will inevitably lead to the liberation of Russia; this is the sine qua non for the freedom of Russia." In accordance with this credo, the "lame prince" fully supported the uprising of 1863. He condemned Muravyev's actions and Katkov's writings, and drew beautiful portraits of Potiebnia and Sierakowski. He wrote to his countrymen, "By assisting the Petersburg government in subjugating the Poles, the Russians are forging chains for their own slavery. The Russians who side with the Poles are acting for Russia's freedom and defending its honor."

Dolgorukov's point of view was the exact opposite of Turgenev's. When we counterpose these two writers' opinions on the Polish issue, it is easy to notice a characteristic split in Russian liberal thinking—a separation of actions from values. Reasoning in pragmatic terms, the Russian liberal would justify the reforms he proposed by referring to the interests of his state; reasoning theoretically, he would refer to a universal order of values. For example, the reform of the franchise on the one hand strengthened the state and on the other implemented the ideals of equality before the law and justice. The Polish insurrection led to a conflict between these two ways of thinking: the interest of the state demanded the rejection of abstract values and principles. Both Turgenev and Dolgorukov attempted to reconcile their ideology with practical demands. The ex-Decembrist underscored his concern with the Poles' national rights, while the "lame prince" explained that the freeing of Poland was in the vital interest of the Russian state. The former had forgotten that only the Poles were in a position to decide the shape of their national rights, whereas the latter did not understand that the interests of the Russian state lie in that which the citizens of that state consider to be their interest. Turgenev chose the pragmatic aspect of the liberal position, while Dolgorukov remained faithful to the universal values of liberalism. They both paid a high price for it: the former Decembrist lost the sympathy of the émigrés and the "lame prince" lost his authority in Russia—something that affected him deeply. Indeed, Dolgorukov knew that he was contradicting the opinions of his compatriots: it was not for nothing that he named his periodical *Le Véridique*.

Other Russian émigrés also sided with the Poles in 1863: Golovin and Pechorin; Blumer and Ogaryov; and also Herzen and Bakunin, who tried to transform their philo-Polish declarations into armed action. Still, siding with the Poles did not mean identifying the interests of the Russian opposition with the Polish rebels. Aleksandr Herzen, the moral leader of the Russian democratic camp, was an ardent proponent of the "Polish cause" and at the same time a partisan of the idea of a Slavic federation. In 1859 he expressed his ideas in the following way:

> Poland . . . has an undeniable and complete right to exist as a state independent of Russia. Do we want a free Poland to distance itself from Russia? This is another matter. No, we do not want this and how could we, when different nationalities and animosity between nations are one of the principal obstacles to the free development of mankind. However much I detest all centralization, I am convinced that federations of related nations give the state much greater opportunities than the dispersion of one family of nations into separate branches. A federal union should be a voluntary gift: Russia has no right to Poland; it should have earned what it has taken by force; it should erase what has been done with its hands. But if Poland does not want an alliance with Russia, we can grieve over it, we can disagree with Poland, but we must leave it the freedom to choose, unless we want to abandon our basic principles.

Two years later, upon learning of the first demonstrations in Warsaw, Herzen repeated his *memento:* "We have talked so many times about a future union of all Slavic tribes, and today we still believe in it—but today this point is not on the agenda. In the immediate future, it is the historical task of all the Slavs to make Poland independent and to unite its torn-up parts."

In undertaking cooperation with the Poles and supporting—despite his dreams of a federation—the Polish irredentists, Herzen was not supporting irredentism "as such," but only a specific part of the Polish independence camp. He did not back the "aristocratic party" of Hôtel Lambert, but only the Central National Committee, which had a progressive and democratic social program. Herzen wrote in *Kolokol* in reply to a letter from the Polish Central National Committee:

> The principles upon which you are calling for an uprising are so broad and so modern and have been formulated so precisely that we

have no doubt that your words will awaken a deep and active sympathy among all Russians who themselves want to cast off the humiliating and degrading fetters of state tutelage. It is easy for us to march together with you. You are granting the peasants the right to own the soil which they cultivate, and all nations the right to determine their fate. Such are also our principles, our dogmas, our banners.

The above argument contains the following reasoning: "We are supporting you, Polish conspirators, because you believe in a social philosophy similar to ours. This is the necessary condition for a Polish-Russian understanding." Other Russian revolutionaries, both at home and abroad, thought alike.

The Poles and the Russians were aware of their fundamentally different political goals. The Russian revolutionaries' political goals could be summed up in the slogan of abolition of autocracy and in the demands for far-reaching social reform. The Poles wanted to win independence. In defining the Polish point of view, the Central National Committee wrote to the editors of *Kolokol:* "Our difference over the peasantry question stems from our different points of departure and the situations in which we find ourselves. The Russian movement is concerned with the land, while ours is national. In Russia a social movement will bring political freedom, whereas in our country a reorganization of society can only be achieved through liberation and restoration of our national independence."

Herzen was also aware of these differences. In reminiscing on his contacts with Poles, he wrote in *My Past and Thoughts:*

We had different points of departure and our paths crossed only at the point of shared hatred for the Petersburg autocracy. The Polish ideal went beyond that; they marched toward their past which had been severed by force, and it was only from there that their path could continue. They had plenty of relics; we had empty cradles. . . . They are striving to revive their dead, while we want to bury ours as quickly as possible. . . . In the obscurity of the prison of Nicholas's reign, as we sat behind locked doors as prisonmates, we empathized rather than knew each other. But when the little window was opened somewhat, we guessed that we had been brought here along different routes and that from here our paths would diverge. We sighed joyously after the Crimean War ended; they were offended by our happiness: the change of climate in Russia reminded them of their losses and not of hopes. We were eager to move forward, ready to break anything; for us the new times began with lofty demands, for them—with church services and mourning prayers. But the government, again, united us. When shots were fired at priests and children, at crucifixes and women, at hymns and prayers, all questions were silenced, all differences were erased.

The Russian Revolution and the Polish Restoration reached agreement in opposing tsarist despotism. The Russian revolutionary camp lent its support to Polish irredentism.

This support was mostly moral and in practice was based on the emigrants' public pronouncements. The opposition in Russia was helpless and decimated through arrests (among those arrested was also an ideologist of the younger generation sympathetic to the "Polish question," Nikolay Chernyshevskii). The officers' conspiracy was uncovered, and the much hoped-for peasant revolts did not occur. Only a small number of Russian officers went over to the rebels. After the wave of repression, the Zemlya i Volya organization was incapable of any action. Longin Panteleyev, a member of that organization's leadership, made the following remark in his diaries on the question of negotiations with Padlewski: "How can we assist them? In no way: we don't even have the capability to commit the slightest act of sabotage to further their cause."

The Russian revolutionaries were helpless. Helplessness, however, did not mean betrayal; Herzen's and Chernyshevskii's followers did not desert the Poles—they did not join the anti-Polish campaign. They paid for their pro-Polish sympathies not only with hard labor and exile but also by losing all popularity among the Russian intelligentsia, whose thinking became muddled by the nationalistic writings of the era. In 1863 Herzen was replaced by Katkov as the moral influence on Russian hearts and minds. By supporting the Polish insurrectionists, the editor of *Kolokol* condemned himself to political solitude.

Herzen's contacts with the Polish émigrés did not compensate for his loss of communication with Russia. The relations between the Polish and Russian émigrés began to sour. Again, the paths of Russian revolution and Polish restoration diverged. The assessments of the effects of the Russian enfranchisement policy in the kingdom created a sharp conflict. For the Poles, understandably—the only criterion for judging this policy was the Russifying edge of Milyutin's decrees; for the Russians—not surprisingly—other aspects of the problem were also taken into account.

To reiterate: for the Russian democrats, the "Polish question" was only one of many important issues, but it was by no means the only or the most important one. Undoubtedly, their most significant concern was the emancipation of the peasantry. The Russian democrats supported Tsar Alexander II's reforming tendency immediately after his access to power, and they sympathized with those politicians who presented the most radical reform programs. Among them was Nikolay Milyutin, called "the red" in court circles. The progressive groups interpreted the rejection of Milyutin's program of emancipation of the peasantry and his removal from the work that prepared the emancipation as regressive for the tsarist reform policies. Pyotr Kropotkin, the famous revolutionary, remarked on this in a characteristic manner in his memoirs. Kropotkin and his comrades were of course aware that Milyutin came from the camp of the opposition; still, from among the enormous tsarist bureaucracy that split into many cliques, Milyutin was closer to the progressive intelligentsia than to conservative politicians, such as Valuyev or Gorchakov, who opposed the antinobility emancipation reforms.

The Poles' reasoning was the exact reverse of this. To them the conservative Berg was much easier to digest, because he was less aggravating than Milyutin, whom they despised most of all. Milyutin they hated perhaps even more than they did the cruel Muravyev, for Muravyev simply hanged people whereas Milyutin used his perfidious "Orthodox socialism" to destroy—or so he thought—the very core of the Polish nation, the nobility.

After the tsarist ukase that decreed the forced sale of estates belonging to the Polish insurrectionists in the so-called annexed territories, *Kolokol* published an article by Nikolay Ogaryov, "On the Sale of

Estates in the Western Country." Calling the policy of expropriation and resettlement of the Poles a crime, Ogaryov remarked that the Russian government gave the right to purchase these estates to "Russian landowners and German schemers" while denying this right to the peasants. Ogaryov wrote:

> Perhaps a need would have been found among the local peasants or among peasants from other *guberniyas* for land in the western country. The local peasants could have been given the opportunity to join into associations in order to buy the estates, in return for annual payments stretched over many years, with the mutual guarantee of the association. . . . Petty farmers from other *guberniyas* should have been asked to move to the western country and to purchase land on the same condition of payments over many years.

This idea provoked sharp reactions among Polish émigrés, who interpreted it as the affirmation of the policy of Russification. Russians also reacted to it. Aleksandr Serno-Solovyevich wrote this in the pamphlet "Question polonaise":

> I want to protest in order to certify that *Kolokol* is no longer the banner of young Russia. . . . I understand the method of implementing socialist theories . . . in a different manner than do the gentlemen who edit *Kolokol*. Before one prescribes a drug, one ought absolutely to prove one's medical qualifications, to be recognized as a doctor. But if I am offered a cure that consists of the whip or the bayonet then I have the right to say: "Either get out of my house or admit that you are robbers and thugs" . . . One of the principal tasks that socialism will resolve in the future is to find a formula for establishing an economic base for society which will thereby give not only every nation but every community the opportunity to exist fully and independently.

Serno-Solovyevich formulated his attitude toward Poland thus:

> I protest in order to prove to the Poles that there still exist people in Russia who blush at the Russians' assumption of the roles of bandits and torturers and who earnestly wish, without having any

ulterior motives, for the complete emancipation of Poland, i.e., the separation of everything Polish from Russia. . . . I am not going to say to the Poles: "Dear brothers, give me your hand because your cause is our cause" and other such platitudes. On the contrary, I will tell them openly: I am very sympathetic to the cause of your nation of heroes, your nation that has been oppressed by the nation to which I belong, but still your cause will not be our cause so long as the Polish movement carries the banner of the aristocrats and priests, as long as the Polish movement does not become a popular movement.

Poland was first to detach itself and only then could it form a free federation—such was Serno-Solovyevich's conclusion: "First a split, then a fraternal alliance."

Aleksandr Serno-Solovyevich's pronouncement bore the traces of the émigrés' "quarrels of the damned." Both Herzen and Ogaryov would certainly have lent their support to his positive program, but their differences had been blown out of proportion (as were Ogaryov's by the Polish critics of this article). It seems certain that Ogaryov did not approve of the policy of Russification. In his article (as Wiktoria and Rene Śliwowski have noted correctly) can be found

the reflections of old illusions, the echoes of a faith in the uninten-tional effectiveness of the authorities' actions, in the involuntary good results of orders from above, in the possibility of exploiting these for the "goals of Russian socialism."

Ogaryov's article had an antinobility and not an anti-Polish edge to it; he stood up for the interests of the peasantry and not for Russification. The editor of *Kolokol* frequently expressed his consistent antiaristo-cratic convictions. He wrote in a letter to a friend:

"If Pugachev shows up here, I will volunteer as his aide-de-camp because the Polish nobility does not arouse in me a hundredth of the hatred that the Russian nobility does. The latter is frivolous, mean, and inseparably attached to the Russian government."

This opinion provides final proof that Ogaryov's statement may have been clumsy, tactless, badly timed, but in no way gave support to Milyutin's anti-Polish policy or to Muravyev's officials in the Kingdom of Poland and in Lithuania—something of which not only Ogaryov but Herzen and Bakunin were accused by many Polish émigrés. Jan Kucharzewski, an outstanding historian and great expert on this question, took up this accusation, generalized it, and made it into a historical truth.

> The hatred of Poles was the putty intended to seal the masses and the government and the different camps, forming a single patriotic front that would march against its enemies as a mass, singing the tsarist hymn. Indeed, it was a peculiar phenomenon: Russian currents that until now have fought each other furiously, when they meet on Polish ground become brothers, shake hands, link up with the unbreakable knot of a shared cause. The fraternal harmony reigning between Muravyev and red Milyutin is an example of this *union sacrée*. The Slavophiles who formed a fronde against the German imperium of Petersburg and reproached the government . . . during the Crimean War that it had been overlooking pan-Slavic goals, now found an outlet for their missionary enthusiasm in Poland. Samarin was to go there . . . , in order to exterminate on the banks of the Vistula the poisonous influence of Rome and of the rotting West. The newly awakened and agitating spirit of popular democracy, . . . dissatisfied with the reform, in search of a way to gain access to the hearts and minds of the Russian peasants, would for the time being be redirected to the annexed lands and to the Congress Kingdom of Poland and there liberate the people from the fetters of their Polish masters. The admirers of Proudhon, the advocates of the slogan that property is theft, would march onto Polish soil and there emancipate; Feuerbach's disciples would fight Catholicism; the pupils of *Zemlya i Volya* would have room to experiment; the nihilistic impulse would find an outlet in the destruction of the Polish culture.

Elsewhere Kucharzewski remarked that the "sociopolitical ideology these *deyatele* took with them to Poland was a reflection of Herzen's Slavophile-populist Messianic spirit."

I consider Kucharzewski's assessment false and oversimplified.

Because this judgment concerns one of Poland's outstanding historians, it requires a brief commentary. I have already cited the opinion of Aleksandr Serno-Solovyevich on the aristocratic-clerical and anti-populist character of the January Uprising. Taken out of context, this opinion at first seems not to differ in any way from Katkov's or the Slavophiles' viewpoints on the issue. But it should be remembered that when two people say the same thing, it need not have the same meaning. In Katkov's or Aksakov's writings, accusations against Polish irreden-tists for their backwardness served as a smoke screen for the practices of Great Russian nationalism and for a specific sociopolitical program. "In the minds of those tsarist bandits and democrats," Kucharzewski aptly noted, "was ingrained an idea characteristic of original despotism, a view of the ruler as the owner of all the land in the country and of his subjects who are tenants thanks to his good graces, which he could always revoke: this was tsarist communism."

Serno-Solovyevich, Bakunin, and the editors of *Kolokol* had differ-ent ideas. In their opinion land should belong to the peasants and be administered by communities. They saw their main task as steering the nation toward a social upheaval that would expropriate land from the landowners and hand it over to the communities; it would also entail a political upturn that would liquidate the tsarist apparatus of oppression. Bakunin's or Herzen's critical attitude toward the 1863 Uprising stemmed from their conviction—shared by many Poles—that the Polish rebels had concentrated on the ideology of independence to the detri-ment of radical slogans for agrarian reform. According to the Russian revolutionaries, the Poles' sole chance lay in transforming the insurrec-tion into an agrarian revolution and a people's war. Only mass partici-pation of the peasantry could make the partisan rebels invincible; only an agrarian revolt could provoke peasant riots in the Ukraine and in Russia itself.

The editors of *Kolokol* grieved that the National Government's inconsequential policies made possible the suppression of the uprising and made it easier for Muravyev or Milyutin to represent their sordid deeds as generosity toward the peasantry. Bakunin described Milyutin's policies as "the most repulsive and dangerous hypocrisy born in our times: the government's democracy and the red bureaucracy." Herzen called those who implemented Milyutin's policies "imperial sans-culottes." About the politics of expropriation itself, he wrote:

> The government's plans are clear: it wants to push *per fas et nefas* the Polish population out of the Western Country and to tie the Ruthenian population to Russia with ties stronger than the essays . . . and philological studies written by the Great Russian patriots. It lacked the courage to opt for the Asian method of mass exile or of forced resettlement; this would be cruel, unjust, but powerful. The sordid method of individual accusations based on informers' reports, i.e., the demoralization of the peasants, appeared more pleasant to the government. Let no one think that the Petersburg government ever fussed over applying these radical measure. Considering itself the owner of the land and people in accordance with Eastern thinking, it never retreated before anything, and without reservations behaved the way the peasant behaves toward his cattle. . . . What do you think: Should I grant the right to ownership as a reward for good behavior? I will give presents to whomever I like! Gracchus Baboeuf went far but neither he nor the Convention of 1794 nor the communists could rise up to where our own Tartar Gracchus arrived naturally. This is what it means to draw super-knowledge directly from Eastern sources.

Such was "Herzen's respect for the Petersburg satraps who distributed land to the Polish peasants," to quote Jan Kucharzewski. According to him, "The patriotic Pole-hating mission is a drug that puts to sleep the Russians' sensitivity to their political slavery; what is more, it elevates this slavery to the heights of sacrifice for Russia's greatness." This, of course, is an accurate remark: campaigns of chauvinism are always a method of resolving internal conflicts, and this is not a specifically Russian phenomenon. It is particularly burdensome and unpleasant when only the chauvinists have a monopoly on expressing their point of view.

The editor of *Kolokol*, accused by the Russian press of treason to the motherland, said:

> We love the Russian nation and Russia, but we are not possessed by patriotic passion or by the boring insanity of Russomania, not

such loathsome methods. The government itself . . . is submerged in some sort of Pugachovism. Concerned simply with the eradication of the Polish uprising, destroying the Polish element in Lithuania, the government, without realizing it, is leading Russia somewhere other than it intends to. . . .

And Herzen explains:

> If the government really does extend these methods of Spartacus to all Russia and finds zealous executors for them, then the people who because we are practiced cosmopolitans but simply because our love of the motherland does not reach . . . that solidarity of the herd which justifies crimes and participates in them. . . . What is going on in Russia now . . . is not an argument against our hopes. This whole orgy of executioners' exploits and of drunken patriotism has merely revealed that the internal movement cannot be halted with proclaim the right of the peasantry to the land and consider the land state property that really does not belong to anyone will also have to formulate an address to Alexander Nikolayevich and thank him for taking upon himself with the state's hands (although clad in Muravyev's gloves) all that is lamentable, coercive, and repulsive— in the future revolt of the peasantry.

It was in this—and solely in this—context that Herzen spoke of the positive effects of the emancipation policies of the tsarist officials in the Kingdom of Poland and in Lithuania.

Similarly limited was the often emphasized (by, among others, Jan Kucharzewski) unity of ideas between Bakunin and the editors of *Kolokol* on one side, and the Pan-Slavic camp on the other. This purported unity was said to concern attitudes toward Western civilization and toward the Slavs. Herzen and Bakunin, unlike Nikolay Chernyshevskii, for example, were not occidentalists. They were both very critical of the bourgeois civilization of Europe. According to Bakunin,

> the social order has degenerated in the West and is barely surviving with sickly effort. . . . In Western Europe, wherever one turns, one can observe incompetence, weakness, lack of hope, and demoralization . . . all stemming from a lack of faith. Starting at the very top

These words of Bakunin's are from his famous "confession," which he wrote in the fortress of Petropavlovsk. Tsar Nicholas wrote on their margin: "What blatant truth."

When one compares these two viewpoints, it is easy to conclude that it was on the issue of hatred toward the "rotten West" that the alliance of Russian conservative and Russian revolutionary groups was formed, all the more so since the phrase "the rotten West" was first used by the Pan-Slavist Shevyriov. Such a conclusion, however, would be a misinterpretation, in my opinion. It is true that the anti-Occidental tendency of a great part of the Russian intelligentsia would later permit

> of the social ladder, not one man, not one privileged class, believes in his calling or his rights; they are all bluffing one another, and no one trusts anyone lower than himself. Privileges, classes, and the authorities are holding out just barely, thanks to their egotism and habits. What a weak dam to hold off the impending storm!

the exploitation of anti-Western slogans and a permanent misrepresentation of the West, that it would lead to the use of this misrepresentation in various ideological contexts. It is also true that later, in different circumstances, Slavophile reactionaries and revolutionary critics of capitalist Europe would meet on an anti-Occidental platform. Bakunin's confession was the first signal of the possibility of such a meeting—still, Bakunin did not support the tsar's policies in practice.

The anti-Occidental motif was also present in Herzen's writings. The editor of *Kolokol* likened Western Europe to ancient Rome and prophesied its fall, which was to resemble the fall of the Roman Empire. "That part of the world," he wrote about Western Europe, "has completed its course; its forces have been exhausted; the nations that inhabit those lands have fulfilled their mission, and are getting slow-witted, lagging behind." In another piece of writing Herzen argued: "The hour has struck for the Slavic world." Herzen believed that Russia's historical mission lay in conquering Constantinople and uniting the Slavic nations. At first glance, this thought is identical to the demands of the Pan-Slavists: they too called for the conquest of Constantinople and the union of the Slavic nations; they too believed that Western civilization was nearing its fall.

Herzen, however, favored agrarian socialism and opposed the tsarist autocracy, whereas Aksakov and other Pan-Slavists repudiated socialism and praised the tsar. In Aksakov's thinking the tsar was to realize the mission of the Slavic nations: they were to be united under his scepter; for Herzen this union could come into being on the ruins of the tsarist empire. Aksakov wanted tsarist Russia to subjugate the Slavic peoples; Herzen supported the conquered Slavs' aspirations for independence, even though some of them were anti-Russian. Bakunin thought like Herzen, and favored the creation of a "great, powerful, and free all-Slavic federation"; at the same time he emphasized: "We want Poland, Lithuania, the Ukraine, Finland, Latvia . . . to regain their full liberty, the right to govern themselves, and to sort things out according to their own will."

The demand for "the right to detach themselves" for the nations conquered by Russia was, in practice, proof of the total discord between the goals of the revolutionaries and the aspirations of the Pan-Slavs. The Pan-Slavs, in the writings of their ideologue Nikolay Danilevskii, supported the conquest of the "noble-Jesuit" Poland and called Poland the "Judas of the Slavs." Poland was excluded from the community of Slavic nations extolled by the Pan-Slavists, who grieved for the fate of the Slavs suffering under the Austrian and Turkish yokes.

The Pan-Slavic propaganda resulted in the Slavic congress that took place in Moscow in 1857, when the Russian Pan-Slavists called upon the representatives of the Slavic nations to "realize fraternity on the Slavic soil." Both Herzen and Bakunin sharply condemned the anti-Polish pronouncements at the congress and emphatically detached themselves from the imperial and chauvinistic slogans of the Pan-Slavists. Bakunin described Pan-Slavism as "an idea that is as horrendous as it is dangerous." He wrote:

> It is true, however, that many of the Slavs under Austrian rule are awaiting rescue and a rescuer out of Petersburg. Horrible, and fully justified, hatred has led them to this madness, and they either cannot remember or are unaware of all the misfortunes suffered by

Lithuania, Poland, Little Russia, and even the Great Russian people itself under the yoke of Muscovite and Petersburg despotism. They expect to be liberated by our all-Russian, tsarist knout.

Every Polish democrat could subscribe to these opinions.

Warsaw, 1978

// Conversation in the Citadel

If you insist on your dreams of nationhood, of an independent Poland, and all of your illusions, you will bring on yourselves a great misfortune.

—Tsar Nicholas I

In order to prevent future disorder in Warsaw, the Warsaw Citadel was erected and paid for by the city, which is guilty of the latest revolt.

—Ivan Paskevich

TO A POLISH MOTHER

O Polish mother, if the radiant eyes
    Of genius kindle in thy darling's face,
If even in his childish aspect rise
    The pride and honor of his ancient race;

If, turning from his playmates' joyous throng,
    He runs to find the bard and hear his lays,
If with bowed head he listens to the song
    Of ancient glory and departed days:

O Polish mother, ill must be his part!
    Before the Mother of Our Sorrows kneel,

Gaze on the sword that cleaves her living heart—
  Such is the craven blow thy breast shall feel!

Though peoples, powers, and schisms a truce declare,
  And though the whole wide world in peace may bloom,
In battle—without glory—must he share;
  In martyrdom—with an eternal tomb.

Soon bid him seek a solitary cave
  And ponder there—on rushes lay his head,
Breathe the foul vapors of a hidden grave,
  And with the envenomed serpent share his bed.

There will he learn to hide his wrath from reach,
  To sink his thought as in the abyss profound,
Slyly to poison with miasmic speech,
  And humbly, like the serpent, kiss the ground.

A child in Nazareth, our Savior mild
  Fondled the cross whereon he saved mankind:
O Polish mother, I would have thy child
  Thus early learn what playthings he will find.

His young arms load with chains, his body frail
  Full soon have harnessed to a barrow, so
Before the headsman's axe he shall not pale,
  Nor at the swinging halter crimson grow.

Not his to venture like a plumèd knight
  And plant the holy cross on pagan soil,
Nor like a soldier of new faith to fight
  In Freedom's cause, and for her sake to toil.

One day an unknown spy will challenge him,
  A perjured court his adversary be,
The jousting-field, a secret dungeon grim;
  A powerful foe the verdict will decree.

And for the vanquished man as monument
  The gallows tree will rear its sullen height;

For glory—but a woman's tears, soon spent,
And fellow patriots' whispered words by night.

—Adam Mickiewicz
[This translation by Jewell Parish and G. R. Noyes]

The gentry felt the Chamberlain spoke true.
No one is ever reconciled, they knew,
Who once has had a quarrel with the Tsar,
But fights or moulders in Siberia.

—Adam Mickiewicz
(*Pan Tadeusz,* Book X, Emigration, Jacek lines 233–236.)

I jotted down the following remarks in a somewhat unusual situation—in a prison cell they refer to as lodging, for prisoners who are called internees. My fellow internees, Warsaw factory workers and students from Warsaw universities, asked me to give a lecture to fill somehow the empty days. What do Poles talk about in jail? About the same things they always have, the same things as their fathers, grandfathers, and great-grandfathers did when they were jailed in the pavilions of the Citadel. Today, the Citadel no longer exists. The jail has been replaced by a museum of the revolutionary movement. But the myth of the Citadel remains, as does the symbol of the Citadel. Now we have Białołęka. Will a commemorative plaque be placed here one day?

It occurred to me that it might be interesting to recount anew our grandfathers' disputes over victories and defeats, over freedom and sovereignty, over programs and ideas; that it might be worth recreating their nocturnal disputes and heartfelt quarrels when, eighty years ago, they were apprehended during a strike, arrested in a street demonstration, taken in after a church service for a free Poland, or caught while posting announcements—and landed in the Citadel where they would await their freedom and better days.

This was to be a series of lectures. But it was interrupted when I was moved into solitary confinement. Here, in idyllic peaceful conditions, I wrote what was supposed to be read aloud. Such are the origins of this text and its title.

The Cradle of the Century

It so happened that in my jail readings I once again reached back to the turn-of-the-century era, to books dealing with the early period of Polish nationalism and Polish socialism.

This was an interesting period: a modern nation was being born; modern conflicts were taking place within this nation, which had modern ideologies. It has been widely accepted that the most important conflict of that time was the dispute between Piłsudski's Polish Socialist party (PPS) and the National League under the leadership of Dmowski, Popławski, and Balicki. Others believe that the key to understanding the tensions of that era lies in the conflict between the proponents of national sovereignty and those who renounced independence. The latter included both the conservative conciliators in the Kingdom of Poland as well as the left-wing leaders of the Social Democracy of the Kingdom of Poland and Lithuania (SDKPiL); opposites were supposed to attract. Still others have defined the meaning of the ideological and political pluralism of that era as an articulation of particular ambitions of different social groups: the bourgeoisie, the proletariat, the peasantry.

Certainly everyone is right to some degree. But personally I believe that it is also valid to discern the meaning of the divisions of that era in the dispute between those who believed that realism entailed activity within the limits defined by the partitioning power and those who favored the concept of building an active Polish politics outside those limits. This at least was the case in the part of Poland ruled by Russia, where the tsarist legal system made it impossible for the Poles to become masters of their own fate. In Galicia and in the German sector things were different. There the Poles had more liberties. But it was precisely the (Russian-dominated) Kingdom of Poland that was the most important region for the artisans of Polish political aspirations.

Conciliation and Its Critics

The dualism of romanticism versus positivism was ingrained in Polish political thought, and the alternatives of armed insurrection versus organic work a part of Polish practice. It was absolutely necessary to overcome these alternatives in order to create a new style of political thinking. Let us remember that the January Uprising [1863] in the Kingdom against Russian rule, its course and its defeat, was a major mental shock that for many years weighed on Polish political life. Facing up to the failure of the insurrection led to a new approach: calls for independence were replaced by programs of political compromise and organic work. The anti-insurrectionist camp was by no means uniform. A great deal divided the conservative Zygmunt Wielopolski from the liberal Spasowicz, or Świętochowski from Sienkiewicz, but they all shared the conviction that, at that moment, thinking about independence was a daydream and a misunderstanding. Poland, they felt, needed not conspirators but doctors and engineers, and only loyalty to the partitioning power's legal system could allow the Poles to gradually undertake actions leading to an improvement of the national fate. The ideals of the insurrectionists were rejected by conservative landowners and Westward-looking bourgeois liberals. They were criticized by writers and industrialists, mocked by freethinkers, and cursed by bishops from their pulpits. The anti-insurrectionary shock was so potent that even the first socialists who revolted against tsarist oppression, Ludwik Waryński's comrades, wrote on their banners: "Down with nationality; long live social revolution." A quarter of a century had to pass, a new generation not contaminated by the shock of the defeat had to mature, for these dogmas to be critically appraised.

The new current was not the outcome of cool intellectual reflection. It was the product of new times, when the plebeian elements were gaining a national consciousness while the nobility was losing its spiritual monopoly. It was a response to new questions arising out of a new situation.

The conciliators would say: we must stand firm on a realistic foundation, we must do what is possible by giving up the impossible, we must recognize the reality of the Russian presence in the Kingdom of Poland and bargain with the Russians over concessions instead of retaining in our minds the absurd plan for an armed struggle for independence. We must renounce illusions—although, they would add, we should not give up our dreams.

But their youthful adversaries would respond that realism is not just the acknowledgment of facts like foreign domination. Realism must recognize as equally real the national striving for sovereignty. A realist is not a person who simply understands the ineffectiveness of insurrectionist activity but rather one who is able to analyze the causes of the defeats of national uprisings, to inscribe the achievements of past freedom fighters in the ethical and political consciousness of his contemporaries, and to build of those actions a living tradition and a weapon more effective than the rebel's double-barreled gun. The realist must understand that the need for national and civic liberty, inherent in the human soul, is no less real than the realities of jail and foreign domination.

The critics of compromise would say that the ineffectiveness of insurrectionist tactics should not lead to the abandonment of the idea of sovereignty but rather to a search for new roads and new ways to achieve independence. The conciliatory camp is drawing the wrong conclusions from its critique of uprisings. Its first mistake is to lower Polish political aspirations to the level of seeking concessions from the partitioning governments; whereas in actuality Poles must not renounce the long-term policy that aims for independence. Its second mistake is to believe that the partitioning powers will make concessions to the Poles only at the cost of surrender and passivity; whereas in reality concessions can only be won through pressure. To be able to impose such pressure, the Poles must first organize themselves to act autonomously.

The National Democratic and the socialist movements were two different methods of constructing this social autonomy.

National Democracy and the Politics of Activism

The early National Democrats (NDs) are described in an excellent book edited by Barbara Toruńczyk.[1] In her book (consisting of a lucid selection of texts, a thorough introduction, and a good chronology of events of that era) the author manages to extract an outline of those national-democratic traditions that have not only been forgotten by the

---

1. *National Democracy: An Anthology of the Political Thought from "Przegląd Wszechpolski" (1895–1905)*, selected, prefaced, and edited by Barbara Toruńczyk (Warsaw: NOWa, 1981; London: Aneks, 1983).

majority of readers but also consciously deformed by national democratic and antinational democratic stereotypes.

Contemporary followers of National Democracy construct in their publications stereotypes based on misrepresentations of their own history, and a vision of the past that is free from mistakes, perplexities, and dramatic choices. The stereotypes assume a continuity from the National League to contemporary anti-Mafia and anti-Semitic aberrations and anti-German obsessions; the approval of a model of national culture based on xenophobia and intolerance in the style of Jędrzej Giertych [contemporary émigré politician]; and the frequent acceptance of false geopolitics that can lead to servility toward the USSR. No one has written a history of ND thought with all its different currents, internal tensions, oppositions, and secessions. Certainly, traces of all these features can be found in the writings of some émigrés (for example, W. Wasiutyński), in some historical works (for example, R. Wapiński's), in the essays of A. Micewski (Dmowski's biographer), and in the articles of A. Hall, a young publicist from Gdańsk. But these are all merely traces of an enormous topic.

The contemporary National Democratic camp lacks a political thought for the present; that is, a diagnosis of current events and a plan for the future. This tendency still wants to function as a coherent political and ideological entity, differing from others by its particular conception of the nation and its collection of phobias and resentments. I propose to look for the origins of these phenomena, marking the demise of ND political thought, in the ideological evolution of this group during the Second Republic, when the originality of its programmatic conceptions was increasingly replaced by a fascination with the successes of the national totalitarian movements in other European countries.

The anti-ND stereotype, especially the leftist one, is equally one-dimensional and primitive. It stresses the national democrats' xenophobia and anti-Semitism, their pro-Russian character, connections with the propertied classes and tsardom, their attraction to the truncheon and to dictatorship, their sympathy for fascism. Let us add here that the downfall of national democratic followers in exile (Giertych, and most of the writing that appears in *Myśl Polska*), at home (Bolesław

Piasecki [Pax leader]), and among the oppositionists (*Samoobrona Polska*) tends to justify this stereotype, enriching and broadening our knowledge of the intellectual horizons of the sleuths of the "Jewish-freemasonic conspiracy."

Yet the existence of stereotypes impoverishes thought, distances it from historical truth, makes it backward and dogmatic. This is especially true of political thought, which requires coolness, distance, and reflection. Indeed, even in my own articles I can detect contamination by the anti-ND stereotype, by the emotions which I am able to rationalize today but which have made it difficult to untangle the Gordian knot of tradition. Yet for someone who learned at school about Hitlerite anti-Semitism and its outcome, and who saw with his own eyes the 1968 attempt to use anti-Semitism politically, the ND's programmatic anti-Semitism did not lend itself to dispassionate reflection.

I therefore saw Barbara Toruńczyk's book as a wise and penetrating polemic against stereotypes: wise because it allows the original texts to speak for themselves; penetrating because it attempts to explain the phenomenon of National Democracy by separating its innovative characteristics from its backward, murky, and provincial ones. Toruńczyk makes an earnest attempt to discern the roots of the greatness and pettiness which are both present in *Przegląd Wszechpolski*, the NDs' theoretical newspaper. She correctly takes as her point of departure the national democrats' unwillingness to conciliate, for it was this that brought out the modes of thought, arguments, and techniques which shook the public from its long social torpor.

This torpor found its political expression in the conciliatory ideas and passivity of the elites. It was said that "Every protest action will only sharpen the repressions and bring new victims." "Illegal actions" (the well-known *liberum conspiro*) were said to destroy in people the sense of law and to lead to irresponsible acts that damage what ought to be protected, such as a legal Polish press and other existing national institutions. Empty spectacular gestures would allegedly only impair the strategy of resistance to denationalization and provoke the authorities to be more vigilant and more repressive.

Roman Dmowski's reply comprised several parts. It would be a mistake, he said, to believe that the resistance movement can be kept within limits that the invader will not notice. Such limits are so narrow that they only allow a semblance of resistance. The authorities tolerate legal institutions as long as these are not dangerous, that is, when they do not fulfill their natural functions in the nation's life. How can one speak of respect for the law in the part of Poland ruled by Russia, when the mere defense of national identity brings one into conflict with it? The right to a dignified national existence can only be won illegally. This is why we must surmount the barrier of legality. Everyone must grow accustomed to living illegally.

> Our policy must be revolutionary. It cannot be "organic work," because it has no legal foundation on which to lean; it cannot become defensive, because the debris that are left do not permit us to live and to grow, and a program limited to defense would be equivalent to a slow death. . . . Those aspects of national life that cannot be developed on legal ground, we will create illegally. We are not allowed to have autonomous and serious press or literature, so we will create a free press and an illegal literature. To counteract the government's schools that aim to deprive us of national identity and to kill both physically and morally, we will have a conspiratorial national school. Next to innocent legal associations, we will develop secret associations in which public life will be centered. Next to the courts that have been imposed on us and that frequently poison our national organism, we will erect our own courts that will denounce all rottenness. To the invader's government that depends on police and bayonets, we will juxtapose our internal national government based on moral strength. . . . Defense against the enemy should be based primarily on fortifying our citadel. Thus, we should aim to create a strict patriotic opinion that would scorn all deviation; to encourage the nation to utilize, for the public good, all those rights still left us; and to habituate people to at least do nothing for the authorities that they are not forced to do by law.

And the victims? Dmowski replies:

> There can be no patriotism without readiness to sacrifice. Whoever wants to save our nation without endangering himself will have to watch it deteriorate slowly. . . . It is ridiculous to count the losses by the numbers of people who are sent into exile for a few years. This is especially ridiculous for a society that has more hands than

it has work, and that voluntarily sends whole legions of its sons to the very same regions of Russia and Siberia to which others are being exiled.

We should also remember the countless victims of conciliatory passivity: the people who are being Russified, corrupted, and degraded in solitude in the face of the omnipotent Russian knout.

The clarity and persuasive power of Dmowski's arguments is striking. They sound oddly familiar to all those who with their own eyes have observed the emergence of new social values from silence and the stormy transformation of public opinion that for years had been used to the philosophy of "leave me alone" and "somehow things will turn out all right."

The vision of anticonciliatory politics of activism was articulated in illegal leaflets and proven on Warsaw's streets. The conflict was obvious: the conciliators festively welcomed the tsar to Warsaw while the NDs organized patriotic demonstrations. Beginning in 1891, these were the first street demonstrations since the 1863 Uprising that carried openly proindependence slogans. For much of society this was a psychological watershed. Conquered Warsaw saw people who wanted independence, and all Poland learned about their existence and their demonstrations. The organizers fell victim to police repression. A new factor in the political landscape had appeared in the consciousness of both the partitioners and the Poles.

Looking at the meaning of those demonstrations after all these years, it is hard not to notice that this emergence from nothingness, this manifestation of a new orientation, had both a propagandistic and a symbolic dimension. It was not merely a question of publicity but of impressing on the public the potential of a new type of activity that went beyond routine attempts made by the camp of conciliation. Moreover, the political circles that took up such actions became visible. The basic arguments against demonstrations (apart from the fear of increased repressions) were limited to evoking the specter of the street demonstrations that preceded the 1863 Uprising. The mobilization of the people in the street, it was said, might lead to an increase in tension, provoke battles with the police, create an avalanche of events whose course and dynamics could not be controlled by anyone, including the organizers. The outcome of such events might prove contrary to the intentions of the organizers as well as inimical to the Polish national interest. It would be added that even if one were to dismiss this dark scenario, the very idea of street demonstrations carries the risk of popularizing a style of political action that appeals only to the crowd's emotions, to spectacular effects and "showy" patriotism. It promotes a style of action aimed at passions, not subordinated to any broader political thought or long-term strategy.

It would be difficult to contend that these arguments lack realism, that they do not correctly diagnose the illnesses inherent in the Polish political style. But these objections can be applied least to the national democrats. The ND leaders knew well how to create a hierarchy of aims. They consciously included street demonstrations in the broad panorama of their strategy and tactics. After all, Kiliński's anniversary[2] stimulated not only further demonstrations in Warsaw but also organizational activity among students and villagers. Illegal self-education circles and libraries of forbidden writings were founded, independent publications were popularized, and far-reaching educational activity got under way. All this was subordinated to the construction of an ideological-political camp that was to create Polish self-determination vis-à-vis the invader's power apparatus.

Self-determination consists of internal national self-organization and external activist policies with determined goals. Internal self-organization means respecting the nation's own norms and demands, independent of the penal code that exists in accordance with the wishes of the partitioning power. It means satisfying a maximum of national needs regardless of the institutions imposed by the invader. It means the positive creation and functioning of an independent public life in which the supreme national ambitions are discussed, formulated, and socially accepted. A conscious politics of activism means the implementation of these goals by both legal and illegal methods—legal ones by seeking out the gaps in the invader's organizational and legal systems, illegal ones by creating secret institutions and organizing actions con-

2. A huge manifestation to celebrate Jan Kiliński (1760–1819), the Polish patriot who participated in the Kościuszko Insurrection, was organized by both the National League and the Polish Socialist party on April 17, 1894, the one-hundredth anniversary of the insurrection.

demned by the legal code. Activist politics also consists of the cool analysis of political situations and their comparison with current tactics and the hierarchy of demands. It requires an assessment of what can be achieved today and what should be put off until later.

By choosing activist politics the NDs did not contradict any of the goals of their fathers or older brothers who had opted for organic work. They were aware of the need to build schools and bridges, to develop industrial cities and modern agricultural techniques. But they believed that the success of these activities would be determined by the creation of independent Polish structures for directing the rhythm of the nation's life. In dealings with the partitioning power they wanted to be a real subject, an organized whole; in this they differed from the organicists. But they did not formulate their goals as if they were present-day programs; they were not stalwart maximalists who would reject every thought of a temporary compromise with the enemy as treason and negation. Nevertheless, they viewed every solution *except independence* as provisional, and they believed that only honest representatives of the people, not the self-appointed leaders of the camp of conciliation, could enter into agreements with the partitioning powers. The NDs promoted broad participation in the movement of national resistance. They aimed to construct a *political camp,* not a party of those who believed in a particular doctrine. This is why they never said "all or nothing" but rather, in every situation, pointed out the activities accessible to every citizen which could improve the nation's lot.

The "politics of activism" formula was not free of dilemmas. Whenever the NDs would call for a boycott of Russian institutions, including schools, the objection would arise instantly (and it is difficult to deny its validity) that Polish society was in no position to build a network of schools that could cover the whole country, and that therefore it was better to take advantage of Russian schools than to increase the illiteracy rates. In practice, a compromise would then be worked out: Students who attended Russian schools would be organized into illegal study groups where gaps in their knowledge would be filled and falsehoods in the official curricula elucidated.

And so realism won out. The authors published by *Przegląd Wszechpolski* continuously strove for a program of political realism both in everyday tactics and in long-term strategy. Political realism consisted in the daily toil of organizing a network of reading rooms, taking over legal newspapers, directing striking high school youth, and creating a vision of a gradual, step-by-step return of sovereignty through the exploitation of changes in the partitioning countries and on the political map of the world. In this conception the fight for independence ceased to be a one-time act (armed uprising, for example) and became a process of change planned over a period of years. In the course of this process the dynamics of the Russian constitutional movement, revolutionary upheavals, the war with Japan, and the growth of Germany's power were followed closely. The consequences of these events, including the instability of the Holy Alliance, were analyzed in detail. These observations and analyses enabled Dmowski, Popławski, and Balicki to elaborate an original doctrine of Polish geopolitics.

Poland's Geopolitics

The Polish situation, said the ND leaders, is determined by the durability of the international situation and the alliance among the states that had partitioned Poland. A conflict within the Holy Alliance may provide an opportunity for the return of "the Polish question" to the international scene. The Russo-German conflict enabled the Poles to represent themselves at negotiations. In Roman Dmowski's view, the Poles' place was on the side of Russia. He saw Germany, a nation only recently organized into one state and full of plans for expansion, as the main enemy. Dmowski feared the power of German civilization and its consequences. As he watched the policies of Germanization in Poznań province, Pomerania, and Silesia, the ND leader was afraid that the fate of the Poles in those territories would not differ much from the fate of the Slavs on the other side of the Elbe. This danger was not posed by the Russians, despite all their Asiatic cruelty. In Russia Dmowski saw not only a threat but also an opportunity. The unity of all Polish territories within the Russian state, as the NDs proposed, was to be one step on the road to independence. Dmowski saw this proposition as realistic in view of the inevitability of a military conflict between Germany and Russia, which he studied in detail. Geopolitical analysis opened up new perspectives and enabled him to construct optimistic scenarios. It imposed a revision of outdated stereotypes but frequently struck at national essentials. Dmowski's pro-Russian orientation upset the public; his tactics were not understood and their aims seemed unclear. But this was due chiefly to flaws in implementation. The essence of geopolitical thinking lay in placing the Polish question against an international background, in rejecting parochial thinking in politics. Dmowski's actions at the Versailles conference were the logical consequence of the effectiveness and wisdom of his thinking.

There is a moral to be drawn from the writings of the early national democrats: In undertaking the task of building internal self-determination, it is necessary to measure strength by intention. Yet when planning a policy for regaining sovereignty, intentions should be judged according to strength. Not all Dmowski's forecasts proved true, not all his analyses were accurate, but his style of diagnosis remains a permanent, perhaps the best, model for analyzing the political situation of the Poles, a nation living between the Russian state and Germany, an obstacle to the interests of others, caught between two expansive powers. The novelty of his geopolitical analysis consisted in departing from traditional calculations about the solidarity of international public opinion with Poland and observing the play of forces and the relationships of interests. Dmowski looked for allies not among those who shared his ideology but rather among people and nations that shared or could share Poland's interests.

Toruńczyk's anthology brings out these characteristics of the political thought of the national democrats. The book's achievement may lie in restoring the heritage of the early national democrats to all of "thinking Poland." Perhaps *Przegląd Wszechpolski* will cease to be the sole property of a single political party, of one political camp and one ideological orientation, and will instead become a part of the shared intellectual heritage of all Poles, an element as equally indispensable as the political writings of Mochnacki, regardless of whether he was connected to the Democratic Society or to Hôtel Lambert.

In Toruńczyk's book the early ND party emerges as the political movement of the radical intelligentsia, a movement oriented toward gaining national sovereignty. It was aware of the deep transformations taking place within Polish society and clearly defined the effects of these changes, the most important of which lay in the demise of the former identification of national ambitions with the interests of the nobility. Moreover, the NDs saw that the Poles were not alone in becoming a modern nation in the territories of the old commonwealth. They observed the burgeoning processes that also gave national consciousness to the Lithuanians, Ukrainians, and Jews. They recognized the competition between Poles and Lithuanians or Poles and Ukrainians—not to mention between Poles and Germans in Silesia, Ermeland, and Pomerania—for victory over the minds of the population of the ethnically-mixed, lacking a defined national identity. The NDs clearly understood the conflict-laden nature of these various national ambitions. They called their point of view "nationalism," that is, a way of defining and achieving national interests through conflict with other nations' interests. This constituted a blatant departure from Poland's heritage of a commonwealth of three nations, but it was also the product of a new era, an era of national struggles for sovereignty. The conflict was both natural and inevitable. It suffices to recall that for both Poles and Lithuanians, Vilna was an indispensable part of a future independent state. The conflict over Vilna was one between two young nationalisms, whose outcome would be determined by force.

The dynamics of nationalistic ambitions were shaped by social groups with a new national identity, devoid of a background of traditions or a knowledge about the advantages of compromise, who felt more comfortable at a rally than at the negotiating table. The countryside was the base for these nationalist ambitions. It was the peasant cart that was to serve as the vehicle for Polish independence, and not the wagonette from the noble's estate, where in the past the elite corps of future revolutionaries and spokesmen for the landed conservatives had grown up. It was the peasant—Polish, Lithuanian, or Ukrainian—who dictated the line of action to ideologues, and so it was not surprising that the political awareness that was being shaped amid territorial, linguistic, or religious conflicts had little in common with the traditional Polish incantation "for our freedom and yours." This also applied to the Jewish population, which in the social structure of the Kingdom of Poland took the place of the third estate. Considering the absence of a Polish bourgeoisie and the poor performance of Poles in trade and the free professions, this was—in the opinion of the national democrats—a real threat for the future of the modern nation as it was being shaped.

A Digression about Socialists

The ND's adversaries, the Polish socialists, were also aware of the nation's internal changes. While the NDs saw the peasant as the heir to national tradition, the socialists viewed the industrial proletariat as the inheritor of the ideas of an independent commonwealth. One should be aware of the scale of this phenomenon: Both the national democrats and the socialists were at first only small groups of young people scattered all over the country and in émigré centers abroad, searching for new forms of political activity. The conflicts of that era touched on secondary issues that had little importance; these people looked primarily for things they could share. Both groups wanted an independent Poland; both rejected passivity and policies of conciliation. It was not an accident that both groups took part in Kiliński's anniversary demonstrations and together landed in the Citadel. They did not expose their differences in their programmatic public statements, and members of the National League for a time belonged to the leadership of the Polish Socialist party (PPS).

Historians of the two parties provide different accounts of the first conflicts between National League and Polish Socialist party. Stanisław Kozicki, the author of a history of the National League and himself a national democrat, claims that the first spectacular difference of opinion emerged over Dmowski's negative attitude toward the suggestion from Moscow University students, addressed to academics in Warsaw, to coordinate a protest action. Dmowski justified his opposition to the idea by his determination to separate Polish issues from general Russian questions, to disengage the Polish struggle for independence from the Russian fight for democratic reforms. This issue was said to reveal the differences in the behavior of the "nationalists" and the "internationalists"—the latter was the name the NDs gave socialists who wanted to act together with their "Muscovite friends."

Historians connected to the Polish Socialist party do not attach much importance to this incident, although it was characteristic of the mentality of the author of *Thoughts of the Modern Pole*. According to these historians, the first public manifestation of the differences between the two parties occurred during the unveiling of the Mickiewicz monument in Warsaw. The monument, erected on the initiative of the camp of conciliation, was conceived as a symbolic bridge between the patriots who paid for the monument and the Russian administration who gave permission for it. The National League chose to support the idea and its members took part in the official ceremony. The Polish Socialist party boycotted the unveiling. Both sides' arguments were transparent and logical. The NDs contended that a national aspect ought to be impressed on this conciliatory undertaking. The PPS (in the writings of Józef Piłsudski) condemned the act, interpreting it as an attempt to draw Adam Mickiewicz into the ranks of the proponents of a pro-Russian orientation. This pseudopatriotic masquerade, wrote the socialists, was aimed at dressing up the flunkies from the camp of conciliation in the coat of romantic tradition. I think both attitudes held important grains of national truth.

Here, in the capital of the "Country on the Vistula," in the city where Mickiewicz's works are repeatedly falling victim to Russian censors, a monument was being constructed for this greatest poet of anti-Russian protest. This would have an effect on the social consciousness, popularizing the poet and his works, virtually legalizing him in a country where Russian policemen during house searches frequently go through closets looking for copies of Mickiewicz's *Poetry* published in Paris or Cracow. The construction of this monument, argued the NDs, is the beginning of a certain course, the course of loosening restrictions, broadening spheres of national liberties, accustoming the public along with the Russian guardians of order to Mickiewicz's presence in every Polish home. It was to serve as a step in the implementation of a long-term program of fighting for Polish schools, official use of the Polish language, and autonomy for the Kingdom.

This scenario had to assume a variety of forms and means of action, compromises and temporary alliances, a combination of pressure on and negotiations with the authorities. It had to allow for street demonstrations and strikes by high school students as well as talks and agreements with the Russian government. The socialists thought differently; they were maximalists. From their point of view all compromise with tsarist Russia was impossible, and the Poles had the duty to fight incessantly, at all times, for every inch of freedom, for every minute torn off the working day. At no negotiating table could the rights of the Polish proletariat and Russian tsarism be discussed.

The Polish socialism of those years—after it broke with the anti-independence phraseology of the "Proletarians"[3]—was a peculiar synthesis of Marxist social doctrine, the ethos of Russian conspirators, and the romantic-insurrectionist tradition of Polish democracy of the nobleman's kind. The theory of class struggle was interwoven with stanzas out of Mickiewicz's poems. At demonstrations workers sang "The Red Banner," while the red-and-white flags they pulled out from under their jackets sported images of Our Lady of Częstochowa. Much time had passed since the Geneva meeting where Waryński declared a break with the insurrectionist tradition. At the end of the nineteenth century, "social revolution" was signing a pact with "irrendentism for independence." Many years later, in 1919, Roman Dmowski still perceived Piłsudski as a "blend of an old Polish romantic and a Muscovite bolshevik." Some historians have questioned whether Piłsudski was ever a socialist. They claim that socialism and the workers' movement served him as a trampoline for independence-oriented activity. Leaving aside the rather academic dispute over the nature of Piłsudski's psychological experiences, it is difficult not to notice that in those days virtually the entire leadership team of the PPS (Wojciechowski, Grabski, Jodko-Narkiewicz, Wasilewski, Sulkiewicz, and Studnicki—and one could add other names to this list) believed in the same model of the socialist idea. The thesis that the people who led the socialist movement were strangers to it does not withstand scrutiny, unless one defines *socialism* narrowly and arbitrarily. Polish socialism had to answer the questions of its time, a time when the modern nation was forming under the unnatural conditions of a foreign invasion. Thus, socialist thought had to synthesize strivings for social liberation and nationalistic ambitions, to form a bridge between the last uprising and the first revolution.

The maximum program—"socialism and independence"—left open questions about priorities, alliances, tactics, and medium-term

---

3. *Proletariat* was the first Polish Socialist party, founded by Ludwik Waryński in 1882.

goals. All the socialists agreed in their uncompromising negation of Russian tsardom, but they had different perspectives. Some saw the Russian revolutionaries as allies and tended to stress their common fate and aspirations, to search for concrete agreements and discuss initiatives and plans. They were willing to treat the demand for democratic elections to the Constituent Assembly as an essential step on the way to realizing their goals. Others noticed the weakness of Russian democracy and the contamination of the Russian revolutionary movement with the "Great Russian" tendency. They also stressed that Polish political and cultural traditions differed from Russian ones. They looked for allies for the "Polish cause" in countries hostile to Russia, especially in the Austro-Hungarian monarchy. In the Russian empire itself they saw as allies the movements among the conquered nations—the Lithuanians, Ukrainians, Georgians—rather than the Russian movement for democratic reform. They counted not on the democratization of the empire but on its disintegration. From these ideas grew a vision of a federated socialist commonwealth made up of the nations living in the western borderlands of the Russian empire.

One of the characteristics of socialist programs—not just in Poland—was their rather abstract character. The language of doctrine replaced the language of reality. Piłsudski, Perl, and Daszyński all had an excellent pragmatic sense and knowledge of political mechanisms, but their practical achievements were usually left outside the sphere of theoretical reflection. Thus, there existed socialist doctrine and the practices of socialists, but there was no Polish socialist thought which could bring theoretical assumptions to bear on everyday practice. No socialist writer managed to present his camp's theses and achievements as clearly and coherently as Dmowski did for his party in his book *The Politics and Reconstruction of the Polish State*.

Social Utopia and the Totalitarian Germ

Socialist ideals included the hope for a classless society based on liberty, equality, and fraternity. This utopia was merged with a class interpretation of historical events. The theory of class struggle located the source of historical change in the transformation of the economic system and the resulting conflicts between those who controlled the means of production and those deprived of property who possessed only their labor-power. The struggle between ideas was treated as a derivative of the class struggle. Every idea from the past could be explained and placed in its historical context. It was only their own utopias that the socialists were unable to examine. According to their declarations, this was the first time that the philosophers' stone had been discovered that would reshape utopia into a scientific program of action, and change dreams into reality. "This will be the last battle, the bloody hardships will be over," they promised in the hymn they sang on their holiday.

But there was also everyday life: the Russian policeman, the Russian school, the Russian imperial power, as well as their own weakness and the conformity of their compatriots. There was only a handful of socialists, and they knew it. So they found for themselves a lay eschatology that helped them endure the years of exile, the time that stretched between the Citadel and the gallows. They had to believe that they were sacrificing their lives for something priceless and sacred. The myth of a Poland of "glass houses," of a just, pure, and passionate Poland, drew its inspiration from this will to believe. But life has its laws and so does politics. It was a winding path that led to this Poland, and the methods that had to be used could not always be pure. A gap came into being between the socialist ideal and everyday practice, one that could not be filled by political reflection. Socialism promised total change, building this promise on the complete negation of a world based on the exploitation and oppression of nations and individuals. This ideological promise was to become reality after the revolution; an era would begin in which today's virtues would be rewarded. It is at this point that ideological promise began to replace objective diagnosis of social conflict and a clear-cut program of reform. A new quality came into being. The germ of totalitarianism was beginning to force its way into the democratic ideology, whether nationalist or internationalist.

The Polish socialists' pretotalitarianism had two faces. It lay, on the one hand, in the nature of the doctrine itself, which attempted to comprehend and embrace the whole wealth of society's life in its categories and concepts. It lay as well in the nature of the organization, the form of which was said to guarantee success in the Polish workers' holy war against Russian autocracy.

To put it another way: the "doctrinaires" viewed the future as a glorious world emerging out of the revolutionary deluge. The revolutionary deluge was the inevitable product of social evolution, an historic necessity. But after the deluge, quarreling nations would become one big family. The people would be free and equal and everybody would be everybody else's brother, regardless of race or skin color. All that was needed was one great effort: the Revolution. This radiant goal allowed the doctrinaires to deny completely the present and the contemporary world of values, to consider all its achievements as unimportant products of a rotting culture. The technique of the revolutionary act itself was morally neutral: "You cannot make an omelette without breaking eggs," the saying went. Hidden behind this saying was not merely approval of moral relativism but also a mental jump from a radically deterministic theory to total voluntarism of practice. "Socialism is the natural outcome of the evolution of production forces and of the relationship of production," the Western European high priests of Marxism would say. This, translated into the language of politics, produced the reformism of the German social democrats. In the Polish situation the radically deterministic view of history was merely a pseudoscientific pseudoguarantee that the outcome of the struggle was not an ideological illusion but rather the necessary product of social phenomena, just like rain coming down from dark clouds covering the sky. But political practice indicated that the tempo of the march of the spirit of history would depend on us and therefore that all methods were permissible, since we were "moving the earth in its foundations." Let us repeat: such was the basis of the conviction that all of society's needs ought to be subordinated to one supreme goal: revolution. This way of thinking gives rise to a particular sort of mentality.

Florian Znaniecki calls the person with this type of mentality "a fanatic of his ideas." He sketches his portrait in the book *Today's People and Tomorrow's Civilization*. This person ascribes an absolute cultural importance to his own mission, and he perceives the whole community from the point of view of its positive or negative role in his efforts.

> Lasting spiritual isolation . . . single-handed setting of his objective tasks, a growing concentration of all activity on these tasks and the

negligence of all others . . . , going counter to the existing order in fulfilling these tasks, which frequently are sharpened by the attitudes of the ordinary society that tends to ascribe to it destructive rather than constructive intentions; all this contributes to a loss of awareness of the relativity of human actions. His own endeavors, on which his whole personality focuses, which are the only thing that gives meaning to his life (since ordinary public roles are meaningless to him), gain absolute importance that cannot be compared to anything. . . . He becomes a fanatic of his ideas, ready—if necessary—to sacrifice for them every existing cultural system so that they can be realized. . . . As he spends long years walking in the wilderness of revolt, encountering passive resistance and active antagonism as he develops and expands his activities, meeting normal people, appreciating the recognition and cooperation of rare supporters . . . , he gradually divides people into friends and adversaries. This division, together with his total devotion to his mission and his fanatical faith in his own ideas, becomes the principal guideline in his life within society. . . . The more difficult his life . . . , the more distinct the contrast between himself and his group on the one hand and the rest of society . . . on the other. His supporters also believe in this attitude. . . . Moreover, as the group's activity genuinely acquires the character of a struggle with opponents, the group often attracts typical fighters who reinforce this activity and make the group into a fighting squad.

Such was the psychological portrait of the revolutionary sketched by a sociologist. This psychology was accompanied by theory. The theory did not need to be internally coherent. The belief in the "automatic collapse of capitalism" accompanied repeated calls for a "general strike," which would bring the "collapse" and "revolution" closer. "Revolution" and "general strike" require effective and disciplined cadres. If the plan of overthrowing the capitalism supported by the tsarist repressive apparatus is to be implemented effectively, these cadres or, to be more precise, party activists have to become "an army of professional revolutionaries." Their awareness must differ from the thinking of "normal" people, workers or craftsmen who live the lives of ordinary bread-eaters and view the world likewise, with a large degree of conservatism and conformism. The bread-eaters who are employed in factories and workshops are burdened with "ordinariness" and are incapable of rising above the political level of trade unionism. Therefore, the cadre of professional revolutionaries must bring into the ranks of the working class a political consciousness from the outside. It is to be the avant-garde of the working class, the expression of its best qualities and its truest long-term interests, even if today the workers are unaware of this. But it is only in this way that the proletariat's revolutionary cadre can identify with the proletariat itself, because the real historical interest of the proletariat is the same as the interest of the party of professional revolutionaries, which has placed the slogan of liberation of the proletariat on its banners.

Such is the essence of the political worldview of the doctrinaires, who also justify these formulas by quoting profusely from Marx, Engels, and other theoreticians of the movement.

The "organizers"—as I will call the proponents of a different orientation—were not very interested in the secrets of Marxist theory or in the Talmudic disputes of the doctrinaires about a "general strike" or the "automatic collapse of capitalism." Their leader confessed once that he never managed to wade through the entangled reasoning of Marx's *Das Kapital*. The organizers were interested in concrete action that would strike at the Russian tsarist system, action whose success would be measured by the recovery of independence or at least by a clear acknowledgment to the world of the Poles' ambition to have a sovereign state. For this they needed an organization that would resemble a fighting squad rather than a democratically run underground workers' party. For the organizers, small teams of trained fighters, capable of undertaking risky armed action, were more valuable than networks of factory organizations. But what if armed action does not bring immediate results? What if it is impossible to overthrow the tsar today? What if it is necessary to wait? What if it is necessary to look for help among the enemies of our principal enemy? In this situation an army-type discipline is all the more necessary, a discipline that creates unconditional trust in the leaders. The mentality of the "fanatic of his ideas," characteristic of the doctrinaires, appears among the organizers in a different conceptual cloak. The leading cadre, the organizers would say, cannot look out for the moods of the conformist public, who "cannot bear hearing glass scratched, yet put up with having their face struck with the Russian whip." On the contrary, these cadres must believe that God himself had entrusted them with the honor of all Poles, that it is they who are the actual realizers of the nation's aspirations, even if the nation itself is not aware of it and is not giving the cadres a mandate for it. Under the partitions this nation lost its instinct for self-preservation and its political reason. That is why this nation must subordinate itself to those who know better, see farther, and—most importantly—are prepared to "throw their lives onto the pyre."

These were the two faces of the pretotalitarian temptations that existed in the Polish socialist camp. One of them would become clearer both in the theory and practice of the Communist party of Poland, the party that attempted to bolshevize Poland during the Second Republic; the other one would be manifest in the political practices of the Sanacja regime, which was crowned by the 1935 Constitution and the programmatic declaration of the Camp of National Unification.

Socialism and Antitotalitarian Thought: Visions and Intuitions

Polish socialist thought was not unaware of these dangers. Daszyński and Kelles-Krauz argued in their writings that Poland's lasting alliance with Russia, even after the overthrow of the tsarist system, would bring Poland a cultural regression, and that Polish historical traditions and cultural models had to lead to another type of political solution in the postrevolutionary state. Autocracy was a Russian tradition and golden liberty a Polish one. Thus, the different spiritual biographies of these nations had to model differently the programmatic visions of political changes. This argument struck at Rosa Luxemburg and her theory of the "organic incorporation" of the Kingdom of Poland into Russia. Luxemburg was considered the leading ideologue of the Social Democracy of the Kingdom of Poland and Lithuania [SDKPiL], the workers' party dominated by the spirit of the doctrinaires, which with true doctrinaire enthusiasm fought the idea of a sovereign Poland and preferred instead a universal utopia. The SDKPiL opted for close cooperation with the Russian workers' movement, especially with the revolutionary wing led by Lenin.

Characteristically, it was with Lenin that Rosa Luxemburg had a dispute about the model for a workers' party. In effect this was an argument over the character of postrevolutionary power. Lenin favored a statute for the social-democratic party which would in effect make it into an organization of professional revolutionaries; this was the Leninist concept of a party of a "new type." Luxemburg accused the leader of the Bolsheviks of "Blanquism," of unconsciously accepting the ideas of the French revolutionary of the early nineteenth century. (Blanqui spent most of his life in prison; he believed that the capitalist system could be overthrown by an underground conspiracy.) Blanquist ideas were in sharp contrast with the theory of a proletarian revolution, which was to be the task of the working masses aware of their aspirations, not the work of a group of conspirators who thought and acted in place of the masses. "Conspiratorial activity has little chance of success," argued Rosa Luxemburg; but her argument did not concern only chance. Even if the plotters did manage to assume power in the country, she claimed, this would not be the rule of the working class but the rule of the conspirators themselves. It would not be proletarian democracy that would triumph but the Jacobinism of the new era, which would give birth to an imperial-bonapartist regime. This regime would be founded on the passivity of the working masses deprived of their civil rights. The party's Central Committee would become something of a collective emperor in the entourage of a pretorian guard protecting safety and order. So much for the idea of a workers' state.

Luxemburg saw all these dangers in the Leninist concept of the party of "professional revolutionaries"—a party composed of "fanatics of ideas," people who are specially chosen and who come from a social margin, a party set apart from the rigors of social order and detached from the everyday life of factory teams, although it speaks in their name. A party of this kind lives its own life, is subject to the mechanisms that govern sects, and creates its own particular interests and goals. These accusations, formulated in 1908, were reiterated by Luxemburg ten years later in her well-known pamphlet about the Bolshevik revolution, in which she again took up her fundamental dispute with Lenin about the value of bourgeois democracy in postrevolutionary conditions. This time, too, she spoke of the deadly threat presented to the working class, passive and deprived of its rights by the party bureaucracy that was monopolizing power.

What is interesting is that Rosa Luxemburg never understood the importance of the nation-creating process, and that she perceived the Poles' goal of independence as a mere anachronism of the nobility. Nonetheless, this same Luxemburg was able to see with uncommon shrewdness the outlines of the Napoleonic hat under the Phrygian cap of the Russian Jacobins, which would be instantly transformed into Monomach's cap with the red star. The spirit of yesterday's and an even earlier Russia defeated the utopia of egalitarianism and democracy.

Rosa Luxemburg was attracted to the Bolsheviks by their revolutionary radicalism and by her conviction that unified Polish-Russian action was necessary. The leaders and theoreticians of the Polish Socialist party sought different solutions. Edward Abramowski, who for a time was closely connected to the PPS, concentrated on the methods used in socialist politics. He believed that methods have a decisive influence on the shape of political change. In order to understand Abramowski's concept one must analyze his idea of "bureaucratic revolution." It was with this phrase that he described every policy that attempted change not through the proletariat's revolutionary activities but through the deeds of the elites that direct socialist parties. The "bureaucratic revolution" is therefore undertaken both by the proponents of the Leninist model of the party of "professional revolutionaries" and by the German social-democratic activists, who substitute direct proletarian action for the parliamentary game and diplomatic endeavors. Changes made in this way are short-lived and superficial; they do not revolutionize social consciousness. Socialist politicians should renounce all reform "from above": they should give up all strategies of wringing reform from bourgeois governments by parliamentary or behind-the-scenes pressure. This strategy conceals a fetishistic attitude toward the institution of the state, with its whole apparatus of political coercion. It also entails the belief that this apparatus can be transformed, through "top-down" changes, from being a tool of antiworker repression into being the guardian of a reformed state. A reform decreed by the government means that the political elites still hold power and the proletariat is still only a political object. In order to be able to govern, the workers must gain experience in the course of the struggle for power. Only during this struggle can they learn about self-organization, attain a political self-awareness, and understand the nature of their most important weapon—worker solidarity. Abramowski termed the belief in change imposed by the state a theory of the "ennobling, redeeming influence of the policeman's knout, when this knout is held in a hand that has been enlivened by the ideals of freedom and the people's welfare."

The revolutionary bureaucracy looks somewhat different when it is the party of professional revolutionaries. Then, the revolution is the work of the party intelligentsia that "after winning support among the masses by any available method has grabbed state power," and with the help of dictatorship has built a new society. This socialist Jacobinism finds especially fertile ground in countries—such as Poland—which have been deprived of political freedom. It is the outcome of concentrating political actions on incessant fighting against police repression. In these conditions the Socialist party's driving force comes not from factories but from conspiratorial cells of professional revolutionaries. The party becomes external in relation to its social base. In a situation of this type, says Abramowski, "Jacobinism" appears as an

> even more necessary, artificial means of conducting a revolution. Indeed, it becomes the only possible means, for the slogans of revolution must somehow be kept up when this revolution is incapable of striking root in people's souls. If it does not have real force it must give them a fictitious force. No wonder then that the tactics of "terror," which in the people's eyes adorns the party with some hidden providence fighting for the people, so frequently returns to the minds of the activists.

This tactic may prove fatal. If the liberation from the outside is not the work of the workers themselves, degeneration is inevitable. Abramowski wrote:

> Let us assume for a moment that there appears some sort of revolutionary providence, a group of conspirators who believe in socialist ideals, succeed in taking over the state mechanism, and who, thanks to the help of police dressed in their new colors, implement communist mechanisms. Let us assume that the people's consciousness plays no role in this, and that it all takes place through the force of the bureaucracy itself. So what happens then . . . The new institutions outlaw the reality of private property, but property remains as

the people's moral need. They liquidate official exploitation in the realm of production, but all the external factors that create human misery are still there. . . . The communist organization would have to use broad state powers to suppress the interests of property. The police would have to replace those natural needs thanks to which social institutions live and develop freely. The defense of the new institutions could only be taken up by a state based on the principles of bureaucratic absolutism, because in a society in which a new system has been imposed by force, democracy would threaten this system with immediate collapse. It would return to all those social laws that continued to live in people's souls not touched by the revolution. In this way communism would not only be superficial and weak but, moreover, would be transformed into a state system that represses the freedom of individuals and that creates two new classes in place of the old ones: the citizens and the bureaucrats, whose antagonism would be apparent in all areas of public life. Thus, even if communism could survive in this artificial form, without the moral transformation of the people, it would in any case contradict itself and become such a social monster, about which no exploited class, especially not the proletariat which stands up for human rights and which is destined by history to liberate man, has ever dreamed.

This extensive quotation well illustrates Abramowski's apprehensions for the future of the socialist movement. What is significant is that while he defined the dangers in terms similar to Rosa Luxemburg's, he looked elsewhere for remedies. In discussion with Lenin, Luxemburg defended the values of bourgeois democracy. She explained that any movement that tramples freedom (in simplest terms, the freedom for opponents to their opinions) inevitably condemns itself to degradation and sterility. Abramowski thought differently; he understood bourgeois freedom as a privilege for elites which can coexist with the subjugation of the working class. He looked for institutional safeguards in the practical negation of the state, which he saw as the apparatus for oppressing the working people and a tool for defending the privileges of the propertied classes. Therefore, Abramowski argued, one ought to boycott the state's institutions (the police force, courts, education) and create independent institutions that in the very process of struggling with the partitioning power will make it possible to construct social mechanisms based on solidarity and ties of friendship. He attached special importance to economic institutions (cooperatives), which were to form an alternative to capitalist enterprises.

The writings of Rosa Luxemburg and Edward Abramowski represent two directions of thought about the totalitarian temptation contained in socialist thinking, in the party programs that combined a plan for social change with the struggle for state power. Let us call these directions "parliamentarian" and "self-governing." The parliamentarians took the existence of state institutions as a given; they were interested in the state's class content and its democratic mechanisms. Luxemburg did not criticize Lenin for not putting into practice the social vision presented in his book *State and Revolution,* in which he predicted that the cook would govern the country. She criticized him for the way the Bolshevik state was organized, for destroying all civil liberties, and for approving the autocratic system of the party apparatus organized into a state. The declared dictatorship of the proletariat in effect turned into the dictatorship of the party over the people and the bureaucratic apparatus over the party.

Abramowski used the sharp blade of his criticism to reach deeper. He argued that the very ambition to take over the state presupposed the belief that the omnipotent state apparatus would become the servant and tool of the working world. Yet he felt that social changes decreed "from above," reforms imposed by the army and police—even if these are controlled by the parliament—are bound to lead to a new sort of captivity. It can be prevented by building up self-determination in civil society, by creating associations from below and avoiding the intermediary role of state institutions in public life.

The similarity of these reflections to Roman Dmowski's ideas is striking. Their differences lay in axiology. In Abramowski's view the development of self-governing institutions was to lead to "the freedom of Poland and the freedom of the individual in Poland." One can easily observe in this phrase the fear (also expressed by Stefan Żeromski) that in a free Poland the policeman with the Romanovs' two-headed eagle on his cap would only be replaced by the gendarme with the Polish crowned eagle.

Politics of Activism and the Dispute over Values

In *Thoughts of the Modern Pole,* Dmowski stated brutally that the person who wants a Poland that will live in harmony with all its neighbors; who is directed by the abstract ideal of justice and not by territorial expansion; who would call it "chauvinism" rather than a healthy national instinct any Polish fight with Ukrainians, Lithuanians, or Jews; who says that he would like a Poland but makes faces at the thought of a Polish police and Polish prisons—that that person is only mocking the idea of sovereignty.

This argument no doubt refers to Abramowski and other socialists. To them Dmowski was the ideologue of an aggressive nationalism, the spokesman for the propertied classes and their interests in the world of violent social conflict. From Dmowski's point of view the socialists were irresponsible aesthetes who spun utopian illusions that, when translated into the concrete language of politics, served Poland's enemies; for example, they subordinated their own strategy to the interests of the German social democrats.

Let us reflect on the meanings hidden in these mutual accusations. Was Dmowski the ideologue of the propertied classes? Dmowski was the ideologue of Polish nationalism, the theoretician of the doctrine that defined the national interest in terms of its conflict with other nations and the principle of iron solidarity within his own nation. To Dmowski the nation was made up of landowners and peasants, industrialists and workers, craftsmen and teachers—all those who try to build a nation-state despite foreign interests and hostile peoples. This form of national structure was natural for Dmowski. Plans for social upheaval were the acts of troublemakers and a way of destroying national unity. National unity, for him, meant the concentration of all Poles around the political camp of the national democrats and the implementation of their program. The revolutionary activity of the workers' parties seemed to Dmowski an "illness," "the work of madmen," "political banditry," "the syphilis of public life." Nationalism was the enemy of social revolution, but it never identified fully with the interests of the bourgeoisie or the landowners. It respected those interests, but it subordinated them to the supreme goal, its own political strategy, which it equated with the general national interest.

Dmowski was wrong in his assessment of the socialist orientation. The PPS activists, including Abramowski, frequently entered into disputes with German and Russian socialists about Polish independence. Their adversaries' arguments that the aim of independence was anachronistic, the Socialists perceived as either stupid authoritarianism or plain hypocrisy that concealed the mentality of imperial nationalism under a patina of universalistic slogans. In this respect Dmowski's criticisms missed the point.

The essence of the dispute, however, seemed to lie in different perceptions of politics. For the socialists politics was a means of putting into practice the socialist ideal; for the national democrats it was the art of accomplishing concrete goals in concrete situations. These were two different philosophies of politics.

The socialists liked to quote Marx, but they drew their quotations from his works the way theologians cite the Bible. They transposed somewhat mechanically onto the terrain of the Polish reality the Marxist network of concepts, elaborated in order to analyze other eras. Meanwhile the spirit of Marx's full-blooded but dispassionate analyses, such as can be found in his *Eighteenth Brumaire* [*of Louis Bonaparte*], was lost. Their studies were tainted with a peculiar blindness that made them "see everything separately." Social conflicts barely meshed with national emotions. Such was the price paid for faithfulness to the language of doctrine. It was difficult to phrase the stipulation for sovereignty in this language. When the socialists talked about national independence, they went back to the language of their grandfathers, the language of rebellious irredentism. The Polish socialists' publications are filled with the eclectic agglomeration of class struggle and national insurrection, of workers' strikes and the rebels' double-barreled guns. This mixture made a perfect emotional whole, but intellectually it concealed a gap, an internal split between the demand for daily economic struggle and a vision of revolution as a definitive watershed, between views of a sovereign state and of a brave new socialist world: a Republic of the Globe.

Dmowski could see this split very well. He understood that the idea of socialism is a product of social conflict, that the belief in the conflictive nature of capitalist societies is this ideology's theoretical foundation. Indeed, social conflict could be seen with the naked eye, since it was inherent in the very essence of Polish existence. But the NDs explained this conflict as a national struggle, the struggle of the Poles against foreigners: Russians, Germans, Ukrainians, Jews. Thus, the solution lay in aiming for a sovereign Polish state, not in the fratricidal quarrel among Poles that the socialists wanted when they proclaimed the class struggle. And a sovereign Poland could not be built in accordance with the socialists' abstract daydreams about justice and humanism. A sovereign Poland had to be "a Poland for the Poles," or to be more precise, "a strong Poland for disciplined Poles." Dmowski constructed the chances for independence on a geographic and ethnic analysis, on a detailed diagnosis of the conflicting interests of Russia and Germany, on careful observation of the young nationalisms growing on the territories of the former commonwealth. Today how can one not admire the perspicuity of the writings of Dmowski or Popławski? There is probably no one in the entire history of Polish political thought who wrote as clearly and lucidly about the conflictive nature of Poland's relations with its neighbors. No one else has dealt as courageously with illusions and self-deceptions, such as the calculations that Europe—both royal and plebeian—would offer disinterested help. No one else so persuasively challenged the naive belief that the motto "For your freedom and ours" could replace political thought, or the equally naive conviction that the various young nationalisms striving for sovereign states in these ethnically mixed lands might not come into conflict.

Regardless of Dmowski's ideological convictions, his practical analyses were accurate. Still, reading his works today, one can at times hardly resist a feeling of intellectual embarrassment and moral shame. One sees not only the greatness but also the poverty of Roman Dmowski's thought. And not only the poverty of his thought but also of this great political tendency. An English diplomat once called Dmowski the personification of not only the best but also the worst in the Polish national character. And I think that this Englishman was not altogether wrong.

Roman Dmowski was an excellent analyst, but he was a prisoner of his phobias. He was the co-founder of Polish proindependence thought and the co-culprit of Polish narrowness. He sowed the seeds of rationality in political thinking, yet carried the germs of xenophobia which caused gangrene in wide areas of intellectual life. He shaped

Polish minds and depraved Polish consciences. He shaped them by developing the idea of a politics of activism, teaching about geopolitics, injecting harsh realism; he degraded them by formulating a concept of the nation and an idea of Polishness that led straight to totalitarian solutions. Let us take a look at Dmowski's description and justification of patriotism.

> Its principal foundation is its moral union with the nation, a union that is independent of the will of individuals. This means that the individual who has blended into one with the nation over whole generations has no free will in a certain broad range of actions, but has to obey the collective will of the nation, of all its generations, expressing themselves through separate instincts.

At the same time he rejected the connection of national aspirations and the right to statehood with a broader, universal principle of human right to freedom and self-determination. For Dmowski only instinct and power counted.

This dispute in essence concerned not only the primacy of national over personal values but also the issue of how the nation would be shaped, how it would be organized internally, what its leading ideals would be. When he defined the Polish national interest, Dmowski advocated external expansion: only that which served Polish expansion concurred with the national interest. We know from history that national expansion had many different shapes. For Dmowski all expansions were equivalent to Polonization: the more people who were turned into Poles (even by force), the more effectively would the Polish national interest be implemented. The nation develops through territorial growth; growth takes place through struggle with other nations. Therefore, a negative attitude toward foreigners, who may halt this growth, is the gauge of nationalist posture.

The context of these ND theses was obvious: struggle with Germanization and Russification, conflict with Lithuanian and Ukrainian nationalist movements. The NDs believed the only solution to be a total struggle of the Polish nation with other nations. They viewed all attempts at compromise as naiveté, weakness, and harmful defeatism. Arguments proving the rights of nations according to the canon of

Christian or liberal European values did not count—only force counted. For a nation to be capable of external expansion, it had to be internally organized. Self-determination was not sufficient; its form was what mattered. Therefore, the NDs claimed, national interest demands that the Poles accept discipline as the principle of their internal organization. The people subordinate themselves to those who "most strongly feel the Polishness inside them": that is, they must subordinate themselves to the national democrats. War should be declared on those who refuse. Who are these people? Who makes up these elements that "are not national enough within the nation," that form obstacles on the national democrats' way to the reign of souls? How can these elements be uncovered and how can the public be turned against them? There is a way to do this. One must find "those who are behind it." One must find the Jews.

ND anti-Semitism aimed at the Jewish community as well as at the part of Polish society that had its roots in the ghetto. Whoever did not accept the ND vision of Polishness was called a Jew, or at least accused of "caving in to Jewish influence." The NDs allowed dispute over tactics—this was the nature of their polemics with the conservatives. But they did not allow dispute over the meaning of Polishness. They viewed their ideological adversaries as mere "half-Poles." The Jewish question was a complex one and is not the subject of discussion here. For us what is important is that in Dmowski's doctrine anti-Semitism served as the cement for the construction of the modern Polish nation. It was in the struggle with the Jewish threat that Polish national unity was to be forged. In this struggle the Polish aristocrat was to meet with the Polish nobleman, the Polish worker with the Polish industrialist, the Polish artisan with the Polish merchant. They were to meet, unite, and organize to fight under the command of the national democrats.

The NDs' attitude toward the Germans or the Russians was the result of their analysis of the international situation. Their attitude toward the Lithuanians or Ukrainians stemmed from their conception of the future state's territorial form. Their attitude toward the Jews derived from their vision of the internal form of the Polish nation. The common denominator in all these attitudes was xenophobia. The National Democrats trained generations of modern Poles in prejudice and distrust of anything related to other nations. They taught a cult of naked force—however inhumane, contemptuous of weakness—however undeserved. Original and independent thinkers themselves, they taught others to think on command, along beaten tracks. Dmowski was not consistent: for example, he denounced the brutality of the German enemies of the Poles. He claimed to have the "moral instinct of civilized man," yet parted with doctrinal purity and made an allowance for traditional Polish customs based on a spirit of universalism and the ethos of knightly virtues. This same ethos was included in the Polish socialists' program of national education. Their proletarian universalism was linked with a vision of Jagellonian Poland, a Poland that was the common motherland of all the nations living in the lands of the former commonwealth. This was an open and tolerant Poland, a Poland that was proud of being a "country without pyres," proud of its principle, "For our freedom and yours." It, too, was an expansionist Poland. But theirs was a different expansionist model than that of the National Democrats. The NDs propounded a looting type of expansionism that relied on the power of the sword; the socialists wanted a cultural expansionism based on the radiance of the values of national culture. Piłsudski's ideal—for he was its principal architect—had the exceptional force of a national myth. And it scored victories the way a myth does. The young generation's most intelligent elements focused on this ideal.

The NDs attacked the ideological myth constructed by Piłsudski with all the fervor of a movement that aspires to "reign over souls." They condemned him for his "anachronism" and "naiveté," for his "parting of ways with reality." To Piłsudski's "Poland of nationalities," they juxtaposed their own myth of a "national Poland," a Poland that was ethnically pure, free of the admixture of other races, religions, and nations. The ND program did not set imaginations on fire to the same extent, but it was easier to translate into the language of daily experience; it was more useful in social and technical terms. In this way it was a more realistic program. But it was a vision of Polishness full of poisonous ideas. Their triumph shoved Polish culture into the hinterlands, into the depths of xenophobia and resentment.

Dmowski always believed that Poland belongs in Europe and that as a great historical nation it must enrich European culture with new values. Yet, all authentic Polish cultural achievements which were to become a permanent part of the European cultural experience were formed in protest against the NDs' vision of Polishness.

According to Dmowski, from the cultural point of view Poland belonged to the West, but from a political point of view it was condemned to be permanently united with Russia. This diagnosis explains much. It contains the recognition of harsh political realities: No assistance could be expected from the West. From the German side the Poles were threatened fatally with denationalization. Russia dominated Poland with its military power, while Poland surpassed Russia with its level of civilization. From Russia, therefore, there was no threat to national identity. Dmowski was contemptuous of Russia, but at the same time he was fascinated by the power of the imperium. He felt himself a part of the Western world that had been hurled deep into the barbarian state of the tsars. He watched Europe closely, but he despised it for turning its back on Poland. He saw in this a conspiracy of Germans, Freemasons, Jews, and socialists.

Dmowski believed in conspiracy as the motivating—albeit hidden—force of history. He thought that mafias ruled the world and made a deal to hurt the Poles. Today, his reflections on the might of the Jewish-Freemasonic mafia are embarrassing even to his most enthusiastic supporters. The question comes to mind: How could a man who was so perceptive and who analyzed the international situation so intelligently believe in such silly nonsense? No rationalization will explain this. The puzzle will not be solved by the argument that Jews and Masons really existed and that Dmowski demonized their role. We stand helpless in the face of this mysterious flaw that was to become a disease of the Polish soul.

The sociotechnical value of the belief in conspiracy lies in the simplicity of its construction. I am poor, oppressed, and overcome; I am incapable of understanding the mechanisms of this world that make me unhappy; I am lost in the entanglement of figures, information, and interpretations. I am lonely. And here comes someone who asks me to be part of a community and at the same time explains to me the causes of my misfortune. He does both in a way I can understand. He tells me that I am a Pole, that this is the supreme value, a value in itself, which I must protect from others. This is my life's duty. I must perform it if

I am to be worthy of being called a Pole. And so I must combat the enemies of Poland, who are also the cause of my unhappiness. They are the Masons and the Jews. It is they who are conspiring to harm us; it is they who in secret are leading us into misfortune. Never mind that I have never seen a Mason, that I would not know how to recognize one. Masons act secretly, deceitfully, but my friends, "real Poles," have uncovered their tricks. They will point them out to me. Actually, Jews are visible. They walk in the streets of our towns, they destroy our trade with their competition, they are lawyers, doctors, financiers. And they are foreign. They speak differently. They dress differently. They pray differently. When you take notice of them, they are arrogant and sassy. What are they doing on our soil anyway? Why are they fighting with us? Why are they stirring things up, destroying the national spirit, spreading destructive cosmopolitan ideas that have been forced on Poland from abroad?

This was the mood which ND leaders endowed with an ideological dimension. Dmowski's thought gives a precise reflection of Poland's anti-Western complex, the complex of rejected love, of the poor cousin who has been banished from the family dining table following a spectacular bankruptcy. It is the schizophrenia of the impresario who dreams about directing the Paris opera but must settle instead for the public theater in an obscure Russian province. Out of such a conflict an aggressive nationalism was born. It drew force from weakness and backwardness. It condemned the aping of Western ideological models, the weakness for liberal and socialist intellectual gossip. What was the use of all that in the country of the tsars? What profit could it bring? In Russia liberal and socialist currents were like a delicate red rose grown out of a stinking latrine, a latrine that had not been renovated in hundreds of years, that was falling apart, but was still run by a brutal policeman.

Dmowski was familiar with Russia and with Russian political circles. He saw the opportunities for rescuing that country with which he tied his fate not in liberal reforms, but in the enhancement of its power. This was why he found it easier to enter into agreements with the "Black Hundreds" than with constitutional democrats. With the "Black Hundreds" he differed on only one issue: their attitude toward the Polish question. They shared phobias, such as the belief in the

Jewish-Freemasonic plots. They shared the holy war they had each declared on cosmopolitans and anarchists. What a paradox: this politician who had the air of a European statesman, who met with premiers and ministers, who frequented top offices and salons in Paris and London, joined together in an ideological aberration with the most anti-Polish circles in Russia. For obvious reasons it was a tactical alliance. Dmowski supported Great Russian nationalism in its attempts to expand the tsarist empire to include the remainder of the Polish territories. And this was where their alliance ended. Trying to convince Russian politicians that the restoration of a sovereign Poland lay in Russia's interest was like explaining to a healthy man that the amputation of an arm is necessary to save his life. Such situations do occur, but persuasion like this is rarely effective.

Dmowski knew very well that in opting for a long-term pro-Russian policy he was going counter to popular expectations. This tactic was challenged not only by socialists; among the National Democrats violent disputes also surfaced. How could further splits be prevented? Dmowski saw the solution in organizing such discipline in the nation so as to guarantee the execution of every order. He attributed the lack of discipline to the Polish national character, inherited from the nobility. He considered "humanitarianism" and "tolerance" toward other peoples to be the Poles' most serious flaws. He scorned their "traditional passivity" and their unwillingness to fight. In Galician attempts at a Polish-Ukrainian understanding Dmowski saw only "mental laziness" and an easy way out. These shortcomings, he felt, led to concessions toward hostile elements, along with a psychology of slavery and the renunciation of national aspirations.

It is interesting that Piłsudski also attacked Polish national shortcomings. He defined these as conformism, intellectual conservatism, and spiritual pusillanimity. What qualities should the Poles acquire? According to Dmowski, these were love of hard work and self-discipline, sobriety (renouncing the romantic-insurrectionist ethos), and national egotism (separating the Polish national interest from the interests of other nations). According to Piłsudski, Poles should continue the insurrectionist tradition and translate it into the present-day language, popularize heroic virtues and the obligation to sacrifice one's life for the motherland, seek the forces that would most effectively put up active resistance against tsarist oppression (the proletariat), look among neighbors for allies in the struggle against tsardom and for the future construction of a just commonwealth of many nations.

Once again, two styles of thought, two value systems, two visions of Polishness came into conflict. Which one was more realistic?

The ideal of a commonwealth of many nations has never been realized. In this sense it was Dmowski who was the greater realist. But Dmowski himself liked to repeat that a nation's politics ought to be planned not only years in advance but decades. From that perspective we can see Piłsudski's ideas as a version of the antitotalitarian community of the nations of the former commonwealth, founded on its shared, essential values.

Dmowski and Piłsudski, the National Democrats and the independence-oriented socialists, offered their ideological concepts to a society that for years had been living in passivity. These parties shared the idea of building social self-determination. Their differences lay in the form self-determination would assume. Whole volumes have been written about the differences between these politicians. Therefore we will concentrate on some similarities.

Although breaking with the psychology of captivity, both of them remained infected with it. Just as the "master" infects the rebellious "slave" with his mentality, tsarist Russia left permanent traces on the mentality of its opponents. The tsarist system has been described many times. It was built on coercion, despotism, contempt for the law; it used intimidation, and brought the humiliation of human dignity. It was unfamiliar with the concept of citizenship: everyone was a subject. Its subjects were taught absolute obedience and trained to pay ritual homage. This is why they lived in a schizophrenic world, where the truth of official life was different from the truth of private life. The subjects were made ignorant: free speech, a free press, and science were all strictly regulated. The system used lies, always and everywhere, toward its subjects and toward foreign ambassadors. In this lay the power of Russian diplomacy and the secret of its successes. The system perfected the techniques of political provocation. It was in the offices of the Russian Okhrana [secret police] that the idea of controlling terrorists by planting agents was first thought up. Documents creating new ideologies, such as the "Protocols of the Elders of Zion," had their origins there, along with plans for bringing these ideologies into practice. It was in Russia that anti-Jewish pogroms were used for the first time as a technique of defusing social tensions.

Such was the system the Poles had to struggle with. The adversary set the rules for this fight. Russia was the metropolis and Poland a province. Not just instructions to *Polizeimeister* but ideological fashions as well traveled from Petersburg to Warsaw. From Russia came the ideas of social revolution and aggressive nationalism. The socialism was tinted with eschatology and terrorism; the nationalism was the ideology of ignorant people for whom national community meant hatred of other groups. One could easily detect traces of these influences of the metropolis in National Democratic nationalism and Polish socialism. What did it matter that the political edge of these programs was anti-Russian when their inner shape was sculpted by everyday life under Russian autocracy? For this reason Polish nationalism contained the peculiar psychology of people entangled in a game with the Petersburg court, with the bureaucratic elite of the army of Russian officials. If you wanted to do well in this game, you had to learn its rules and its language; you had to don the mask of a person from those circles, a legitimate player in the game. But such behavior exacted its price. Since the mask fit tightly on your face, it was difficult to tear it off later. You learned their language so carefully that you forgot your own; you began to use their rules of the game in everyday life, even with your friends. Such was the road from "Christ's Calvary to the Kremlin."

In the Russian empire the socialist was condemned to be an eternal conspirator. The psychology of "underground" people is shaped by fear of arrest and fear of provocation. This breeds fanaticism and distrust. It creates contempt for normalcy, for a life without conspiracy. It leads to a belief in one's own perfection and omniscience, and to the dangerous conviction that today's total suffering will be rewarded by tomorrow's total power.

Captivity depraves everyone: masters, slaves, and rebels, individuals and communities, political camps and nations. Years later Karl Jaspers would write:

> The fighting man sometimes comes to resemble his adversary. If in
> the struggle against totalitarianism one uses totalitarian methods, one

imperceptibly alters the shape of one's cause. In the struggle against a monster, one can become a monster oneself. In such a case, even if one scores a victory, the battle is lost because a kingdom of monsters is created for oneself. Were it to happen that the external thing one fights ruins one internally, the struggle would have no meaning.

Dmowski and Piłsudski were full of contempt for the psychology of slavery, the product of tsarist rule. This was gradually transformed into contempt for those people who still suffered this psychology. Yet weren't these the same people whom the leaders wanted to educate toward self-determination? Dangerous traits were present in the political programs of that day; traits in which *from today's perspective* it is easy to see the mark of pretotalitarianism. Indeed, these were concepts of self-determination that by their very nature (and out of necessity) had to be imposed from above. This was to be the self-determination of a nation that had been organized into a fortified citadel, prepared for constant battle. Such self-determination therefore had to take on the institutional form of a disciplined and hierarchical organization in which obedience and self-sacrifice, not plurality and tolerance, were the principal virtues. In other words, the rules by which the nation's life was internally organized more closely resembled army regulations than norms of a democratically governed community.

This was understandable, but it also had many consequences. An army rules in times of war. In times of peace it sits in the barracks. Peacetime requires different principles of social coexistence than does wartime. Dmowski's and Piłsudski's concepts came to a natural end with the regaining of independence, but the logic of political events was different. In the Second Republic these two camps came to dominate public life. In the course of the struggle for power the pretotalitarian temptations took on different dimensions. Dmowski's national camp, which had been shaped in the struggle for self-determination, became the Camp of Great Poland, an organization with a totalitarian internal structure and a totalitarian program, destined to fight for complete state power. Piłsudski's independence-oriented camp, which had been formed by conspiracy and by the legions' armed action, was transformed into a supraparty camp of the Marshal's followers who wanted to destroy the parliamentary system and promote authoritarianism. In both cases the political programs were based on visions of autonomy of the state, depriving its people of their sovereignty. Again, the nation was to be organized into a military fortress. The state's might was to be created at the expense of civil rights and society's self-determination.

Edward Abramowski had warned of such a turn of events earlier. At the turn of the century he contrasted his own plan for winning self-determination with Dmowski's and Piłsudski's ideas. His plan was in part opposed to theirs, in part complementary. His cooperative program was aimed both at the practices of the National Democrats and the program of the socialists.

Let us recall that in Abramowski's view both these political formations conducted policies aimed at assuming state power. Such policies are directed by political elites that become autonomous, whereas the broad social masses become the object of manipulation. Reforms imposed from above did not give power to the people but rather to new elites that exercise it through traditional methods, including the whip. Political parties as well as military organizations are traditional means for winning state power. Abramowski contrasted this with the idea of a cooperative, voluntary association of producers that would function within the existing structures. The cooperative was to foster the creation of new forms of management, a new work ethic, new moral values. A broad cooperative movement, built from below, based on the full self-determination of individual links in the chain, was to create a new type of social self-determination and a new moral consciousness. This would allow a boycott of the state, with its apparatus of coercion. These were the essential attributes of a movement of social liberation, a movement of the people, elected by the people, and governed for the people.

It was also a program of national rebirth and liberation. Against the National Democratic idea of hostility toward other nationalities, Abramowski counterposed a program of national enrichment through cooperative organizations and aimed at positive work. This was to lead to the liberation of Poland from economic domination by foreign capital, particularly German and Jewish. To achieve this—Abramowski reproached the National Democrats—"it was not enough to organize boycotts of foreign goods and to preach to the Polish people." Unlike the NDs, Abramowski wanted to immerse the cooperative movement in the spirit of "ties of friendship." In the name of humanist values he wanted to overcome the merciless atmosphere of his time; the same merciless atmosphere that Dmowski used as the cornerstone of his worldview.

Abramowski was naive. He appeared so to the National Democrats and the socialists, and he was so in reality. His plan for a "cooperative republic" was crushed on the battlefields of the world war. Poland regained its sovereignty by other means and its political shape was different. But Abramowski could be described in another way: he was trusting. He trusted the good in the human condition, he trusted the sense of humanist values, he trusted the potential of man's labor, he trusted friendship. He did not trust ideologies based on hatred or on political practices that degraded man to the role of an unthinking creature that must be ruled by coercion and inspired by tribal or class passions.

How much we need Edward Abramowski's trust and distrust today!

The Catholic Church and the Politics of Activism

The society to which the ideologues such as Dmowski, Piłsudski, and Abramowski appealed was Roman Catholic. This meant that people, in their everyday lives, as well as on Sunday, believed in the Catholic value system and in the educational mission of church institutions. They believed in the integrating role of a religious community that in effect served the function of a fortress of national consciousness. The solidarity of the nation with the clergy and the clergy with the conquered nation gave rise to a new psychological essense: the moral model of the Polish-Catholic, an alloy of religious faith and patriotic awareness. This was a specific Polish version of the political reduction of Christian religion. It was not the first time that the political reduction of this religion took place. Ryszard Przybylski, in an essay on Polish poetry, recounts:

> In the sixteenth century the popes themselves practiced it; in the eighteenth century the partitioning powers did it. The partitioning was done in the name of the Holy Trinity. The Holy Alliance, which brought about an inhumane and unbearable triumph of falseness,

mediocrity, and crime, abused the name of Christ. It was an exceptionally abhorrent and dangerous process. Christianity was made into a tool of absolutist imperial policies. The ill-treatment of man and of whole nations was justified with religious principles, which concealed the lawlessness of the autocratic states. At the time, Rome was incapable of understanding this threat. The conflict between the Holy See and the Polish poets, much like the split with Western European socialism, simply contributed to the uncovering of Christianity.

With Western socialism the Church differed on social issues; it sided with the royal courts in their conflict against plebeian demands. With the Polish poets it differed over the Polish question. It was the time of "Syllabus"[4] and the lost fight for a church-dominated state; a time of Rome's unconcealed political aspirations and the dispute over the shape of the Holy See's policies. The plebeian movements struck at this Church. Their ideologies were full of anticlerical and areligious aspects, such as demands for a secularized public life and for the separation of Church and state. And it was of this Roman Church that Polish Catholicism was a part. But in Poland everything was different. In Poland the Church was persecuted. The Pole-Catholic was conservative and hostile to all free-thinking and revolutionary novelty. He was a tough defender of the Catholic faith and the Polish proprietary status, which to him were threatened by the partitioning power's repressive actions and Godless subversive propaganda that had been dragged into the Polish lands from the East or West. This Pole was molded by the Church during religious holidays that were frequently transformed into patriotic demonstrations. Sometimes priests would be exiled to Siberia.

In Poland the faithful tended to associate the Church with the spirit of the catacombs in which the persecuted Christians hid, not with an alliance between the altar and the throne. But it was not a Church of the catacombs. The political practice of the Catholic Church in the Kingdom of Poland consisted of striking a balance between the demands made by the Russian authorities and the national aspirations of the people, between the Petersburg court and the conspiratorial meetings

4. A collection containing the principal errors of our times as noted in the Allocutions, Encyclicals and other Apostolic Letters of our Holy Father, Pope Pius IX. December 8, 1864.

on Polish landed estates. Only in this way could the continuity of this powerful religious and social institution be assured. The Church was the only authentically independent institution in the despotic state. This independence irritated the Russian administration. In the struggle against continuing attempts to Russify religious rituals and to detach the Church from Rome, the consistent attitude of the clergy and of the faithful constituted a definite model of self-determination and national resistance. Self-determination meant gathering around the Church and the Holy Virgin of Częstochowa, the Queen of Poland, despite the pressure of Orthodox priests and government officials, teachers and policemen. National resistance meant the defense of the faith, the language and the customs of fathers and grandfathers; it meant blocking, through passive resistance, the persistent attacks on the national identity.

The socialists and National Democrats battled against this model of national self-determination, presenting in its place a concept of the Polish politics of activism. Bohdan Cywiński wrote about the history and the dialectics of this dispute several years ago in his *Genealogy of the Unhumbled,* a book that ought to be compulsory reading for every Pole who struggles with his history and with the present that surrounds him. I agree with most of Cywiński's theses, and I will talk only about two secondary issues.

The socialists viewed the Church as a pillar of the social order they wanted to overthrow, the ally of oppressors and proprietors, an enemy of progress and public enlightenment, a fortress of the Dark and Ignorant City. The Church paid them back in kind. It cursed them from the pulpits, guarding the sheepfold from the wolf dressed in the red riding hood of socialist ideology. A peculiar mixture of mutual phobias thus arose, but it revealed itself one way in political and worldview disputes and another way in everyday experience.

Noting ironically the image of the Virgin Mary of Częstochowa on socialist banners, Dmowski pointed to the peculiar split in the psychology of the Polish socialists. For they had spiritually matured at the crossing of two traditions, of two ideological systems. As the proponents of the theory of class struggle and the active combatants in it, they believed in socialist universalism and repeated Waryński's credo: "Down with national insurrection; long live social revolution." The Polish "social revolution," however, was nothing else but a new uprising; in undertaking it the Polish socialists took their place in the long line of heroes of national struggle, accepting its chivalrous ethics, symbols, and spiritual atmosphere. The young adherents of socialism, breaking with the estates of the nobility or the homes of the bourgeois— (Stefan Żeromski wrote about this in his diaries)—could consider it absolutely necessary to blow up the Częstochowa cloister because they saw it as a fortress of ignorance and backwardness. Their pamphlets expressed a materialist worldview, negated the existence of God and religion, and announced that human life was the supreme value. They taught the class character of morality and announced the anachronism of national aspirations. But in practice the Polish socialists were giving their lives for the cause which they considered greater than life itself. In accordance with the traditional code of chivalrous virtues they bravely perished in the cells of the Citadel or went to Siberia in the footsteps of their fathers and grandfathers who had participated in defeated Polish uprisings.

In the early twentieth century, Stanisław Brzozowski wrote in his book, *Flames*, about a meeting between the Russian revolutionary Zhelabov and the Warsaw worker, Tur, an activist of *Proletariat*.

They talked about myths.

Zhelabov frowned and said with animosity: "It's always the Queen of Poland, Virgin Mary of Częstochowa."

A crack was heard; it was Tur crushing the arm of his chair. . . . He stood up before Zhelabov, looking at him with burning eyes. His nostrils flared up, his body leaned forward, ready to jump.

"Hands off, you scoundrel," he said in a hoarse voice.

Zhelabov lifted himself up. It almost seemed that they would leap at one another. A strange smile, both sad and mocking, flashed across Zhelabov's face.

"I understand," he said, "you want forgiveness." Tur grabbed my arm.

"You tell him, your little Muscovite, not to talk to me about forgiveness. Him! I can still hear the creaking of the gallows. Hands off! Hands off this! It's mine! Can he hear, it's mine! I don't pray, but She's mine. Damn it," and he slammed his fist on the table so hard that the glasses rattled.

How characteristic! This short dialogue gives an excellent illustration of the strange attitude of the Polish socialist to national-religious symbolism. The traditional national archetypes were permanent; it was impossible to remove them from the Polish consciousness. In other words, alongside the declarations of doctrine was the mentality of the people. The achievements of Polish socialism were marked with the specific stamp of the Polish, chivalrous, freedom-oriented tradition which consistently reappeared in the ideology of the workers' revolution. This atmosphere remained in the PPS as long as the party existed.

The National Democrats' relationship with the Church was completely different. The street demonstration to celebrate Kiliński (that I mentioned earlier) started with a Mass for the freeing of the "sick child." This sick child was Poland. The priest who said the Mass was involved in the plan for a patriotic demonstration [which was to follow the Mass]; he was punished by his bishop for participating in the ND scheme. At the base of the relationship between the National Democrats and the Church lay conflict. This conflict had many faces. No doubt the conservative bishop saw the action of the young NDs as a reckless act, an echo of old insurrectionist ideas, a reflection of contemporary political currents. The conservative bishop did not like social innovation, which he saw, for instance, in the ND publications on agrarian topics. The conservative bishop did not want to expose the Church to new conflicts with the Russian administration in the already complex situation facing the Church. Why should he do it, anyway? For the undertakings of some careless youths for whom he foresaw no future? In addition, the conservative bishop must have been quite irritated by the frequent admonishments of the ND publicists.

In 1898 *Przegląd Wszechpolski* wrote openly that "an important part of the clergy in the Russian sector is morally and politically demoralized and led astray. The blame for this demoralization lies in large part with the Church hierarchy, partly with the Curia in Rome, and primarily with the leaders and ecclesiastic and lay apostles of the politics of conciliation." The source of this was the illusory faith in the Catholic Church's diplomatic agreements with the Russian government, whereas in fact the Russian government exploited every agreement as a new means of fighting Catholicism.

We do not shy away from fighting; as a matter of fact we deem it desirable not only for the national cause but also for the cause of Catholicism. The militant Church has sometimes suffered great losses, but it has never been defeated by government repression, whereas the Church that has tried diplomatic methods and signed pacts with the enemy has always lost. Policies of compromise and concession are contrary to the principles and the absolute spirit of the Catholic Church, which is expressed most powerfully by the memorable *non possumus*. A fight cannot take place without sacrifice, loss, and pain, but these sacrifices and losses will be redeemed tenfold by the strengthening of the solidarity of the national cause and the Church's cause. Indeed, after every fight, the Catholic Church in the Russian sector came out internally stronger than it had been previously. It was hardened, cleansed in the heat of battle of its weaknesses and its flaws.

There is no doubt that the Russian government will take revenge on the recalcitrant clergy, above all on the bishops. They will be exposed to various harassment, maybe even exile. But are these bishops molded of a different clay than their predecessors who suffered that same fate, those thousands of priests and laymen who, for the national cause and the Church's cause, went to jail, were tortured, sent into the misery of exile and wandered homeless among foreigners? They are called spiritual leaders, so let them lead their armies to battle. As a matter of fact, exile to Russia and salary cuts are still not synonymous with martyrdom, for which Christ's servants and righteous Poles should be prepared. This is our civic duty, which we should perform without pride or fear. . . . Let the Russian government start the fight it is destined to lose; the Polish community is not afraid of it and the clergy should not be afraid either.

This is an example of the admonishments addressed to the Catholic bishops by the National Democrats. At the same time Dmowski openly rejected ultramontanism, condemned attempts at the subordination of Polish interests to the policies of Catholic Rome, and uncovered unholy intentions among some of the Holy See's political actions. The Catholic bishops identified Polish interests with the interests of the Holy See. There was, therefore, a dispute over how to define Polish national interests. But apart from that, it was also a dispute of two visions of Christianity. Dmowski was personally indifferent to religion. To him the Church was a powerful hierarchical institution that could not become the guarantor of the spiritual unification of the Poles. In his idea the Church was to "govern souls" while the National Democrats were to govern politics. This was accompanied by the belief, frequently repeated by the ND leader, in the dual character of moral norms: personal lives were to be governed by the Ten Commandments and public life by the ethical norms of "national egotism." We discussed these norms earlier. Thus, the National Democratic criticism of the bishops' political line included the offer of an alliance. Within this alliance the Church was to openly renounce the belief that biblical principles concerned politics. It was to give up its universal spirit and morally sanction political concepts of nationalism which had been built on hatred and xenophobia. For their part the National Democrats offered to participate in a crusade against anticlericalists, atheists, and destroyers of moral order who paraded with red flags on May Day. The offer was attractive but not fully acceptable. The NDs could count on the favorable attention of the princes of the Church but never on their identification with National Democratic politics.

What was the problem? The Polish-Catholic's political reduction of Christianity made the Church into a true national institution. It performed many nonreligious functions because it was the sole open and legal bastion of the captive people's national aspirations. But in the ND conception the political reduction of Christianity was deeper and took a different turn. The Church was to be made into a tool for the implementation of particular policies; in effect it was to be subordinated to the policies of the National Democrats. This political line presupposed an abandonment of the demand to apply biblical values to political life and the subordination of the Ten Commandments to the National Democrats' political strategy.

The Church could not do this—because it was entangled in its own tactics of resistance to the invader; because by the nature of its mission it had to occupy a supraparty position in the nation's life; because the commands of faith made the bishop repeat: "My kingdom is not of this world." The National Democrats accused the bishops of excessive conciliatory tendencies. But how could the Church throw its authority and its long-term religious mission onto the scale of a particular political contest? This is the dilemma always faced by the shepherd whose flock desires liberation from oppressive terror. The Church must be united with the persecuted. But the Church must exist forever, even when a particular battle has been lost, because the flock also needs its shepherd after a defeat. The politics of the Church always hovers between moral testimony and cold calculation. There is no ready-made solution for this dilemma. One thing is certain, however: when the flock of sheep straighten their backs to fight for dignity and freedom, the shepherd must not do as Pilate did. What is also certain is that the Church can defend the natural rights of its flock in different ways, but the reduction of Christianity to a political program is never appropriate.

The differences were significant. But the National Democrats scored an important victory. Taking advantage of the clergy's intellectual and conceptual weakness, they were able to instill a particular content into Polish Catholicism. In the practices of the Church's pastoral ministry, this content, translated into a concrete language of politics, lay closer to Dmowski's *Thoughts of a Modern Pole* than to the teaching of the gospel. The alliance of Catholicism and nationalism had a purely negative foundation. They had enemies in common: the atheistic liberal and the social revolutionary, foreigners and believers in other gods. The arguments were interchangeable; when adjusted to a mass audience, they were made appropriately primitive. Thus, self-determination was based on reducing an important part of the population to the status of objects. Followers were treated as an easily manipulated clay, and opponents were viewed as Satan's litter. It was in this intellectual climate that the pamphlets revealing the rule of a "Jewish-Freemasonic mafia" were produced and read.

But it was not only the National Democrats who interacted with Polish Catholicism. They themselves—haphazardly—gave in to its influence, to its concept of the human being, to its antitotalitarian principle of separating what was God's from what was Caesar's. I believe that this was one of the important reasons why ND programmatic thought did not become fully totalitarian, not even in the 1930s, when the poison of chauvinism and the germ of totalitarianism seemed to penetrate all the ranks of the disciplined youths, when brass knuckles were used to resolve political disputes, when young NDs openly empathized with fascism, accusing the Sanacja regime in the era of Brześć and Bereza of rotten liberalism. Even then one of the creators of National Democratic thought, Roman Rybarski, wrote: "Without the internal unity of emotion and effort, the nation will not remain in a leading position. But does the strength of the nation require the complete political unity of its members? Is it necessary for everyone to hold the same political belief and wear the same uniform? Or do internal disputes, based on the foundation of national unity, not lead more successfully to the blossoming of the nation?"

Conclusion

I did not intend these reflections to reconcile in some suprahistorical way the traditions of the National Democrats with those of the independence-oriented socialists. I intended to interpret these traditions anew, to decipher their message, to reflect on the lessons inherent in those conflicts. Barbara Toruńczyk's book, which I have cited throughout, served as my inspiration; but such reflection is also stimulated by knowledge about subsequent events, about successors, about the blossoming and degeneration of those ideologies. I was also led to these thoughts by the belief that the past few years in Polish public life have been marked by a renaissance of nonconformist attitudes. Their common denominator lies in the goal of self-determination and the formation of a program for a Polish politics of activism. Reflection on analogous endeavors from some eighty years ago can create an intellectual bridge between the era of our ancestors and now, when it is our turn to strive for independence. All the more so since an important element of the struggle for self-determination lies in an authentic knowledge of our own history. It is necessary to develop one's own approach to the national heritage, to form one's own ideological tradition and place oneself in it. Disputes over history are frequently equivalent to quarrels over our identity. At times, we were limited to this form of discussion by the censor's pencil, at times by the paralysis of our own tongues. This also applies to my ruminations here. They too ought to contribute to the discussion about the shape of our national fate.

It seems to me that much detailed inspiration and a handful of general teachings can be extracted from those past issues. I will try to summarize them.

The chief characteristic of the political programs I have described was the goal attained: Poland regained its independence. The efforts and achievements of all the participants in the polemics that I have described contributed to it. It was they who shaped the nation that was capable, after 120 years of captivity and division, to exist on its own. They developed its political awareness, its modern ideologies, its pluralistic internal structure. Despite captivity, this pluralism determined the richness and maturity of Polish life, even though not all those who took part in it were aware of this. But the form and intensity of Polish disputes were indeed saddening. Each one of the discussants claimed political reason and patriotic honesty only for himself—and his camp. The mutual accusations were brutal and unfair. They weighed heavily on Polish political life. It is important always to remember this truth, especially now when we are engaged in an internal dispute over what policies we need today.

We need self-determination. We must save our self-organization, our union structures, our uncensored newspapers, our unwritten moral codes. We must save our own course of civic life which is independent of the government. This will cost us—as it already has—many sacrifices, but such is the price of freedom. Our unofficial life is our authentic life. So long as we have self-organization we will retain self-knowledge and the soul of a free nation, even if we are held captive.

We need politics of activism. This means politics that will enable us to resist the temptations offered by the totalitarian power and to work resolutely for the attainment of the most important national goals. Such a policy requires determination and patience, courage and a keen ability to compromise, a sober geopolitical analysis and a flexible tactic of forcing internal changes. A politics of activism means a realistic assessment of one's place in the world. It means firmly holding on to the realities of life and rejecting idealistic illusions. It means the readiness to fight selflessly for the right to a sovereign existence for one's own national community. But this is not the same as the conviction that the good of my own nation requires fighting with other nations. It is not the same as the view, formulated many years ago, that "the idea of struggle is as old as life itself, for life goes on solely due to the fact that other life perishes in the struggle. . . . In this conflict it is the stronger and more talented ones who win and the weak and less talented who lose. Struggle is the father of the universe. . . . Man lives and is capable of surviving beside the animal world not because of humanitarian principles but by using solely and exclusively the most brutal methods of struggle."

Let us read these words carefully. These words were not spoken by a Polish politician, although many could have pronounced them. These words were uttered by Adolf Hitler. We should think about their consequences.

Politics of activism is not the same as fanaticism and cruelty. Politics of activism is the conscious attempt to overcome Poland's vicious circle, the cycle "from one 'renewal' to the next," from an explosion to an uprising.

We need the Catholic Church—a church that will teach us moral values, defend national and human dignity, provide an asylum for trampled hopes. But we do not expect the Church to become the nation's political representative, to formulate political programs and to sign political pacts. Whoever wants such a Church, whoever expects these things from Catholic priests, is—whether he likes it or not—asking for the political reduction of the Christian religion. For we do not need a Church that is locked up, that is hidden behind the walls of a particular political ideology. We need an open Church, a Church that "takes the whole world onto the arms of the Cross." It is such a Church, I think, that all Poles need today: those who believe in the "madness of the Cross," those who are blindly searching for the meaning of Christian transcendence, those who define the meaning of their lives in the categories of lay humanism.

We need national solidarity. As its basis we must have respect for differences, diversity, and pluralism. As a condition for it we must have concern for the positive development of our nation, for its collective ethos and its spiritual dimension. The threat that hangs over it consists in hatred for other nations, contempt for other cultures, and a megalomaniac belief in one's own perfection. National solidarity provides a shelter for spiritual homelessness; it is the declaration of war against human solitude in the face of the communist Leviathan. But it must in no way entail the formation of social ties on the model of a military hierarchy. Solidarity is not the same as discipline. There can be no national solidarity without tolerance and pluralism, without the belief that it is precisely pluralism that serves as testimony to the wealth of a nation's culture.

We need socialism. Leszek Kołakowski has aptly written:

> We need a living tradition of socialist thought which in proclaiming the traditional values of social justice and freedom appeals solely to human forces. But here we do not need the ideas of any socialism. We do not need crazy dreams of a society from which all evil temptations have been removed or dreams of a total revolution which all at once will bring us a bliss of final redemption in a world devoid of conflict. What we need is a socialism that will help us find our way in the complex reality of the brutal forces that operate in human history, a socialism that will strengthen our readiness to fight poverty and social injustice. We need a socialist tradition conscious of its own limitations, because the dream of final redemption is despair dressed in the cloak of hope, the greed for power clothed in the gown of justice.

We need freedom. As we walk toward freedom we carry in us the seeds of captivity. No one comes out innocent from the war declared on the Prince of Darkness. Freedom can be threatened in different ways. Some of us are hungry for the freedom of others, whereas others are afraid of the burden of their own freedom. Such is the inheritance of long years of slavery, and there is no way that this can be overcome overnight. One must be mature enough for freedom. One must learn freedom. It is true: freedom has been imprinted on our hearts and minds. But how can one read one's insides accurately?

Freedom is self-creation. I mold myself, I forge my fate for the price of my own life. It can be the fate of a slave or the fate of a free man. In the latter case I have the freedom of choice. I can cross out all of the tradition of my fathers and grandfathers. I can spit on all the monuments of my culture. I can do all of the above.

> At the same time, this whole historical process of man's awareness and choices is closely connected with the living tradition of his nation, in which Christ's words, the testimony of the gospel, the Christian culture, the customs born of faith, hope and love resound with a living echo across generations. Man chooses consciously,

through his inner freedom. Tradition does not create a limit, it is a treasure, a spiritual resource, a great common good, all of which are confirmed by every choice, by every noble deed, by every life lived in a genuinely Christian fashion. Can one push all this aside? Can one say no? Can one reject Christ and all that He has contributed to man's history?

Of course one can. Man is free. Man can say no to God. But—and this is the essential question—is one allowed to? And "allowed to" in the name of what? What argument of reason, what value of the will and the heart can one present to oneself, to one's loved ones, to one's compatriots, to the nation, so as to reject and say no to all that has enabled us to live for a thousand years?! Or to all that has formed the foundation of our identity and has always been there? (John Paul II)

This is why in a free nation, reason is truly fulfilled. It is the living and present spirit, in which the individual has found his destiny, his general individual being, not just something that is expressed and given as a thing, but which in itself is its own being, and which has fulfilled his mission. This is why the greatest of the ancient wise men said that *wisdom and virtue mean living in harmony with the customs of one's nation.* (G. W. F. Hegel)

July 1982

Epilogue

I wrote "Conversation in the Citadel" in peculiar circumstances. I only had a few colleagues whom I could ask for comments. They all had enough to keep them busy, but nevertheless gave me much of their time and attention. Let me thank Jacek Kuroń, Anatol Lawina, Janusz Onyszkiewicz, and Henryk Wujec.

The first criticism concerned the organization of the text and its skewed proportions. In the words of one of my friends, "An extremely positive picture of the National Democrats emerges from this text, while the legacy of the socialist camp is not shown. Yet it too developed a vision of self-determination and a politics of activism. It organized education, an illegal culture, a cooperative movement, etc."

But I did not intend to paint a complete, textbook picture of that era. From such a viewpoint my text is useless. I attempted to ask new questions—formulated from today's perspective—of that era, of its testimony and documents. This is why my argumentation is in the form of an essay, perhaps too disorganized. The socialists' intellectual output is quite well known; much has been written about it, objectively and competently. My own views on it were expressed years ago in my essay "Shadows of Forgotten Ancestors," in which I drew an ideological sketch of Józef Piłsudski. By my nature, by my ideological choice and biographic tradition, I consider the ethos of the Polish Socialist Party to be my own. I have identified publicly, on many occasions, verbally and in writing, with the tradition of independence-oriented and democratic socialism. The intention behind "Conversation in the Citadel" was somewhat perverse: I wanted to interpret anew—through the eyes of one who had been formed by leftist tradition—the content in the political concepts of the National Democrats and to uncover the values hidden beneath the thick layers of insult, resentment, and falsehood. I naturally concentrated on those motifs that characterize the wisdom and shrewdness of the National Democrats' political thought. Ideological polemics—the logic of political disputes—always make people exaggerate their adversaries' flaws and whitewash their own mistakes. This may be why I applied the opposite method in this article: I saw my own tradition in the crooked mirror of its dangers and deformations, and the National Democratic tradition in the brightness of its virtues. But I also pointed out the shadows in the thinking of the National Democrats, although admittedly I tried to understand their origins instead of unmasking their symptoms. I therefore attempted to fish out of Dmowski's writings an acute prognosis for the conflict between Polish and Lithuanian or Ukrainian nationalisms rather than view the conclusions drawn by the ND leader merely as the product of his own nationalistic beliefs. It is difficult to separate in his writings the current of objective diagnosis from the ideological and political agitation; the two are united, entangled. Looking at them from today's perspective, however, one must conclude that false ideological messages do not preclude a correct diagnosis of political situations.

National Democracy was not a uniform creation. It was a camp made up of many currents, undergoing an evolution, full of internal tension. But I was interested in its universal characteristics, typical of a political style of thought. This is probably why I avoided the important problem of ND propaganda, dominated by a primitive and cheap demagogy that awakened passions and gained votes. The transformation of this political thought as a result of its mass popularization is a topic for another study. The ND program expressed in the pages of *Przegląd Wszechpolski* seemed very different from the way it was used in speeches by local agitators made at preelection rallies. The brutal phraseology of national hatred replaced subtle geopolitical analysis. A similar phenomenon would happen in the socialist camp: the concept of "class struggle" ceased being the tool for analyses of historical processes as it turned into a demagogic slogan, often justifying the plunder of others' property. Emotions and popular expectations had an effect on the political ideologues: they reduced them and led to fanaticism and hatred. The type of fanatic ideologue described by Florian Znaniecki did not appear only among the socialists.

In the opinion of my friends I did not contrast clearly enough my positive assessment of the National-Democratic camp with the totalitarian threat born of National-Democratic ideology. According to them, I noted the totalitarian germ only among the socialists.

I believe the evolution of nationalist movements into totalitarianism has been described many times, mostly on the German and Hitlerite example. These things are well known, so I would prefer if someone who openly claims adherence to the ND tradition (for example Wojciech Wasiutyński, Wiesław Chrzanowski, or Aleksander Hall) were to look at the totalitarian germ contained in the nationalist programs and ideologies.

Henryk Wujec wrote to me:

> You show the depravation of Dmowski and Piłsudski, along with their idea of self-determination, which was incurred in the struggle with the tsarist system. But I believe that at the heart of Dmowski's idea of self-determination, which you describe in such a positive fashion, lies a real illness that denies this self-determination. For Dmowski, self-determination is to concern Poles only, while other

groups are to be subordinated, inferior. According to Dmowski, self-determination does not affect all citizens of the Polish state. It is a more dangerous affliction than those caused by the struggle with the tsarist system and the habits picked up by the fighters, because it lies at the source of the doctrine.

I consider the above thoughts to be basically sound. This aspect of the National-Democratic doctrine was a particularly ominous burden on the public life of the Second Republic. But let us recall the heart of the matter. Dmowski, himself a nationalist and himself understanding the dynamics of other nationalisms, did not believe in a conflict-free arrangement of Polish-Lithuanian or Polish-Ukrainian relations in the future Polish state. The political conclusions he drew were undeniably wretched, although his diagnosis in itself was correct. The Ukrainians could not be satisfied with any equality before the law in a Polish state; they wanted a sovereign Ukraine. And one can hardly be surprised at this. For this reason I believe that to create a program for a federation it was necessary to recognize Ukrainian national aspirations. It was not enough to feed on the vision of a tolerant "Jagellonian Poland" and the idea of a "state without pyres." In other words, Dmowski sinned with the brutality of his program of Polonization and with the narrowness of his vision of Polishness, whereas his antagonists in the PPS and in the Belvedere camp sinned through their naiveté.

One friend asked me: "Did you not neglect the importance of the 'unrealistic' and romantic program of the Polish Socialist Party for the regaining of independence?" To me this question is based on a semantic misunderstanding. The idea that triumphed in 1918 had been wholly unrealistic at the beginning of the century. But in its objective of striving for independence, the National Democrats did not differ from the PPS. Their dispute concerned the methods and means for reaching independence. These means were different, but one could not argue that Piłsudski's actions were not realistic and calculated. The point is that this realistic political practice was not accompanied by a clearly formulated political thought, such as was present in Dmowski. The Poles owe many things to Piłsudski: a sense of dignity, faith in independence, readiness to make sacrifices, familiarity with values. But they do not owe him thanks for a systematic political thought presented in his writings. From Roman Dmowski, however, Poles could learn how to think about politics.

"Socialism is a thoroughly discredited term. Is it good that you use it in your conclusions?" Janusz Onyszkiewicz wrote to me.

I don't know how to give an unequivocal answer to this question, even to myself. Because, indeed, in Poland the word *socialism* is both discredited and ambiguous. From this point of view it should be abandoned. Nonetheless, the Polish workers' movement and its party, the PPS, which upheld the ideals of the rights of working people and of national independence, the principles of "Poland's freedom and the freedom of man in Poland," used the word for decades. It is true that the PPS's socialism was the child of another era, the product of different social and intellectual circumstances. But isn't the overall form of those ideological conflicts an archival phenomenon? Do we not often argue about the past, thinking that we are arguing about the truths of the present? Is it not the case that out of the melting pot of the past, new programs, new ideologies, new expressions of old conflicts are bound to emerge? Is it not the case that the plans which are being made today for a self-governing republic must be a synthesis of the motifs that clashed yesterday and could not be reconciled, but which today are complementary and natural allies, mutually enriching each other?

I believe that this is exactly the case today. That is why I used the concept of "socialist tradition," in which I see an indispensable factor of our present-day hopes.

And this is why I wrote "Conversation in the Citadel."

Warsaw, 1982

// Index

"Horizontal structures," and Communist Party, 92, 118, 128

Hôtel Lambert, 174, 263–264, 288; defined, 231n; policies of politicians in, 231, 232, 235, 238–239, 241, 243, 246

Humanism, 137

Human rights, 52–53, 142; linked with American foreign policy, 97; violations of, 93

Hungarians, books by, 91

Hungary, 27, 37, 49, 81; repercussions of Soviet intervention in, 143; revolution in, 87, 125

Husák, Gustav, 38, 50, 81; "model" of, 37–38

Imprisonment, 97; of Adam Michnik, x, xi, xiii, xix–xx, xxi, 2, 65, 68, 85, 98, 155–156, 204n, 277–278; attitudes toward and experience of, 68, 74, 76–77, 277–278; compared with freedom, 3–4; effects of, 41; opportunities for release from, 3, 65. *See also* Emigration; Internees; Loyalty declarations

Independence of Poland, 205, 225–226, 242–243; compared with Russian revolutionary goals, 263–264; Russian advocates of, 261–264; in Russian nineteenth-century foreign policy, 253–254, 258–259, 261–264; viewed after January 1863 Uprising, 279–280. *See also* National Sovereignty

Independent institutions, creation of, xxvi, xxvii, 144–145, 151–153

Independent Publishing House (NOWa), xx, 188. *See also* Publishing houses

"Instant change" vs. "Long March" strategy, 55–58

Institut Littéraire in Paris, 18n

Insurrectionists, 12–13, 235; expropriation of estates of, 267; vs. organicists

and organic work concept, 12, 173, 174, 225–226, 232–233, 278–279

Intellectuals, 178–191; alliance with workers, xi; attitudes toward Józef Piłsudski, 222; dilemma of, 220; evaluated by Józef Piłsudski, 210–211; imprisoned in 1945, 202; relations with Catholic Church, x–xi; revisionism advocated by, 137, 138; role in opposition movement, xxvii, 78, 147–148; and Stalinism, 184; and traditions of "insubordinate" intelligentsia, 147; under rule of Leading System, 178–191

Interfactory Founding Committee, 127

Interfactory Strike Committee, 124

"Internal emigration," 45

International brotherhood, xii, 248

International Labor Organization, conventions of, xiii

International proletarian movement, xiii

International Red Cross, 10

Internees, 40, 83; conversations of and potential lectures to, 277; ill treatment of, 65; policies on release of, 3, 16, 21, 22, 65, 85; released after Amnesty Act, 85; role in election campaigns, 73–74; and separation of political prisoners from common criminals, 66. *See also* Imprisonment

Irreality (K. Brandys), 178–179

Irredentism, 242, 248, 249; Russian attitudes on, 257, 258, 262, 264

Iwanow, Zbigniew, 33, 118, 128

Jacobinism, 301

"Jagellonian Poland," 332

Jagielski, Mieczysław, 112, 119, 124

January 1863 Uprising, 223, 225, 236–237; effect on Russian policies on Poland, 249, 260, 261, 269; failure of, 279; interpretations of, 243, 260, 261; suppression of, 269

Jaroszewicz, Piotr, 106, 120

Studies in Society and Culture in East-Central Europe

General Editors
Jan T. Gross
Irena Grudzinska-Gross

Jan Jozef Lipski, *KOR: A History of the Workers' Defense Committee in Poland, 1976–1981*

Adam Michnik, *Letters from Prison and Other Essays*

Designer:	Paula Schlosser
Compositor:	Prestige Typography
Printer:	Edwards Brothers
Binder:	Edwards Brothers
Text:	10/13 Times Roman
Display:	Bauer Bodoni Bold